Pilimin

D0875697

ADVANCES IN

EXPERIMENTAL
SOCIAL PSYCHOLOGY

VOLUME 9

Equity Theory:
Toward a General Theory of Social Interaction

CONTRIBUTORS TO VOLUME 9

J. Stacy Adams

William Austin

Ellen Berscheid

Sara Freedman

John G. Holmes

George C. Homans

L. Rowell Huesmann

Melvin J. Lerner

Gerald S. Leventhal

George Levinger

Dale T. Miller

Mary Kristine Utne

Elaine Walster

G. William Walster

Equity Theory: Toward a
General Theory of Social Interaction

ADVANCES IN

Experimental
Social Psychology

EDITED BY

Leonard Berkowitz
DEPARTMENT OF PSYCHOLOGY
UNIVERSITY OF WISCONSIN
MADISON, WISCONSIN

and

Elaine Walster
DEPARTMENT OF PSYCHOLOGY
  AND SOCIOLOGY
UNIVERSITY OF WISCONSIN
MADISON, WISCONSIN

VOLUME 9

ACADEMIC PRESS   New York San Francisco London   1976

A Subsidiary of Harcourt Brace Jovanovich, Publishers

ACADEMIC PRESS, INC.
111 Fifth Avenue, New York, New York 10003

United Kingdom Edition published by
ACADEMIC PRESS, INC. (LONDON) LTD.
24/28 Oval Road, London NW1

LIBRARY OF CONGRESS CATALOG CARD NUMBER: 64-23452

ISBN 0-12-015209-6

PRINTED IN THE UNITED STATES OF AMERICA

CONTENTS

New Directions in Equity Research

Elaine Walster, Ellen Berscheid, and G. William Walster

Equity Theory Revisited: Comments and Annotated Bibliography

J. Stacy Adams and Sara Freedman

The Distribution of Rewards and Resources in Groups and Organizations

Gerald S. Leventhal

Deserving and the Emergence of Forms of Justice

Melvin J. Lerner, Dale T. Miller, and John G. Holmes

Equity and the Law: The Effect of a Harmdoer's "Suffering in the Act" on Liking and Assigned Punishment

William Austin, Elaine Walster, and Mary Kristine Utne

Incremental Exchange Theory: A Formal Model for Progression in Dyadic Social Interaction

L. Rowell Huesmann and George Levinger

Commentary

George C. Homans

CONTRIBUTORS

Numbers in parentheses indicate the pages on which the authors' contributions begin.

J. Stacy Adams, *Graduate School of Business Administration, University of North Carolina, Chapel Hill, North Carolina* (43)

William Austin, *University of Virginia, Charlottesville, Virginia* (163)

Ellen Berscheid, *University of Minnesota, Minneapolis, Minnesota* (1)

Sara Freedman, *University of North Carolina, Chapel Hill, North Carolina* (43)

John G. Holmes, *University of Waterloo, Waterloo, Ontario, Canada* (133)

George C. Homans, *Department of Sociology, Harvard University, Cambridge, Massachusetts* (231)

L. Rowell Huesmann, *University of Illinois, Chicago Circle, Chicago, Illinois* (191)

Melvin J. Lerner,* *University of Waterloo, Waterloo, Ontario, Canada* (133)

Gerald S. Leventhal, *Wayne State University, Detroit, Michigan* (91)

George Levinger, *University of Massachusetts, Amherst, Massachusetts* (191)

* On Sabbatical leave: East-West Culture Learning Institute, East-West Center, Honolulu, Hawaii.

Dale T. Miller,* *University of Waterloo, Waterloo, Ontario, Canada* (133)

Mary Kristine Utne, *University of Wisconsin, Madison, Wisconsin* (163)

Elaine Walster, *University of Wisconsin, Madison, Wisconsin* (1, 163)

G. William Walster, *University of Wisconsin, Madison, Wisconsin* (1)

*Present address: University of Western Ontario, London, Ontario, Canada.

PREFACE

A new mood of optimism is emerging in social psychology.

Social psychologists have always been painfully aware that social psychology desperately needs a general theory of social behavior, one that can integrate the myriad of elegant little mini-theories which now exist. Although social psychologists agree that we need a general theory, they have, until recently, assumed that it is far too early to try to develop one.

Recently, however, a number of optimistic, or foolhardy, social psychologists have begun to challenge this assumption. For example, Bem's "self-perception model" attempts to integrate the Skinnerian paradigm and dissonance theory. Heider, Jones, and Kelly's "attribution theory" attempts to integrate data generated by Skinnerians, dissonance theorists, Schachterians, motivational theorists, and so forth. Equity theory was developed in the hope of providing the glimmerings of the general theory that social psychologists so badly need. It attempts to integrate the insights of reinforcement theory, cognitive consistency theory, psychoanalytic theory, exchange theory, etc.

Adams argues that this equity integrative attempt has been strikingly successful. He observes:

> The theory in its present form (Walster *et al.,* 1973) strikes us as having a well articulated structure, being parsimoniously elegant, and having an increased predictive range. These are characteristics that bode well for progress, for as Kuhn (1962) and Rosenberg (1972) have noted, the growth of a discipline, scientific or technological, is intimately tied to the existence and quality of theory (p. 44, this volume)

Equity theory has been applied to predict men's reactions in such diverse interactions as industrial relations, exploiter/victim relationships, philanthropist/ recipient relationships, intimate relationships, and the like. Walster, Berscheid, and Walster review the wide-ranging and voluminous equity research in the forthcoming volume, *Equity Theory and Research* [Allyn & Bacon (in press)].

This encyclopedic review of past research is complemented by the present volume, in which major equity theorists attempt to foresee emerging theoretical and research directions.

In the first article [New Directions in Equity Research], Walster and her colleagues present an introduction to equity theory and research by providing a brief overview of equity theory and a review of the hundred or so equity studies which have been conducted.

In the second through the sixth articles, equity theorists offer their speculations as to where they think equity theory *should* go, and will go, as we progress toward Year 2000.

Adams and Freedman, in the second review [Equity Theory Revisited: Comments and Annotated Bibliography], argue that equity theorists must now confront four critical problems: (1) Researchers must learn more about such equity/inequity produced emotions as "contentment," "anger," "feelings of betrayal," "hurt," "guilt," and "shame" and their relationships to behavior. (2) They should study the *process* by which people restore equity. (3) They should explore the ways in which people manipulate equity/inequity to get the things they want. (4) They must make equity theory a more precise theory; they must develop quantitative measures of "inputs" and "outcomes" and develop alternative mathematical definitions of equity/inequity.

In the second section of their paper, Adams and Freedman provide an extensive annotated bibliography of theoretical, review, and research papers— published and unpublished—on equity.

In the third article [The Distribution of Rewards and Resources in Groups and Organizations], Leventhal provides a brilliant analysis of the factors allocators must consider when they are deciding how to distribute human material and resources. He points out that allocators must weigh a variety of competing considerations when deciding how to allocate resources. Should an allocator divide resources equitably? Attempt to meet the competition? Stimulate employees' performance? Focus on keeping everyone happy? Leventhal details some of the cost/benefit considerations that seem to affect allocators' decisions.

In the fourth paper [Deserving and the Emergence of Forms of Justice], Lerner and his colleagues point out that competing themes of "deserving" and "justice" pervade the fabric of our society. Mythology and religion assure us that industry and goodness triumph over laziness and evil. Yet, their insistence that this is a "just world" is strikingly juxtaposed against vivid evidence of institutionalized injustice. The authors offer some provocative suggestions about the factors that determine how people react to the suffering of others; they also provide an up-to-date review of research in this area.

In the fifth review [Equity and the Law: The Effect of a Harmdoer's "Suffering in the Act" on Liking and Assigned Punishment], Austin and his colleagues speculate about equity's possible usefulness in illuminating the legal process. Legal philosophers have never been able to agree on why society punishes criminals. Do we punish men to restore equity? To rehabilitate them? To protect society by isolating them? To set a harsh example for other potential criminals? They cannot agree. In spite of philosophers' disagreements, however, most people feel that to some extent, wrongdoers must be punished to "set things right." The authors ask: Do judges', jurors', and spectators' notions of what is equitable affect their judicial reactions and decisions? When judges and jurors discover that a defendant has partially paid for his crime by mental, physical, or financial suffering, do they feel he has, at least in part, "set things right," and thus deserves a lighter sentence? The authors review the sparse anecdotal, survey, and empirical research which provide the glimmerings of an answer to this timely question.

Huesmann and Levinger, in the sixth article [Incremental Exchange Theory: A Formal Model for Progression in Dyadic Social Interaction], explore new frontiers. A general mathematical model of social interaction is presented along with a computer program called "RELATE." The authors provide examples of RELATE's ability to predict the form social interaction should take in four specific topic areas: "altruistic" relations, interpersonal similarity and attraction, self-disclosure, and romantic involvement.

In the final chapter [Commentary], Homans, with his usual irrepressible wit, offers an elegant and insightful commentary on all of the papers.

Hopefully, the authors' provocative speculations will stimulate readers to do some speculating of their own as to where the social sciences should go as they, and we, move inexorably toward Year 2000.

Leonard Berkowitz
Elaine Walster

ACKNOWLEDGMENTS

We would like to thank Ms. Suzanne Touton for her help in editing and typing this manuscript.

In addition, we would like to thank the American Psychological Association for giving us permission to reprint "New Directions in Equity Research."

The editing of this volume was supported in part by National Science Foundation Grant GS30822 (to Walster).

CONTENTS OF OTHER VOLUMES

ADVANCES IN

EXPERIMENTAL
SOCIAL PSYCHOLOGY

VOLUME 9

Equity Theory:
Toward a General Theory of Social Interaction

NEW DIRECTIONS
IN EQUITY RESEARCH[1,2]

Elaine Walster

UNIVERSITY OF WISCONSIN
MADISON, WISCONSIN

Ellen Berscheid

UNIVERSITY OF MINNESOTA
MINNEAPOLIS, MINNESOTA

G. William Walster

UNIVERSITY OF WISCONSIN
MADISON, WISCONSIN

This article consists of four sections: The first section elucidates a general theory of social behavior—equity theory. Equity theory consists of four propositions designed to predict when individuals will perceive that they are justly treated and how they will react when they find themselves enmeshed in unjust relationships. The second section summarizes the extensive research that has been conducted to test equity theory. The third section points out the ways in which equity theory interlocks with other major social psychological theories. The final section hints at some ways in which equity theory can be applied to understanding social problems.

The Theoretical Formulation

The proposition that individuals seek for themselves maximum reward at minimum cost is hardly startling. Theories in a wide variety of disciplines rest on

[1] This article originally appeared in *Journal of Personality and Social Psychology* 1973, Vol. 25, No. 2, 151–176.
[2] Preparation of this article was financed in part by National Institute of Mental Health Grants MH 16729 and MH 16661.

1

the assumption that "Man is selfish." Psychologists believe that behavior can be shaped by the careful application of reinforcements. Economists assume that individuals will purchase desired products at the lowest available price. Moral philosophers conclude that the ideal society can only be one which insures the "greatest good for the greatest number." Politicians contend that "Every man has his price." Equity theory, too, rests on the assumption that man is selfish.

Thus, our first proposition states:

Proposition I: Individuals will try to maximize their outcomes (where outcomes equal rewards minus costs).

If everyone were unrestrained in his attempts to get what he wanted, everyone would suffer. Every man would attempt to monopolize community resources; every man would be continually confronted by rivals bent on reclaiming these resources. Only by working out a compromise can the group avoid continual warfare and maximize collective reward.

This fact is acknowledged in Proposition IIA:

Proposition IIA: Groups can maximize collective reward by evolving accepted systems for "equitably" apportioning rewards and costs among members. Thus, members will evolve such systems of equity and will attempt to induce members to accept and adhere to these systems.

If group members are to be effective in inducing their fellow members to behave equitably, they must make it more profitable for the individual to behave equitably than inequitably (see Proposition I). Thus, Proposition IIB proposes that groups will insure the profitability of equitable behavior in the following way:

Proposition IIB: Groups will generally reward members who treat others equitably and generally punish (increase the costs for) members who treat others inequitably.

WHAT CONSTITUTES AN EQUITABLE RELATIONSHIP?

In Proposition IIA we argued that every culture must institutionalize systems for equitably apportioning resources among its members (see De Jong, 1952). We must admit, however, that the perception of *what* is equitable varies enormously between cultures. In spite of the fact that different societies have established strikingly different procedures for partitioning their resources, we have found a single general principle to be useful in characterizing these widely diverse conceptions about what is equitable (see Adams, 1965; Blau, 1967; Homans, 1961; Walster, Berscheid, & Walster, 1970).

We define an "equitable relationship" to exist when the person scrutinizing the relationship (i.e., the scrutineer—who could be Participant A, Participant B, or an outside observer) perceives that all participants are receiving equal relative outcomes from the relationship, i.e.

$$\frac{\text{Outcomes}_A - \text{Inputs}_A}{(|\text{Inputs}_A|)^{k_A}} = \frac{\text{Outcomes}_B - \text{Inputs}_B}{(|\text{Inputs}_B|)^{k_B}}$$

Definition of Terms

Outcomes (O) are defined as the positive and negative consequences that a scrutineer perceives a participant has incurred as a consequence of his relationship with another. Following Homans (1961), we shall refer to positive outcomes as "rewards" and negative outcomes as "costs." The participant's total outcomes in a relationship are equal to the rewards he obtains from the relationship minus the costs he incurs.

We defined inputs (I) as "the participant's contributions to the exchange, which are seen (by a scrutineer) as entitling him to rewards or costs." The inputs that a participant contributes to a relationship can be either assets—entitling him to rewards—or liabilities—entitling him to costs.

In different settings, different inputs are seen as entitling one to rewards or costs. In industrial settings, assets such as "capital" or "manual labor" are seen as relevant inputs—inputs that legitimately entitle the contributor to reward. In social settings, assets such as physical beauty or kindness are generally seen as assets entitling the possessor to social reward. Social liabilities such as boorishness or cruelty are seen as liabilities entitling one to costs.

Definitional Formula[3]

Adams proposed the simple formula

$$\frac{O_A}{I_A} = \frac{O_B}{I_B}$$

for designating an equitable relationship, where O_A and O_B are A's and B's outcomes from the relationship, and I_A and I_B are A's and B's inputs to the relationship. Unfortunately, this simple notation is adequate only so long as all participants have positive inputs. This formula is *not* suitable in social relations where inputs may be negative as well as positive. For example, according to the preceding formula, a relationship would be calculated as equitable if $I_A = 5, O_A = -10, I_B = -5$, and $O_B = 10$. Substituting in the formula:

$$\frac{O_A}{I_A} = \frac{-10}{5} = -2 \quad \text{and} \quad \frac{O_B}{I_B} = \frac{10}{-5} = -2$$

[3] When this article was originally published in *JPSP*, two critical exponents, k_A and k_B, were omitted from the Definitional Formula. In reprinting this paper, we present the formula as it *should* have appeared.

Obviously neither Adams nor we would feel such a relationship was, in fact, equitable.

In place of Adams's formula, we have chosen the following formula[4] for calculating whether or not a relationship is equitable:

$$\frac{O_A - I_A}{(|I_A|)^{k_A}} = \frac{O_B - I_B}{(|I_B|)^{k_B}};$$

where O designates a scrutineer's perception of A's and B's outcomes, I designates his perception of A's and B's inputs, and $|I|$ designates the *absolute value* of A's and B's inputs (i.e., the perceived value of A's and B's inputs, disregarding sign). The exponents k_A and k_B take on the value +1 or −1, depending on the sign of A and B's inputs and A and B's gains (Outcomes–Inputs). [k_A = sign (I_A) × sign $(O_A - I_A)$ and k_B = sign (I_B) × sign $(O_B - I_B)$.][5] A participant's relative outcomes will be zero if his outcomes equal his inputs. His relative outcomes will be positive if his $O > I$, and negative if his $O < I$. Thus, the sign and the magnitude of this measure indicates how "profitable" the relationship has been to each of the participants.

Recall the preceding example, where $I_A = 5$, $O_A = -10$, $I_B = -5$ and $O_B = 10$. Substituting in our formula

$$\frac{O_A - I_A}{(|I_A|)^{k_A}} = -15 \times 5 = -75; \qquad \frac{O_B - I_B}{(|I_B|)^{k_B}} = 15 \times 5 = +75.$$

Unlike Adams's formula, our formula properly reveals that B is reaping undeservedly large outcomes from his relationship with A.

WHO DECIDES WHETHER A RELATIONSHIP IS EQUITABLE?

In Propositions IIA and IIB we argued that societies develop norms of equity and teach these systems to their members. Thus, in any society there will be a consensus as to what constitutes an equitable relationship. However, the preceding formulation makes it clear that ultimately, equity is in the eye of the beholder. An individual's perception of how equitable a relationship is will depend on *his* assessment of the value and relevance of the various participants' inputs and outcomes. Participants themselves, even after prolonged negotiation with one another, will not always agree completely as to the value and relevance of various inputs and outcomes. One person may feel that a distinguished family name is a relevant input, entitling him to positive outcomes. His partner might

---

[4] The restriction of this formula is that $|I| > 0$.

[5] The exponent's effect is simply to change the way relative outcomes are computed: If $k = +1$ then we have $(O - I)/|I|$, but if $k = -1$ then we have $|I| \times (O - I)$. Without the exponent k, the formula would yield meaningless results when $I < 0$ and $O - I > 0$, or $I > 0$ and $O - I < 0$.

disagree. Aesop acidly observed that "The injuries we do and those we suffer are seldom weighted on the same scales." If participants do calculate inputs and outcomes differently—and it is likely that they will—it is inevitable that participants will differ in their perceptions of whether or not a given relationship is equitable. Moreover, "objective" outside observers are likely to evaluate the equitableness of a relationship quite differently than do participants.

DO PEOPLE GENERALLY BEHAVE EQUITABLY?

Proposition I states that individuals will try to maximize their outcomes. We might rephrase this proposition as:

Corollary I.1: So long as individuals perceive that they can maximize their outcomes by behaving equitably, they will do so. Should they perceive that they can maximize their outcomes by behaving inequitably, they will do so.

In Propositions IIA and IIB we observed that society will try to insure that members recognize that they can maximize their outcomes by behaving equitably. There is some evidence that individuals do generally behave equitably. A number of experiments demonstrate that individuals will spontaneously share rewards with others. Individuals who are given more than their share of reward voluntarily surrender some benefit to their deprived partners. Deprived individuals, on the other hand, are quick to demand the reward they deserve (see, e.g., Leventhal, Allen, & Kemelgor, 1969; Marwell, Ratcliffe, & Schmitt, 1969; Schmitt & Marwell, 1970[6]).

In spite of the consistent evidence that individuals do behave equitably, we must remember that individuals will behave inequitably with some regularity[7] (Corollary I.1).

We have just argued that individuals now and then treat others in ways they perceive to be *inequitable.* How should the socialized individual react when he finds himself in an inequitable relationship?

We have argued that individuals are often punished when they treat their colleagues inequitably. We pointed out that the person who extorts greater outcomes than he deserves will be punished. Conversely, the person who acquiesces in receiving fewer outcomes than he deserves will be punished—by depriva-

---

[6] Unpublished study entitled "Cooperation and Inequity: Behavioral Effects," 1971. Address requests to D. R. Schmitt, Department of Psychology, University of Washington, Seattle, Washington 98106.

[7] There are two reasons why we would expect a participant in a relationship to behave in a way that he acknowledges is inequitable. First, an individual should behave inequitably whenever he is confident that in a given instance he can maximize his outcomes by doing so. Second, it is to the individual's long-range benefit to behave inequitably now and then. Only by varying the equitableness of his behavior can a participant ascertain whether or not sanctions against inequity are still operating. (Only by testing limits occasionally can one adapt to a changing world.) Thus, an individual can maximize his total outcomes if he tests equity norms now and then.

tion (and possibly by his peers as well). Thus, individuals should quickly come to associate "participating in an *inequitable* relationship" with punishment.

As a consequence of these inevitable socialization experiences, we propose Proposition III.

Proposition III: When individuals find themselves participating in inequitable relationships, they become distressed. The more inequitable the relationship, the more distress individuals feel.

Experimental evidence supports both our Proposition III and Homans' contention that individuals participating in inequitable relationships do feel distress regardless of whether they are the victims or the beneficiaries of the inequity. Experiments by Walster *et al.* (1970), Leventhal *et al.* (1969), Jacques (1961), and Thibaut (1950) indicated that those who receive less than they deserve feel distress (usually in the form of anger). Experiments by Jacques (1961), Adams and Rosenbaum (1962), Adams (1963), and Leventhal *et al.* (1969) demonstrated that those who receive more than they deserve feel distress (usually in the form of guilt).

Evidence also exists to support the contention that the greater the inequity, the more distress participants feel (see Leventhal *et al.,* 1969; Leventhal & Bergman, 1969).

Proposition IV: Individuals who discover they are in an inequitable relationship attempt to eliminate their distress by restoring equity. The greater the inequity that exists, the more distress they feel, and the harder they try to restore equity.

There are two ways that a participant can restore equity to an inequitable relationship: He can restore actual equity to the relationship, or he can restore psychological equity.

A participant can restore "actual equity" by appropriately altering his own outcomes or inputs or the outcomes or inputs of the other participants. For example, the ghetto black who feels his boss underpays him can reestablish actual equity by becoming a slacker (thus lowering his inputs), by forcing his employer to work harder (thus raising his employer's inputs), by demanding a raise or stealing from the company (thus raising his own outcomes), or by sabotaging company equipment (thus lowering his employer's outcomes). The ingenious ways individuals contrive to bring equity to inequitable relationships are documented by Adams (1963).

A participant can restore "psychological equity" by appropriately distorting his perception of his own or his partner's outcomes and inputs.[8] For example,

---

[8] We can, of course, detect whether or not participants are "distorting" by (a) examining how participants' assessments of relevant inputs and outcomes compare to those of observers, who are not so motivated to distort their perceptions of participants' relative outcomes, or (b) by examining whether or not the perceptions of participants suddenly shift in predictable ways as soon as they discover they are participating in an inequitable relationship.

an exploitative employer may convince himself that his inequitable relationship with his underpaid and overworked secretary is in fact equitable by appropriately distorting reality. He can restore psychological equity to their relationship if he can sufficiently minimize her inputs ("You wouldn't believe how stupid she is."), exaggerate her outcomes ("Work gives her a chance to see her friends."), exaggerate his own inputs ("Without my creative genius the company would fall apart."), or minimize his outcomes ("The tension on this job is giving me an ulcer.").

Equity theorists concur that people try to maximize their outcomes (Proposition I). A group of individuals can maximize their total outcomes by agreeing on some equitable system for sharing resources. (A relationship is defined as equitable when a scrutineer perceives that all participants are securing equal relative outcomes, $(O - I)/|I|$, from the relationship, that is,

$$\frac{O_A - I_A}{(|I_A|)^{k_A}} = \frac{O_B - I_B}{(|I_B|)^{k_B}}$$

Groups try to insure that members can maximize their outcomes by behaving equitably; they reward members who behave equitably and punish members who behave inequitably. When individuals socialized by this system participate in inequitable relationships, they experience distress. Participants reduce their distress either by restoring actual equity or by restoring psychological equity to the relationship.

Applications of Equity Theory

Researchers have applied the equity framework to four major areas of human interaction: (a) business relationships, (b) exploitative relationships, (c) helping relationships, and (d) intimate relationships.

Equity Theory and Business Relationships

The vast majority of equity research has been conducted in industrial settings. Since excellent and recent summaries of this material are available elsewhere (see Adams, 1965; Lawler, 1968; Opsahl & Dunnette, 1966; Pritchard, 1969; Weick & Nesset, 1969), we will not review this literature here.

Equity Theory and Exploitative Relationships

At first researchers were preoccupied with testing equity theory in industrial settings. Eventually they realized that the theory could be applied to social as well as to business exchanges. The first social relationships to come under their scrutiny were "exploitative" relationships—relationships in which one participant received far greater relative outcomes than did another.

The decision to focus on exploitative relations was a natural one. It is easy to analyze exploitative relations within the equity framework. We can reasonably define a "harmdoer" as "one who commits an act which causes his partner's relative outcomes to fall short of his own." The participant whose relative outcomes are reduced is the "victim" of the inequitable action.

Let us first consider how harmdoers have been found to respond after treating another inequitably.

Reactions of the Harmdoer

According to our theory (Proposition III), an individual who receives higher outcomes than he knows he deserves will feel distress. Compelling evidence exists to support the contention that individuals do feel intense distress after injuring another. Theorists have labeled this distress as "guilt," "fear of retaliation," "dissonance," "empathy," or "conditioned anxiety." Basically, however, a harmdoer's distress is presumed to arise from two sources: fear of retaliation and threatened self-esteem. Presumably, both retaliation distress and self-concept distress have their roots in the socialization process.

Retaliation distress. Children are usually punished if they are caught injuring others. Soon they come to experience conditioned anxiety when they harm another or even contemplate doing so. [Aronfreed (1964) provides a description of the development of conditioned anxiety in children.] By the time the normal individual reaches adulthood, he experiences some distress whenever he harms another. How much anxiety he experiences in a given harmdoing situation depends first on how similar the stimuli associated with harmdoing are to those stimuli previously associated with punishment, and second on the magnitude and timing of previous punishment.

The conditioned anxiety that one experiences when he harms others may be labeled by the harmdoer as fear that the victim, the victim's sympathizers, legal agencies, or even God will restore equity to the harmdoer/victim relationship by punishing the exploiter.

Self-concept distress. Harmdoing often generates a second kind of discomfort: self-concept distress. In most societies, nearly everyone accepts the ethical principle that "one should be fair and equitable in his dealings with others" (cf. Fromm, 1956, for an interesting discussion of the pervasiveness of the "fairness" principle). Harming another violates a normal individual's ethical principles and conflicts with his self-expectations. When the normal individual violates his own standards, he experiences self-concept distress.

In arguing that the "normal" individual accepts norms of "fairness," we are *not* arguing that everyone internalizes exactly the same code, or internalizes it to the same extent and follows that code without deviation. Juvenile delinquents and confidence men, for example, often *seem* to behave as if the exploitation of others was completely consonant with their self-expectations. Evidence suggests, however, that even deviants do internalize standards of fairness, at least to some extent. It is true that they may repeatedly violate such standards for financial or social gain, but such violations do seem to cause at least minimal distress. Exploitation evidently causes deviants enough discomfort that they spend time and effort trying to convince others that their behavior is "fair." Anecdotal evidence on these points comes from interviews with confidence men (see Goffman, 1952) and delinquents (see Sykes & Matza, 1957).

The distress that arises when one performs unethical or dissonant acts has been discussed in great detail by guilt theorists and by cognitive dissonance theorists. See, for example, Maher (1966), Arnold (1960), and Bramel (1969) for these two points of view.

THE GREATER THE INEQUITY, THE GREATER THE DISTRESS

In Propositions III and IV we proposed that the more inequitable a relationship, the more distress the participants will feel, and the harder they will try to restore equity. There is some indirect evidence to support the notion that the more one harms another, the more distressed he will be. Brock and Buss (1962, 1964) recruited student assistants to shock other students each time the students made a learning error. The authors discovered that the more painfully one required the assistant to shock his fellow student, the more the student tried to foist responsibility for administering the shock onto the supervisor. Lerner and Simmons (1966) found that the more one allows another to suffer, the more one will derogate the hapless victim. Lerner and Matthews (1967) concluded that the more responsible subjects feel for another's suffering, the more they will derogate the victim. If we assume that a harmdoer will be especially distressed when his victim suffers a great deal or when the harmdoer is obviously responsible for the victim's suffering, these findings are consistent with Propositions III and IV.

There is also much compelling evidence available to support the contention (Proposition IV) that participants involved in inequitable relations will try to eliminate their distress by restoring either actual equity or psychological equity to their relationship.

RESTORATION OF ACTUAL EQUITY

Harmdoers can restore equity in a straightforward way: They can *compensate* their victims. When we think of "compensation," we usually envision acts designed to increase the victim's outcomes. However, one can also compensate the victim by allowing him to lower his inputs. The underpaid and overworked secretary, for example, may be encouraged to "take Monday off" by her uneasy boss.

Cynics such as Junius have acidly observed that even "a death bed repentance seldom reaches to restitution." This pessimism is not always warranted. Recent studies verify the fact that harmdoers do commonly compensate their victims: Walster, Walster, Abrahams, and Brown (1966), Walster and Prestholdt (1966), Brock and Becker (1966), Berscheid and Walster (1967), Freedman, Wallington, and Bless (1967), Carlsmith and Gross (1969), and Berscheid, Walster, and Barclay (1969).

Theoretically, a harmdoer can restore actual equity to his relationship with the victim by using a second strategy—*self-deprivation*. The harm-doer could voluntarily reduce his own relative outcomes to the victim's level; one could curtail his own outcomes from the relationship or increase his inputs.

The anecdotal and clinical literature provide support for the notion that individuals sometimes do react to the commission of harmful acts by administering punishment to themselves or by seeking punishment from others. Indeed, Sarnoff (1962) has suggested that "punishment is the only kind of response that is sufficient to reduce the tension of guilt [p. 351]." Attempts to demonstrate self-punishment in the laboratory have been uniformly unsuccessful, however. In the view of our assumption that individuals prefer to maximize their rewards whenever possible (Proposition I), we would expect individuals to restore equity by employing self-punishment only as a last resort. The data indicate that self-deprivation is not a popular strategy for equalizing our relations with others.

RESTORATION OF PSYCHOLOGICAL EQUITY

As we noted earlier, by distorting reality, one can restore psychological equity to his relationship with another. If the harmdoer can aggrandize the victim's relative outcomes or minimize his own, he can convince himself that his inequitable relationship is, in fact, equitable. Some distortions which harmdoers have been detected using include derogation of the victim, minimization of the victim's suffering, or denial of one's own responsibility for the victim's suffering.

Derogation of the Victim

An act which injures another is not inequitable if the victim deserves to be harmed. Thus, an obvious way in which a person who has harmed another can persuade himself that his act was equitable is by devaluating the victim's inputs.

That harmdoers will often derogate their victims has been demonstrated by Sykes and Matza (1957), Davis and Jones (1960), Berkowitz (1962), Davidson (1964), Glass (1964), and Walster and Prestholdt (1966). In a typical experiment, Davis and Jones (1960) found that students who were hired to humiliate other students (as part of a research project) generally ended up convincing themselves that the student deserved to be ridiculed. Sykes and Matza (1957) found that juvenile delinquents often defend their victimization of others by arguing that their victims are really homosexuals, bums, or possess other traits which make them deserving of punishment. In tormenting others, then, the delinquents can claim to be the restorers of justice rather than harmdoers.

Minimization of the Victim's Suffering

If a harmdoer can deny that the victim was harmed, he can convince himself that his relationship with the victim is an equitable one. Sykes and Matza (1957) and Brock and Buss (1962) demonstrated that harmdoers consistently underestimate how much harm they have done to another. Brock and Buss, for example, found that college students who administer electric shock to other students soon come to markedly underestimate the painfulness of the shock they are delivering.

Denial of Responsibility for the Act

If the harmdoer can perceive that it was not his behavior but rather the action of someone else (e.g., the experimenter or fate) that caused the victim's suffering, then *his* relationship with the victim becomes an equitable one. (The person who is unjustly assigned responsibility for reducing the victim's outcomes will now be perceived as the harmdoer, and it will be *his* relationship with the victim, not the harmdoer's relationship, that is perceived as inequitable.)

That harmdoers often deny their responsibility for harmdoing has been documented by Sykes and Matza (1957) and by Brock and Buss (1962, 1964). In daily life, denial of responsibility seems to be a favorite strategy of those who are made to feel guilty about exploiting others. War criminals protest vehemently they were "only following orders."

The research results enumerated in this section document the eagerness with which harmdoers restore equity after injuring others. Equity theory provides an orderly framework for cataloguing the possible reactions of harmdoers. But this is not enough. Researchers are more interested in prediction than in description.

Prediction of a Harmdoer's Response

To predict which of many potential techniques harmdoers will use, researchers adopted a simple strategy. They tried to (a) condense the multitude of potentially equity-restoring responses into a few meaningful categories and (b) isolate variables which determine which class of responses a harmdoer will choose.

CONDENSATION OF RESPONSES INTO A FEW CATEGORIES

Prediction was facilitated when researchers eventually realized that harm-doers' responses generally fall into two distinct categories: Harmdoers tend either to *compensate* their victims (and to restore actual equity) or to *justify* the victims' deprivation (and restore psychological equity). Harmdoers rarely use both techniques in concert; compensation and justification seem to be alternative, rather than supplementary, techniques for restoring equity.[9]

Logically, it should be difficult for a harmdoer to use compensation and justification techniques in concert. It should be difficult for the harmdoer to simultaneously acknowledge on the one hand that he is at fault for the victim's undeserved suffering and thus exert himself in an attempt to assist the victim while on the other hand convincing himself that his victim deserves to suffer, that he is not really injured, or that the harmdoer is not responsible for the victim's suffering.[10]

There is empirical evidence that individuals generally *do not* use compensation and justification in concert. Walster and Prestholdt (1966) led social work trainees to inadvertently harm their clients. Subsequently trainees were asked to evaluate the clients and asked to volunteer their free time to help them. Compensation and justification responses were found to be negatively related; the more trainees derogated their clients, the *less* time they volunteered to help them. Lerner and Simmons (1966) found that observers only derogated a victim when they were powerless to aid him in any way. When it was clear that compensation would occur, no derogation was detected. Thus, we can conclude:

Conclusion I: The harmdoer will avoid using justification techniques and compensation techniques in concert.

ISOLATING VARIABLES WHICH INFLUENCE A HARMDOER'S RESPONSE

Once researchers discovered that (a) a hodge-podge of equity-restoring techniques could be classified into two distinct categories—compensation or justifica-

---

[9] It is possible, of course, for individuals to use compensation and justification techniques *in sequence*. For example, a harmdoer may attempt to make compensation, find it impossible, and then resort to justification. Or he may attempt to justify his behavior, have his rationalizations challenged, and then accede to demands for compensation. However, individuals do not generally use compensation and justification techniques simultaneously.

[10] Although victims generally do not use compensation and justification techniques in concert, it is, of course, possible for them to do so. For example, a harmdoer could inadequately compensate the victim (thus partially restoring actual equity) and minimize the harm he had done the victim. Distorting the victim's outcomes would allow the harmdoer to deceive himself that this inadequate compensation had completely restored equity.

tion—and (b) compensation and justification tend to be mutually exclusive techniques for restoring equity, their task was vastly simplified. It is easier to detect the antecedents of two alternative responses—compensation or justification—than to ferret out the antecedents of a multitude of disorganized responses.

In addition, the recognition that harmdoers generally compensate *or* justify made it evident that it is practically, as well as theoretically, important to identify the variables which push harmdoers toward one or another response.

Any society has a vested interest in encouraging harmdoers to voluntarily compensate their victims rather than derogating them. If a harmdoer refuses to make restitution, the victim is left in sad straits. Not only has he been deprived of material benefits which he deserves, but he must face both the indignity of derogation and the added difficulty that the harmdoer, because of his derogation, may *continue* to treat him unjustly (see Berscheid, Boye, & Darley, 1968). Societies should naturally prefer that their citizens restore actual equity after committing injustices rather than engaging in a series of justifications which end in shared bitterness and possible further harmdoing. For theoretical and practical reasons, then, we are interested in identifying those variables that encourage harmdoers to make voluntary compensation and those variables which encourage justification.

Two situational variables have been found to be important: (a) the adequacy of the existing techniques for restoring equity and (b) the cost of the existing techniques for restoring equity. We would expect people to prefer techniques that *completely* restore equity to techniques that only *partially* restore equity. and to prefer techniques with little material or psychological cost to techniques with greater cost. More precisely we would expect:

Corollary IV.1: Other things being equal, the more adequate a harmdoer perceives an available equity-restoring technique to be, the more likely he is to use this technique to restore equity.

Corollary I.2: Other things being equal, the more costly a harmdoer perceives an available equity-restoring technique to be, the less likely he is to use this technique to restore equity.

Adequacy of Equity-Restoring Techniques

The "adequacy" of a technique is defined as the extent to which that technique will *exactly* restore equity to the harmdoer/victim relationship. As we pointed out in Proposition III, participants in inequitable relations feel uncomfortable and the more inequitable the relationship, the worse participants feel. Harmdoers thus have a vested interest in reestablishing as equitable a relationship as possible.

Data support the contention (Corollary IV.1) that individuals are more likely to compensate their victim if adequate compensation is available than if it is not.

Adequacy of Compensation

By definition, an adequate compensation is one that can exactly balance the harm done. Both *insufficient* compensations and *excessive* compensations lack adequacy; thus, harmdoers should be reluctant to make such compensations.

Why should a harmdoer be reluctant to make an insufficient compensation? (Certainly his victim would prefer insufficient compensation to no compensation at all.) If insufficient compensation is the *only* way by which a harmdoer can reduce his distress, rather than do nothing, he will probably choose to restore at least partial equity to his relationship with the victim. But insufficient compensation is *not* the only equity-restoring technique open to the harmdoer. A technique incompatible with compensation is available to him. The harmdoer can always completely eliminate his distress by *completely* justifying the victim's suffering. Thus, as available compensations become increasingly insufficient, justification techniques should become increasingly appealing to the harmdoer.

Making an excessive compensation is also an unsatisfactory way to restore equity. An excessive compensation eliminates one kind of inequity by producing another. The harmdoer who compensates his victim excessively does not restore equity; he simply becomes a victim instead of a harmdoer—a most undesirable transformation.

Berscheid and Walster (1967) tested the hypothesis that a harmdoer's tendency to compensate his victim will be an increasing function of the adequacy of the compensations available to him. Their results provide support for Corollary IV.1. In this experiment, women from various church groups were led to cheat fellow parishioners out of trading stamps in a vain attempt to win additional stamps for themselves. When the women were subsequently given an opportunity to compensate the victim (at no cost to themselves), it was found that adequacy of compensation was crucial in determining whether or not the women chose to compensate. Women who could compensate with an adequate compensation (exactly restoring the number of books the partner had lost) were much more likely to make restitution than were women limited to insufficient compensation (a few stamps) or to excessive compensation (a great many stamp books). This finding was replicated by Berscheid *et al.* (1969).

The hypothesis that individuals are predisposed to make adequate compensation and to resist making inadequate or excessive compensations has some interesting implications. In life, exploited individuals sometimes try to impress on those in a position to make restitution how much they have suffered in the hope of eliciting increased restitution. It is natural to assume that the better a case one makes for his claim, the more likely it is that he will be compensated. The preceding research, however, indicates that in some instances, it might be a more effective strategy for a victim to minimize his suffering than to aggrandize it.

The greater the inequity a victim documents, the more restitution the harmdoer should be willing to make—up to a point. However, at some point, the described inequity will become so large that the harmdoer will despair of *ever* being able to make complete restitution. Once this point is reached, it is no longer profitable for the victim to exaggerate his suffering. Further exaggeration will *not* elicit increased restitution—the harmdoer has already reached his limit. In fact, the more additional suffering the victim describes, the more inadequate the compensations available to the harmdoer become, and thus the more unwilling he should become to provide any compensation at all.

The preceding reasoning may provide some insight into the public reaction to demands for compensation. Most Americans probably feel that no matter how hard they try they cannot make adequate restitution to blacks for their centuries of exploitation. Black leaders have argued that citizens should at least take some step toward restoring equity. However, the idea of making a small step toward restoring equity, making a small compensation, is not very attractive to many citizens. The effort to make a partial compensation mocks their rationalizations that no harm was done or that blacks deserved their treatment. If one cannot compensate enough to reduce his own distress, he is perhaps happier with his rationalizations. If we generalize shamelessly from the preceding findings, we might speculate that an effective strategy for deprived minorities may be to *minimize* their description of their suffering and to make it clear that if *available* compensations are extended, it will completely *eliminate* the debt owed to them. While this is not true, it may be a profitable strategy since it would insure that blacks would receive at least minimal compensation.

Adequacy of Justifications

To restore complete psychological equity in his relationship with a victim, a harmdoer must be able to conceive of justifications that (a) adequately justify the harm done and (b) are plausible to himself, the victim, and to others. (Only if the harmdoer believes his own distortions will he be able to eliminate self-concept distress; only if he imagines that the victim accepts his justifications will he be able to eliminate fear of retaliation.)

Little is known about what causes an excuse to be seen as "adequate justification" for a harmful act. Once a harmdoer conceives of an adequate justification, however, we know a great deal about the factors which determine how plausible or *credible* a given justification is (see McGuire, 1968). For a delightful and extensive account of excuses that work, see Scott and Lyman (1968).

In this article we describe only two factors that have been found to determine how plausible, and thus how readily used, various justifications are.

1. A harmdoer will perceive a potential justification to be more credible when it requires little distortion of reality than when it requires a great deal of

reality distortion. The more serious or extensive a distortion of reality required by a justification, the less credible these justifications should be to the victim, the harmdoer, and others. A justification that no one believes is not very effective in restoring equity. Some tangential support for this proposition comes from Rosenberg and Abelson (1960), who provide evidence that individuals prefer to distort reality as little as possible.

2. The more contact the harmdoer has had (or anticipates having) with the victim or the victim's sympathizers, the less likely he will be to justify his harmdoing.

There are two reasons why one should be more reluctant to distort an intimate's relative outcomes than to distort those of a stranger: First, the more intimate we are with someone, the more likely we are to have voluminous information about that person. Thus, when one tries to distort an intimate's characteristics, he will soon find himself in trouble. The harmdoer's fine rationalizations will keep bumping up against recalcitrant facts. However, it will be easy for one's fantasies about a stranger to proliferate boundlessly.

Virtually all of the cognitive consistency theorists (Abelson & Rosenberg, 1958; Cartwright & Harary, 1956; Festinger, 1957; Rosenberg, 1960; Zajonc, 1960) acknowledge it is easier to change beliefs that exist in isolation. Walster, Berscheid, and Barclay (1967) demonstrated that one is more likely to avoid distortions when future objective evidence may contradict these distortions than when objective evidence will be unavailable. Both these observations are consistent with the expectation that it is harder to distort the familiar than the unknown.

There is a second reason why one should be more reluctant to distort an intimate's relative outcomes than those of a stranger. One should expect more difficulty *maintaining* an adequate distortion when the distortion involves an intimate than when it involves a stranger. If one engages in a massive distortion of an intimate's character, he must anticipate that his friend will have more opportunities (than a stranger would) to confront him, challenge his rationalizations, and perhaps retaliate against him.

For two reasons, then, familiarity with the victim should breed accuracy and discourage justification as a distress-reducing technique. Data are available to support this hypothesis. Davis and Jones (1960) found that subjects who ridicule another student, derogate him more when they do not expect to see him again than when a meeting is expected. Davis and Jones assumed that they secured this result because subjects who anticipate future contact plan to "neutralize their harmdoing" by explaining that their negative evaluation does not represent their true feelings. However, since the victim has already suffered by the time neutralization occurs, this explanation is not totally satisfactory. An equally plausible interpretation is that distortion becomes more difficult and less likely to occur when future interaction is anticipated.

Ross (1965) conducted an experiment in which students were led to choose to consign their partner to electric shock to avoid painful shock themselves. In some conditions, the students believed they would work with their partner only once. In other cases they believed they would work with him on many tasks. Ross discovered that when the student allowed the other to be injured, derogation occurred more often when subsequent contact was not anticipated. This finding is, of course, satisfactorily explained by the hypothesis that we only distort the characteristics of those individuals who can be kept "out of sight and out of mind."

This conclusion suggests that the exploited might do well to harrass their exploiters. For example, so long as exploited minorities are geographically and socially segregated, an exploiter can conveniently reduce whatever vague feelings of guilt he might have by justifying his exploitation. It is easy for him to maintain that minority members deserve their exploitation ("The poor are shiftless and lazy and don't want a steady job.") or that they are not really suffering ("A Chicano can live better on a dollar than a white can can on five dollars."). We might expect that integrated housing and forced association will make use of such rationalizations more difficult. Until such integration occurs, however, minority members could arrange "symbolic integration." Welfare mothers who feel that suburban whites reinforce one another's "preposterous rationalizations," could arrange to expose the taxpayers to reality. They might travel to the suburbs, talk to suburbanites about their plight, confront shoppers, speak up in suburban Parents Teachers Associations, etc.

We proposed that two variables determine how a harmdoer chooses to restore equity to his relationship with the victim: (a) the adequacy of existing techniques for restoring equity (Corollary IV.1), and (b) the cost of the existing techniques for restoring equity (Corollary I.2). In the last section we provided data showing that adequate compensations and justifications are preferred to inadequate ones. In the next section, we present evidence that the greater the cost of an equity-restoring technique, the less likely a harmdoer is to use that technique to restore equity.

Cost of Equity-Restoring Techniques

In Proposition I, we stated that individuals try to maximize their outcomes. In Proposition II, we stated that groups try to arrange things so that individuals can maximize their outcomes by behaving equitably, that is, by insuring that their partner receives relative outcomes equal to their own.

On the basis of these two propositions, we can make the following derivation:

Derivation I: Other things being equal, the harmdoer will use that equity-restoring technique that allows the pair to maintain the highest possible relative outcomes.

This conclusion is similar to Adams's (1956) assumption that a person "will reduce inequity, insofar as possible, in a manner that will yield him the largest outcomes" (p. 284). Adams presented evidence supporting the validity of his hypothesis (Adams, 1963; Adams & Rosenbaum, 1962). This hypothesis is also supported by the results of an experiment concerning preferences among forms of equity resolution in fictitious work situations (see Weick & Nesset, 1969).

Derivation I is consistent with the observation that self-punishment seems to be an unpopular way for harmdoers to restore equity to a relationship. Theoretically, both compensation to the victim and self-punishment are equally adequate techniques for restoring actual equity to a relationship. In practice, however, one rarely finds harmdoers restoring equity by self-punishment. Derivation I reminds us of the reason for the aversion to this equity-restoring technique; harmdoers resist lowering their outcomes unnecessarily.

Anecdotal evidence (Jon Freedman, personal communication, 1970) supports the proposition that subjects in laboratory experiments energetically resist restoring equity by self-punishment. A very few experiments have demonstrated that individuals are more willing to perform unpleasant altruistic acts following commitment of harmful acts (e.g., Darlington & Macker, 1966; Freedman *et al.*, 1967). However, in these experiments the experimenters have made it difficult or impossible for the harmdoer to compensate the victim. In addition, the guilt-inducing procedures used in these experiments are such that justifications (denial of responsibility for the harm, denial that the harm was done, or perception that the act was just) were difficult, if not impossible. Thus, evidence of self-punishment following harmdoing has been restricted to situations in which compensation and justification techniques are almost totally unavailable. The frequency with which use of self-punishment is found, if either compensation or justification is available and perceived as adequate, is unanswered.

Restoration of Equity by the Victim and Outside Agencies

The preceding discussion has focused on the means by which the harmdoer may restore equity to his relationship with the victim. However, the harmdoer is not the only possible agent of equity restoration. The victim, the victim's sympathizers, social workers, the courts, etc., may all intervene to improve the victim's lot. What effect does such intervention have on the harmdoer's perception of the equitableness of his relationship with the victim? The following conclusion seems most reasonable:

Conclusion II: When the victim or an external agency restores equity to a relationship, the harmdoer's distress is reduced, and he is less likely to use additional equity-restoring techniques.

Evidence for this conclusion comes from diverse sources:

Retaliation

Victims do not always sit placidly by, waiting for the harmdoer to decide how to react. Sometimes victims take matters into their own hands and restore equity to the relationship. They may restore equity by seizing that portion of reward they deserve. They could provide the exploiter with ready-made excuses for his behavior (as some Uncle Toms have been known to do), or they can "get even" with the harmdoer by retaliating against him. How does a harmdoer respond under such conditions?

The data available support Conclusion II. When the victim restores equity, it eliminates the harmdoer's need to do so.

Berscheid, Boye, and Walster (1968) conducted an experiment designed to assess the effect that a victim's retaliation has on the exploiter's tendency to justify the victim's suffering by derogating him. The results of this study indicate that a victim can indeed restore equity through retaliation against the exploiter. In this experiment, individuals were hired to administer severe electric shocks to another person. If the victim could not retaliate against the harmdoer, the harmdoer subsequently derogated the victim. However, when the exploiter expected retaliation for his harmful act, the derogation process was arrested; the harmdoer did not derogate the victim.

It is also interesting that the relationship between retaliation and derogation was diametrically opposed for control subjects who merely observed the victim's suffering; those observers who expected to be hurt by the victim in the future liked him less than did those who did not expect to be hurt.

The insight that a victim can restore equity to a victim/harmdoer relationship simply by retaliating has interesting implications: The victim naturally prefers that equity be restored by receiving compensation. Frequently, however, it becomes obvious to the victim that compensation is unlikely to be forthcoming. In such circumstances the victim must realize that the harmdoer is likely to justify the victim's suffering. This is not a pleasant prospect. The exploiter's justifications are potentially dangerous to the victim. The harmdoer who justifies his actions will end up with a distorted and unreal assessment of his own actions. If he distorts the extent to which the victim deserved to be hurt, for example, or minimizes the victim's suffering as a consequence of the act, he may commit further acts based on these distortions (Berscheid, Boye, & Darley, 1968). When a harmdoer uses justification technique, then the victim is left in sad straits. Not only has he been hurt, but as a result of the harmdoer's justification, the probability has increased that he will be hurt again. Thus, speculating from the little we know, one could argue that once it becomes obvious that the harmdoer is not about to compensate the victim, the victim might well retaliate against the harmdoer before he justifies what he has done.

Civil rights leaders have sometimes made similar speculations. James Baldwin (1964), in a statement concerning the blacks' struggle for minority rights in this country, argued that "Neither civilized reason or Christian love would cause any of these people to treat you as they presumably wanted to be treated; only fear of your power to retaliate will cause them to do that, or seem to do it, which was (and is) good enough" (p. 34). Black militants have taken an even stronger position. They have argued that widespread black violence is necessary to restore blacks to full citizenship. The variables they discuss sound much like those we have considered. They talk of the "white devil," his guilt, his denial of racial injustices, and the equity-establishing effects of violence. However, if extrapolation from our findings is relevant, we might suggest that retaliation, or the anticipation of retaliation, will be beneficial *only* if the recipient of the violence feels that he is in some way directly responsible for blacks' suffering. Retaliation against those who feel themselves to be innocent observers of injustices would seem to be a disastrous strategy.

Forgiveness

The victim can restore equity to the harmdoer/victim relationship in a second way: He can "forgive" the apologetic harmdoer.

Harmdoers often apologize to their victim in the hope that the victim will forgive him. If the victim forgives him, this implies that their relationship can proceed again on an equitable basis.

An "apology" is not a single strategy for restoring equity but comprises several quite different strategies.

1. An apology is often a persuasive communication designed to convince the victim that the harmdoer's justifications are plausible. (The harmdoer may point out "You hit me first"; "I didn't mean it"; or "He made me do it.") If the victim agrees that these justifications are plausible, the relationship becomes a *psychologically* equitable one and can proceed as before. [Scott & Lyman (1968) provide a devastating description of how one goes about devising a compelling excuse.]

2. An apology may be designed to *convince* the victim that their relationship is actually equitable. For example, a harmdoer may profusely verbalize how much personal suffering and guilt he has endured as a consequence of his unjust treatment of the victim. If his description is heart-rending enough, the victim may conclude that his score with the harmdoer is settled.

The common television scenario of the careless driver rushing to the hospital room of his victim to express his anguish and remorse becomes explicable through this reasoning. A person not familiar with the common "I'm sorry"– "You're forgiven" sequence might wonder what benefit is conferred upon a dying victim or what wrong is righted by such a demonstration of the harmdoer's personal suffering as a consequence of his act. The answer is none. The act is performed not for the victim's benefit but for the harm-doer's. To say "I'm sorry" is to imply personal suffering and to beg for forgiveness to end one's distress.

The notion that a description of one's remorse and suffering, if convincing, may, in fact, attenuate the wrath and retaliatory intentions of the victim and others has been supported by an experiment conducted by Bramel, Taub, and Blum (1968).

An effusive apology may make a relationship *actually* more equitable in another way. During his apology the harmdoer may humble himself and exalt the victim. This redistribution of esteem may provide a valuable reward to the victim and thus even his score with the harmdoer.

When apologies, self-derogation, and exaltation of the victim do not elicit forgiveness, it is interesting that harmdoers often switch with ease to another technique—often justification techniques.

3. Finally, an apology may be a way in which a harmdoer can acknowledge that the participants' relationship has been inequitable but point out that nothing can be done to remedy the preceding injustice. The harmdoer may ask that the victim "forgive and forget" the injustice so that the relationship can begin anew.

Intervention by Outside Agencies

Outside agencies often intervene when relationships become disturbingly inequitable (see Baker, 1969). Legal and religious agencies sometimes insist that clients make restitution to their victims or punish them when they do not. Social welfare agencies and insurance companies compensate the disadvantaged. What are the effects of such intervention? Undoubtedly, they depend on whether the intervening agency encourages harmdoers to compensate, punishes them, pre-empts their plans to compensate, or simply provides a residual source of compensation for neglected victims.

Society's first intervention attempts are usually directed toward inducing harmdoers to voluntarily compensate their victims. This is a wise policy. Everyone benefits when individuals are motivated to voluntarily compensate those they have injured. The harmdoer who voluntarily decides to compensate becomes a stauncher advocate of the equity norm (see Mills, 1958). The voluntary compensator also serves as a behavioral model for others; observers should be likely to imitate his equitable behavior when they find themselves in a similar situation (see Bandura, 1965).

If it becomes evident that an agency is not going to be able to induce the harmdoer to behave equitably, it probably is beneficial for it to escalate and to force him to make restitution. The person who is forced to compensate at least is dissuaded from justifying his inequitable behavior and is prevented from serving as a negative model for others.

A state can prod an individual into making restitution in a variety of ways. For example, in the Hungarian and Norwegian legal systems, whether or not harmdoers have made restitution is taken into account when determining sentences and granting paroles. When a prisoner's freedom is contingent on whether or not he makes restitution, restitution is obviously not really voluntary. However, the Hungarians consider it better, from a rehabilitative point of view, to elicit semivoluntary restitution than none at all.

Macaulay and Walster (1971) pointed out that in the United States both formal and informal techniques are used to induce restitution:

> the common-law of torts consists of rules which say a wrong-doer must compensate his victim. In addition, the legal system in operation has more avenues to restitution than merely its formal rules. There is a wide variety of procedures which may encourage compensation. . . . Some criminal sanctions are used as leverage to induce restitution: A police officer may decide not to arrest a shoplifter if the wrong-doer is not a professional thief and if the stolen items are returned; a district attorney may decide not to prosecute if the amounts embezzled are returned. (p. 179)

In other systems, restitution is simply extracted from the harmdoer (i.e., money may be deducted from his prison earnings).

The psychological literature (i.e., Brehm & Cohen, 1962) and the observations of penal theorists (e.g., Del Vecchio, 1959; Schafer, 1960; Spencer, 1874) provide some support for the contention that if one induces "fair" behavior, "fair" attitudes will follow.

Sometimes restitution cannot be elicited. (For example, those who injure others are often unknown or are indigent.) In such cases, it may be wise for the community to reconcile itself to the fact that an injustice has occurred and simply intervene to alleviate the victim's suffering. Such intervention is consistent with our notion of fairness (the innocent victim is recompensed) and is expedient (the legitimacy of equity norms is affirmed by society).

Some legal theorists (i.e., see Fry, 1956) have proposed that, in the interests of justice and efficiency, the state should *routinely* assume responsibility for compensating victims of criminal violence. They argue that the state could save time and money if instead of tracking down harmdoers and prodding them into making restitution, it simply provided automatic compensation to the disadvantaged.

We argue that a society should be wary of introducing a compensation procedure that erodes individuals' responsibility for restoring equity, thus weakening their adherence to equity norms. If the harmdoer knows that the outside agency will reestablish equity at no cost to himself, he should have little motivation to initiate his own equity-restoring responses. In addition, it is probable that an agency set up to "right all wrongs" would soon find that it was incapable of fulfilling this mandate. Agencies set up to provide social justice are always meagerly funded. Although citizens may be unanimous in their agreement that social justice is desirable, they seldom agree that society ought to pursue this goal at all costs. Inevitably, agencies are forced to do the best they can with limited funds. Social welfare agencies thus soon evolve into agencies of "social compromise" rather than agencies of perfect "social justice" (see Macaulay & Walster, 1971, for a lengthy discussion of this problem).

For these reasons, public compensation is seen as a residual source of equity restoration, resorted to only when attempts to induce the exploiter to compensate have failed.

PERSONALITY

Throughout the previous section we have taken the nomothetic approach and have attempted to provide a framework to guide prediction of how the average individual will respond following his commission of a harmful act.

In spite of the fact that equity researchers have focused on the nomothetic approach, we should not assume that personality differences are unimportant. It is clear that personality variables will affect how participants evaluate both their own and their partner's inputs and outcomes, how much distress harmdoers feel after injuring another, and how the harmdoer and the victim respond to their shared distress.

For example, we have proposed that after injuring another, a normal harmdoer experiences distress from two sources: (a) He experiences self-concept distress, since his harmful act is inconsistent both with his own good opinion of himself and with his moral principles; and (b) he experiences fear of retaliation distress. Interest in individual differences leads to the obvious conclusion that harmdoers who have high self-esteem (e.g., harmdoers who think they are foresightful, kind, nonexploitative people), and who have strongly internalized ethical standards will feel more self-concept distress after harming another than will individuals who have low self-esteem and poorly internalized ethical standards. A high-self-esteem individual, then, will be expected to make a greater effort to restore equity—either actual or psychological—after harming another than a low-self-esteem individual.

There is some experimental evidence to support this derivation. In an experiment by Glass (1964), an individual's self-esteem was experimentally raised or lowered by providing him with "authoritative" information about his own personality. After harming another, high-self-esteem subjects justified their harmdoing (by derogating their victims) more than did low-self-esteem subjects.

Profitable and interesting attempts to identify some of the individual difference variables that are related to or affect a harmdoer's reaction have been made by Aronfreed (1961), Weinstein, De Vaughan, and Wiley (1969), Lawler and O'Gara (1967), Blumstein and Weinstein (1969), Schwartz (1968), Glass and Wood (1969), and Tornow (1970). Such studies may be expected to considerably sharpen prediction in individual situations.

Reactions of the Exploited

DISTRESS

If an inequitable relationship is distressing to the exploiter, it is doubly distressing for the exploited. Although an exploiter must endure the discomfort of knowing he is participating in an inequitable relationship, he at least has the consolation that he is benefiting materially from his discomfort. The victim has no such comfort—he is losing in every way from the inequity. He is deprived of deserved outcomes, he must endure the discomfort of participating in an inequitable relationship, and he is faced with the unsettling realization that unless he can force the harmdoer to provide compensation, he is likely to justify the inequity by derogating him.

Propositions I, II, and III lead to the following derivation:

Derivation II: A participant will be more distressed by inequity when he is a victim than when he is a harmdoer.

Several theorists have noticed that those who materially benefit from inequity are more tolerant of inequity than are those who materially suffer from it (see Adams, 1965; Blumstein & Weinstein, 1969; Homans, 1961; Lawler, 1968).

Researchers have also documented that those who materially suffer from inequity are quicker to demand a fair distribution of resources than are those who do not (see, e.g., Andrews, 1967; Leventhal & Anderson, 1970; Leventhal & Lane, 1970; Leventhal, Weiss, & Long, 1969).

DEMANDS FOR COMPENSATION

Undoubtedly the victim's first response to exploitation is to seek restitution (see Leventhal & Bergman, 1969; G. Marwell, D. P. Schmitt, & R. Shotola, 1970[11]). If the victim secures compensation, he has restored the relationship to equity, and he has benefited materially. It is easy to see why this is a popular response.

---

[11] Unpublished study entitled "Cooperation and Interpersonal Risk," 1970. Requests should be sent to G. Marwell, Department of Sociology, University of Wisconsin, Madison, Wisconsin.

RETALIATION

A second way a victim can restore equity is by retaliating against the harmdoer (and thereby reducing the harmdoer's outcomes to the level he deserves). Ross, Thibaut, and Evenbeck (1971) demonstrate that when given the opportunity, victims will retaliate against those who have treated them inequitably.

The more inequitably they perceive they were treated, the more they will retaliate. Evidence from Berscheid, Boye, and Walster (1968) suggests that appropriate retaliation will cause the harmdoer (as well as the victim) to perceive that the relationship is again an equitable one.

JUSTIFICATION OF THE INEQUITY

Sometimes a victim finds that it is impossible either to elicit restitution or to retaliate against the harmdoer. The impotent victim is then left with only two options: He can acknowledge that he is exploited and that he is too weak to do anything about it, or he can justify his exploitation. Often, victimized individuals find it less upsetting to distort reality and justify their victimization than to acknowledge that the world is unjust and that they are too impotent to elicit fair treatment (Lerner & Matthews, 1967).

Victimized individuals have been found to restore psychological equity in several ways: Victims sometimes console themselves by imagining that their exploitation has brought compensating benefits ("suffering brings wisdom and purity"), or they console themselves by thinking that in the long run the exploiter will be punished as he deserves ("The mill of the Lord grinds slowly, but it grinds exceedingly fine."). Victims may also convince themselves that their exploiter actually deserves the enormous benefits he receives because he possesses previously unrecognized inputs. Recent data demonstrate that the exploited will justify the excessive benefits of others. Jecker and Landy (1969), Walster and Prestholdt (1966), and A. Hastorf and D. Regan (personal communication, February 1962) pressured individuals into performing a difficult favor for an unworthy recipient. They found that the abashed favor-doer tries to justify the inequity by convincing himself that the recipient is especially needy or worthy.

Reformers who have worked to alleviate social injustices, at great personal sacrifice, are often enraged to discover that the exploited themselves sometimes vehemently defend the status quo. Black militants encounter "Uncle Toms," who defend white supremacy. Women's liberation groups must face angry housewives who threaten to defend to the death the current status of women. Reformers might have more sympathy for such Uncle Toms and "Doris Days" if they understood the psychological underpinnings of such reactions. When one is treated inequitably but has no hope of altering his situation, it is often less degrading to deny reality than to face up to one's humiliating position.

Equity Theory and Helping Relationships

In spite of the fact that social observers reproach individuals for not helping others as much as they "ought" to help, the fact remains that individuals do help one another to a remarkable extent. Public assistance agencies help welfare recipients, parents care for children and elderly parents, Boy Scouts help little old ladies across the street, Congress aids underdeveloped nations, and eager suitors urge gifts on overdeveloped maidens.

On the surface, relationships between benefactors and recipients seem quite different from relationships between victims and exploiters. Conceptually, however, both relationships can be analyzed in the same terms. Let us assume that initially participants are in an equitable relationship. Then the benefactor helps the recipient. Now the previously equitable relationship becomes an inequitable one. The benefactor, like the victim, is now a participant in an inequitable—and unprofitable—relationship. The recipient, like the exploiter, is now a participant in an inequitable—and profitable—relationship. Equity theory leads us to expect that benefactor and recipient, like harmdoer and victim, should experience vague discomfort when they discover they are participating in an inequitable relationship. As Proposition IV indicates, they should alleviate their distress by restoring either actual equity or psychological equity to their relationship.

Research indicates that those in philanthropic relations do respond much as do those in harmdoing relations (see, e.g., Leventhal *et al.*, 1969).

Much of the research investigating the impact of helpful acts on the gift giver and his recipient has been conducted by "action psychologists." The research of these psychologists was generally not designed to test theoretical propositions but to enable practitioners to devise better welfare programs, construct better foreign aid programs, etc. As a consequence of their practical orientation, helping researchers focused on very different variables than have harmdoing researchers. This difference in focus has produced unusual theoretical benefits. Helping researchers enable us to document the importance of variables which harmdoing theorists have contended were theoretically important but which they had totally neglected to investigate empirically. Let us consider two variables which helping theorists have found to be important determinants of participants' responses: intentionality and ability to repay.

Intentionality

Proposition III stated that when individuals find themselves participating in inequitable relationships, they will become distressed. It seems plausible to argue that an individual who feels *responsible* for creating an inequity should feel more distressed than an individual who *inadvertently* finds himself in an inequitable relationship. The intentional harmdoer should experience both self-concept distress *and* fear of retaliation distress. At most, the inadvertent harmdoer should experience only retaliation distress.

A few harmdoing theorists observed that the person who deliberately provokes an inequity *should* become more distressed than the person who accidentally behaves inequitably (see, e.g., Davis & Jones, 1960; Glass, 1964). Unfortunately, harmdoing researchers can call up little evidence to document this contention. Few studies have investigated the reactions of voluntary harmdoers. Instead of focusing on the reactions of voluntary harmdoers, researchers have focused on the reactions of individuals who were prodded into injuring others. The reason for this is simple. Laboratory researchers found it almost impossible to induce subjects to voluntarily harm others. Even intensely provoked subjects would refuse to treat another inequitably. To induce subjects to harm another, the experimenters had to practically force them to behave inequitably. By necessity, then, rather than by design, harmdoing researchers were confined to studying the reactions of inadvertent and reluctant harmdoers.

Helping researchers, on the other hand, have not encountered such problems. Their research finally enables us to document the importance of intentionality in determining how a benefactor and a recipient respond to inequity. The data they provide lead to the following conclusion:

Conclusion III: When the inequity is intentionally produced, participants in an inequitable relationship will experience more distress and will have stronger desires to restore equity to the relationship than if the inequity occurs inadvertently.

Some support for Conclusion III comes from Thibaut and Riecken (1955), Goldner (1960), Goranson and Berkowitz (1966), Greenberg (1968), and Greenberg and Frisch (1972). Their research demonstrates that when one is intentionally helped, he has a much stronger desire to reciprocate (and thus to restore equity to his relationship with the benefactor) than when he is helped accidentally.

A typical experiment was conducted by Greenberg and Frisch (1972) in which they recruited subjects to participate in an experiment ostensibly designed "to identify personality characteristics associated with success in the business world." Subjects were promised extra credit if they were successful on a task. During the course of the experiment, the subjects discovered that they had little chance of succeeding unless they received help from their partners. (Their partners possessed graph cards which the subjects needed to successfully complete their tasks.) In all cases the partner helped the subject: In some cases this help was intentional; in other cases it was not. In the high-intentionality condition, the partner sent the subject the graph cards he needed along with a note: "I have some duplicates that probably belong to you. I'm sending them over since you can probably use them." In the low-intentionality condition, the partner sent the needed graph cards, but they were accompanied by a note which made it clear that the partner did not realize that he was helping the subject. The note said: "Some of my cards don't have the month on them. Can you help me and identify them for me?" Before the subjects could reply, however, the inadvertent benefactor sent him another note saying: "Forget it. I found the cards I was missing."

The subject's eagerness to restore equity to his relationship with the partner (by repaying the help he had received) was then assessed. As predicted, subjects were more eager to pay back the intentional helper than the inadvertent helper.

Ability to Repay

A second variable has an important impact on how an altruistic act affects the benefactor and his recipient, that is, the beneficiary's ability to make restitution. Earlier (see Corollaries IV.1 and I.2) we argued that the adequacy and the cost of available equity-restoring techniques would determine how individuals would restore equity. The same rationale is applicable here: If a recipient has *no* ability to repay his benefactor or has the ability to make only a most *inadequate* compensation, he is unlikely to try to restore equity via compensation techniques. He is more likely to justify his windfall instead. On these grounds, we would expect ability to make restitution to be a theoretically important variable.

A variety of researchers have testified that ability to repay is a potent determinant of how helping affects the benefactor-recipient relationship. Those researchers who have investigated the reactions to help on the part of welfare clients, underdeveloped nations, and the physically handicapped have dealt with recipients who know they will never be able to repay their benefactors. Researchers who have investigated the reactions to help of receivers of holiday gifts, members of the kula ring (a complex institution of international ceremonial exchange), and the kindness of neighbors have dealt with donors and recipients who know that each helpful act will be reciprocated in kind. The differing reactions of participants in reciprocal versus nonreciprocal relations underscore the importance of the recipient's "ability to repay" in determining how help affects a relationship. Ability to repay seems to determine whether favor-doing generates pleasant social interactions or discomfort and rationalization.

Research supports *Conclusion IV:* Undeserved gifts produce inequity in a relationship. If the participants know the recipient can and will reciprocate, the inequity is viewed as temporary, and thus it produces little distress and little need to justify the inequity. If the participants know the recipient cannot or will not reciprocate, however, a real inequity is produced; the participants will experience distress and will therefore need to restore actual or psychological equity to the relationship.

Evidence in support of Conclusion IV comes from three diverse sources:

1. On the basis of ethnographic data, Mauss (1954) concluded that three types of obligations are widely distributed in human societies in both time and space: (a) the obligation to give, (b) the obligation to receive, and (c) the obligation to repay. Mauss (1954) and Dillon (1968) agreed that when individuals are prevented from discharging their obligations, mutual distress is the result. They noted that while reciprocal exchanges breed cooperation and good feelings, gifts that cannot be reciprocated breed discomfort, distress, and dislike. The authors observed that some societies have worked out exchange systems in which everyone can be both a donor and a receiver. (The kula ring is an example.) Harmonious stable relations are said to be the result. They contrasted these societies with those in which no mechanisms for getting rid of obligations by returning gifts is provided. For example, Dillon (1968) noted:

> Instead of the *kula* principle operating in the Marshall Plan, the aid effort unwittingly took on some of the characteristics of the potlatch ceremony of the 19th Century among North Pacific Coast Indians in which property was destroyed in rivalry, and the poor humiliated. (p. 15)

Volatile and unpleasant relations are said to be the result of such continuing inequities. These authors, along with Blau (1955) and Smith (1892), agreed that the ability to reciprocate is an important determinant of how nations will respond to help from their neighbors.

2. There is evidence that individuals are more likely to *accept* gifts that can be reciprocated than gifts that cannot.

Greenberg (1968), Berkowitz (1968), and Berkowitz and Friedman (1967) demonstrated that people are reluctant to ask for help if they cannot repay it.

Greenberg (1968) told subjects that they would be participating in a study of the effects of physical disability on work performance. Subjects were told that on the first task they would have restricted ability to use their arms. It was obvious to them that this restriction would make it difficult for them to perform the task they had been assigned. If the incapacitated subject wished, however, he knew he could solicit help from another subject on this task. Half of the subjects believed that the fellow subject would need their help on a second task and that they would be able to provide assistance. The remaining subjects believed that the fellow subject would *not* need their help and that, in any case, they would be unable to provide much help. The subjects' expectations about whether or not they could reciprocate any help provided to them strongly affected their willingness to request help. Subjects in the no-reciprocity condition waited significantly longer before requesting help than did those in the reciprocity condition. Greenberg and Shapiro (1971) replicated these findings.

There are three reasons why individuals may be reluctant to accept help when they are unable to reciprocate in kind: (a) Individuals probably avoid accepting undeserved benefits because such benefits place them in an inequitable relationship with the benefactor. As we indicated in Proposition III, inequitable relationships are unpleasant relationships, and individuals avoid unpleasantness. (b) Individuals may avoid accepting help which they cannot repay in kind, because to accept such help means one is obligated for an indefinite period to repay the benefactor in unspecified ways. The recipient might reasonably be worried that his benefactor may attempt to extract greater repayment than the recipient would have been willing to give, had the conditions of the exchange been known ahead of time. Democritis (in the fourth century B.C.) said: "Accept favors in the foreknowledge that you will have to give a greater return for them." The recipient may be unwilling to extend such unlimited blanket credit to his benefactor. [See Blau (1967) for a discussion of this point.] (c) Or, the recipient may have more specific fears. He may worry that the benefactor will demand excessive gratitude or constant acknowledgment of his social or moral superiority from the recipient.

Homans (1961) observed that "anyone who accepts from another a service he cannot repay in kind incurs inferiority as a cost of receiving the service. The esteem he gives the other he foregoes himself" (p. 320). The recipient may be unwilling to risk being assigned so menial a status as a consequence of accepting help. [See Blau (1967) for further discussion of this point.]

3. Research also demonstrates that gifts that can be reciprocated are *preferred* to gifts that cannot be repaid. Gergen (1968) questioned citizens in countries that had received United States aid as to how they felt about the assistance their country received. Gergen noted that international gifts, when they are accompanied by clearly stated obligations, are preferred either to gifts that are not accompanied by obligations or gifts that are accompanied by excessive "strings." Presumably, gifts that can be exactly reciprocated (by fulfilling clearly stated obligations) are preferred to gifts that cannot be reciprocated or to gifts which require excessive reciprocation.

In laboratory research, Gergen (1968) found additional support for the conclusion that individuals like a benefactor more when they know they can reciprocate his help than when they know they cannot return his generosity.

Gergen investigated the reactions of male college-age students in the United States, Japan, and Sweden to inequitable situations. Students were recruited to participate in an experiment on group competition. Things were arranged so that during the course of the game, the subject discovered that he was losing badly. At a critical stage (when the student was just about to be eliminated from the game), one of the "luckier" players in the game sent him an envelope. The envelope contained a supply of chips and a note. For one-third of the subjects (low-obligation-condition subjects), the note explained that the chips were theirs to keep, that the giver did not need them, and that they need not be returned. One-third of the subjects (equal-obligation-condition subjects) received a similar note, except that the giver of the chips asked the subject to return an equal number of chips later in the proceedings. The remaining subjects (high-obligation-condition subjects) received a note from the giver in which he asked for the chips to be returned with interest and for the subject to help him out later in the game.

At the end of the game, subjects were queried about their attraction toward various partners. The results support Conclusion IV: Those partners who provided benefits without ostensible obligation or who asked for excessive benefits were both judged to be less attractive than were partners who proposed that the student make exact restitution later in the game.

J. Gergen, P. Diebold, and M. Seipel[12] conducted a variation of the preceding study. Just as subjects were about to be eliminated from a game because of their consistent losses, another "player" in the game loaned the subject some resources. The donor loaned the chips with the expectation that they would be paid back. However, in subsequent play, only half of the subjects managed to retain their chips. Thus, half of the subjects were unable to return the gift; half were able to do so. In subsequent evaluations of the donor, recipients that were unable to repay the donor evaluated him less positively than did recipients that were able to repay. These results were replicated in both Sweden and the United States. These results are consistent with Tacitus's observation that "Benefits are only acceptable so far as they seem capable of being requited: Beyond that point, they excite hatred instead of gratitude."

Equity Theory and Intimate Relations

When equity theorists argue that business or neighborly relationships will endure only so long as they are profitable to both participants, few demur. Yet, when one argues that intimate relations—relations between husband and wife, parent and child, or best friends—might be similarly dependent on the exchange of rewards, objections are quickly voiced. People insist their intimate relations are "special" relations—relations untainted by crass considerations of social exchange.

For example, Liebow (1967) reported the sentiments of Tally, a black "streetcorner man":

> The pursuit of security and self-esteem push him to romanticize his perception
> of his friends and friendships. . . . He prefers to see the movement of money,

---

[12] Study in preparation entitled "Intentionality and Ability to Reciprocate as Determinants of Reactions to Aid."

goods, services and emotional support between friends as flowing freely out of
loyalty and generosity and according to need rather than a mutual exchange
resting securely on a quid pro quo basis. . . . (p. 34)

Yet, in spite of Tally's insistence that his relationship with Wee Tom
transcended selfish considerations, an outsider would be skeptical of this contention. Liebow, for example, pointed out that Tally and Wee Tom's relationship
quickly disintegrated when mutual reinforcement faltered. When Tally won
$135 on numbers and refused to lend his "walking buddy" any more than $5,
their friendship began to disintegrate (Liebow, 1967, pp. 176–177).

Anticipating inevitable opposition, then, we still contend that even in the
most intimate relations, considerations of equity will influence strongly the
viability and pleasantness of a relationship.

A variety of equity theorists have voiced similar conclusions: Blau (1967)
argued it is inevitable that people generally end up paired with those partners
they "deserve." He pointed out that if one wants to reap the benefits of
associating with another, he must offer his partner enough to make it worthwhile for him to stay in the relationship. The more the partner has to offer, the
more demand there will be for the partner's company, and the more one will
have to offer before he can hope to win the other's friendship. Thus, market
principles insure each person will get as desirable a friend as he "deserves."

On the basis of such reasoning, Backman and Secord (1966), Homans
(1961), and Blau (1968) proposed a "matching hypothesis"—they predicted that
the more equitable a relationship is, the more viable it will be.[13]

Backman and Secord (1966) argued that (in groups) "The final structure
that emerges is always a compromise. The group structure moves toward an
equilibrium in which each person's position in the affect structure is the best he
can obtain in terms of his reward-cost outcomes" (p. 190). Thus, they proposed
that partners of similar value tend to pair up.

Homans (1961) argued that people choose intimates who are about equal to
them in status.

Theorists have even suggested that equity considerations affect one's most
intimate choices—one's choice of a romantic and marriage partner.

A number of experimenters have investigated this proposition. Their data
lead to the following conclusion:

Conclusion V: (a) Individuals' romantic choices are influenced by equity
considerations. They tend to choose and prefer partners of approximately their

[13] In previous sections, we discussed established relationships which are disturbed by
an inequitable act. We then examined various techniques by which participants can restore
equity to their relationships. Now we are suggesting that equity considerations may have a
strong impact on whether or not a group will even form and whether or not it will
disintegrate once formed.

own "social worth." (b) There is a constant upward bias in one's choices. Individuals persist in trying to form relations with partners who are somewhat more desirable than themselves.

One's romantic choices thus seem to be a delicate compromise between the realization that one must accept what he deserves and the insistent demand for an ideal partner.

Evidence for Conclusion V comes from several sources: Walster, Aronson, Abrahams, and Rottman (1966) found evidence that dating preferences are sometimes influenced by equity considerations and are sometimes determined by the unlimited aspirations of participants.

The authors had predicted that equity considerations would affect *all* dating choices. They initially proposed two hypotheses: (a) The more "socially desirable" an individual is (i.e., the more physically attractive, personable, famous, or rich, etc., he is), the more socially desirable he or she will expect a "suitable" romantic partner to be; (b) couples who are similar in social desirability will more often continue to date one another and will better like one another than will couples who are markedly mismatched.

Figure 1 depicts graphically the prediction that participants will prefer dates of approximately their own attractiveness.

The authors' hypotheses were tested in a field study. College freshmen were invited to attend a dance. They were told that their partner would be assigned by computer.

Physical attractiveness was chosen as the indicant of participants' social desirability. (Data indicate that physical attractiveness is strongly correlated with popularity, self-esteem, and other indexes which comprise "social desirability.") The freshman's physical attractiveness was then evaluated by four students while

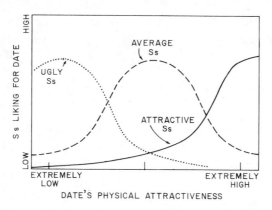

Fig. 1. Amount of liking predicted for dates of various attractiveness by ugly, average, and attractive subjects.

he or she was purchasing a ticket. Whether or not students expected and preferred partners of approximately their own social desirability was assessed in the following ways.

First, when freshmen signed up for the dance, they were asked how socially desirable they expected their date to be. (They were asked how physically attractive, how personally attractive, and how considerate they expected their date to be.) Equity theory predicts that the more attractive the freshman, the more desirable his date should be expected to be. This prediction was confirmed.

Second, freshmen were randomly assigned to dates, whom they met for the first time at the dance. Equity theory predicts that the more similar the dates are in attractiveness, the more viable their relationship will be. The validity of the relationship was assessed in three ways: First, during intermission, students were asked how much they liked their partner and, second, how eager they were to continue the dating relationship. Third, whether or not couples actually continued to date was determined by interviewing all participants 6 months after the dance.

Once partners had met one another, equity theory predictions were not supported. Everyone, regardless of his or her own social desirability, best liked and most often attempted to continue to date the most desirable dates available. Equity considerations seemed not to limit the participants' aspirations in any way.

To make things even worse for the theory, these findings were replicated by Brislin and Lewis (1968). Walster (1970) secured additional support which further weakens the conclusion that equity considerations influence romantic preferences. In accord with equity theory, she predicted that when an individual's self-esteem is lowered, he lowers his romantic aspirations. When his self-esteem is raised, he raises his romantic aspirations. Two studies failed to find any support for this contention.

Kiesler and Baral (1970) did find support for the equity theory predictions. The authors recruited male college students for a study on intelligence tests. The experimenter told the men that he was perfecting a new intelligence test that had already been successfully used on hundreds of students. Men were then given a difficult test. Men in the high-self-esteem condition were led to believe that they were doing extremely well on the test. (The experimenter nodded and smiled at their answers and mentioned that other men had much more trouble with the questions.) Men in the low-self-esteem condition were led to believe that they were doing badly on the test. (The experimenter made it apparent that he was displeased with their performance. He frowned, looked away, and mentioned that other subjects had performed better.)

During a break in testing, the experimenter and the subject visited a nearby canteen. When they entered the canteen, the experimenter recognized a girl (actually an experimental confederate). In one condition (the attractive condition), the confederate was made-up to be very physically attractive. She wore becoming make-up and fashionable clothing. In the unattractive condition, she was far less attractive. She wore no make-up, heavy glasses, and had her hair pulled back with a rubber band. Her skirt and blouse clashed and were arranged sloppily.

The girl sat down and chatted with the experimenter and the subject. After a minute, the experimenter excused himself to make a phone call. While he was gone, the confederate continued to engage the subject in conversation for ½ hour. She acted in a friendly and interesting way toward all subjects.

The dependent variable was the extent to which the male indicated to the female confederate that he was romantically interested in her and the extent to which he attempted to prolong their relationship. The confederate kept track of whether the man asked her for a date, asked for her phone number, offered to buy her a snack or coffee, offered her a cigarette, complimented her, or, finally, ignored her when at the end of the prescribed time she said that she should get back to work.

Kiesler and Baral found strong support for the matching hypothesis. When the man's self-esteem had been lowered, he behaved most romantically with the moderately attractive confederate. When the man's self-esteem had been raised, he behaved in a far more romantic way with the attractive confederate than with the unattractive one.

Other support for the matching hypothesis comes from Berscheid, Dion, Walster, and Walster (1971).

At the present time, then, data do not consistently support either equity theory *or* the notion that individuals' intimate social choices are unchecked by reality. Thus, Conclusion V can merely state that individuals' social choices are a compromise between two conflicting pressures.

The conclusion that one's social choices are a compromise between fantasy and reality seems to be consistent with our own observations in the daily world.

Sometimes individuals talk and act as if they have unlimited social inputs and thus are deserving of perfection. They talk as if the fact that they had to compromise in selecting a marriage partner is an inequity. For example, we can all think of prestigious but aging professors who leave their wives and marry beautiful, young, graduate students. Often, within a short time, our professor may begin to lament his protege's shortcomings. "If only she were more intelligent and more considerate," he complains. Observers sometimes smile, because they are more atuned to the operation of exchange processes in determining social pairings than is the participant in the relationship. They are smugly aware that if his lady were smarter, she would not have to settle for the company of the aging professor.

Sometimes, however, individuals are aware of equity considerations. The man with the undeservedly beautiful wife often manifests vague uneasiness—

whether the uneasiness is generated by his own recognition that he has married a better women than he deserves, or whether his uneasiness is generated by the fact that she constantly reminds him that he has married too well, we do not know.

Intimate relations, then, seem to be influenced in part by equity considerations and in part by fantasy.

Equity Theory and Social Psychology

Social psychological theory is generally acknowledged to be in a chaotic state. A number of mini-theories exist. Rigorous research supports all of them, at least some of the time. Yet, the relationships between these theories are vague. Thus, when we wish to predict how people in a given situation will respond, we often discover that several mini-theories can make predictions—and often they make different predictions. We are often left in the embarrassing state of being able to predict anything, anytime.

Obviously, what is needed is a general comprehensive theory and rules of transformation which tell us how the various mini-theories fit into the general framework. In equity theory we have made an effort to synthesize various theoretical approaches rather than follow the more usual (and more entertaining) procedure of setting up crucial confrontations between the mini-theories.

For example, equity theory proposes that individuals enmeshed in inequitable relationships feel distress. When discussing the genesis of this distress, we tried to synthesize the insights of learning theory, cognitive consistency theory, and Freudian theory. In the future, we must try to continue this process of synthesis. We must try to formally relate existing social psychological theory to equity theory. (Two areas of research which could be profitably related to equity theory may have already occurred to the reader.)

On Establishing the Relationship

Equity theory describes how individuals enmeshed in inequitable relationships respond. To predict how an individual will respond, one merely has to ascertain whether the scrutineer perceives participants to be in a relationship and how he calculates the participants' relative outcomes.

The theory has no need to know *why* the scrutineer perceives individuals to be in a relationship; it is enough to know that he does. Yet, a mini-theory, telling us *when* individuals will perceive participants to be in a *relationship* and when they will not, could be a useful addition to the theory.

A body of literature exists which tells us *when* individuals perceive themselves in a relationship with, and compare their outcomes with, others. In the future, it would be profitable to attempt to formally relate this mini-theory to equity theory.

Theorists such as Stouffer, Suckman, Devinney, Star, and Williams (1949), Festinger (1954), Merton (1957), Homans (1961), Gurr (1970), and Latané (1966) provide us with some insights as to when people compare individuals' (or groups') outcomes and when they do not.

Homans (1961) said that when "Person" is trying to decide whether or not distributive justice prevails, he goes through the following mental procedures:

> Am I getting as much as other men in some respect like me would get in circumstances in some respect like mine? And is Other giving me as much as other men, in some respect like Other, would give? When it comes, moreover, to comparisons with other men, the most important other man is the particular one with whom exchange is now taking place. (p. 76)

Festinger (1954) in discussing the question of whom a person chooses to compare his own opinions with said:

> Given a range of possible persons for comparison, someone close to one's own ability or opinion will be chosen for comparison. (p. 121)
> The more attractive a group is to a member, the more important that group will be as a comparison group for him. (p. 131)

Merton (1957) argued that soldiers compare themselves with [a] "Others with whom they were in actual association, in sustained social relations. . . ." [b] "Men who are in some pertinent respect of the same status or in the same social category." [c] "Men who are in some pertinent respect of different status or in a different social category. . . ."

Merton argued that

> some similarity in status attributes between the individual and the reference group must be perceived or imagined, in order for the comparison to occur at all. Once this minimal similarity is obtained, other similarities and differences pertinent to the situation will provide the context for shaping evaluations. (p. 242)

He also suggested that people compare themselves with those they admire.

Finally, Merton argued that structural variables determine with whom one compares himself:

> If the structure of a rigid system of stratification, for example, is generally defined as legitimate, if the rights, prerequisites and obligations of each stratum are generally held to be morally right, then the individuals within each stratum will be the less likely to take the situation of the other strata as a context for

appraisal of their own lot. They will, presumably, tend to confine their comparisons to other members of their own or neighboring social stratum. If, however, the system of stratification is under wide dispute, then members of some strata are more likely to contrast their own situation with that of others, and shape their self-appraisals accordingly ... the *range* of groups taken as effective bases of comparison in different social systems may well turn out to be closely connected with the degree to which legitimacy is ascribed to the prevailing social structure. (p. 267)

In brief, these writers suggest that comparisons take place with those who are (a) in an actual physical relationship with Person at the time, (b) perceived as similar to Person along salient dimension, or (c) attractive, looked up to, or admired in some way. There is the further suggestion that the less structured the situation, the broader the spectrum of individuals with whom it is possible to make a comparison.

In the future, it might be valuable to restate these insights into a propositional form which is consistent with equity theory. This set of propositions could then be used to tell us when the scrutineer is likely to see participants as being "in a relationship."

On Evaluating Rewards and Costs

A second important element in equity theory is the scrutineer's perceptions of the *rewards* and *costs* that participants are securing as a consequence of interacting with one another. In experiments one can manipulate the scrutineer's perception of the rewards and costs participants are incurring, and then determine the effect these manipulations have on his behavior. In field studies, one can measure participants' perceptions of the outcomes they are receiving as a consequence of their relationship with another. Such procedures work well when one is testing a theory. But what about applying the theory? How does one calculate inputs and outcomes then?

Once again, an impressive body of research already exists to guide us in calculating how costly or rewarding various stimuli will be perceived to be (see Homans, 1961 Thibaut & Kelley, 1959). This formulation could be valuably incorporated into equity theory.

Given the relevance of many social psychological findings to equity theory, the next step in equity research should be to integrate these social psychological findings into equity theory in a formal way, in the hope of further increasing the breadth of the equity theory predictions.

REFERENCES

Abelson, R.P., & Rosenberg, M.J. Symbolic psychologic: A model of attitudinal cognition. *Behavioral Science,* 1958, **3,** 1–13.
Adams, J.S. Toward an understanding of inequity. *Journal of Abnormal and Social Psychology,* 1963, **67,** 422–436.

Adams, J.S. Inequity in social exchange. In L. Berkowitz (Ed.), *Advances in experimental social psychology*. Vol. 2. New York: Academic Press, 1965.

Adams, J.S., & Rosenbaum, W.E. The relationship of worker productivity to cognitive dissonance about wage inequity. *Journal of Applied Psychology*, 1962, 46, 161–164.

Andrews, I.R. Wage inequity and job performance: An experimental study. *Journal of Applied Psychology, 1967*, 51, 39–45.

Arnold, M.B. *Emotion and personality: Vol. 2. Neurological and physiological aspects.* New York: Columbia University Press, 1960.

Aronfreed, J. The nature, variety and social patterning of moral responses to transgression. *Journal of Abnormal and Social Psychology*, 1961, 63, 223–240.

Aronfreed, J. The origin of self-criticism. *Psychological Review*, 1964, 71, 193–218.

Backman, C.W., & Secord, P.F. The compromise process and the affect structure of groups. In C.W. Backman & P.F. Secord (Eds.), *Problems in social psychology*. New York: McGraw-Hill, 1966.

Baker, K.A. An experimental analysis of third-party justice behavior. *Journal of Personality and Social Psychology*, 1974, 30, 307–316.

Baldwin, J. *The fire next time.* New York: Dial, 1964.

Bandura, A. Vicarious processes: A case of no-trial learning. In L. Berkowitz (Ed.), *Advances in experimental social psychology*, Vol. 2. New York: Academic Press, 1965.

Berkowitz, L. *Aggression: A social psychological analysis.* New York: McGraw-Hill, 1962.

Berkowitz, L. The frustration-aggression hypothesis revisited. Paper presented at the meeting of the Western Psychological Association, San Diego, March 1968.

Berkowitz, L., & Friedman, P. Some social class differences in helping behavior. *Journal of Personality and Social Psychology*, 1967, 5, 217–225.

Berscheid, E., Boye, D., & Darley, J.M. Effects of forced association upon voluntary choice to associate. *Journal of Personality and Social Psychology*, 1968, 8, 13–19.

Berscheid, E., Boye, D., & Walster, E. Retaliation as a means of restoring equity. *Journal of Personality and Social Psychology*, 1968, 10, 370–376.

Berscheid, E., Dion, K., Walster, E., & Walster, G.W. Physical attractiveness and dating choice A test of the matching hypothesis. *Journal of Experimental Social Psychology*, 1971, 7, 173–189.

Berscheid, E., & Walster, E. When does a harm-doer compensate a victim? *Journal of Personality and Social Psychology*, 1967, 6, 435–441.

Berscheid, E., Walster, E., & Barclay. A. Effect of time on tendency to compensate a victim. *Psychological Reports*, 1969, 25, 431–436.

Blau, P.M. *The dynamics of bureaucracy: A study of interpersonal relations in two government agencies.* (Rev. ed.) Chicago: University of Chicago Press, 1955.

Blau, P.M. *Exchange and power in social life.* New York: Wiley, 1967.

Blau, P.M. Social exchange, In D.L. Sills (Ed.), *International encyclopedia of the social sciences.* Vol. 7. New York: Macmillan, 1968.

Blumstein, P. W., & Weinstein, E. The redress of distributive injustice. *American Journal of Sociology*, 1969, 74, 408–418.

Bramel, D. Interpersonal attraction, hostility, and perception. In J. Mills (Eds.), *Experimental social psychology.* Toronto: Macmillan, 1969.

Bramel, D., Taub, B., & Blum, B. An observer's reaction to the suffering of his enemy. *Journal of Personality and Social Psychology*, 1968, 8, 384–392.

Brehm, J.W., & Cohen, A.R. *Explorations in cognitive dissonance.* New York: Wiley, 1962.

Brislin, R.W., & Lewis, S.A. Dating and physical attractiveness A replication. *Psychological Reports*, 1968, 22, 976.

Brock, T.C., & Becker, L.A. Debriefing and susceptability to subsequent experimental manipulations. *Journal of Experimental Social Psychology*, 1966, 2, 314–323.

Brock, T.C., & Buss, A.H. Dissonance, aggression, and evaluation of pain. *Journal of Abnormal and Social Psychology,* 1962, **65,** 192–202.

Brock, T.C., & Buss, A.H. Effects of justification for aggression in communication with the victim on postaggression dissonance. *Journal of Abnormal and Social Psychology,* 1964, **68,** 403–412.

Carlsmith, J.M., & Gross, A.E. Some effects of guilt on compliance. *Journal of Personality and Social Psychology,* 1969, **11,** 232–239.

Cartwright, D., & Harary, F. Structural balance. A generalization of Heider's theory. *Psychological Review,* 1956, **63,** 277–293.

Darlington, R.B., & Macker, C.E. Displacement of guilt-produced altruistic behavior. *Journal of Personality and Social Psychology,* 1966, **4,** 442–443.

Davidson, J. Cognitive familiarity and dissonance reduction. In L. Festinger (Ed.), *Conflict, decision, and dissonance.* Stanford: Stanford University Press, 1964.

Davis, K.E., & Jones, E.E. Changes in interpersonal perception as a means of reducing cognitive dissonance. *Journal of Abnormal and Social Psychology,* 1960, **61,** 402–410.

De Jong, J.P.B. De Josselin. *Levi-Strauss's theory on kinship and marriage.* Leiden, Holland: Brill, 1952.

Del Vecchio, G. The problem of penal justice (imprisonment or reparation of damage). *Revista Juridica de la Universidad de Puerto Rico,* 1959, **27** (Trans. by Silving).

Dillon, W.S. *Gifts and nations.* The Hague: Mouton, 1968.

Festinger, L. A theory of social comparison processes. *Human Relations,* 1954, **7,** 117–140.

Festinger, L. *A theory of cognitive dissonance.* Evanston, Ill.: Row, Peterson, 1957.

Freedman, J.L., Wallington, S.A., & Bless, E. Compliance without pressure: The effect of guilt. *Journal of Personality and Social Psychology,* 1967, **7,** 117–124.

Fromm, E. *The art of loving.* New York: Harper & Row, 1956.

Fry, M. Justice for victims. *Journal of Public Law,* 1956, **8,** 155–253.

Gergen, J. Altruism from the recipient's viewpoint: Individual and international perspectives. Swarthmore College: Author, 1968. (Mimeo)

Glass, D.C. Changes in liking as a means of reducing cognitive discrepancies between self-esteem and aggression. *Journal of Personality,* 1964, **32,** 531–549.

Glass, D.C., & Wood, J.D. The control of aggression by self-esteem and dissonance. In P.G. Zimbardo (Ed.), *The cognitive control of motivation.* Glenview, Ill.: Scott Foresman, 1969.

Goffman, E. On cooling the mark out: Some aspects of adaptation to failure. *Psychiatry,* 1952, **15,** 451–463.

Goldner, A.W. The norm of reciprocity. *American Sociological Review,* 1960, **25,** 165–167.

Goranson, R.E., & Berkowitz, L. Reciprocity and responsibility reactions to prior help. *Journal of Personality and Social Psychology,* 1966, **3,** 227–232.

Greenberg, M.S. A preliminary statement on a theory of indebtedness. Paper presented at the meeting of the Western Psychological Association, San Diego, March 1968.

Greenberg, M.S., & Frisch, D.M. Effect of intentionality on willingness to reciprocate a favor. *Journal of Experimental Social Psychology,* 1972, **8,** 99–111.

Greenberg, M.S., & Shapiro, S.P. Indebtedness: An aversive aspect of asking for and receiving help. *Sociometry,* 1971, **34,** 290–301.

Gurr, T.R. *Why men rebel.* Princeton: Princeton University Press, 1970.

Homans, G.C. *Social behavior: Its elementary forms.* New York: Harcourt, Brace & World,: 1961.

Jacques, E. *Equitable payment.* New York: Wiley, 1961.

Jecker, J., & Landy, D. Liking a person as a function of doing him a favor. *Human Relations,* 1969, **22,** 271–378.

Kiesler, S.B., & Baral, R.L. The search for a romantic partner: The effects of self-esteem and physical attractiveness on romantic behavior. In K. Gergen & D. Marlowe (Eds.), *Personality and social behavior*. Reading, Mass.: Addison-Wesley, 1970.

Latané, B. (Ed.) Studies in social comparison. *Journal of Experimental Social Psychology*, 1966, **2**, Supplement 1, 1–115.

Lawler, E.E., III. Equity theory as a predictor of productivity and work quality. *Psychological Bulletin*, 1968, **70**, 596–610.

Lawler, E.E., & O'Gara, P.W. Effects of inequity produced by underpayment on work output, work quality, and attitudes toward work. *Journal of Applied Psychology*, 1967, **51**, 39–45.

Lerner, M.J., & Matthews, G. Reactions to the suffering of others under conditions of indirect responsibility. *Journal of Personality and Social Psychology*, 1967, **5**, 319–325.

Lerner, M.J., & Simmons, C.H. Observer's reaction to the 'innocent victim": Compassion or rejection? *Journal of Personality and Social Psychology*, 1966, **4**, 203–210.

Leventhal, G.S., Allen, J., & Kemelgor, B. Reducing inequity by reallocating rewards. *Psychonomic Sciences*, 1969, **14**, 295–296.

Leventhal, G.S., & Anderson, D. Self-interest and the maintenance of equity. *Journal of Personality and Social Psychology*, 1970, **15**, 57–62.

Leventhal, G.S., & Bergman, J.T. Self-depriving behavior as a response to unprofitable inequity. *Journal of Experimental Social Psychology*, 1969, **5**, 153–171.

Leventhal, G.S., & Lane, D.W. Sex, age, and equity behavior. *Journal of Personality and Social Psychology*, 1970, **15**, 312–316.

Leventhal, G.S., Weiss, T., & Long, G. Equity, reciprocity, and reallocating the rewards in the dyad. *Journal of Personality and Social Psychology*, 1969, **13**, 300–305.

Liebow, E. *Tally's corner*. Boston: Little, Brown, 1967.

Macaulay, S., & Walster, E. Legal structures and restoring equity. *Journal of Social Issues*, 1971, **27**, 173–187.

Maher, B.A. *Principles of psychopathology: An experimental approach*. New York: McGraw-Hill, 1966.

Marwell, G., Ratcliff, K., & Schmitt, D.R. Minimizing differences in a maximizing difference game. *Journal of Personality and Social Psychology*, 1969, **12**, 158–163.

Mauss, M. *The gift: Forms and functions of exchange in archaic societies*. Glencoe, Ill.: Free Press, 1954.

McGuire, W.J. The nature of attitudes and attitude change. In G. Lindzey & E. Aronson (Eds.), *The handbook of social psychology*, (2nd ed.). Reading, Mass.: Addison-Wesley, 1968.

Merton, R.K. *Social theory and social structure*, (Rev. ed.) Glencoe, Ill.: Free Press, 1957.

Mills, J. Changes in moral attitudes following temptation. *Journal of Personality*, 1958, **26**, 517–531.

Opsahl, R.L., & Dunnette, M.D. The role of financial compensation in industrial motivation. *Psychological Bulletin*, 1966, **66**, 108–118.

Pritchard, R.D. Equity theory: A review and critique. *Organizational behavior and human performance*, 1969, **4**, 176–211.

Rosenberg, M.J. An analysis of affective-cognitive consistency. In M.J. Rosenberg & C.I. Hovland (Eds.), *Attitude organization and change*. New Haven, Yale University Press, 1960.

Rosenberg, M.J., & Abelson, L.P. An analysis of cognitive balancing. In M.J. Rosenberg & C.I. Hovland (Eds.), *Attitude organization and change*. New Haven: Yale University Press, 1960.

Ross, A. Modes of guilt reduction. Unpublished doctoral dissertation, University of Minnesota, 1965.

Ross, M., Thibaut, J., & Evenbeck, S. Some determinants of the intensity of social protest. *Journal of Experimental Social Psychology*, 1971, 7, 401–418.

Sarnoff, I. *Personality dynamics and development*. New York: Wiley, 1962.

Schafer, S. *Restitution to victims of crime*. London: Stevens & Son, 1960.

Schwartz, S.H. Words, deeds, and the perception of consequences and responsibility in action situations. *Journal of Personality and Social Psychology*, 1968, 10, 235.

Scott, M.B., & Lyman, S.M. Accounts. *American Sociological Review*, 1968, 33, 46–62.

Smith, A. *The theory of moral sentiments*. London: Bell, 1892.

Spencer, H. *Essays: Moral, political and aesthetic*. New York: Appleton, 1874.

Stouffer, S.A., Suckman, E.A., Devinney, L.C., Star, S.A., & Williams, R.M. *The American soldier: Adjustment during army life*. Vol. 1. Princeton: Princeton University Press, 1949.

Sykes, G.M., & Matza, D. Techniques of neutralization: A theory of delinquency. *American Sociological Review*, 1957, 22, 664–670.

Thibaut, J.W. An experimental study of the cohesiveness of underprivileged groups. *Human Relations*, 1950, 3, 251–278.

Thibaut, J.W., & Kelley, H.H. *The social psychology of groups*. New York: Wiley, 1959.

Thibaut, J.W., & Riecken, H.W. Some determinants and consequences of the perception of social causality. *Journal of Personality*, 1955, 24, 113–133.

Tornow, W.W. Differential perception of ambiguous job characteristics as inputs or outcomes moderating inequity reduction. Unpublished doctoral dissertation University of Minnesota, 1970.

Walster, E. Effect of self-esteem on liking for dates of various social desirabilities. *Journal of Experimental Social Psychology*, 1970, 6, 248–253.

Walster, E., Aronson, V., Abrahams, D., & Rottman, L. Importance of physical attractiveness in dating behavior. *Journal of Personality and Social Psychology*, 1966, 4, 508–516.

Walster, E., Berscheid, E., & Barclay, A. A determinant of preference for modes of dissonance reduction. *Journal of Personality and Social Psychology*, 1967, 7, 211–215.

Walster, E., Berscheid, E., & Walster, G.W. Reactions of an exploiter to the exploited: Compensation, justification or self-punishment? In J.R. Macaulay & L. Berkowitz (Eds.), *Altruism and helping behavior*. New York: Academic Press, 1970.

Walster, E., & Prestholdt, P. The effect of misjudging another: Overcompensation or dissonance reduction? *Journal of Experimental Social Psychology*, 1966, 2, 85–97.

Walster, E., Walster, G.W., Abrahams, D., & Brown, Z. The effect on liking of underrating or overrating another. *Journal of Experimental Social Psychology*, 1966, 2, 70–84.

Weick, K.E., & Nesset, B. Preferences among forms of equity. *Organizational Behavior and Human Performance*, 1968, 3, 400–416.

Weinstein, E.A., Devaughan, W.L., & Wiley, M.G. Obligation and the flow of deference in exchange. *Sociometry*, 1969, 32, 1–12.

Zajonc, R.B. The concepts of balance, congruity, and dissonance. *Public Opinion Quarterly*, 1960, 24, 280–286.

EQUITY THEORY REVISITED: COMMENTS AND ANNOTATED BIBLIOGRAPHY

J. Stacy Adams

and

Sara Freedman

UNIVERSITY OF NORTH CAROLINA
CHAPEL HILL, NORTH CAROLINA

I. Introduction

In 1973, following twelve years of research on equity by some 170 different authors, Walster *et al.* (1973) pleaded for, and contributed significantly to, the expansion of equity theory into a major social psychological theory. The theory, they argued, had the capacity to explain and to predict a broad spectrum of social behavior.

Our review of the literature bearing directly on equity theory reveals four general phenomena. First, the annual growth rate of publications is an exponentially increasing one showing no sign of asymptoting. Second, the number of *new* authors each year is also increasing exponentially. Third, from an initial research emphasis on social behavior involving monetary exchanges, which continues today, an increasing amount of work has been directed to other social relationships. As if anticipating the plea by Walster and her associates, researchers with interests as diverse as child development, coalition formation, bargaining, and social protest, among many others, have found the theory predictively useful. Finally, major derivations from the original theory have been tested, with the consequence that it has been corrected, expanded, and made relevant to a wider range of phenomena. A comparison of the papers of Homans (1961) and Adams (1963) with the theoretical and review paper of Walster, Berscheid, and Walster (1973) provides unambiguous testimony to this.

The convergence of these phenomena, which are not necessarily interdependent, suggests that equity theory may, indeed, eventually result in a comprehensive theory of social relationships. The theory in its present form (Walster *et al.*, 1973) strikes us as having a well articulated structure, being parsimoniously elegant, and having an increased predictive range. These are characteristics that bode well for progress, for as Kuhn (1962) and Rosenberg (1972) have noted, the growth of a discipline, scientific or technological, is intimately tied to the existence and quality of theory.

This chapter is divided into two parts. The first offers a few comments on existing theory and research. Notwithstanding the optimism generated by equity theory, there are lacunae that appear to deserve attention. In particular, theoretical and research effort might profitably be directed to the phenomenological experience of inequity, how inequity may be used instrumentally, the analysis of the interactive dynamics of inequity reduction, and the quantification of inequity. The second part consists of an extensive annotated bibliography of theoretical, review, and research papers, published and unpublished, on equity. The annotations for research papers describe the essential contents: tasks, independent and dependent variables, results, and, for populations of possible special interest, subject characteristics. Preceding the bibliography is an index to theoretical and review papers, to independent and dependent variables, and to subjects. The bibliography and index will hopefully constitute a useful reference.

II. Comments

A. THE NATURE OF INEQUITY "DISTRESS"

Equity theorists, as other cognitive consistency theorists, posit that a set of conditions, in the case at hand labeled "inequity," results in tension or distress which, in turn, the person experiencing it will be moved to reduce (Adams, 1963, 1965, 1968; Walster *et al.*, 1973). As most frequently used by equity theorists, the conceptual status of distress is that of a hypothetical construct rather than that of an intervening variable (MacCorquodale & Meehl, 1948). The concept of distress has been typically endowed with existential characteristics and surplus meaning. For example, it is stated to have the characteristics of anger and guilt in inequitable situations. Yet, research on the phenomenological quality of distress produced by inequity is not to be found. Perhaps, as McGuire (1973) has suggested, we are prey to our research methods and models.

Determining empirically the existence and quality of distress is potentially fruitful in testing equity theory. Failing to do so would be equivalent to not having searched for Pluto after Kepler had hypothesized its existence to account for the orbital paths of visible planets. It is not *necessary* to search for equity theory's "Pluto" and to establish its characteristics, except that a central element of the theory would remain untested and that better differentiated predictions might be precluded.

It is implicit in existing research and explicit in various theoretical statements that different initial conditions should produce distress of different quality and, consequently, that different behavior should obtain. At a fairly macro level of prediction it has been stated that advantageous inequity produces feelings of guilt, whereas disadvantageous inequity induces anger (Adams, 1963, 1965; Homans, 1961; Walster *et al.*, 1973). Certainly many findings are consistent with this, but in only a few studies, each concerned with disadvantageous inequity, can one comfortably infer anything about the character of the distress experienced. Notable among these are the studies by Thibaut (1950), Homans (1953), and Ross, Thibaut, and Evenbeck (1971), in which anger is manifest. Direct evidence of guilt feelings among persons who are advantaged is lacking.

The limits of distress are surely not anger and guilt. A range of qualitatively different experiences is probable and with each form of distress a different distribution of equity-restoring responses should be associated. Let us consider a few examples, first, in regard to disadvantageous inequity. A group of female clerks paid the same wage includes a half dozen whose status is greater than that of the others (cf. Homans, 1953). They are angry; they attempt to increase their outcomes and eventually try to obtain union representation. In a similar situation, a single clerk is disadvantaged. She, too, is angry. She confronts her supervisor and takes him personally to task for an invidious action. Anger is present in both cases, but the phenomenological quality is different in each. In the second case self-esteem is wounded, whereas in the first it is not. In the second, a supervisor is personally unjust; in the first, management or management policies are unfair. Two similar conditions of disadvantageous inequity result in qualitatively different subjective experiences, in different responses, and, in this case, different loci of causality and response targets.

In the next example a couple is happily married for several years. The husband has an extramarital affair. A previously equitable intimate social relationship is unbalanced. The wife is, no doubt, distressed. But the character of her distress will be quite different if it is merely a casual, sexual relation than if the husband has "fallen in love" with another woman. The inequity in the first instance would be less of an affront to the wife's self-esteem, and could be easily reduced by a variety of psychological justifications. The second kind of infidelity would be much more wounding; it strikes directly at the wife's characteristics and self-worth. Reduction of this inequity could not be reduced by psychological means; more likely are "leaving the field," decreasing her contributions to the relationship, and increasing the husband's costs—making his life a lifelong hell.

Or consider this example. A man is cheated in a poker game, in one case by a stranger, in the other by a buddy. The private experience and the inequity-reducing response will vary systematically with the circumstances. The act of the stranger elicits anger and instant demand for restitution, perhaps with appeal to the other players. The anger is simply the anger of unfair transactions. But the experiential quality of being cheated by a friend has strong components of "hurt," bitterness, and betrayal: "He is not my buddy, after all." The overt response, in part because it would be public, would be less obviously emotional than in the first case, less likely to demand restitution, and more likely to result in severing an existing social relationship.

Advantageous inequities may be a product of chance, responsibility, or intention. The last two, although generally treated together in contrast to chance, can be usefully distinguished. One may, for example, be responsible for harm done to another, but without intent. The cause may be negligence, as when one forgets a close friend's birthday. However, one might also deliberately withhold a gift. In the first instance, embarrassed guilt, followed by compensation, are probable. In the second case, guilt might be totally absent since the intentional act presumably had a prior "justification." Or guilt, regret, and retaliation-anxiety (Berscheid *et al.*, 1968) might be felt and lead to equity-restoring behavior, despite prior "justification" for the intended harm done. Having a "reason" to commit the act does not preclude feelings of guilt, but if guilt *is* experienced, considerable cognitive dissonance is predictable. This, in turn, would probably result in additional, but now post-act, justifying behavior.

Chance advantageous inequity has been reviewed recently by Walster *et al.* (1973). Such "inequities" may either not be perceived as inequitable or, alternatively, be so perceived but not be productive of guilt feelings. An accidental overpayment may be viewed as good fortune in a not totally predictable world. Studies by Garrett and Libby (1973) and Leventhal, Weiss, and Long (1969) suggest this may be so, but their data do not allow us to conclude why accidentally overrewarded subjects do not compensate their partners when intentionally overrewarded subjects do. We suspect that chance inequities are perceived, but not as injustices productive of guilt, though perhaps eliciting empathy and compassion for a victim.

The quality of the response to inequity, we propose, is important to the prediction of how persons will attempt to reduce inequities. This does not imply that the nature of distress experienced by an individual would account for more variance than has been accounted for by the host of variables investigated by equity researchers, but rather that additional variance might be explained.

B. INSTRUMENTAL USES OF INEQUITY

Research on inequity has focused almost entirely on means of inequity reduction as dependent variables. The model guiding research has taken the production of inequity, in any of several forms, as an antecedent condition. A worker was underpaid, a child was overrewarded, a woman was led to deprive a friend of stamps, one person helped another, so producing inequities that, largely in accord with theory, were reduced by less work, reallocation of reward, voluntary donations, compensation, justification, giving help, and other means. This dominant focus of the research appears to have inhibited discussion of the instrumental uses of inequity, despite Jones' (1964) suggestive work on its strategic uses by ingratiators.

If, as has been demonstrated repeatedly, people incur costs in the service of inequity reduction, one may reasonably conclude that they find inequity distressing. It follows—without needing to assume anything about the perversity of Man's nature!—that persons may perceive inequity as having uses in influencing the behavior of others.

The creation of injustices may serve several instrumental functions. First, an inequity may *signal* to a second party that the focal person perceives the existing social exchange relationship as inequitable. If a person, *P,* is disadvantaged in his relationship with *O,* it does not follow that *O* will perceive the inequity. Indeed, it is likely that *O* will not over a range of low to moderate inequities because the threshold for advantageous inequity is higher than for disadvantageous inequity (Adams, 1965; Jaques, 1961; Weick & Nesset, 1968). Producing an inequity for *O* may signal to him that *P* views the social exchange as unjust. There is a suggestion of such instrumental use of inequity in an experiment by Leventhal and Bergman (1969). Subjects who were moderately underrewarded by their partner tended to redress the inequity by taking some of their partner's money when given an opportunity to reallocate the moneys. Some extremely under-rewarded subjects, on the other hand, *increased* the advantaged partner's funds. This behavior is paralleled by an observation at La Guardia Airport: A man alighting from a taxi gave the driver several dollar bills. Having received his change, the passenger gave the driver a dime tip. The driver returned the dime to the man with the comment, "I think you need it more than me, Mister!"

Signaling disadvantageous inequities is not limited to unmistakable over-payment. One of the authors, when subjected to especially poor restaurant service, leaves a three-penny tip to communicate his perception of an unfair transaction. Leaving no tip might not have the intended effect: The waitress might all too easily attribute the event to forgetfulness or cheapness. Three pennies eliminate the first possibility and make the second highly improbable, for no one is that stingy and there is an intentional quality to leaving three pennies that is not conveyed by, say, a nickel. Somewhat in the same vein, managers occasionally signal displeasure with a subordinate by creating special kinds of disadvantageous inequities. Two cases come to mind. In the first, a manager caused a subordinate manager's carpet (an important status symbol in this company) to be removed to indicate his dissatisfaction with the employer–employee exchange. The action did not have the purpose of redressing an inequity, which could have been accomplished less perversely by a salary decrease or the like, but had the calculated intent of signaling the manager's felt inequity. In the second case, which is far more cruel, inequities are built by systematically withholding normal pay increases and promotions over a period of time in hope of that an employee will resign as the organization's "message" impresses itself. Analogous to this is the snubbing, derogation, and abuse poured on an "undesirable" family that has moved into a residential neighborhood. No doubt comparable tactics are also employed in forcing the severance of intimate relationships that are perceived as so inequitably disadvantageous that they are unreducible.

Quite different purposes may also be served by deliberately created inequities. Equity research findings are impressive witnesses to the proposition that persons suffering the distress of advantageous inequity will behave so as to establish equity. A person could, therefore, use inequity instrumentally for personal gain by creating *obligations* or indebtedness in another person. As Jones (1964) has noted, this may be accomplished by causing another person to perceive that one's inputs or costs are greater or one's outcomes are smaller than previously perceived by the other, or that the other person's inputs or costs are smaller or the other's outcomes are greater than initially perceived. The creation of obligations by these means is part of every salesman's and advertiser's psychotechnology. Indeed, public sensitivity to the technique has made it necessary to promise "No obligation!"

The creation of obligation is not limited to sales, however. It is useful in all social relationships. A wife's tears may artfully produce perceived advantageous inequity in a husband. Feigning greater harm than has been incurred may exaggerate the inequity perceived by a harm-doer and stimulate him to increase compensation. Gifts and compliments to a date or to a client may induce a need to reciprocate in appropriate terms, which in such situations are typically not the same as the terms of manipulation. In *The Godfather* (Puzo, 1969), Don Corleone created an eventually frightful debt merely by granting a favor to Amerigo Bonasera. On a somewhat different familial level, the legendary "Jewish mother" makes and acts out sacrifices for her children and for the rest of her life plays on their guilt (Greenberg, 1968; Roth, 1969). This type of long-term control is not limited to the western world. Mead (1951) reports that New Guinean men remain in debt to their relatives for years because they were bought a wife at immense cost.

But let the obligator beware! The inequity created must never be greater than the target person's perceived ability to reduce the inequity—to reciprocate, to compensate, to give. The same warning in a somewhat different context is sounded and given empirical support in Walster *et al.* (1973). Failure to observe this bit of practical psychology exposes the obligator to a break in the relationship, to derogation, or to both.

If inequities may be used instrumentally in the control of behavior, it is logical that equity theory has the capacity to be generalized to social influence and social learning. In respect to the latter there is an obvious similarity between the structure of equity theory and of some learning theories. In bare-bone form, the theories postulate antecedent conditions, such as deprivation, that lead to certain states of the organism (e.g., drive), which, in turn, the organism attempts to reduce. Interestingly, equity theory is not limited to antecedent operations like deprivation. Indeed, it predicts that reverse operations—surfeits, if you please—will produce conceptually equivalent organismic states. All this is perhaps too conjectural. Nevertheless, discussion of the theoretical parallels may be productive.

C. DYNAMIC ASPECTS OF INEQUITY REDUCTION

Theorists postulate that inequities in social exchange are a function of the participants' *perceptions* of their inputs and outcomes (Adams, 1963, 1965; Walster *et al.*, 1973). As a consequence there may be poor obverse symmetry in the inequities experienced by the interacting persons. The logical implication that the partner of a person suffering disadvantageous inequity necessarily experiences advantageous inequity has no psychological validity. Two persons may each experience disadvantageous inequity, for example. Interactors may not only weight their own and the other's inputs and outcomes differently, but the relevance of particular imputs to and outcomes from an exchange may be quite different. Also, even given perfect correspondence of perceptions, the threshold value for perceiving advantageous and disadvantageous inequity may be different.

Assume that two persons, P and O, experience advantageous and disadvantageous inequity, respectively, in their relationship. Each feels "distress" and is motivated to act to reduce the inequity and to continue the relationship. In the unlikely limiting case of perfect correspondence of perceptions of inputs and outcomes and of their relevance, if P and O each have five equiprobable practical and psychological means[1] of reducing their *own* inequity, there are only four chances in one hundred that their preferred means of reduction would be compatible.

It is evident from this simplified illustration that achieving *joint* equity requires coordination—by normative rule or bargaining, for example. Without coordination there is a high probability that new kinds of inequities will be created. Suppose, continuing the example, that *P* opts to increase his inputs, increasing *O*'s outcomes in the process, and that *O* decreases his inputs. The net result may be that disadvantageous inequity has shifted from *O* to *P*. A possible derivative consequence is that *P* will perceive the new inequity as much more distressing than *O* perceived the original one, for his "altruism" was met by "ingratitude."

If some of the simplifying assumptions in our example are removed and more realistic ones are substituted, it becomes evident that achieving joint equity is more complex and difficult. For example, one might assume that *P* and *O* prefer to reduce inequity at least loss of outcomes and most gain, respectively, and that some of the constituent components of outcomes and inputs for the two are different. The first assumption implies that transfer of transferable outcomes (not all are, such as respect) will be resisted if other solutions are available. The second may turn inequity resolution into a game of "Go Fish." In relation to this point, Tornow (1971) has demonstrated that different individuals may perceive identical job elements as inputs *or* as outcomes. The complexity of resolving inequity under such circumstances is obvious. Indeed, one wonders if the pervasive inequities observed in work situations are not partly a function of the fact that, for a given job held by several people (e.g., welders), job evaluation and pricing practices weight job elements identically for each employee. Analogous problems exist in a broader social context: for instance, a courtesy extended by a man to a woman may constitute today either an outcome or a cost for the woman.

From the foregoing comments one may conclude that the joint resolution of inequity may be a complex, difficult, and unstable process. Research on the restoration of equity has resorted almost exclusively to a simple linear causal experimental design: Inequity was produced for *P* under systematically varied conditions and *P*'s responses were observed, *in vitro*, so to speak. Subjects have been isolated from real interaction with another person, when in a wide range of inequities the interactive nature of the relationship may be essential to under-

---

[1] For *P*: (1) decreasing own and (2) increasing *O*'s outcomes; (3) increasing own and (4) decreasing *O*'s inputs; (5) distorting own and *O*'s inputs and outcomes. The reverse means apply for *O*. Distortion is considered a single means in the present context of matching inequity-reducing mechanisms since they are private. Stated differently, if *P* and *O* both use distortion, the specific nature of the distortions is irrelevant—both will have achieved equity.

standing inequity resolution. This does not, of course, vitiate the research findings, but it leaves us uninformed about the interactive dynamics of inequity-reducing processes and about the coordinating mechanisms required for the attainment of relatively stable, equitable exchange relationships.

Consider an intimate relationship between a man and wife, P and O: P has very low self-esteem, believes he is dull, is not a good provider, and so on; he thinks his wife is the brightest, most beautiful, admirable woman in the world. O, on the other hand, perceives herself as intelligent, attractive, and competent and thinks of P as a kind, hardworking, honest, and tender man with whom she has a comfortable relationship. P experiences advantageous inequity and feels he does not "deserve" O; O perceives no inequity in the relationship and is content. One could reproduce P's inequity in the laboratory and observe the subject increasing his inputs (e.g., taking on an additional task for money) with the object of increasing a "confederate's" outcomes. Fine. But would the finding represent the ultimate resolution of P's felt inequity in the intimate relationship we described? Had P and O interacted over time, the following might have been observed: (1) P increases his inputs and O's outcomes, as in the fictitious experiment; (2) assuming that O perceives the connection between P's extra work and a new washer she receives, O initially feels somewhat overrewarded but later begins to feel considerable *disadvantageous* inequity as she is left alone at night while P works; she complains to P; (3) P is hurt; he now perceives negative attributes of O, "bitching" and ingratitude; he keeps his second job but is less affectionate and becomes occasionally surly. . . . The rest of the script could be left to the imagination. More usefully, however, could we not *predict* the oscillating process and the ultimate resolution of P and O's inequitable relationship by extending equity theory? For example, propositions about the correspondence of P's and O's perceptions of their inputs and outcomes and about coordination mechanisms in reducing inequity would improve the predictability of dynamic processes.

Given the substantial body of knowledge on equity, the time is propitious to expand theory and to adopt more dynamic experimental designs (cf. McGuire, 1973). Dynamic designs employing two subjects (not a subject and a confederate) interacting in an inequitable relationship appear quite fruitful. They permit observation of the *process* of inequity resolution over time as a function of variables manipulated either initially or in the course of interaction. Such experimental designs, though approximating reality better, are difficult to deal with, particularly in regard to making observations and analyzing them. But they are feasible. For example, Stephenson and White (1968), *inter alios*, set up the appropriate conditions for observing the process of inequity reduction but stopped short of doing so.

In this context, Adams recalls an attempt with John Arrowood in 1960 to produce inequity in two equally paid subjects who were seated on each side of a "partners' desk" and whose related clerical tasks were performed sequentially. Inequity was to be produced, we hoped, by manipulating the demand character-istics of the tasks—high for one subject, low for the other. Among other task characteristics that were varied was the means of adding numbers. The "high input" subject was required to add by head-and-hand (high effort); the "low input" subject used an electric calculator (low effort). Finding, to our chagrin, absolutely no differences in productivity after running several pairs of subjects, we turned clinician and interviewed the subjects in depth. The reason for the inferred absence of inequity, we discovered, was that all subjects viewed using a calculator as demanding skill, if not effort. At this stage of the development of equity theory, we were not prepared to deal with such slippery phenomena, abandoned the experiment, and returned to simpler designs! Equity researchers today are more sensitive to the potential of dynamic design structures, have a better understanding of equity, and should consider picking up where we left off in 1960.

D. QUANTIFICATION OF INEQUITY

There is a striking absence of attempts to quantify the magnitude of inputs and outcomes, and thus of inequities, in the research literature on equity, despite the implication of a need for quantification in Adams (1965) and, more recently, in Walster *et al.* (1973). Because the boundaries of inquiry have been extended well beyond relationships involving monetary exchanges, quantifica-tion appears especially desirable. The earliest studies focused on monetary exchanges principally because outcomes were thereby roughly quantifiable, as were inputs such as productivity. In retrospect this was a tactical error because, by arousing curiosity in counter-intuitive overpayment phenomena, rapid expan-sion of research into more socially significant areas may have been inhibited. Be that as it may, the point is that as equity theory matures and its relevance extends to the domains of exploitative, intimate, and helping social relationships (see review in Walster *et al.* 1973) and of legal justice (Legant, 1973b; Macaulay & Walster, 1971), more precise measurement of variables and parametric investi-gations appear desirable.

Equity research to date has aimed principally at establishing the truth value of theoretical propositions and predictions. This was accomplished, first, by inducing inequity through strong manipulation of one objective outcome or input, occasionally both, not by manipulating total, net outcomes or total inputs. Second, the experiments employed factorial designs in which variables were typically manipulated at two or three levels. The first practice established the existence of certain phenomena and validated particular propositions *in general* by statistical tests of differences between means—which is immensely useful, of course. But, more often than not, the amount of variance in the dependent variables that is accounted for by manipulated input and outcome variables is not impressive. An obvious possible explanation for this is that a manipulation, of an outcome for example, has quite variable effects on the *inequity* experienced by subjects.

In a given situation, a subject will perceive a variety of outcomes, positive and negative,[2] and different subjects may perceive a different set of relevant outcomes and value identical outcomes differently. Indeed, Tornow's (1971) work gives evidence that what is an outcome to one person is evaluated by another as an input and vice versa. There are also intersubject differences in the utility of manipulated outcomes, as is suggested in an experiment by Lawler *et al.* (1968) in which subjects' need for money was correlated with piecework productivity. Obviously, the manipulation of an outcome may produce varying net outcomes among subjects. Similarly, there are undoubtedly intersubject differences in the relevance and evaluation of inputs. Finally, subjects vary in their perceptions of other subjects' outcomes and inputs. The resultant of these experimentally uncontrolled variations is that the magnitude, and perhaps the quality, of experienced inequity varies among subjects. The variation may be treated as error variance, but, in fact, it is not. It is the very substance of equity theory.

Development in any science is contingent, in part, upon precise measurement of variables. Equity theory is no longer at the stage of establishing basic functional relationships. Some research effort must be devoted now to measurement, not only in order that the theory might better be tested and refined, but so that it might be confidently applied to social problems. Concern for social justice has never been keener and more pervasive, and equity theory has obvious relevance to possible solutions. Yet, it is doubtful that theorists could contribute more than sound general principles to those responsible for social programs. An important reason is that we cannot yet measure with precision the magnitude of existing social injustice, much less the effects of a program proposed to reduce felt injustice (cf. Bauer, 1966). A priority, then, is the development of psychometric technology for the measurement of the components of inequity.

A first step in that direction is to establish a unit of measurement common to both inputs and outcomes. A possible approach is Stevens' magnitude estimation procedure (Stevens, 1955; Galanter, 1962) that has been used, for example, by Ruch and Holmes (1971) to measure pleasant and unpleasant life changes that produced stress. Another possibility are the multivariate paired comparison procedures discussed by Bock and Jones (1968). Ideally, the unit of measurement established would measure equally well a person's own inputs and outcomes and his perceptions of a comparison person's inputs and outcomes.

---

[2] Negative outcomes are equivalent to "costs" in Homans (1961) and Walster *et al.* [(1973), reprinted in this volume—see the first article].

Whatever the measurement procedure used, it is assumed that what are inputs and what are outcomes would be identified by subjects, not experimenters, for reasons stated earlier.

Given a unit of measurement and a psychometric technology, the next logical move is to determine the additivity functions for inputs and outcomes. It is very unlikely that they are linear. Inputs may add at a greater than linear rate, whereas outcomes probably add at a slower than linear rate if one is to judge from studies on the utility of money by Galanter (personal communication, 1967). It is also possible that particular inputs among themselves, outcomes among themselves, and inputs and outcomes in combination interact in peculiar ways. Attesting to this, Bock and Jones (1968) observed in a group of industrial employees that pay and certain fringe benefits interacted in unique ways. The additivity rules for positive and negative outcomes (gains and costs) may also have peculiarities. Suppose that we were able to measure objectively the positive and negative outcomes of persons A and B and that we found the resultant net outcomes equal. Suppose further that A's net was a result of positive outcomes of 10 and negative outcomes of 9, whereas B's net resulted from positive and negative outcomes of 2 and 1, respectively. Is there much doubt that the subjective utility of B's net outcome is greater?

Recent work by Einhorn (1971) bears a significant relationship to how subjects aggregate inputs and outcomes. It suggests that persons may use non-linear, noncompensatory models for combining information. The noncompensatory aspects are particularly germane because compensation is inherent in equity theory, in the sense that outcomes constitute compensation for inputs. It appears quite plausible (and testable) that a person experiencing disadvantageous inequity would perceive that certain forms of compensation from another person were inappropriate and were, therefore, not outcomes. For example, if P in an intimate relationship had been insulted by O, a gift by the latter might not be seen as an equity-restoring outcome, whereas a verbal apology would. Non-compensatory processes may also occur with respect to the aggregation of positive and negative outcomes, in the sense that the existence of certain negative outcomes nullify positive outcomes, although they are arithmetically smaller. An illustration is the man who declares, "No amount of money and research support would cause me to move to New York" or states "No degree of participative management can substitute for pay!"

To conclude this comment on measurement let us return to the practice of limiting manipulations to two or three levels of a variable. It is parsimonious and may often be necessary in the absence of better than nominal or ordinal measures of the variables. However, there is a risk of losing information if a function is limited to two or three points. Importantly, predictable discontinuities cannot be tested. One might hypothesize, by way of illustration, that the probability of a person's severing an existing relationship is a step function of the magnitude of inequity experienced, being near zero over low to moderately high magnitudes and then "stepping" to a high probability at high magnitudes. Clearly, a parametric investigation is required to test such a hypothesis. With the exception of a study by Leventhal, Allen, and Kemelgor (1969), we have found no study with a comparable hypothesis and with the appropriate parametric experimental design. It is possible, of course, that more hypotheses like this have been inhibited by the inability to quantify inequity. Only the development of measurement can test *this* hypothesis!

E. A CONCLUDING OBSERVATION

For reasons discussed in the previous section, equity theory appears weakly prepared to be applied to social problems, although it has great relevance to inequities in economic, legal, interpersonal, and intergroup relationships. This relevance should be made more publicly visible, for it is not foolishly optimistic to believe that public understanding of inequity would make a difference in ameliorating conflicted relationships.

A vast array of social conflicts are perceived fundamentally as problems of inequity. Petroleum consumers feel unjustly abused by producers as scarcer gasoline increases in price; the producers are outraged by the unfair attacks upon them by the public. Women and ethnic minorities voice unjust discriminatory treatment, while other portions of the public claim that remedies for discrimination forces them to bear inequitable costs. Comparably stressed relationships exist between labor and management, the public and government, the public and recipients of welfare, former prison inmates and potential employers, and so on, endlessly. Underlying each instance is a perceived injustice. Frequently, if not invariably, the inequity experienced by one party is a direct result of the other party's first proclaiming an injustice or taking action to eliminate one.

If a person or group, *P,* alleges that another party, *O,* has, however, vaguely or however long ago, caused it harm, *O* instantly accrues some negative outcomes psychologically if *O* does not believe this is so. Thus, *P* has created an inequity for *O* by merely proclaiming its own felt inequity. *P*'s allegation of disadvantageous inequity need not, of course, be real; it may be instead a tactic to achieve gains, as discussed earlier in this chapter. Whether *P*'s claim be true or not, the short-term consequences for *O* are the same. Initially true allegations of injustice by *P* may become false ones employed solely for instrumental purposes. This appears to be the case in many labor negotiations in which periodic claims of inequity by both parties become ritualized and the years between negotiations are spent gathering or shaping statistical evidence of inequities. Quite aside from the objective merit of the claims by the two parties, periodic formal negotiations are an important mode of coordinating inequity-reducing responses in the process of achieving joint equity (*vide supra*).

Other conflicts result from one party's taking action, directly or through a third party, to redress felt inequities. Examples are Blacks boycotting neighborhood stores and pressing for school bussing to achieve racial balance. The effects on some other persons are to reduce some positive outcomes and raise their negative outcomes, psychologically and otherwise. Again, the consequence is that two parties experience disadvantageous inequity.

As society grows, its social components become increasingly differentiated, the number of relationships among components increases (De Greene, 1973; Emery & Trist, 1965), and potential conflict between persons, groups, organizations, and institutions rises. In the circumstances, a consequential opportunity to provide understanding is placed before equity theorists.

III. Annotated Bibliography and Index

The following sources were employed in compiling the bibliography: the *Science Citation Index* at North Carolina State University; psychology, sociology and other journals not indexed in the above; references cited in equity articles previously identified and references in newly identified ones, iteratively; *Dissertation Abstracts;* APA Convention *Proceedings; Psychological Abstracts;* the authors' file of unpublished papers; and generous colleagues, especially Dr. Enno Schwanenberg, University of Frankfurt, West Germany, for searching the European literature. Every paper identified through these sources was not included in the bibliography in an attempt to limit its length. Excluded, for example, were articles that merely referred to equity theory. Others were excluded because they were judged only moderately relevant. We tried to use good judgment and hope we have in most cases.

The annotation of research papers is limited to brief descriptions of task, subjects, if of special interest, independent and dependent variables, and results. In some instances tasks, variables, and results were either unavailable in detail or so long that only a brief general description is given. The bibliographic items are alphabetically ordered and numbered sequentially. The researcher wishing to identify theoretical or review articles, independent or dependent variables, or subject populations in research papers need only search the index and note the bibliographic reference number.

A. INDEX TO BIBLIOGRAPHY

1. Theoretical Papers

Cognitive dissonance, 1, 3
Cognitive inconsistency, 6
Distributive justice, 1, 3, 9, 22, 58, 164, 165
Equity, 1, 3, 9, 59, 60, 61, 83, 134, 150, 151, 152, 167

*Only subject populations that may be of particular interest are identified.

Employees
  business and industry, 4, 27, 31, 44, 57, 67, 73, 121, 144
  public institutions, 37, 125
Nationality
  Austrian, 110, 111
  Canadian, 121
  Dutch, 160
  English, 140, 141
  Italian, 43, 123
Schizophrenic, 139

B. ANNOTATED BIBLIOGRAPHY

1. Adams, J.S. Toward an understanding of inequity. *Journal of Abnormal and Social Psychology*, 1963, 67, 422–436. (a)

   Presents general theory of inequity based on social exchange, social comparison, and cognitive dissonance theories.

2. Adams, J.S. Wage inequities, productivity and work quality. *Industrial Relations*, 1963, 3, 9–16. (b)

   Task: Public interviewing in 3 experiments. *IV:* (1) *S*s paid at hourly or piece rate; (2) *S*s induced to feel qualified or unqualified for pay rate. *DV:* (1) Productivity; (2) work quality. *Results:* Unqualified hourly paid Ss' productivity was higher than qualified hourly paid Ss'. Unqualified piece rate *Ss'* work quality was greater and their productivity was lower than the qualified piece rate *Ss'*.

3. Adams, J.S. Inequity in social exchange. In L. Berkowitz (Ed.), *Advances in experimental social psychology*, Vol. 2. New York: Academic Press, 1965. Pp. 267–299.

   Extends equity theory first presented in Adams (1963a). Social exchange, relative deprivation, distributive justice, and other related theories are discussed.

4. Adams, J.S. The effects of pay inequities. Paper presented at the McKinsey Seminar on Managerial Motivation and Compensation, Tarrytown, New York, 1967.

   Reviews effects of pay inequities and presents data on pay comparisons made by large samples of industrial employees.

5. Adams, J.S. Effects of overpayment: Two comments on Lawler's paper. *Journal of Personality and Social Psychology*, 1968, 10, 315–316. (a)

   Critique of Lawler (1968a) paper. *Vide infra.*

6. Adams, J.S. A framework for the study of modes of resolving inconsistency. In R.P. Abelson, E. Aronson, W.J. McGuire, T.M. Newcomb, M.J. Rosenberg, & P.H. Tannenbaum (Eds.), *Theories of cognitive consistency: A sourcebook*. Chicago: Rand McNally, 1968. Pp. 655–660. (b)

   Presents a general conceptual scheme for the development and analysis of cognitive consistency theories and research, including equity theory.

7. Adams, J.S., & Jacobsen, P.R. Effects of wage inequities on work quality. *Journal of Abnormal and Social Psychology*, 1964, **69**, 19–25.

   Task: Proofreading galleys, piece rate pay. *IV:* (1) Male Ss paid 30¢/page and either told they were qualified or unqualified for task, or told they were unqualified and thus paid at reduced rate of 20¢/page; (2) Ss told work might be available for several months or that it would not. *DV:* (1) Productivity; (2) work quality. *Results:* Unqualified Ss paid 30¢/page produced less but higher quality work than qualified Ss paid 30¢/page and unqualified Ss paid 20¢/page reduced rate. The latter two groups did not differ.

8. Adams, J.S., & Rosenbaum, W.B. The relationship of worker productivity to cognitive dissonance about wage inequities. *Journal of Applied Psychology*, 1962, **46**, 161–164.

   Task: Public interviewing. *IV:* (1) In 2 experiments, Ss told they were qualified or unqualified for interviewing; (2) hourly or piece rate pay. *DV:* Productivity. *Results:* Unqualified Ss produced more than qualified Ss when paid hourly. Unqualified piece rate Ss produced less than qualified piece rate Ss.

9. Anderson, B., Berger, J., Zelditch, M., & Cohen, B.P. Reactions to inequity. *Acta Sociologica*, 1969, **12**, 1–12.

   Theoretical discussion of relative deprivation, distributive justice, and equity from sociological viewpoint.

10. Anderson, B., & Shelly, R.K. Reactions to inequity, II: A replication of the Adams experiment and a theoretical reformulation. *Acta Sociologica*, 1970, **13**, 1–10.

    Task: Proofreading, hourly pay. *IV:* (1) Ss told they were qualified or underqualified for task; (2) underqualified Ss were told either than qualification test usually or always predicts proofreading success. *DV:* (1) Productivity; (2) quality of work. *Results:* No differences found between experimental groups.

11. Anderson, B., & Shelly, R.K. Reactions to inequity, III: Inequity and social influence. *Acta Sociologica*, 1971, **14**, 236–244.

    Fails to obtain empirical support for the hypothesis that inequity dissonance will occur only among overrewarded Ss if they receive or expect to receive signs of disapproval from an authority figure or equitably rewarded group members.

12. Andrews, I.R. Wage inequity and job performance: An experimental study. *Journal of Applied Psychology*, 1967, **51**, 39–45.

    Task: Interviewing or data checking, piece rate pay. *IV:* (1) Interesting (interviewing) or dull (data checking) task; (2) underpay (15¢), equitable (20¢) pay, or overpay (30¢); (3) S's previous wage experience. *DV:* (1) Productivity; (2) work quality. *Results:* Underpaid Ss produced more but at a lower quality level than equitably paid Ss. Overpaid Ss produced less but at higher quality than equitably paid Ss. Ss' previous wage experience was positively related to productivity and negatively to quality within piece rate groups. No effect of task interest.

13. Andrews, I.R., & Valenzi, E.R. Overpay inequity or self-image as a worker: A critical examination of an experimental induction procedure. *Organizational Behavior and Human Performance,* 1970, 5, 266–276.

Task: Using role projection method, Ss watched an induction procedure in which a job applicant was unqualified for the pay he would receive. *DV:* Ss' responses to questions about how they would feel if they were the applicant. *Results:* 59 of the 80 Ss responded in terms of their self-image. No Ss responded in terms of inequity. Ratings of structured alternatives indicated Ss felt self-image responses were most plausible and wage inequity responses least plausible.

14. Arrowood, A.J. Some effects on productivity of justified and unjustified levels of reward under public and private conditions. Unpublished doctoral dissertation, University of Minnesota, 1961.

Task: Public interviewing; pay for 3 hours given before task performance. *IV:* (1) Pay too high or about right relative to qualifications; (2) S's work either returned or not to payer. *DV:* Productivity. *Results:* From equity theory, Ss who perceived pay too high relative to their qualifications more productive than those whose pay was about right. From reinforcement theory, Ss whose work was available to source of pay more productive than Ss whose work was not available to source.

15. Austin, W., & Susmilch, C. Comment on Lane and Messé's confusing clarification of equity theory. *Journal of Personality and Social Psychology,* 1974, in press.

Attempt to clarify the conceptual status and definition of comparison "Other" in equity theory. Critique of Lane and Messé (1972). *Vide infra.*

16. Bass, B.M. Ability, values, and concepts of equitable salary increases in exercise compensation. *Journal of Applied Psychology,* 1968, 52, 299–303.

Graduate business students asked to recommend annual salary increases for 10 hypothetical engineers with varying characteristics. *Results:* Ss with lower intelligence and achievement who had strong social and religious values and who were generous with company money for other purposes made higher salary recommendations.

17. Benton, A.A. Productivity, distributive justice, and bargaining among children. *Journal of Personality and Social Psychology,* 1971, 18, 68–78.

Task: Following preliminary tasks, boys in pairs and girls in pairs bargained over division of reward. *IV:* (1) S passed or failed reading test; (2) pairs were friends, non-friends, neutral; (3) sex of pair. *DV:* Allocation of reward. *Results:* Girls prefer equality norm, but adopt equity norm if equal division impossible. Boys prefer equity norm, but this may be overridden by competitive achievement motivation.

18. Berman, S.M. An investigation of the effects of inequitable rewards on student performance and expected performance. Unpublished doctoral dissertation, University of Delaware, 1969.

Ss working in pairs were overrewarded or underrewarded; Ss then worked individually. Ss' expected performance was related to inequity, actual performance was not.

19. Berscheid, E., Boye, D., & Walster, E. Retaliation as a means of restoring equity. *Journal of Personality and Social Psychology,* 1968, **10,** 370–376.

> *Task:* Ss allegedly participated as "trainers," administering shocks, or "observers" in study of shock on verbal performance of confederate peer ("victim"). *IV:* (1) Harm-doer (exp. gp.) or observer (control gp.); (2) expect or do not expect victim to be able to administer shock. *DV: Ss'* derogation of victim. *Results:* Harm-doers derogate victim less when they expect retaliation than when they do not, but observers respond in reverse manner.

20. Berscheid, E., & Walster, E. When does a harmdoer compensate a victim? *Journal of Personality and Social Psychology,* 1967, **6,** 435–441.

> *Task:* Female Ss were led in the course of a game to deprive a fellow church member (victim) of green stamp books. In a second game they had a chance to compensate the victim. *IV:* (1) Insufficient, adequate, or excessive compensation available to Ss; (2) chance to award compensation to victim (exp. gp.) or to crippled child (control gp.). *DV:* Choice to compensate. *Results:* Experimental Ss more likely to compensate victim if available compensation was adequate than if the compensation was insufficient or excessive. This not found among control Ss.

21. Berscheid, E., Walster, E., & Barclay, A. Effect of time on tendency to compensate a victim. *Psychological Reports,* 1969, **25,** 431–436.

> *Task:* Ss played question-answering game in which they deprived their partner of green stamp books. In second game, they could give bonus to partner. *IV:* (1) S able to inadequately, adequately, or overcompensate their partner (victim); (2) S required to choose to compensate immediately or after a delay. *DV:* Whether or not Ss compensated victims. *Results:* Ss in the immediate condition compensated the victim regardless of the adequacy of compensation. Ss in the delay condition were more likely to compensate in the adequate compensation condition than Ss in the inadequate and excessive compensation conditions.

22. Blau, P.M. *Exchange and power in social life.* New York: Wiley, 1964.

> The concepts of justice, fair exchange, and distributive justice are discussed on pp. 151–160 and elsewhere.

23. Blumstein, P.W., & Weinstein, E.A. The redress of distributive injustice. *American Journal of Sociology,* 1969, **74,** 408–418.

> *Task:* Ss and confederate partners wrote questionnaire items. *IV:* (1) Partner did large or small proportion of work; (2) S's partner claimed to have done 1/3 or 2/3 of the work; (3) Ss' scores on Machiavellianism; (4) Ss' scores on Need for Approval; (5) Ss' sex. *DV:* (1) The amount of work claimed by S on a second set of items; (2) S's evaluation of partner. *Results:* Ss who benefited from the partner's claim redressed the injustice more than Ss who were victims. Females and Ss high on Machiavellianism and Need for Approval did not redress in reward allocation when they were victims.

24. Brickman, P., & Bryan, J.H. Evaluation of theft, charity, and disinterested transfers that increase or decrease equality. *Journal of Personality and Social Psychology,* 1974, in press.

Task: 5th grade girls viewed movie of 7th grade girl who surreptitiously modifies distribution of rewards in 4-person group. *IV:* (1) Girl in movie increases or decreases equality among group members by her transfers; (2) girl in movie either increases her own resources (theft), decreases her own resources (charity), or changes the rewards of 2 other group members in disinterested way. *DV:* (1) *Ss'* attitudes toward the 7th grade girl; (2) *Ss'* ratings of fairness of final distribution. *Results:* Charity transfers rated more favorably if they increased equality. This was not true of thefts. Disinterested changes in rewards of two other members were rated more favorably if they increased equality than if they decreased equality.

25. Burnstein, E., & Wolosin, R.J. The development of status distinctions under conditions of inequity. *Journal of Experimental Social Psychology,* 1968, **4**, 415–430.

    Task: Pairs of *S*s worked on a group reaction-time task in which each *S* initially had equal responsibility for joint outcome. *IV:* (1) *S*s told performance reflected important or unimportant skill, or was chance; (2) one *S* 50% successful, other 50%, 70%, or 90%. *DV:* *Ss'* decisions on how much responsibility each member should have in determination of joint outcomes. *Results:* *S*s divided responsibility for maximum joint outcomes. Redistribution of responsibility slower when performance difference between *S*s was smaller and task was important.

26. Callahan, C.M., & Messé, L.A. Conditions affecting attempts to convert fate control to behavior control. *Journal of Experimental Social Psychology,* 1973, **9**, 481–490.

    Task: Same sex pairs of one *S* and one confederate worked for 3 periods, respectively, as supervisor and worker in simulated industrial situation in which worker addressed envelopes and supervisor paid him according to his assessed performance. *IV:* (1) Sex of pairs; (2) high or low fate control of *S;* (3) worker had counterpower or no counterpower in affecting *S*'s pay; (4) worker performance (low in 3 periods vs. low in first and medium in last 2); (5) work period. *DV:* (1) *S*'s pay allocation to worker; (2) *S*'s reasons for allocation. *Results:* Males (not females) paid workers most when they had high fate control and worker had counterpower. *S*s moved by equity considerations when worker had no counterpower. Males more concerned with behavior control, females with equity.

27. Clark, J.V. A preliminary investigation of some unconscious assumptions affecting labor efficiency in 8 supermarkets. Unpublished doctoral dissertation, Harvard University, 1958.

    Studied supermarket checkout counters manned by "ringer" (cashier) and "bundler." *Results:* Inequities resulting from bundler (low status) having higher inputs than ringer (higher status) were inversely related to labor efficiency.

28. Cohen, R.L. Mastery and justice in laboratory dyads: A revision and extension of equity theory. *Journal of Personality and Social Psychology,* 1974, **29**, 464–474.

    Task: Pairs of *S*s jointly performed group reaction time task; success rate for one *S* was 80%, 50% for other; the pair allegedly competing against other groups. *IV:* (1) Success rate wholly under voluntary control of *S*s or partially under uncontrollable factor; (2) high, medium, low criterion of group success to beat other groups. *DV:* Distribution of bonus reward. *Results:* Inferior members (50%) in nonvoluntary condition were given more of bonus reward than in voluntary condition. Also given more as criterion of group success increased.

29. Cook, K.S. An experimental study of the activation of equity processes. Unpublished doctoral dissertation, Stanford University, 1973.

Presents a theory specifying the conditions and processes leading to activation of equity processes. Data on questionnaire and allocation responses support equity theory.

30. Cook, T.D. Temporal mechanisms mediating attitude change after underpayment and overpayment. *Journal of Personality,* 1969, 37, 618–635.

Task: Proofreading, hourly pay. *IV:* Ss underpaid, equitably paid, or overpaid in relation to expected pay. *DV:* (1) Productivity; (2) work quality; (3) attitudes toward task. *Results:* Perceived and actual performance higher among overpaid Ss than other Ss. A time and payment interaction found for attitude toward the task. Underpaid Ss initially liking task material more, then disliking it, and finally liking it as much as equitably paid Ss.

31. Dansereau, F., Cashman, J., & Graen, G. Instrumentality theory and equity theory as complementary approaches in predicting the relationship of leadership and turnover among managers. *Organizational Behavior and Human Performance,* 1973, **10**, 184–200.

In a longitudinal correlational study of 261 salaried managers, high performers who were not differentially compensated in comparison to low performers were much more likely than average to leave the organization. In contrast, when performance and compensation were contingently related, managers were more likely than average to stay.

32. Day, C.R. Some consequences of increased reward following establishment of output-reward expectation level. Unpublished master's thesis, Duke University, 1961.

Task: Children pushed plunger for M & M candies. Number of candies (between 1 and 6) was dependent on pressure exerted on plunger. After responses stabilized, 25 candies received by S on last 5 trials. *DV:* Pressure exerted on overrewarded trials. *Results:* Ss increased pressure when overrewarded.

33. Day, G.J. The behavioral effects of wage inequity in work groups. Unpublished doctoral dissertation, Indiana University, 1961.

Varying degrees of inequity were created in 3-person work groups. Some equity theory predictions failed, but production help and pay reallocation within groups were significant means of reducing inequity; the use of these means increased as inequity increased.

34. Deci, E.L. Intrinsic motivation, extrinsic reinforcement, and inequity. *Journal of Personality and Social Psychology,* 1972, **22**, 113–120.

Task: Ss worked on puzzles, after which they were free to do several things, including work on puzzle. *IV:* (1) Verbal or no verbal reinforcement for puzzle solving task; (2) no payment for task vs. overpayment at the end of the task vs. overpayment after the free-choice period following the task; (3) sex. *DV:* Time spent working on puzzles during free-choice period. *Results:* Ss worked on puzzles more during free time when paid before free-choice period and less when paid after the period than Ss who were not paid.

35. Evan, W.M., & Simmons, R.G. Organizational effects of inequitable rewards: Two experiments in status inconsistency. *Administrative Science Quarterly,* 1969, **14,** 224–237.

   Task: In 2 experiments, *S* proofread galleys in publisher's premises, hourly pay. *IV:* Equitably paid, overpaid, or underpaid in relation to induced competence or to induced authority. *DV:* (1) Productivity; (2) work quality. *Results:* No differential effects of pay-authority discrepancies. Pay-competence discrepancies resulted in underpaid *S*s producing more, but poorest quality work.

36. Evans, M.G., & Molinari, L. Equity, piece rate overpayment, and job security: Some effects on performance. *Journal of Applied Psychology,* 1970, **54,** 105–114.

   Task: Interviewing, piece rate pay. *IV:* (1) High or low job security; (2) *S*s told they were qualified or underqualified for pay rate. *DV:* (1) Productivity; (2) quality of work. *Results:* There was a trend among unqualified (overpaid) *S*s in both secure and insecure conditions to produce better quality work than qualified *S*s. Security and qualification interacted such that productivity was greater among qualified secure *S*s than unqualified secure ones, whereas productivity was greater among unqualified insecure *S*s than qualified insecure ones.

37. Finn, R.H., & Lee, S.M. Salary equity: Its determination, analysis, and correlates. *Journal of Applied Psychology,* 1972, **56,** 283–292.

   Professional and scientific employees in Federal Public Health Service answered questionnaire measuring demographic and work history information, perception of job inputs, salary treatment, and job-related attitudes. *S*s' immediate superiors also completed questionnaire. *Results:* *S*s in inequitably treated subsample displayed less favorable job-related attitudes and had a higher propensity to quit their job than *S*s in equitably treated subsample. Multiple-regression model predicted equitable salaries ($R = .933$).

38. Flynn, M.S. Power imbalance, justice, and exchange in a minimal social situation. Unpublished doctoral dissertation, University of North Carolina at Chapel Hill, 1972.

   Task: Female *S*s worked with fictitious partner on button pushing task. *S* and partner must agree to work one of three buttons which gave *S* equal money reward as partner but required unequal work. *IV:* One of three different sets of ratios of work requirements for *S* and partner. *DV:* Choices of button. *Results:* *S*s maximized outcomes at cost of violating equity and maximizing dependency of partner.

39. Friedman, A., & Goodman, P. Wage inequity, self-qualifications, and productivity. *Organizational Behavior and Human Performance,* 1967, **2,** 406–417.

   Task: Interviewing, hourly pay of $3.50. *IV:* (1) *S*s told they were qualified or underqualified; (2) *S*'s perceptions of his qualifications. *DV:* Productivity. *Results:* The qualification induction did not affect productivity. When *S*s were classified according to their perceived qualifications, however, qualified *S*s produced more than unqualified *S*s.

40. Garland, H. The effects of piece rate underpayment and overpayment on job performance: A test of equity theory with a new induction procedure. Unpublished manuscript, Cornell University, 1972.

Task: Proofreading material containing errors, piece rate pay. *IV:* (1) *S*s hired at 15¢, 30¢, or 60¢/page rate and told by a confederate worker that his pay was 30¢/page; (2) sex. *DV:* (1) Productivity; (2) work quality. *Results:* Underpaid males and females produced more work whereas when overpaid they produced less work than equitably paid *S*s. Overpaid males produced better quality work but poorer quality work if underpaid. Underpaid females did poorer work than equitably paid females, but the overpaid females' work was not better than the latter's.

41. Garrett, J.B. Effects of Protestant ethic endorsement upon equity behavior. Paper presented at the meeting of the American Psychological Association, Montreal, August, 1973.

    Task: *S*s asked to allocate $15.40 among 4 hypothetical work group members varying systematically in effort and performance. *IV:* (1) High or low *S* scores on Mirels-Garrett Protestant Ethic Scale; (2) performance and effort description of member: Hi-hi, hi-lo, lo-hi, lo-lo. *DV:* Amount of money allocated to each of 4 work group members. *Results:* *S*s with high Protestant Ethic Scale scores used equity as a basis of reward allocation more than low scorers.

42. Garrett, J.B., & Libby, W.L., Jr. Role of intentionality in mediating responses to inequity in the dyad. *Journal of Personality and Social Psychology,* 1973, **28,** 21–27.

    Task: 9th graders performed proofreading task with hypothetical partner who allocated reward after task. *S* then allowed to allocate bonus. *IV:* (1) *S*s told reward allocation by partner was chance or intentional; (2) after performing equally with partner, *S* was overrewarded or underrewarded. *DV:* (1) *S*'s allocation of bonus; (2) *S*'s rating of partner (good-bad, fair-unfair). *Results:* *S*s distributed bonus to restore equity when partner's initial allocation was intentional. Bonus allocated about equally, ignoring the first reward allocation, when partner's initial allocation was by chance.

43. Gergen, K.J., Morse, S.J., & Bode, K. Overpaid or overworked? Cognitive and behavioral reactions to inequitable payment. Unpublished manuscript, Swarthmore College, 1971.

    Task: American and Italian *S*s attempted to identify words (English or Italian) transmitted with noise over a speaker. *IV:* (1) *S*s told they would receive same pay as, 40% or 80% more, or 40% less than they felt was correct for task. *DV:* (1) Performance; (2) evaluation of task difficulty; (3) perceived fair rate of pay for task. *Results:* Overpaid *S*s' evaluation of task difficulty and fair rate of pay increased compared to equitably paid *S*s. No systematic effects of pay on task performance.

44. Giles, B.A., & Barrett, G.V. Utility of merit increases. *Journal of Applied Psychology,* 1971, **55,** 103–109.

    Sixty-four professional employees in electronics company responded to questionnaire on merit increases and satisfaction. *Results:* Satisfaction with pay increases was better predicted by the ratio of merit increase to perceived equitable merit increase than by merit increase proper, percentage merit increase, and salary plus increase.

45. Goodman, P.S., & Friedman, A. An examination of the effect of wage inequity in the hourly condition. *Organizational Behavior and Human Performance*, 1968, **3**, 340–352.

  Task: Questionnaire scoring, hourly pay. *IV:* Six pay conditions: (1) Ss overpaid with emphasis on quantity of questionnaires scored. (2) overpaid with quality emphasis. (3) overpaid Ss with quantity emphasis told the production rate of qualified scorers. (4) Ss paid at reduced rate because of lack of qualifications. (5) Ss paid at reduced rate because of lack of qualifications and told the production rate of people with similar qualifications. (6) Ss told they were qualified and paid equitably. *DV:* (1) Productivity; (2) work quality. *Results:* Overpaid Ss produced more than equitably paid Ss. Emphasis on quantity or quality affects Ss' emphasis during performance. Known production rates reduced the production variance of Ss.

46. Goodman, P.S., & Friedman, A. An examination of quantity and quality of performance under conditions of overpayment in piece rate. *Organizational Behavior and Human Performance*, 1969, **4**, 365–374.

  Task: Questionnaire scoring, piece rate pay. *IV:* (1) Ss told they were qualified or underqualified for task; (2) E's emphasis on quality or quantity. *DV:* (1) Productivity; (2) work quality. *Results:* Underqualified Ss reduced inequity by increasing productivity or quality depending on E's emphasis. Production differences between quality and quantity emphasis conditions greater for underqualified than for qualified Ss.

47. Goodman, P.S., & Friedman, A. An examination of Adams' theory of inequity. *Administrative Science Quarterly,* 1971, **16**, 271–288.

  Discusses equity theory and research and effects of inequity on performance and allocation of rewards.

48. Gordon, M.E. An evaluation of Jaques' studies of pay in the light of current compensation research. *Personnel Psychology,* 1969, **22**, 369–389.

  Critique of Jaques (1961). Reviews research on span of discretion and responsibility in relation to equitable compensation.

49. Greenberg, J., & Leventhal, G.S. Violating equity to prevent group failure. *Proceedings, 81st Annual Convention,* APA, 1973, 215–216.

  Task: Ss considered a business case in which two 2-man groups working on special projects were described. Ss were asked to recommend money bonus for each worker. *IV:* (1) One worker in each group had above average performance, the other below average; (2) one group, it was stated, would definitely fail if it continued to perform as it had, while the other group would easily succeed; (3) half the Ss were instructed to award bonus on basis of performance, the others so as to motivate workers; (4) sex. *DV:* Bonus allocations. *Results:* Ss instructed to motivate workers gave greater bonuses to workers of failing groups than did Ss instructed to maintain equity. This resulted also in higher bonuses for failing than succeeding groups. Ss instructed to reward for performance rewarded succeeding groups more than failing ones. Better performing members within groups were allocated larger bonuses.

50. Greenberg, M.S., Block, M.W., & Silverman, M.A. Determinants of helping behavior: Person's rewards versus other's costs. *Journal of Personality*, 1971, 39, 79–93.

    Task: S and confederate role-played disabled workers performing task in which S required help. In second task confederate was potential recipient of help from S. *IV:* Confederate's help in first task resulted in high extra reward for S at low cost to confederate, low extra reward for S at moderate cost to confederate, or no extra reward for S at high cost to confederate. *DV:* Amount of help S gave confederate on second task. *Results:* Ss were more likely to help if confederate's previous help had resulted in high or moderate rewards for S than if help resulted in low or no rewards.

51. Greenberg, M.S., & Frisch, D.M. Effect of intentionality on willingness to reciprocate a favor. *Journal of Experimental Social Psychology*, 1972, 8, 99–111.

    Task: Male Ss were required to complete a sales forecast for which they needed help from a fictitious other; then Ss performed personnel task for which help was requested by other. *IV:* (1) Help given by other was deliberate or accidental; (2) much or little help given by other. *DV:* Help given by S on second task. *Results:* More help given in deliberate than accidental condition. More help given in high help than low help condition.

52. Greenberg, M.S., & Shapiro, S.P. Indebtedness: An adverse aspect of asking for and receiving help. *Sociometry*, 1971, 34, 290–301.

    Task: S with his arm in sling and confederate with an eye patch and sunglasses were asked to first assemble boxes, then to proofread copy for errors. *IV:* (1) S anticipated he would or would not be able to reciprocate help; (2) sex. *DV:* Ss willingness to ask for help from confederate. *Results:* Ss unable to reciprocate help less likely to ask for it from confederate than Ss who anticipated they could help confederate on second task.

53. Haccoun, R.R., Wood, M.T., & Smith, J.E. Explicit versus abstract referents in equity inductions and reversals: A new procedure. *Proceedings, 81st Annual Convention, APA*, 1973, 565–566.

    In a 3-stage experiment with piece rate pay, Ss working with a confederate were first induced to believe their rate was the same, greater, or lower than confederate's. E then equalized pay. *Results:* Underpaid Ss produced more. Productivity was greater when confederate's pay rate was changed to equal S's than when S's was changed to equal confederate's.

54. Heslin, R., & Blake, B. Performance as a function of payment, commitment, and task interest. *Psychonomic Science*, 1969, 15, 323–324.

    Task: Ss signed up for task for which they would be paid by the hour. *IV:* (1) Interesting (puzzle) vs. boring task (packing); (2) underpayment, usual payment, or overpayment; (3) high vs. low commitment. *DV:* Productivity. *Results:* Committed Ss produced more than noncommitted Ss.

55. Hinton, B.L. The experimental extension of equity theory to interpersonal and group interaction situations. *Organizational Behavior and Human Performance*, 1972, 8, 434–449.

    Task: Groups of 9 Ss checked and collated IBM cards. *IV:* (1) Ss on hourly pay:

underpaid, overpaid, or equitably paid; (2) Ss on piece rate: underpaid, overpaid, or equitably paid; (3) Ss worked independently, in task-dependent subgroups of 3 with 3 subgroups paid differently, or in task-dependent subgroups of 3 with each member receiving different pay but subgroups receiving same pay. *DV:* (1) Productivity; (2) work quality. *Results:* Hourly paid Ss produced less but higher quality work than piece rate Ss. Availability of relevant referents and group setting were important in determining performance.

56. Hinton, B.L., & Barrow, J.C. The use of economic and evaluative reinforcements as a function of one's own reinforcement. Unpublished manuscript, Indiana University, 1973.

In a laboratory experiment of superior-subordinate reciprocal reinforcement, the reluctance of a superior to use equal negative reinforcements when his own are negative suggests that equity motivation may not operate in the negative range of outcomes.

57. Homans, G.C. Status among clerical workers. *Human Organization,* 1953, **12**, 5–10.

In an observational study of female clerical workers, equal pay among clerks of different status was perceived as inequitable and resulted in dissatisfaction and efforts to bring pay in line with status.

58. Homans, G.C. *Social behavior: Its elementary forms.* New York: Harcourt, Brace & World, 1961.

Chapter 12 presents the author's theory of distributive justice.

59. Jaques, E. *Measurement of responsibility.* London: Tavistock Publications, 1956.

Presents relationship between concepts of span of discretion and responsibility and perceived equitable wage payment.

60. Jaques, E. *Equitable payment.* New York: Wiley, 1961.

Vide supra Jaques (1956).

61. Jaques, E. Equity in compensation. In H.L. Tosi, R.J. House, & M.D. Dunnette (Eds.), *Managerial motivation and compensation: A selection of readings.* East Lansing, Michigan: Michigan State University Business Studies, 1972. Pp. 170–206.

Vide supra Jaques (1956).

62. Johnson, D.A. Equity theory and overpayment: The behavior of children of differing socio-economic backgrounds. Unpublished manuscript, University of California, 1973.

Task: 6th graders coded questionnaires. *IV:* (1) Piece rate or hourly pay; (2) equity, mild inequity, or strong inequity. *MV:* S's socio-economic status, high or low. *DV:* (1) Productivity; (2) work quality. *Results:* Equity theory predictions supported among higher SES but not lower SES Ss.

63. Johnson, W.T. Social exchange: Dependency, communication, and inequity. Unpublished doctoral dissertation, University of Washington, 1969.

Pairs of Ss allowed to exchange tasks (listen to music, manipulate plunger) do so more frequently when plunger responses/minute requirements are low and equitable than when high and inequitable.

64. Kahn, A. Reactions to generosity or stinginess from an intelligent or stupid work partner: A test of equity theory in a direct exchange relationship. *Journal of Personality and Social Psychology,* 1972, **21,** 116–123.

Task: Pairs of Ss first worked on proofreading as group and "partner" distributed reward; they then worked individually on second proofreading task and "subject" allocated rewards. *IV:* (1) Partner's qualifications, high or low; (2) sex; (3) S overpaid, equitably paid or underpaid after first task. *DV:* S's allocation of rewards after second task. *Results:* Underpaid Ss took more and overpaid Ss took less of the second reward than equitably paid Ss. Equity-restoring allocations were only partial; a bias toward equal allocation was observed.

65. Kalt, N.C. The temporal resolution of inequity: An exploratory investigation. Unpublished doctoral dissertation, University of Illinois, 1969.

Task: Interviewing for 3 one-hour sessions at $2/hr. *IV:* Ss told they had done well (equitably paid) or poorly (overpaid) on selection test. *DV:* (1) Productivity; (2) quality of work; (3) job ratings. *Results:* Overpaid Ss produced more on first day than equitably paid Ss. Ss more productive on first session rated their qualifications more favorably on next two sessions than less productive Ss.

66. Kessler, J.J., & Wiener, Y. Self-consistency and inequity dissonance as factors in undercompensation. *Organizational Behavior and Human Performance,* 1972, **8,** 456–466.

Task: Word manipulation, hourly pay. *IV:* (1) Ss told they were qualified or overqualified; (2) Ss believed they were working on ego-oriented task dependent on intelligence or on simple clerical task. *DV:* (1) Productivity; (2) work quality. *Results:* Productivity was lower among overqualified Ss than qualified Ss. Work quality higher among overqualified Ss.

67. Klein, S.M. Pay factors as predictors to satisfaction: A comparison of reinforcement, equity, and expectancy. *Academy of Management Journal,* 1973, **16,** 598–610.

To determine the relative predictive value of equity, expectancy, and reinforcement theories, questionnaires were given to blue collar workers to measure their past salary reinforcement, expected future salary treatment, and perceived equity. *Results:* Equity and expectancy predicted job satisfaction, equity being the more powerful predictor.

68. Lane, I.M., & Coon, R.C. Reward allocation in preschool children. *Child Development,* 1972, **43,** 1382–1389.

Task: Sticker pasting with fictitious partner; Ss divided team reward after task. *IV:* (1) 4- or 5-year-old Ss; (2) sex; (3) S-partner inputs: 5-5, 5-15, 15-5, 15-15 stickers. *DV:* Reward allocation by S. *Results:* 4-year-old Ss allocate rewards on basis of self-interest; 5-year-old Ss allocate rewards on basis of equality, not equity.

69. Lane, I.M., Coon, R.C., & Lichtman, R.J. Developmental trends in the principles employed by children to allocate rewards to others. Paper presented at the meeting of the American Psychological Association, Montreal, August, 1973.

Task: Children viewed video-taped TV program of 2 adults playing a ball game for which they would receive money in relation to their performance. Awards allocated to players by *S*s. *IV:* (1) *S*s in kindergarten, 2nd, 4th, or 6th grade; (2) insufficient, sufficient, or oversufficient rewards available for *S*s' distribution to the winner and loser of game; (3) *S*'s sex. *DV:* Reward distribution. *Results:* *S*s allocated a greater proportion of reward to the winner in the insufficient and oversufficient conditions than in the sufficient condition. With insufficient rewards, older *S*s distributed rewards more equitably than younger *S*s. Generally, the norm of equity was the most important determiner of reward allocation.

70. Lane, I.M., & Messé, L.A. Equity and the distribution of rewards. *Journal of Personality and Social Psychology,* 1971, **20,** 1–17.

Task: In 2 experiments, *S*s completed various paper and pencil instruments, then distributed rewards to selves and partners when both had equal inputs (first exp.) and when their inputs varied systematically (second exp.). *DV:* Reward distribution. *Results:* Equity theory predictions generally upheld with respect to frequency of allocation responses. Allocations in second experiment principally influenced by inputs of partner.

71. Lane, I.M., & Messé, L.A. Distribution of insufficient, sufficient, and oversufficient rewards: A clarification of equity theory. *Journal of Personality and Social Psychology,* 1972, **21,** 228–233.

Task: *S* and confederate partner worked on industrial relations questionnaire. *IV:* (1) *S* and partner worked for varying amounts of time; (2) different amounts of money for *S* to allocate to self and partner. *DV:* *S*'s allocations. *Results:* *S*s allocated money equally when contributions were equal, but only if total money available was consistent with internal standard of fair pay. If the total amount was more or less than this, *S*s allocated proportionately more to themselves.

72. Lane, I.M., Messé, L.A., & Phillips, J.L. Differential inputs as a determinant in the selection of a distributor of rewards. *Psychonomic Science,* 1971, **22,** 228–229.

Task: Answering questionnaires. *IV:* *S*s in triads in which one *S* worked 3 hours, one *S* 2 hours, and one *S* 1 hour on proportionate number of questionnaires. *DV:* (1) Each *S*'s allocation of $12; (2) which other *S* in the triad would *S* vote for to allocate rewards. *Results:* *S*s allocated rewards equitably in terms of hours worked. *S*s voted for other *S*s in the triad whose hour inputs were the highest and most similar to their own to allocate rewards.

73. Lawler, E.E., III. Managers' perception of their subordinates' pay and of their superiors' pay. *Personnel Psychology,* 1965, **18,** 413–422.

Managers from government and private organizations responded to questionnaire about pay. *Results:* *S*s reported that the difference between their pay and pay of their superiors and subordinates was too small. *S*s overestimated subordinates' pay.

74. Lawler, E.E., III. Effects of hourly overpayment on productivity and work quality. *Journal of Personality and Social Psychology,* 1968, **10,** 306–313. (a)

Task: Public interviewing, hourly pay. *IV:* *S*s overpaid (low qualifications for task), overpaid by circumstance (qualified), or equitably paid (qualified). *DV:* (1) Productivity; (2) work quality; (3) *S*'s desire to prove his competence. *Results:* Overpaid *S*s produced more but lower quality work. *S*s overpaid by circumstance did not differ from equitably paid *S*s. Overpaid *S*s scored higher on desire to prove competency than other *S*s.

75. Lawler, E.E., III. Equity theory as a predictor of productivity and work quality. *Psychological Bulletin*, 1968, 70, 596–610. (b)

Compares the value of equity theory and expectancy theory in predicting work performance.

76. Lawler, E.E., III, Koplin, C.A., Young, T.F., & Fadem, J.A. Inequity reduction over time in an induced overpayment situation. *Organizational Behavior and Human Performance*, 1968, 3, 253–268.

Task: Public interviewing for three 2-hour periods, piece rate pay. *IV:* (1) *S*s told they were qualified (equitably paid), or underqualified (overpaid) for task; (2) *S*s' need for money earned. *DV:* (1) Productivity; (2) work quality; (3) perceived qualifications. *Results:* Overpaid *S*s produced less but higher quality work than equitably paid *S*s in first period, but not next two. Instead, their perceptions of their qualifications increased. *S*s' need for money correlated with productivity among both overpaid and equitably paid.

77. Lawler, E.E., III, & O'Gara, P.W. Effects of inequity produced by underpayment on work output, work quality, and attitudes toward the work. *Journal of Applied Psychology*, 1967, 51, 403–410.

Task: Interviewing for 2 hours, piece rate pay. *IV:* *S*s underpaid (10¢ rate) or equitably paid (25¢ rate). *DV:* (1) Productivity; (2) work quality; (3) attitudes toward job. *Results:* Underpaid *S*s produced more interviews, but of lower quality, and perceived job as more interesting but less complex, important, and challenging than equitably paid *S*s.

78. Legant, P. Equity theory and the law: Suggestions for future research. Symposium presented at the meeting of the American Psychological Association, Montreal, August, 1973.

79. Lerner, M.J. Evaluation of performance as a function of performer's reward and attractiveness. *Journal of Personality and Social Psychology*, 1965, 1, 355–360.

Task: Female *S*s listened to tape of 2 students working equally well at joint anagram task. One worker was more attractive than other. *IV:* The attractive or less attractive worker paid $3.50 for his work, the other paid nothing. *DV:* *S*s' performance ratings of workers. *Results:* *S*s rated rewarded worker as having contributed more than the unrewarded worker. The ratings of work group contribution were lower and *S*s were more uncomfortable when the less attractive worker was rewarded.

80. Lerner, M.J. The desire for justice and reactions to victims. In J. Macaulay and L. Berkowitz (Eds.), *Altruism and helping behavior*. New York: Academic Press, 1970. Pp. 205–229.

A review of the author's work, including data, on the behavior of persons toward victims and on the concept of justice in such contexts.

81. Lerner, M.J. The justice motive: "Equity" and "parity" among children. *Journal of Personality and Social Psychology*, 1974, **29**, 539–550.

Task: In 3 experiments, kindergarten, 1st, and 5th grade *S*s performed manual tasks with fictitious partner as a team or individually. *S*s then assumed supervisor role and allocated rewards to selves and partners, or *S*s simply determined own share. *IV:* (1) *S* produced more or less than partner; (2) team vs. individual instructions. *DV:* Reward allocations. *Results:* Kindergartners based allocations on equality rather than equity.

82. Leventhal, G.S. Equity and the economics of reward distribution. Paper presented at the meeting of the American Psychological Association, Honolulu, September, 1972. (a)

Task: S to recommend pay increases for 4 hypothetical employees who had received outside job offer. *IV:* (1) High or low productivity of employees; (2) high or average attractiveness of outside offer working conditions and benefits; (3) instructions to *S*s to make counter offers to weed out worst and retain best employees; instructions to retain all employees; or no instructions. *DV: S*s' recommendation for pay increase to each employee. *Results: S*s offered high productivity workers more than low productivity workers and more when outside offer was highly attractive than when it was average. Difference between amount offered to high and low productivity workers greater for *S*s told to weed out worst and retain best than for *S*s told to retain all.

83. Leventhal, G.S. Reward allocation in social relationships. Paper presented at the meeting of the Southeastern Psychological Association, Atlanta, April, 1972. (b)

Presents a framework for conceptualizing allocator-recipient relationships.

84. Leventhal, G.S. Reward allocation by males and females. Paper presented at the meeting of the American Psychological Association, Montreal, August, 1973.

Reviews a large body of literature to determine the effects of subject sex on the distribution of rewards. Males generally deviate more on the exploitative side of equity; females display generosity generally, preferring equality or deviations from equity that are unfavorable to themselves. Sex differences in achievement motivation may provide a partial explanation.

85. Leventhal, G.S., Allen, J., & Kemelgor, B. Reducing inequity by reallocating rewards. *Psychonomic Science*, 1969, **14**, 295–296.

Task: S and partner (confederate) performed arithmetic task for group pay of $1.40 allocated by partner. *S* then allowed to change allocation. *IV:* Amount allocated by partner to *S:* $1.20, 95¢, 70¢, 45¢, 20¢, 5¢, or 2¢. *DV:* (1) *S*'s changing allocation of reward; (2) *S*'s tension and anticipatory behavior toward partner. *Results: S*s receiving too much (too little) relative to their work inputs decreased (increased) their own rewards. *S*s receiving 70¢ did not change allocation. Five *S*s suffering extreme inequity (5¢ and 2¢ allocations) *decreased* their rewards. *S*s' tension level increased as size of the inequity increased; *S*s planned to compensate for inequity on future trials.

86. Leventhal, G.S., & Anderson, D. Self-interest and the maintenance of equity. *Journal of Personality and Social Psychology,* 1970, **15**, 57–62.

   Task: Preschool children pasted stars with fictitious partner. *IV:* (1) Ss told their performance was superior, equal, or inferior to partner's; (2) Ss' sex. *DV:* (1) Reward allocation; (2) Ss' reports of each member's performance. *Results:* Boys took more reward when their performance was superior than when it was equal to partner's. Girls did not. Neither boys nor girls in inferior performance conditions took less than half of reward, but both minimized partners' performance.

87. Leventhal, G.S., & Bergman, J.T. Self-depriving behavior as a response to unprofitable inequity. *Journal of Experimental Social Psychology,* 1969, **5**, 153–171.

   Task: S and confederate worked equally on arithmetic task. *IV:* (1) Confederate gave S 40¢ or 5¢ of $1.40 reward after task; (2) confederate sent S message with high or low status threat. *DV:* S's reallocation, either increasing or decreasing his reward up to 5¢. *Results:* Ss awarded somewhat less than half of reward increased their share, whereas Ss awarded much less decreased their share. Extreme unprofitable inequity increases self-depriving behavior.

88. Leventhal, G.S., & Lane, D.W. Sex, age, and equity behavior. *Journal of Personality and Social Psychology,* 1970, **15**, 312–316.

   Task: Ss worked with fictitious partners on multiplication problems for which the pair received money. Ss allowed to divide earnings afterward. *IV:* (1) Ss told their performance was inferior or superior to partner's; (2) Ss' sex. *DV:* (1) Allocation of earnings; (2) perceptions of inputs. *Results:* Males allocated rewards equitably on the basis of performance. Females in superior performance condition took approximately half the reward; those with inferior performance took much less than half. Superior performance females tended to belittle their performance.

89. Leventhal, G.S., & Michaels, J.W. Extending the equity model: Perception of inputs and allocation of reward as a function of duration and quantity of performance. *Journal of Personality and Social Psychology,* 1969, **12**, 303–309.

   Task: Ss worked with confederates on jigsaw puzzles and then allocated rewards earned. *IV:* Ss required: (1) to work for longer or shorter duration than confederate, and (2) to complete smaller or greater quantity of work. *DV:* (1) Reward allocation; (2) perceptions of inputs. *Results:* With amount of work constant, Ss who worked longer took less reward than Ss who worked for shorter duration. When amount of work and duration were proportional for each member, Ss divided reward equally.

90. Leventhal, G.S., & Michaels, J.W. Locus of cause and equity motivation as determinants of reward allocation. *Journal of Personality and Social Psychology,* 1971, **17**, 229–235.

   Task: Ss judged extent to which 16 hypothetical persons should be rewarded for performance in vertical jumps. *IV:* Attributes of hypothetical persons: (1) high or low jump performance; (2) high or low effort; (3) tall or short body height; (4) useful or unuseful training. *DV:* How deserving of reward persons were. *Results:* With performance held constant, persons whose height and training helped them in jumping were rated as less deserving than those whose height and training did not help. Ss rated individuals with high effort as more deserving than those with low effort.

91. Leventhal, G.S., Michaels, J.W., & Sanford, C. Inequity and interpersonal conflict: Reward allocation and secrecy about reward as methods of preventing conflict. *Journal of Personality and Social Psychology,* 1972, **23,** 88–102.

Task: In 2 experiments, Ss allocated rewards to 4 hypothetical group members. *IV:* Group members varied as to (1) high or low performance and (2) high or low effort; (3) Ss instructed to allocate rewards in way to prevent conflict among members, to prevent conflict between experimenters and members, to ignore possibility of conflict, or given instructions without reference to conflict. (4) Group members would know (no secrecy) or not know (secrecy) rewards others received. *DV:* Amount of reward to members. *Results:* Ss gave higher rewards to better performers. They increased worst performer's share at expense of best under instructions to prevent member conflict; inflation of worst performer's rewards was smaller under secrecy than no secrecy. Ss' desire to conceal reward distribution was greatest in case of members given low reward.

92. Leventhal, G.S., Popp, A.L., & Sawyer, L. Equity or equality in children's allocation of reward to other persons? *Child Development,* 1973, **44,** 753–763.

Task: In 2 experiments, children performed pegboard (or block) task and were rewarded. Ss then asked to award picture seals to 2 fictitious children who had performed similar task, the results of which were shown. *IV:* (1) Small or large performance difference between 2 children; (2) allocate rewards as Ss thought best or as a teacher evaluating the results would think best; (3) Ss' sex. *DV:* Reward allocation. *Results:* Ss, especially boys, gave greater rewards to better performer when performance difference between children was large. Boys gave greater rewards to better performers when using own judgment than when expecting teacher to evaluate allocation.

93. Leventhal, G.S., Weiss, T., & Buttrick, R. Attribution of value, equity, and the prevention of waste in reward allocation. *Journal of Personality and Social Psychology,* 1973, **27,** 276–286.

Task: In 2 experiments, Ss could reward with rolls of film or paperbacks 2 fictitious telephone interviewees who were equally good respondents. *IV:* (1) High or low previous purchase and use of film; (2) E stressed spoilage of unused film or omitted mention of this; (3) systematic variations in purchase and reading of books. *DV:* Reward allocation. *Results:* Interviewees more likely to be given film by S if they had used film at high rate in past and if S was in spoilage condition. S gave more books if interviewee had high past rate of usage, but only if past usage rate of interviewees was greatly different.

94. Leventhal, G.S., Weiss, T., & Long, G. Equity, reciprocity, and reallocating rewards in the dyad. *Journal of Personality and Social Psychology,* 1969, **13,** 300–305.

Task: S and fictitious partner proofread materials; partner then allocated $2 reward. S then had opportunity to reallocate reward. *IV:* (1) Ss told that partner allocated reward intentionally or by chance; (2) S underrewarded (60¢) or overrewarded ($1.40). *DV:* (1) Ss modification of the reward allocation; (2) responses to questionnaire. *Results:* Ss overrewarded intentionally decreased their share of reward more than Ss overrewarded by chance. Ss underrewarded by chance increased their reward to same extent as Ss underrewarded intentionally.

95. Leventhal, G.S., & Whiteside, H.D. Equity and the use of reward to elicit high performance. *Journal of Personality and Social Psychology,* 1973, *25,* 75–83.

Task: Ss awarded mid-term grades to 8 hypothetical students whose exam perfor-mance was constant. *IV:* (1) High or low aptitude of students; (2) students, fore-warned or not, were expected to perform at their best; (3) Ss instructed to grade fairly or to elicit highest possible future performance. *DV:* Grade allocation. *Results:* Ss gave higher grades to students with lower aptitude. This was more pronounced when Ss were trying to motivate high future performance and when students had been warned to do their best.

96. Leventhal, G.S., Younts, C.M., & Lund, A.K. Tolerance for inequity in buyer-seller relationships. *Journal of Applied Social Psychology,* 1972, **2,** 308–318.

Task: In 2 experiments, household consumers were sold a cleaning product by *E* and then offered a rebate. *IV:* (1) Consumers told rebate was from salesman or from company; (2) consumers told rebate was from salesman, from an individual supplier of the salesman, from a group of suppliers, or from the company. *DV:* Consumers' acceptance of rebate. *Results:* Householders accepted rebate from company more than from others.

97. Libby, W.L., & Garrett, J. Role of intentionality of mediating children's responses to inequity. *Developmental Psychology,* 1974, in press.

Task: 1st and 5th graders worked on timed proofreading, believing that another child was doing same task in another room and that they would jointly receive 10 pennies for working. Partner divided 10 pennies, then *S* distributed 10 bonus pennies. *IV:* (1) Ss underrewarded (3¢) or overrewarded (7¢); (2) Ss told that the partner's allocation was intentional or chance; (3) school grade. *DV:* (1) Ss alloca-tion of 10 bonus pennies; (2) fairness and goodness ratings of partner. *Results:* Overrewarded Ss split bonus in half with partners; underrewarded Ss awarded only 3¢ to partner. Neither intentionality nor grade had an effect on bonus division.

98. Lincoln, A., & Levinger, G. Observers' evaluations of the victim and the attacker in an aggressive incident. *Journal of Personality and Social Psychology,* 1972, **22,** 202–210.

Task: Ss observed slides of white policeman and black civilian. *IV:* (1) Policeman in slides attacking civilian (aggression) or not (nonaggression); (2) Ss' ratings to be used only by *E* (no consequence) or by investigative interracial commission (conse-quence). *DV:* (1) Ratings of perceived injustice; (2) rating of policeman and black civilian. *Results:* In no-consequence condition, civilian rated lower under aggression than nonaggression. Reverse obtained in consequence condition. In consequence condition, ratings of civilian positively correlated with perceived injustice.

99. Long, G.T., & Lerner, M.J. Deserving, the "personal contact," and altruistic behavior by children. *Journal of Personality and Social Psychology,* 1974, in press.

Task: 4th grade Ss engaged to "market test" a game for 70¢ pay. They were then given opportunity to donate some of pay to a child charity. *IV:* (1) Donation to charity would be known to no one, to E and teacher, or to future younger Ss; (2) overpaid or properly paid; (3) Ss' scores on delay of gratification test. *DV:* Donation to charity. *Results:* Overpaid Ss donated more than properly paid Ss. Ss with high tolerance for delayed gratification gave more when overpaid and less when properly paid. No effect of who would know of donation.

100. Macaulay, S., & Walster, E. Legal structures and restoring equity. *Journal of Social Issues,* 1971, **27,** 173–188.

In a review of relevant research, examines factors that promote or inhibit the restoration of equitable relationships between harmdoer and victim. Discusses legal practices in this context.

101. Marwell, G., Ratcliff, K., & Schmitt, D.R. Minimizing differences in a maximizing difference game. *Journal of Personality and Social Psychology,* 1969, **12,** 158–163.

Task: Pairs of Ss played 2-person games in 2-stage experiment. *IV:* (1) Games played in first stage produced inequity or equity between Ss; (2) sex of Ss. *DV:* Ss' noncooperation in the second stage Maximizing Difference Game. *Results:* Ss behind their partners in first stage made more noncooperative responses than their "ahead" partners, thus minimizing the difference between players and increasing equity. The effect was stronger among females.

102. Masters, J.C. Effects of social comparison upon subsequent self-reinforcement behavior in children. *Journal of Personality and Social Psychology,* 1968, **10,** 391–401.

Tasks: In 3 experiments, 4-year-old Ss played question game with younger partners for which they received reward tokens. Then (Exp. I) S played game alone and took as many rewards as he wanted; (Exp. II) replayed question game with E and S divided reward tokens; or (Exp. III) S replayed game with partner and S divided rewards. *IV:* (1) Ss received fewer, the same, or more reward tokens than partner; (2) Ss' sex. *DV:* (1) Amount of reward Ss gave themselves in second game; (2) Ss' willingness to replay game. *Results:* Children receiving fewer and girls receiving more rewards than partner took more rewards in second game both when alone and when allocating rewards for replaying game with E.

103. Masters, J.C. Social comparison, self-reinforcement, and the value of a reinforcer. *Child Development,* 1969, **40,** 1027–1038.

Task: 4- to 5-year old Ss played question game with younger partner for which they received reward-tokens. Then Ss replayed question game with E and divided rewards. *IV:* (1) Ss received fewer, the same number, or more reward tokens than partner; (2) Ss' sex. *DV:* Number of reward tokens Ss gave themselves when replaying game with E. *Results:* Ss receiving fewer and girls receiving more tokens than partners took more tokens in the second game.

104. McArthur, L.A., Kiesler, C.A., & Cook, B.P. Acting on an attitude as a function of self-percept and inequity. *Journal of Personality and Social Psychology,* 1969, **12,** 295–302.

Task: After completing 2 "bogus" tasks, Ss received feedback and were promised pay for a future one-hour test. *IV:* (1) Low ($1.50) or high ($10) promised payment; (2) feedback to Ss: had "doer" personality entitling them to payment; had "doer" personality, but entitled to payment because of task performance; or entitled to payment because of performance. *DV:* Ss' response to request by a second experimenter to pass out antipollution leaflets. *Results:* High payment Ss were more willing to pass out leaflets than low payment Ss. Ss told they were paid for having "doer" personality were more willing to pass out leaflets than Ss in other feedback conditions.

105. McCranie, E.W., & Kimberly, J.C. Rank inconsistency, conflicting expectations and injustice. *Sociometry*, 1973, **36**, 152–176.

Distinguishes between 2 distinct processes resulting from rank inconsistency: conflicting expectations and feelings of injustice. Data providing support for the distinction are reported.

106. Messé, L.A. Equity in bilateral bargaining. *Journal of Personality and Social Psychology*, 1971, **17**, 287–291.

Task: Ss first performed questionnaire task for varying lengths of time; they were then paired to bargain using Morgan-Sawyer bargaining board with 9 possible outcomes. Ss spending more time in pretask assigned high payoff side of board. *IV:* Amount of time spent on questionnaire task, 0, 40, 50, 60, or 80 minutes. *DV:* Agreed-upon outcomes in bargaining. *Results:* Equity mediated the bargaining conflict. Ss agreed upon outcomes on the basis of amount of time spent on pretask.

107. Messé, L.A., Dawson, J.E., & Lane, I.M. Equity as a mediator of the effect of reward level on behavior in the prisoner's dilemma game. *Journal of Personality and Social Psychology*, 1973, **26**, 60–65.

Task: PD game bargaining. *IV:* (1) Ss either worked for $1\frac{1}{2}$ hours on prebargaining task or did not; (2) low or high-reward PD matrix; (3) Ss told or not told how many PD trials they would play. *DV:* Amount of cooperation in PD game. *Results:* Ss who worked on pretask made more cooperative responses in high-reward PD game than in the low-reward game, resulting in more equitable payment. Ss who did not work on pretask made more cooperative responses in low-reward than high-reward game.

108. Messé, L.A., & Lane, I.M. Rediscovering the need for multiple operations: A reply to Austin and Susmilch. *Journal of Personality and Social Psychology*, 1974, in press.

Vide supra Austin and Susmilch (1974).

109. Messé, L.A., & Lichtman, R.J. Motivation for the reward as a mediator of the influence of work quality on allocation behavior. Paper presented at the meeting of the Southeastern Psychological Association, Atlanta, April, 1972.

Task: Multiplication problems done with fictitious co-worker. *IV:* (1) Sex; (2) quality of S's performance, superior or inferior to co-worker; (3) S worked longer or shorter time than co-worker; (4) S recruited by promise of money or research credit. *DV:* S's reward allocation to himself and co-worker. *Results:* Promise of research credit led to work quality as basis for reward allocation more than promise of money. Females allocated more to partners than to themselves.

110. Mikula, G. Gewinnaufteilungsverhalten in Dyaden bei variiertem Leistungsverhältnis. *Zeitschfirt für Sozialpsychologie,* 1972, **3**, 126–133. (a)

The relative task performance of pairs of Austrian servicemen were varied in the ratios 75/25, 62.5/37.5, and 55/45. Upon task completion Ss allocated points for money. Allocation was proportional to performance in the 55/45 condition; in the other conditions allocations fell between equality and equity, with a bias favoring the inferior performer.

111. Mikula, G. Gewinnaufteilungsverhalten in gleichgeschlechtlichen Dyaden: Eine Vergleichsstudie österreichischer und amerikanischer Studenten. *Psychologie und Praxis,* 1972, **16,** 97–106. (b)

Cross-cultural (Austrian, American) study of reward distribution among pairs of children, in which one's performance exceeded the other's or was equal. More reward distributed to superior performer among Austrian, American, and male, female Ss.

112. Mikula, G. Die Entwicklung des Gewinnaufteilungsverhaltens bei Kindern and Jugendlichen: Eine Untersuchung an 5-, 7-, 9- and 11 jährigen. *Zeitschrift für Entwicklungspsychologie und Pädagogische Psychologie,* in press.

(Not available for review.)

113. Milardo, S.G. Modes of reducing inequity: Distortion or compensation? Unpublished doctoral dissertation, University of Georgia, 1971.

Ss who administered shock to a partner were more likely to increase the latter's outcomes than to distort their characteristics or the harm they suffered. Anticipation of future association with the victims had no effect.

114. Moore, L.M., & Baron, R.M. Effects of wage inequities on work attitudes and performance. *Journal of Experimental Social Psychology,* 1973, **9**, 1–16.

Task: Proofread galleys, piece rate pay. *IV:* (1) "Standard," greater, or lesser pay; (2) Ss told they were qualified or unqualified for task. *DV:* (1) Productivity; (2) work quality; (3) Ss' work attitudes. *Results:* Unqualified Ss produced higher quality but lower quantity than qualified Ss. Overpaid qualified Ss did poorer quality work than standard pay qualified Ss. No main effects of pay on productivity. Unqualified Ss more dissatisfied than qualified Ss. Overcompensated Ss perceived the work as more important than undercompensated Ss.

115. Morgan, W.R., & Sawyer, J. Bargaining, expectations, and the preference for equality over equity. *Journal of Personality and Social Psychology,* 1967, **6,** 139–149.

Task: Using a game board, 5th and 6th grade boys bargained for monetary rewards with a partner. Possible rewards for each differed. *IV:* (1) Ss did or did not have information about partners' expectations; (2) partners were friends or non-friends. DV: (1) Duration of bargaining; (2) outcomes. *Results:* Ss preferred equality of outcomes. Knowledge of partner's expectations facilitated bargaining.

116. Morris, S.C., & Rosen, S. Effects of felt adequacy and opportunity to reciprocate on help seeking. *Journal of Experimental Social Psychology,* 1973, **9,** 265–276.

Task: Ss assumed role of disabled person (arm in sling), performed manual task, and told they could not meet quota. Later told electricity would be cut off, affecting help they could give to visually handicapped co-worker. *IV:* (1) *S*s told they performed well or poorly for manually handicapped person; (2) told it would be possible or impossible to help visually handicapped co-worker. *DV:* *S*s help-seeking from co-worker on first task. *Results:* *S*s told they performed poorly were less likely to seek help. Effects of opportunity to help co-worker later were mixed.

117. Nielsen, J.O.M. Experimental analysis of equitable and inequitable social exchange. Unpublished doctoral dissertation, University of Washington, 1972.

> In a situation in which *S* could earn money in exchanges with partner, *S*s continued to engage in exchange behavior, whether or not the exchange was equitable, so long as alternatives to it were not more profitable. If *S* had the opportunity to take part of partner's earnings, the development of exchange behavior was reduced.

118. Nystrom, P.C. Equity theory and career pay: A computer simulation approach. *Journal of Applied Psychology,* 1973, 57, 125–131.

> Based on career salaries of 100 persons, a computer model finds support for Jaques' theory of equitable payment.

119. Opsahl, R.L., & Dunnette, M.D. The role of financial compensation in industrial motivation. *Psychological Bulletin,* 1966, 66, 94–118.

> General review and critique of the role of monetary compensation in the motivation and performance of industrial workers. Includes discussion of wage equity considerations.

120. Overstreet, R.E. Social exchange in a 3-person game. *Journal of Conflict Resolution,* 1972, 16, 109–123.

> Using a 3-person political coalition game, *S*s gave evidence that equity processes may account for the formation of some coalitions.

121. Patchen, M. *The choice of wage comparisons.* Englewood Cliffs, New Jersey: Prentice-Hall, 1961.

> Report of survey data obtained in a Canadian oil company. Especially relevant are data on workers' choices of wage comparisons and satisfaction with pay.

122. Pepitone, A. The role of justice in interdependent decision making. *Journal of Experimental Social Psychology,* 1971, 7, 144–156.

> Task: In 2 experiments pairs of *S*s played PD game. *IV:* One of 2 *S*s given $2 bonus on the basis of merit test, given bonus arbitrarily, or given no bonus. *DV:* *S*s' choices in PD game. *Results:* *S*s made maximizing choices with a frequency such that equity obtained.

123. Pepitone, A., Maderna, A., Caporicci, E., Tiberi, E., Iacono, G., Majo, G., Perfetto, M., Asprea, A., Villone, G., Fua, G., & Tonucci, F. Justice in choice behavior: A cross-cultural analysis. *International Journal of Psychology,* 1970, 5, 1–10.

> Task: In 2 experiments, pairs of American and Italian *S*s took an aptitude test and played PD game; *E* made initial award to one *S;* then *S*s resumed play. *IV:* *E* gave

one S in pair monetary award based on aptitude test score (equity) or arbitrarily without reference to test score (inequity). *DV:* S's PD game response choices after E award. *Results:* American Ss in inequity condition who received award made fewer gain maximizing choices than partners; in equity condition, Ss' choices maintained test-related award inequality. Italian Ss behaved similarly in inequity, but not equity condition.

124. Piaget, J. *The moral judgment of the child.* Glencoe: Free Press, 1948. (Republished New York: Free Press, 1965.)

Chapter 3, "Cooperation and the Development of the Idea of Justice," is relevant to research on equity and distributive justice among children.

125. Planz, C.A. Perceived equity and its relation to attrition among early career male teachers in selected school districts. Unpublished doctoral dissertation, State University of New York at Buffalo, 1970.

Male teachers who had stayed in or left 2 school districts with differing reward structures were interviewed. *Results:* Stayers perceived a higher degree of equity than leavers. Above average performance was correlated with perceived equity.

126. Pritchard, R.D. Equity theory: A review and critique. *Organizational Behavior and Human Performance,* 1969, **4,** 176–211.

127. Pritchard, R.D., Dunnette, M.D., & Jorgenson, D.O. Effects of perceptions of equity and inequity on worker performance and satisfaction. *Journal of Applied Psychology,* 1972, **56,** 75–94.

Task: Male Ss worked on clerical task in simulated company for 7 half-days. *IV:* (1) Hourly or modified piece rate pay, pay mode reversed after 3 sessions; (2) equitable, over-, or underpayment. *DV:* (1) Performance; (2) job satisfaction. *Results:* Overpayment and underpayment resulted in higher and lower performance, respectively. Over- and underpaid Ss more dissatisfied than equitably paid Ss.

128. Radinsky, T.L. Equity and inequity as a source of reward and punishment. *Psychonomic Science,* 1969, **15,** 293–295.

Task: S and alleged other played game with 2 possible responses, one of which resulted in "equitable" outcomes and other in unfavorable inequity outcomes. *IV:* (1) S given knowledge of own and other's outcomes or only of own outcomes; (2) S's sex. *DV:* Number of times each of 2 possible choices made. *Results:* Ss' responses in comparison and noncomparison conditions suggest that equity and inequity have reward and punishment effects, respectively. Female Ss more sensitive to equity-inequity than males.

129. Regula, C.R. The effects of inequity and responsibility on helping behavior. Unpublished doctoral dissertation, State University of New York at Buffalo, 1969.

Task: 4 Ss worked on a joint task. S was asked by another (confederate) for help with his work. *IV:* (1) Confederate's pay the same, higher, or lower than S's pay; (2) S believed he was the only one helping confederate or was sharing the responsibility with another S. *DV:* (1) Amount of work; (2) liking for confederate.

Results: Ss produced and liked confederate more when pay inequity was advantageous to them than when it was disadvantageous. Ss produced more when jointly responsible than when solely responsible for helping.

130. Rosen, B., & Jerdee, T.H. Factors influencing disciplinary judgments. *Journal of Applied Psychology,* 1974, 59, 9–14.

Task: Ss read one of 8 versions of a case describing a salesman who "padded" his expense account. Ss then recommended the most appropriate disciplinary action. *IV:* Padding was $10–15 or $80–100 monthly; (2) company paid among the highest or lowest commissions in the industry; (3) salesman's performance was 10% above or 10% below previous year's. *DV:* (1) Severity of recommended discipline; (2) perceived seriousness and unethicality of "padding"; (3) perceived responsibility for offense. *Results:* Discipline was less severe for salesman in low paying company than in high paying one. Perceived seriousness and unethicality of offense and the salesman's responsibility for it were lower in the low paying company.

131. Ross, M., Thibaut, J., & Evenbeck, S. Some determinants of the intensity of social protest. *Journal of Experimental Social Psychology,* 1971, 7, 401–418.

Task: Pairs of boys ("workers") pulled a rope to match a target force that increased over trials. Fictitious "managers" allocated points to workers and to themselves. Points to workers progressively increased in first 2/3 of trials, then decreased. Finally, Ss could transmit neutral signals or painful noise to either of two managers to obtain preferred prizes, one manager being responsible for point reversal. *IV:* (1) Evaluative feedback signalling competence or incompetence; (2) points earned on each trial were contingent or noncontingent on evaluations. *DV:* Duration of noise sent to managers. *Results:* More painful noise transmitted by competent Ss. Ss suffering greater inequity in outcomes also delivered more punishment to "managers."

132. Rothbart, M. Effects of motivation, equity, and compliance on the use of reward and punishment. *Journal of Personality and Social Psychology,* 1968, 9, 353–362.

Task: In 2 experiments Ss acting as "supervisors" of a fictitious worker were to increase the latter's performance on letter-cancelling task by using threat of monetary punishment or promise of reward. E controlled information about worker performance. *IV:* (1) High ($4) or low (nothing stated) motivation of supervisor; (2) Ss believed worker would receive only monetary rewards given by supervisor or $2.50, regardless. *DV:* Use of reward or punishment by S. *Results:* Ss in high motivation condition used punishment more when they believed worker would receive $2.50, when the earnings discrepancy between the two was least.

133. Sampson, E.E. Studies of status congruence. In L. Berkowitz (Ed.), *Advances in experimental social psychology,* Vol. 4. New York: Academic Press, 1969. Pp. 225–270.

Status congruence is discussed as specific case of the functioning of mastery and of justice. Justice is composed of both equity and equality principles.

134. Sayles, L.R. *Behavior of industrial work groups: Prediction and control.* New York: Wiley, 1958.

See Chapter 4, "Dynamics of Work Group Behavior," in particular, in which social comparisons and inequity are discussed.

135. Schmitt, D.R., & Marwell, G. Withdrawal and reward reallocation as responses to inequity. *Journal of Experimental Social Psychology,* 1972, 8, 207–221.

Task: In 3 experiments, pairs of Ss worked on cooperative or individual tasks; rewards for cooperation greater than for individual work, but favorably inequitable. Withdrawal from cooperative to lower-paying individual task was the only alternative to cooperation. *IV:* (1) Large, moderate, or small inequity; (2) in moderate inequity condition, Ss could either give money to or take money from each other. *DV:* (1) Amount of time spent cooperating; (2) transfer of money. *Results:* Withdrawal from cooperation was an increasing function of inequity. When allowed to transfer rewards, most subjects transferred enough to produce equity or near equity.

136. Shapiro, E.G. Equity and equality in the allocations of rewards in a dyad. Unpublished doctoral dissertation, University of Michigan, 1972.

Following manipulation of Ss' inputs and social distance, Ss allocated rewards to themselves and a partner. High input Ss allocated themselves more than half, low input Ss less than half. High input Ss allocated more to themselves when social distance was high.

137. Simmons, C.H., & Lerner, M.J. Altruism as a search for justice. *Journal of Personality and Social Psychology,* 1968, 9, 216–225.

Task: In 2 experiments, female Ss were supervisors whose pay depended on a fictitious partner who made checkerboards. In a second task, Ss were workers making envelopes. *IV:* (1) Ss had been rewarded or "betrayed" by the partner's high or low production of checkerboards or had worked independently (control); (2) Ss believed their supervisor in second task had been rewarded or betrayed on first task. *DV:* Envelopes made. *Results:* Previously rewarded Ss produced more for betrayed supervisors and least for rewarded supervisors.

138. Solomon, D., & Druckman, D. Age, representatives' prior performance, and the distribution of winnings with teammates. *Human Development,* 1972, 15, 244–252.

Task: Pairs of boy "representatives" and "partners" played games to divide the representatives' winnings in prior games with other representatives. *IV:* (1) Representative's prior winnings greater than opponents'; (2) age: 7–9, 10–12, or 13–15; (3) first, middle or last phase of game. *DV:* (1) Outcome of games; (2) competitiveness. *Results:* Representatives who made less than opponent prior to final game made less than partners in final game in 7–9 dyads, made the same in 10–12 dyads, and made more in 13–15 dyads.

139. Stefanowicz, J.P. The resolution of inequity by outpatient schizophrenics. Unpublished doctoral dissertation, Iowa State University, 1969.

Task: Outpatient schizophrenics sorted and assembled data cards. *IV:* Over-, under-, or equitable compensation. *DV:* Productivity. *Results:* No significant effects.

140. Stephenson, G.M., & Fielding, G.T. An experimental study of the contagion of leaving behavior in small gatherings. *Journal of Social Psychology,* 1971, **84,** 81–91.

Task: In 2 experiments, English *S*s constructed words from letters in another word. *IV:* (1) *S*s in groups or alone; (2) presence of collaborators who left after certain time or stayed until all *S*s had left; (3) *S*s told they would receive less, more, or same pay as participants in previous experiments. *DV:* Length of time *S*s worked on task. *Results:* After one person left a group, others left sooner than if alone. Deprived *S*s more likely to leave after collaborator left than other *S*s.

141. Stephenson, G.M., & White, J.H. An experimental study of some effects of injustice on children's moral behavior. *Journal of Experimental Social Psychology,* 1968, **4,** 460–469.

Task: English boys played model racing car games, some racing, and some retrieving cars. They were then given opportunity to win prizes by cheating on a car racing quiz. *IV:* *S*s raced cars whole time ("privileged"); raced and retrieved half the time ("equity"); retrieved only for *adult* racers ("relative deprivation"); or retrieved only for other boys ("absolutely deprived"). *DV:* Cheating on quiz. *Results:* Cheating greatest among the absolutely deprived and greater among the relatively deprived than among the equitably treated. Privileged *S*s did not cheat less than equitably treated.

142. Stouffer, S.A., Suchman, E.A., DeVinney, L.C., Star, S.A., & Williams, R.M., Jr. *The American soldier: Adjustment during army life.* Princeton, New Jersey: Princeton University Press, 1949.

The concept of relative deprivation is introduced on pp. 105–154 to explain anomalous findings on soldier satisfaction.

143. Taynor, J., & Deaux, K. When women are more deserving than men: Equity, attribution, and perceived sex differences. *Journal of Personality and Social Psychology,* 1973, **28,** 360–367.

Task: Male and female *S*s read descriptions of male or female stimulus person behaving appropriately in civic emergency situation previously shown to be more masculine than feminine. *S*s then rated stimulus persons. *IV:* (1) *S*'s sex; (2) sex of stimulus person; (3) presence or absence in emergency situations of non-acting person whose sex was opposite to stimulus person's. *DV:* (1) How deserving of reward stimulus person is; (2) ratings of stimulus person. *Results:* Female stimulus persons were perceived as deserving more reward than males in the same situation, and their ratings were correspondingly inflated.

144. Telly, C.S., French, W.L., & Scott, W.G. The relationship of inequity to turnover among hourly workers. *Administrative Science Quarterly,* 1971, **16,** 164–172.

Hourly employees in high and low turnover shops in a large company responded to questionnaire about inequity pertaining to pay, supervision, leadmen, security, advancement, working conditions, and intrinsic and social aspects of the job. Inequity correlated with turnover.

145. Tornow, W.W. The development and application of an input-outcome moderator test on the perception and reduction of inequity. *Organizational Behavior and Human Performance*, 1971, 6, 614–638.

Proposes that ambiguous job elements may be perceived by Ss as either inputs or outcomes. Based on responses to a 120-item questionnaire, Ss who had previously participated in an equity experiment (*vide supra* Pritchard, Dunnette & Jorgenson, 1972) were classified as Type I (job elements perceived as inputs) and Type O (elements viewed as outcomes). The general findings are that perceptions of job elements improves the predictability of Ss' responses to over- and underreward. Underrewarded Type I Ss feel more underrewarded than underrewarded Type O Ss and overrewarded Type I Ss feel less overrewarded than overrewarded Type O Ss.

146. Valenzi, E.R., & Andrews, I.R. Effect of hourly overpay and underpay inequity when tested with a new induction procedure. *Journal of Applied Psychology*, 1971, 55, 22–27.

Task: Ss hired at hourly pay rate for clerical work. *IV:* After working one session, Ss' pay was decreased (underpay), increased (overpay), or left the same (control). *DV:* (1) Productivity; (2) work quality. *Results:* No significant differences between the 3 pay conditions. 27% of underpaid Ss quit; no Ss quit in other pay conditions.

147. Vroom, V.H. *Work and motivation.* New York: Wiley, 1964.

Equity is discussed as a determinant of job satisfaction (pp. 167–172) and of effective job performance (pp. 252–260).

148. Wahba, M.A. Preferences among alternative forms of equity: The apportionment of coalition reward in the males and females. *Journal of Social Psychology*, 1972, 87, 107–115.

Using 3-person coalition formation task, preferences for 3 forms of equity were tested: (1) equality of outcomes, regardless of inputs; (2) proportionality of outcomes according to relative inputs; (3) equality of gains after repayment of inputs. Females preferred the first, males the third form.

149. Walster, E., & Austin, W.G. Reactions to confirmations and disconfirmations of expectancies of equity and inequity. *Journal of Personality and Social Psychology*, 1974, in press.

Task: Ss, expecting normal $2 pay, proofread pages, believing a second person did similar task and that a supervisor would evaluate work and distribute $4 between the 2 proofreaders. *IV:* (1) Having learned partner and he had performed equally well, S led to expect equitable or inequitable payment; (2) S equitably, over- or underpaid. *DV:* Ss' contentment and distress as measured by Mood Adjective Check List before and after. *Results:* Equitably paid Ss were more content than over- or underrewarded Ss. Overrewarded Ss were more content than underrewarded. Ss expecting inequity were less distressed with inequity than Ss expecting equity.

150. Walster, E., Berscheid, E., & Walster, G.W. The exploited: Justice or justification? In J. Macaulay and L. Berkowitz (Eds.), *Altruism and helping behavior.* New York: Academic Press, 1970. Pp. 179–204.

Harmdoing is discussed as producing inequity between 2 people. Theory and data are presented which predict when a harmdoer will provide restitution to a victim and when he will justify his act.

151. Walster, E., Berscheid, E., & Walster, G.W. New directions in equity research. *Journal of Personality and Social Psychology*, 1973, **25**, 151–176.

By revising, extending, and generalizing previous equity theory, the authors present a general theory of social behavior. Previous equity research is reviewed and the relationship of equity theory to other major social psychological theories is examined.

A correction to and elaboration of the equity formula presented in this paper is available from the authors.

152. Walster, E., & Piliavin, J.A. Equity and the innocent bystander. *Journal of Social Issues*, 1972, **28**, 165–189.

Discussed in the context of equity theory are how bystanders respond to emergencies involving a victim and how, in turn, victims may react to bystanders.

153. Weick, K.E. Reduction of cognitive dissonance through task enhancement and effort expenditure. *Journal of Abnormal and Social Psychology*, 1964, **68**, 533–539.

*S*s working for an experimenter who had lured them to work for no credit evaluated their task more highly than *S*s who worked for normal course credit, thus increasing their net total outcomes.

154. Weick, K.E. The concept of equity in the perception of pay. *Administrative Science Quarterly*, 1966, **11**, 414–439.

Discusses ambiguities and limitations of early formulations of equity theory and suggests extensions of the theory.

155. Weick, K.E., & Nesset, B. Preferences among forms of equity. *Organizational Behavior and Human Performance*, 1968, **3**, 400–416.

*S*s were presented with pairs of fictitious work situations in each of which they and another person were described as to wages and job. The work situations varied systematically as to type of equity comparison processes and basis of pay inequity. *S*s chose the preferred situation in each pair. *Results:* Preferences gave clear support to a social comparison model of equity, as well as evidence for differential thresholds for under- and overpayment inequity.

156. Weick, K.E., & Prestholdt, P. Realignment of discrepant reinforcement value. *Journal of Personality and Social Psychology*, 1968, **8**, 180–187.

Task: "Motor-coordination" marble dropping task. During the task *S*s were offered choices to receive social or monetary reinforcements. *IV:* Underpay ($0), control ($1), or overpay ($3). *DV:* (1) *S*'s choice of monetary or social reinforcement; (2) productivity. *Results:* Underpaid and overpaid *S*s were more productive than control *S*s. Underpaid *S*s showed less preference for monetary reinforcements than other *S*s.

157. Wicker, A.W., & Bushweiler, G. Perceived fairness and pleasantness of social exchange situations: Two factorial studies of inequity. *Journal of Personality and Social Psychology,* 1970, **15**, 63–75.

I. *Task:* Ss rated 18 2-person work situations. *IV:* (1) Person liked or disliked a co-worker; (2) was more, less or equally valuable to employer as co-worker; (2) earned more, less, or the same as co-worker. *DV:* Ss' ratings of fairness and pleasantness of the situation. *Results:* Fairness related to the inputs and outcomes of workers. Pleasantness ratings related to liking of co-worker.

II. *Task:* Female Ss and confederate worked on oral-analogies test. *IV:* (1) Ss received more or less money than confederate; (2) Ss told they had made more or fewer correct responses than co-worker; (3) co-worker made remarks to cause S to either like or dislike her. *DV:* Ss' ratings of the fairness and pleasantness of the situation. *Results:* Same as above.

158. Wiener, Y. The effects of "task-" and "ego-oriented" performance on 2 kinds of overcompensation inequity. *Organizational Behavior and Human Performance,* 1970, **5**, 191–208.

Task: Word manipulation, hourly pay. *IV:* (1) Equitable pay–$2 or $3; input overcompensation–Ss told they were unqualified but received standard pay of $2; or outcome overcompensation–Ss told they were qualified but received higher than standard pay, $3; (2) Ss told task was mental alertness test (ego-oriented) or psycholinguistic project (task-oriented). *DV:* (1) Productivity; (2) work quality. *Results:* Ego-oriented Ss produced more than task-oriented Ss. Outcome over-compensated Ss produced more than equitably paid Ss. Input overcompensated Ss produced more than equitably paid Ss in ego-oriented condition, but not in task-oriented condition.

159. Wilke, H., & Lanzetta, J.T. The obligation to help: The effects of amount of prior help on subsequent helping behavior. *Journal of Experimental Social Psychology,* 1970, **6**, 488–493.

Task: Ss allocated trucks and railroad cars for shipping goods for 40 trials. Ss worked in pairs and believed they could help each other. *IV:* S was helped 0, 2, 4, 6, 8, or 10 times during the first 20 trials, 10 of which could be completed without help. *DV:* S's responses to partner's 10 requests for help in second block of 20 trials. *Results:* Help-giving was proportional to prior help received.

160. Wilke, H., & Steur, T. Overpayment: Perceived qualifications and financial compensation. *European Journal of Social Psychology,* 1972, **2**, 273–284.

Task: Dutch Ss decoded personality questionnaires, hourly pay. *IV:* (1) Ss told they had low, medium or high qualifications; (2) overpaid or equitably paid. *DV:* (1) Productivity; (2) work quality. *Results:* Overpaid and equitably paid Ss did not differ in productivity and work quality. Low qualified Ss produced more.

161. Wood, I., & Lawler, E. E. Effects of piece rate overpayment on productivity. *Journal of Applied Psychology,* 1970, **54**, 234–238.

Task: Ss read articles aloud, piece rate pay. *IV:* Ss told they were qualified or underqualified for task. *DV:* (1) Amount of time S read aloud; (2) quality as determined by Ss' choice of difficult or easy articles to read. *Results:* Overpaid Ss produced less than equitably paid Ss. Lower productivity could not be attributed to striving for higher quality.

162. Wyer, R.S., & Malinowski, C. Effects of sex and achievement level upon individualism and competitiveness in social interaction. *Journal of Experimental Social Psychology,* 1972, 8, 303–314.

Task: Pairs of Ss first participated in achievement task, received feedback on their performance, then interacted in a series of 2-person game situations. *IV:* (1) Same or different sex pairs; (2) negative or positive feedback on achievement task performance. *DV:* (1) S's response choices in 2-person games; (2) S's perception of partner as friendly and competitive. *Results:* For pairs of same sex, Ss' response choices reduced inequities in outcomes.

163. Yuchtman, E. Reward distribution and work-role attractiveness in the Kibbutz - Reflections on equity theory. *American Sociological Review,* 1972, 37, 581–595.

Questionnaires were used to measure reward distribution and work-role attractiveness of managers and workers in 26 Kibbutzim. *Results:* Managers received more intrinsic job satisfaction and power-related rewards but were less attracted to their jobs than workers. The findings are explained by equity theory.

164. Zaleznik, A., Christensen, C.R., & Roethlisberger, F.J. *The motivation, productivity and satisfaction of workers.* Boston: Harvard University, 1958.

The theory of distributive justice is discussed in detail on pp. 50–56 and 291–321, together with a number of illustrative cases.

165. Zaleznik, A., & Moment, D. *The dynamics of interpersonal behavior.* New York: Wiley, 1964.

The concepts of distributive justice and relative deprivation are discussed in the context of job satisfaction on pp. 395–399.

166. Zedeck, S., & Smith, P.C. A psychophysical determination of equitable payment: A methodological study. *Journal of Applied Pschology,* 1968, 52, 343–347.

An adaptation of the Method of Limits protocols were administered to junior executives and secretaries in a large midwestern academic institution to determine perceived equitable payment and just meaningful difference of payment. *Results:* Perceived equitable payment and just meaningful difference were greater for executives than secretaries.

167. Zelditch, M., Berger, J., Anderson, B., & Cohen, B.P. Equitable comparisons. *Pacific Sociological Review,* 1970, 13, 19–26.

Discusses equity comparisons. In "local" comparisons, a person compared himself with a particular person. In "referential" comparisons, a comparison is made in the context of a stable frame of reference.

THE DISTRIBUTION OF REWARDS AND RESOURCES IN GROUPS AND ORGANIZATIONS[1]

Gerald S. Leventhal

WAYNE STATE UNIVERSITY
DETROIT, MICHIGAN

[1] Preparation of this paper was supported by National Science Foundation Grant GS-3171.

I. Introduction

A. REWARDS, RESOURCES, AND SOCIAL ROLES

Every social system contains rewards and resources that are used to achieve group goals and satisfy individual needs. Members of the system occupy different roles in relation to these resources and rewards. Some individuals serve as allocators who dispense them while other individuals are recipients. For example, the chairman of a psychology department who assigns research space is an allocator and the experimenters who use the space are recipients. Similarly, a father who gives his child allowance money is an allocator and his child is a recipient. Allocators typically control a variety of rewards and resources. For example, the chairman of an academic department may allocate material resources such as money, office space, and research equipment. In addition, he may distribute human resources. Thus, a chairman may provide a faculty member with a secretary or teaching assistants. Allocators are likely to hold positions of high status and power. In many instances, the allocator's role requires him to oversee the recipients' behavior. He is charged with the task of ensuring that recipients' activities are productive and beneficial to the social system. Correspondingly, a recipient's role often requires him to comply with the allocator's wishes. Thus, a manager who allocates pay and promotion to employees, or a teacher who allocates grades to students, deals with them in the broader context of a supervisor–subordinate relationship.

This paper sketches a framework for predicting the behavior of persons who occupy the allocator's role. The framework takes account of other persons insofar as they influence the allocator's decisions about rewards and resources. Persons of higher rank who are the allocator's superiors may strongly influence his decisions, and so may the recipients who are subordinate to him. In addition, other parties who observe the allocator may influence his decisions.

Our analysis assumes that groups deal with problems emanating from the external task environment and problems emanating from the interpersonal environment within the group (Bales, 1950, 1965; Collins & Guetzkow, 1964; Homans, 1950; Thibaut & Kelley, 1959). Rewards and resources serve three main functions in relation to these problems, namely: (1) resources are required for the conduct of activities that solve task or socio-emotional problems; (2) rewards reinforce and strengthen recipient behavior that contributes to the solution of these problems; and (3) rewards and resources make group membership attractive to recipients and strengthen their loyalty. An allocator uses rewards and resources to steer recipients' behavior in directions that contribute to the solution of group problems. In the language of Thibaut and Kelley (1959), he converts his control over recipients' fate into control over their behavior.

An analysis of allocation behavior must deal with the fact that many rewards and resources are controlled by several allocators. These co-allocators may make group decisions about the distribution of resources. For example, studies of family decisions about spending (e.g., Blood & Wolfe, 1960) suggest that some decisions are made primarily by one spouse alone, while others are made jointly by husband and wife. Similarly, a chairman of a university department may make many allocation decisions on his own, but make other allocation decisions in close cooperation with faculty members whose control over the decision is as great as his own.

Burnstein and Katz (1972) suggest there are important differences between individual and group allocation decisions. In line with their view, we shall simplify our task by not giving detailed consideration to allocation situations in which co-equal individuals make joint decisions about the distribution of resources and rewards. An adequate analysis of such allocation decisions would require extensive examination of studies of bargaining and group decision-making which space does not allow. We shall therefore restrict ourselves to instances in which the power of decision rests primarily with a single individual. Fortunately, this restriction does not prevent us from considering cases in which the allocation process involves a sequence of separate decisions, a sequence in which several allocators enter the decision process at different points in time, with each exerting independent influence. For example, it is not unusual for an allocator of higher rank to establish a general policy which is followed by a lower-ranking allocator who is free to execute that general policy as he sees fit. Thus, a husband in a traditional family may ask his wife to spend less money on household items but leave it to her judgment to carry out his request in the most sensible way. Or, a department chairman may formulate general policies about the allocation of research space or the allocation of subjects from a subject-pool but appoint a faculty coordinator to make specific decisions about these matters. In the present framework, it is possible to perform separate analyses of the allocation decision of the higher-level decision-maker who establishes a general policy, and the allocation decision of his subordinate who actually implements that policy on a case-by-case basis.

B. EQUITY THEORY

The equity model proposed by Stacy Adams (1963, 1965) has strongly influenced the views set forth in this paper. Basically, equity theory suggests that an allocator will deliver rewards and resources to recipients in proportion to the usefulness of their actions. Numerous studies confirm this basic implication of the model (e.g., Lane & Messé, 1971; Lane, Messé, & Phillips, 1971; Leventhal & Michaels, 1969, 1971). Other research stimulated by equity theory suggests that an allocator's decisions about rewards and resources often cause postdecisional changes in his perception and evaluation of recipients (e.g., Berscheid, Boye, & Walster, 1968; Berscheid & Walster, 1967; Graf & Green, 1971; Walster, Berscheid, & Walster, 1970, 1973). Still other studies influenced by the equity model indicate that group allocation decisions often conform with equity theory predictions (e.g., Benton, 1971; Burnstein & Wolosin, 1968; Messé, 1971; Pepitone, 1971).

The equity model identifies important psychological processes and causal variables that must be taken into account in the study of allocation behavior. However, by itself, the model provides too limited a framework for a comprehensive analysis of allocation behavior. Adams' (1965) statement of equity theory and Walster, Berscheid, & Walster's (1973) recent restatement of the theory, deal primarily with the influence of a single normative rule which dictates that rewards and resources be distributed in accordance with recipients' contributions. However, many other motivational and cognitive factors influence an allocator's decisions. For example, the rule of equity is only one of several possible norms the allocator may follow. Thus, instead of rewarding recipients in accordance with their inputs, an allocator may follow a rule of allocating in accordance with their needs, or a rule of equal distribution. For this reason, we shall treat equity theory as only one member of a large family of constructs about social motivation which are required for the analysis of allocation behavior.

II. Equity and the Use of Rewards to Elicit High Performance

A. THE INSTRUMENTAL VALUE OF ALLOCATION NORMS

Allocation decisions are instrumental acts through which the allocator tries to achieve various goals. Accordingly, our analysis takes account of a wide range of goals and motives which affect his decisions. Allocation norms constitute one important class of such motivational factors. An *allocation norm* may be defined as a social rule which specifies criteria that define certain distributions of rewards and resources as fair and just. As Lerner (1974a, b) and Pruitt (1972) suggest, an allocator may follow a number of alternative allocation norms. For example, he may follow a rule of equity and distribute rewards and resources in accordance with recipients' contributions; follow a norm of equality and give all recipients the same, regardless of their contributions; follow a norm of reciprocity and treat recipients as they have treated him; follow norms of responsiveness to need and give more to recipients with greater need; or follow a norm of "adhering to commitments" and allocate in accordance with prior agreements between himself and the recipients. Typically, several allocation norms are salient at one time. And, if several of these rules of fair allocation favor the same allocation decision, they may summate to produce a very strong response. Thus, if one of two recipients had better performance and was also more needy than the other, the allocator would be inclined to give him much higher reward. However, different allocation norms often favor different allocation decisions and arouse incompatible response tendencies. In such cases, the allocator must reconcile conflicting rules of fairness and decide which norm or weighted combination of norms to follow. Often, the presence of opposing allocation norms will produce a compromise response that partially satisfies the requirements of each. Thus, if one of two recipients had poorer performance but was more needy than the other, an allocator might be inclined to give them similar reward.

The social system typically favors some allocation norms more than others. Prevailing rules and practices may encourage the allocator to follow certain norms and ignore others. Thus, conformity pressure and modeling processes dispose him to follow allocation norms which are socially approved and have been followed by other allocators [see, for example, Blake, Rosenbaum, & Duryea, 1955; Macaulay & Berkowitz (in Berkowitz, 1972a); Midlarsky & Bryan, 1972; Midlarsky, Bryan, & Brickman, 1973; Rosenhan & White, 1967; Staub, 1972]. Yet, the social environment is far from monolithic. It offers the individual a variety of alternative models to imitate and a range of alternative cues and rules to follow (Bandura, 1969). Such diversity in the social environment tends to legitimize a variety of alternative actions and may allow considerable flexibility of behavior. Thus, notwithstanding the influence of models and conformity pressures, an allocator may have considerable freedom in deciding which allocation norms to follow. Even if one rule of fair allocation is more widely accepted than others, he may ignore it and follow another norm which is more compatible with his desires.

The basis for the pervasive influence of allocation norms on an allocator's decisions is of central importance in the present analysis. Sometimes, the norms derive their impact from the allocator's commitment to an ideal of treating recipients fairly and justly. However, it seems unlikely that the power of such norms stems solely or even primarily from his desire for fairness and justice as ends in themselves. Rather, the impact of allocation norms probably stems from the benefits they produce, both for the allocator and for other members of the system. Certain benefits are common to all norms. For example, compliance with any norm tends to make interaction more predictable and less costly (Thibaut & Kelley, 1959, pp. 130–135). But beyond such common benefits, each allocation norm produces a specific pattern of benefits that is somewhat different from those produced by other norms. It facilitates certain goals that others do not. Thus, an allocator's decision to comply with one allocation norm rather than another, represents not only an attempt to be fair and just, but also an attempt to gain the unique pattern of instrumental benefits that is associated with following that norm.

B. THE INSTRUMENTAL VALUE OF EQUITABLE ALLOCATIONS

We have suggested that an allocator elects to follow one allocation norm rather than another primarily because following that norm has beneficial effects. For example, there is reason to believe that equitable allocations help foster high levels of task performance. A large body of theory and research suggests that delivering high reward to good performers and low reward to poor performers often facilitates productivity (e.g., Bales, 1950; Burnstein, 1969; Collins & Guetzkow, 1964; Homans, 1961; Lawler, 1971; Porter & Lawler, 1968; Steiner, 1972). Numerous studies conducted in laboratory and field settings indicate that reward systems which closely tie a recipient's rewards to his performance often elicit better performance (see Lawler, 1971, pp. 118–128). Thus, an allocator who follows the rule of equity as a criterion of fair distribution is likely to elicit high productivity from recipients. This view of the utility of equitable allocations is consistent with Sampson's suggestion that "where justice . . . is achieved through a principle of equity, then both mastery and justice can be obtained simultaneously" (Sampson, 1969, p. 266). In fact, it seems likely that an allocator who distributes rewards equitably frequently does so more because he desires to maximize long-term productivity than because he desires to comply with an abstract standard of justice. His decisions are based on an expectancy that equitable distributions of reward will elicit and sustain high levels of motivation and performance.

An allocator's expectancies about the effects of rewards on recipients' behavior are derived from his past experience, both as an allocator and as a recipient. We hypothesize that allocators *believe* a policy of allocating rewards and resources in accordance with recipients' contributions elicits and sustains high performance in the following ways.

1. Equitable allocations ensure that recipients whose behavior is most useful have greatest access to essential resources. Consequently, they are able to carry out their activities effectively and continue making large contributions.

2. Equitable allocations strongly reinforce those recipients whose behavior is most useful and beneficial. Consequently, their tendency to perform effectively and continue their membership in the group is strengthened.

3. Equitable allocations deliver low reinforcement to recipients whose behavior is least useful. Consequently, poor performers are likely to change their behavior in order to obtain higher reward (Kelley, Thibaut, Radloff, & Mundy, 1962). Ideally, they will increase their effort and performance. Alternatively, inferior performers may become so dissatisfied with their lot that they will terminate their membership in the group (Lawler, 1971; Thibaut & Kelley, 1959). Their departure from the system will upgrade the overall quality of performance by reducing the relative frequency of nonproductive behavior.[2]

---

[2] As we see later, there are important exceptions to the assertion that giving low reward to poor performers causes them either to improve or quit. Instead of leaving the

4. Equitable allocations demonstrate to recipients they can increase their rewards by working harder and improving their performance. This perception of a strong link between performance and rewards must be present before a merit (equitable) reward system can facilitate productivity (Atkinson, 1964; Porter & Lawler, 1968; Lawler, 1971).

1. Counterproductive Effects of Equitable Allocations

It has been suggested that allocators believe equitable allocations help maximize recipients' productivity. Their belief derives from the fact that performance is facilitated when recipients are rewarded in accordance with their contributions. However, there are notable exceptions to this rule. Equitable allocations do not always foster high productivity. For example, rewarding recipients in accordance with their apparent contributions may be counterproductive if it is difficult to assess individual contributions accurately, or if a high level of cooperation among recipients is essential for effective performance (Lawler, 1971, p. 170; Steiner, 1972, p. 155). Miller and Hamblin (1963) report that when interdependence is high, group members in direct competition for a reward may disrupt one another's task activity. In addition, many authors have suggested that an unmitigated policy of distributing rewards on the basis of merit may arouse considerable tension and antagonism, particularly among recipients who receive relatively little (e.g., Collins & Guetzkow, 1964; Goldner, 1965; Goode, 1967; Homans, 1961; Lawler, 1971; Steiner, 1972). Such antagonism may disrupt productivity when task performance requires a high degree of cooperation. Yet, other studies indicate that even under such circumstances, equitable distributions of reward can facilitate productivity (Julian & Perry, 1967; Weinstein & Holzbach, 1973). In summary, much evidence and opinion supports the view that equitable allocations will foster high productivity over the long run, but there are important exceptions to this general rule.

Allocators probably recognize that productivity is not always facilitated by a strict policy of rewarding recipients in accordance with their contributions. Consequently, we may expect to find instances in which an allocator deviates markedly from the equity norm even though his primary goal is to elicit a high level of performance. The existence of such exceptions is not incompatible with our assertion that allocators believe a policy of allocating equitably is usually an effective method for maximizing recipients' performance.

The fact that equitable allocations may arouse negative feelings in poor performers points to the importance of distinguishing between allocation strategies that cope with task problems and allocation strategies that cope with socio-emotional problems. It has been suggested that an allocator follows the equity norm to cope with task problems, i.e., to maximize recipients' perfor-

---

system or responding constructively, they may engage in hostile and negativistic actions which damage group effectiveness (Lawler, 1971).

mance. However, strict adherance to the rule of equity may cause socio-emotional problems by arousing dissatisfaction and resentment among poor performers. Consequently, an allocator whose primary concern is to cope with socio-emotional problems and minimize negative responses may often move away from adherence to the equity norm.

2. Conformity as a Cause of Equitable Allocations

It has been suggested that allocators distribute rewards equitably because they believe equitable allocations foster productivity. However, if this were the only basis for an allocator's decision to reward recipients in accordance with their performance, he would have no reason to distribute rewards equitably when no further performance was anticipated, i.e., if all task activity was complete. Yet, many studies have shown that allocators do distribute rewards in accordance with recipients' performance even when no further task activity is expected (e.g., Lane & Messé, 1971; Lane, Messé, & Phillips, 1971; Lerner, 1974a; Leventhal & Anderson, 1970; Leventhal & Lane, 1970; Leventhal & Michaels, 1969; Leventhal, Popp, & Sawyer, 1973; Messé & Lichtman, 1972; Mikula, 1974; Shapiro, 1972). Because no further task activity could occur in these studies, it makes little sense to assume subjects distributed rewards equitably in order to maximize future performance. However, these results are easily accounted for by the assumption that subjects followed the equity norm because they were conforming with the experimenters' wishes. In each of the studies just cited, a commitment to follow the rule of equity was built into the basic fabric of the exchange between the experimenters who provided rewards and the performers who received them. It was clear to the subjects who served as allocators, and to the recipients, that the reason for giving reward was to provide an incentive that would induce recipients to perform and do their best. Thus, the allocator's superiors, i.e., the experimenters who instructed the subjects, created a social structure in which subjects believed they were expected to give high reward in exchange for good performance. Accordingly, subjects followed the equity norm not because they desired to maximize future productivity, which was impossible, but because they were conforming with an established policy of distributing rewards in accordance with performance.

C. USING REWARDS AND RESOURCES TO MAXIMIZE PRODUCTIVITY

The preceding analysis suggested two major reasons why allocators distribute rewards equitably. First, the allocator's desire to conform with rules and practices established by his superiors may lead him to reward recipients in accordance with their contributions. Thus, in many studies, subjects have distributed rewards equitably because the social structure defined the equity norm as the appropriate rule of allocation. Second, allocators may distribute rewards equitably because they believe that equitable allocations foster productivity. An allocator follows the equity norm for the latter reason only if he expects recipients to continue performing task activities.

The suggestion that an allocator follows the equity norm in order to maximize productivity is quite speculative. Nevertheless, this conception of the instrumental value of equitable allocations brings order to data obtained in several types of situations in which allocators are concerned about maximizing recipients' performance. Four such situations are considered below.

1. Providing Essential Resources

Allocators must often supply recipients with resources essential for the conduct of task activities. More productive recipients use resources more effectively and may also use them at a faster rate. Consequently, the allocator who desires to maximize productivity is likely to follow the equity norm and give more resources to better performers. Such a policy would facilitate their task activities and tend to maximize group output. In contrast, giving large amounts of resources to poorer performers would probably yield only modest increases in output, and could prove very wasteful and inefficient.

A study by Pondy and Birnberg (1969) demonstrates that allocators more readily supply essential resources to highly productive recipients. Subjects played the role of a chief budget officer who approved or rejected requests for company funds. The recipients of the funds were hypothetical managers whose past recommendations differed in profitability and accuracy. The subjects were readier to allocate financial resources to recipients with better past performance. They approved more spending requests by managers whose past recommendations were highly profitable and accurate.

2. Control of Group Membership

An allocator can improve group productivity by using rewards to regulate group membership. Equitable distributions of reward make group membership more attractive for recipients who contribute more. Highly rewarded superior performers will tend to remain in the group and poorly rewarded inferior performers will be inclined to terminate their membership. Consequently, over a period of time, an allocator who follows the rule of equity and rewards recipients in accordance with their performance will maximize group effectiveness by increasing the proportion of highly capable performers in the group.

The allocator's use of reward to control group membership is strongly influenced by recipients' access to attractive alternative relationships. The greater the attractiveness of such alternative relationships the more the allocator's relationship with the recipient is jeopardized (Lawler, 1971; Thibaut & Kelley, 1959). To keep recipients from leaving the relationship, the allocator is likely to increase their rewards in order to overcome the appeal of attractive alternatives. The more attractive the outside alternatives the more he will increase the recipients' rewards (Landau & Leventhal, in press; Leventhal, 1972; Thibaut, 1968; Thibaut & Faucheux, 1965; Thibaut & Gruder, 1969).

Results obtained by Landau & Leventhal (in press) indicate that an allocator who desires to upgrade group membership is especially likely to follow the equity norm. Subjects recommend monetary counteroffers to hypothetical workers who received an outside job offer which promised a substantial increase in salary. The workers had either high or low productivity. As expected, subjects made much higher counteroffers to highly productive recipients. They offered these recipients more than the amount promised by the outside offer, and offered nonproductive recipients less than the outside offer. Clearly, this pattern of allocation would encourage good performers to remain in the group and poor performers to accept the offer and leave.

Landau and Leventhal obtained further support for the view that an allocator who desires to upgrade the membership of a work force is very likely to follow the equity norm. Some subjects were instructed to make counteroffers that would help weed out inferior performers and retain the best. In comparison to controls, these subjects showed a strong increase in the tendency to distribute reward in accordance with performance. In particular, they offered much less to poor performers. This response suggests an attempt to induce poor performers to quit the group.

An allocator may also use the strategy of giving low reward with non-monetary incentives. For example, he may induce an unwanted recipient to leave the system by assigning him only to unpleasant tasks, or by preventing him from using facilities which make work easier and more satisfying. Such allocation decisions may be highly effective means of motivating a recipient to seek alternative work relationships.

Several factors probably limit an allocator's tendency to use a strategy of giving low reward to force nonproductive recipients from the group. First, it may be very difficult or costly to obtain and train competent replacements (Caplow & McGee, 1958; Goode, 1967; Homans, 1961; Leventhal, 1972). Second, a strategy of giving low reward may be ineffective because nonproductive recipients lack viable alternative relationships. The environment may provide few work opportunities for them, either because few jobs are available or because their incompetence makes them unattractive to others (Lawler, 1971, pp. 235, 262). Third, other recipients may object and resist a policy of weeding out incompetents. Such objections may stem from feelings of sympathy and friendship, or from other recipients feeling threatened by the allocator's use of powers that could be turned against them later (Goode, 1967). Finally, there are many groups in which membership is permanent or near-permanent, regardless of the members' individual contributions. In such cases, group norms are likely to prohibit allocators from attempting to expel nonproductive recipients—even by such indirect means as giving them low reward.

Attracting New Members. In many respects, the problems faced by an allocator who desires to attract new members are similar to those involved in keeping old group members from leaving. In both cases the allocator must consider the alternative relationships available to the recipient and offer him enough reward to overcome the appeal of these alternatives. For example, just as an allocator gives higher reward to encourage highly competent performers to remain in the group, Baskett's (1973) results suggest he will give higher reward to encourage such individuals to join the group. However, there may be some important differences between the response of an allocator who is using reward to preserve a relationship and an allocator who is using it to establish a relationship.

Results from a study by Beth Vershure (1974) suggest that certain variables may have different effects on the two types of allocation decisions. Subjects recommended salary raises for hypothetical employees who differed in age (29 or 55 years old) and productivity (high or low). Each subject made two separate allocation decisions. In one case, the raises he gave were counteroffers to current employees who had received an outside job offer. In the other, the raises he offered were inducements to encourage prospective employees to join the company. Information about productivity had the same effect for both types of allocation decision. The more productive recipient was offered higher pay, whether the aim was to induce him to remain or induce him to join. However, information about recipients' age had different effects in the two cases. When subjects were offering raises to induce competent prospective employees to join the company, they gave higher raises to younger workers. However, when subjects were offering raises to deter current employees from leaving, they did not treat younger workers more favorably. One possible explanation for these results is that prospective employees are viewed solely in terms of their future usefulness to the organization, and older persons are downgraded because of alleged deficits in ability and motivation (Nardi, 1973). However, older persons who are current employees may be evaluated more sympathetically and protected (Goldner, 1965; Goode, 1967).

Other studies do not allow direct comparisons between the behavior of an allocator who is trying to induce current members to remain and one who is trying to induce prospective members to join. However, there are probably other important differences. For example, an employer probably assumes his employees are enmeshed in a web of relationships and behavioral commitments from which they find it difficult to disengage. The effort and uncertainty that go with terminating old relationships and entering new ones often deters an employee from leaving his present job (Lawler, 1971, p. 188). Such factors operate to reduce employees' mobility. Consequently, an employer probably feels it is unnecessary to greatly increase his employees' rewards in order to retain their services. However, in the case of a prospective employee who is currently employed elsewhere, a similar network of forces would deter him from leaving his present position. Consequently, an employer might feel it was necessary to offer him a very large salary increase in order to induce him to change jobs and join the employer's organization.

3. Evaluating Recipients' Performance

An allocator who is attempting to elicit high performance by following the equity norm must evaluate the worth of each recipient's contribution. Social comparisons play a critical part in this evaluation process. Thus, an allocator often rewards recipients in accordance with their performance relative to that of other recipients. However, Leventhal and Michaels (1969, 1971) and other investigators (e.g., Taynor & Deaux, 1973) have suggested that an allocator's performance expectancies also play an important part in determining his evaluation of recipients' contributions. The allocator's expectancies vary for different types of performers. On a given task, the allocator expects certain categories of individuals to perform better than others. For example, he may expect better performance from adults than from children, or better performance from more intelligent persons. His performance expectancies serve as an alternative standard for evaluating the worth of a given recipient's contributions. Expectancies permit the allocator to evaluate performers relative to their own potential. The recipient is evaluated in accordance with the extent to which his performance approaches the maximum of which he is capable. The more the recipient utilizes his full capacity the more reward he is given (Leventhal & Michaels, 1971).

The influence of performance expectancies on an allocator's decisions is well-documented by studies which show that an allocator often evaluates and rewards recipients relative to their own ability. For example, when recipients have similar performance, a recipient with lower ability is seen as more deserving and given higher reward (e.g., Lanzetta & Hannah, 1969; Leventhal & Michaels, 1971; Taynor & Deaux, 1973; Weiner & Kukla, 1970; Wiggins, Dill, & Schwartz, 1965). The findings of Weiner and Kukla (1970) are typical. Their subjects played the role of teachers and evaluated hypothetical students. The students differed in ability and in exam performance. The influence of social comparison was demonstrated by the fact that subjects gave higher reward to students with better exam performance. The influence of performance expectancies was demonstrated by the fact that, at each level of exam performance, students with lower aptitude were judged more deserving of reward than students with higher aptitude. Presumably, students with lower aptitude were evaluated more favorably because they were utilizing their potential more fully and performing closer to their maximum.

An allocator probably tends to reward recipients relative to their own ability because a complete disregard for differences in ability would be counterproductive in certain respects. Expectancy theories of motivation (Atkinson, 1964; Lawler, 1971; Vroom, 1964) and analyses of achievement behavior (e.g., Atkinson, 1957; 1958) suggest that a policy of distributing rewards solely on the basis of social comparisons would tend to discourage recipients with low ability and reduce their motivation to work. When all performers are trying to do well, a recipient with low ability will not perform as well as a recipient with high ability. It will be difficult for less capable performers to improve their relative standing in the population, no matter how hard they try. As a result, a recipient with low ability would have little incentive for trying to improve because he would see little chance of doing as well or earning as much as recipients with higher ability.

An allocator might prevent less able performers from being discouraged by placing greater emphasis on his performance expectancies when rewarding them. If the allocator based his decision primarily on whether the recipient was utilizing his full potential, the chance of the recipient earning high reward would depend more on his effort than on his ability. Differences in ability would not penalize the less capable, or advantage the more capable. Regardless of his ability, each recipient could obtain high reward if he performed near his maximum. Thus, an allocator who desires to motivate all recipients, including those with less ability, is likely to distribute rewards not only on the basis of comparisons between recipients, but also on the basis of whether each recipient is doing his best. By taking account of recipients' potential and rewarding them relative to their ability, the allocator could sustain the motivation and performance of recipients with modest ability. Furthermore, such a policy might help elicit truly superior performance from some recipients with high ability who might otherwise coast along without using their full potential.

Leventhal and Michaels' (1969, 1971) original formulation concerning the effect of performance expectancies on an allocator's decisions was based on a limited conception of the equity norm which failed to consider the facilitative effect of equitable allocations on recipients' performance. They viewed the equity norm only as a standard of justice and neglected its implications for the problem of task mastery. However, the preceding analysis suggests that an allocator's tendency to take account of performance expectancies depends on the extent to which he is attempting to motivate all recipients to do their best. This suggestion has been confirmed by Leventhal and Whiteside (1973) who demonstrated that an allocator who desires to motivate all recipients is especially likely to reward them relative to their own ability. Subjects were given information about the ability and exam performance of several hypothetical students. All students had similar exam performance, but students with lower ability had performed at their maximum while students with higher ability had performed below their maximum. The subjects then assigned a mid-term grade to each student. They graded the students two times, once under instructions to grade so as to motivate each student to do his best and once under instructions to grade as fairly as possible. In accordance with the preceding analysis, subjects who were instructed to motivate the students displayed a significantly stronger tendency to award higher grades to students with lower ability, i.e., to give higher reward to students who were performing at their maximum. Hence, an allocator's tendency to reward recipients relative to their own ability is intensified when he is very concerned about motivating recipients to do their best. This conclusion may explain why many studies have found some tendency for subjects to reward each recipient relative to his own ability. Typically, the experimental procedures in these investigations have probably aroused strong interest in maximizing recipients' motivation and performance. Consequently, the influence of performance expectancies on subjects' allocation decisions was enhanced.

Research indicates that even when an allocator desires to motivate all recipients, performance expectancies have much less effect than social comparisons on his allocation decisions. Results obtained by Weiner and Kukla (1970), Kaplan and Swant (1973), and Rest, Nierenberg, Weiner, and Heckhausen (1973) suggest that allocators base their decisions more on differences between recipients' performance than on discrepancies between individual ability and performance. Experimental manipulation of recipients' performance relative to that of other recipients (with ability held constant) generally has greater effect on subjects' allocation decisions than experimental manipulation of recipients' ability (with performance held constant). Thus, variation in performance expectancies has less impact on an allocator's response than variation in social comparison information.

The prepotency of social comparisons over performance expectancies in determining allocation decisions is not surprising. In spite of the beneficial effect of rewarding poor performers relative to their own ability, task activity could be seriously disrupted if an allocator distributed rewards and resources solely on the basis of whether each recipient was performing at his maximum. Such a policy would often fail to provide greater reinforcement and resources for individuals whose actual contributions were greatest. Consequently, the motivation and performance of individuals with high ability might be disrupted and their loyalty and attraction to the group would decline. An allocator's concern about such potentially negative effects probably predisposes him to rely primarily on social comparison information rather than on performance expectancies when distributing rewards and resources to recipients.

In summary, the greater is the allocator's concern about motivating poor performers, the greater will be the influence of his performance expectancies and the more he will tend to reward recipients relative to their own ability. However, the magnitude of such effects is likely to be small. In each case, the allocator will balance the possible advantages gained by rewarding recipients relative to their own ability against the attendant disadvantages of deviating from a policy of rewarding recipients in accordance with their relative standing in the population.

The more serious are the anticipated difficulties resulting from such deviations the more the allocator will disregard his performance expectancies and distribute rewards solely on the basis of the recipient's performance relative to that of other recipients. Such considerations may explain why investigators have sometimes found that information about recipients' ability has little effect on an allocator's decisions (e.g., Rest, Nierenberg, Weiner, & Heckhausen, 1973). However, it should be noted that an allocator may disregard information about recipients' ability for other reasons. First, he may disregard such information because he is unconcerned about maximizing recipients' performance and productivity. Second, he may disregard it because he doubts its validity. Third, he may not have the time or ability to process large amounts of information about each recipient.

4. Using Overreward to Maximize Productivity

We have suggested that an allocator distributes rewards and resources in accordance with recipients' contributions because he believes such a policy helps maximize productivity. However, the time perspective in which the allocator views the recipients' behavior and the temporal span within which his own goals are defined probably have important effects on his allocation decisions (Weick, 1966). In fact, an allocator's strategies for sustaining productivity over the long term may differ from those he uses to bring about rapid improvement. Sometimes, allocation policies which produce high gains over a short period may have undesirable long-term effects. For example, a corporate manager who considers only the maximization of immediate profit when making decisions about the allocation of financial and human resources may produce an exceptionally high level of short-term gain but destroy his organization's capacity to operate profitably in the future (Rhode & Lawler, 1973, p. 159). However, the short-term benefits derived from certain allocation policies may be great enough to risk incurring longer-term costs. For example, an allocator may sometimes believe that the counterproductive effects of departing briefly from the equity norm will be more than offset by an immediate and sizeable improvement in the productivity of some recipients in the group.

Earlier, we suggested that an allocator believes that giving low reward to poor performers may lead them to improve in order to earn higher reward. However, an extensive body of opinion and research suggests that a punitive strategy of withholding or reducing rewards is often counterproductive as a means of influence (e.g., Collins & Guetzkow, 1964; Day & Hamblin, 1964; Deutsch & Krauss, 1962; Leventhal & Whiteside, 1973; Raven & Kruglanski, 1970; Rothbart, 1968; Yukl, 1971). Instead of arousing renewed efforts, the poor performer who receives low reward may feel dissatisfied and behave less cooperatively. Giving him low reward may actually produce further decrements in his performance. In addition, a number of studies indicate that overrewarding a recipient may improve his productivity. Often, the recipient who is paid more than he deserves performs at a substantially higher level, either in terms of the quantity or quality of his performance (e.g., Adams, 1963; Adams & Jacobsen, 1964; Goodman & Friedman, 1968, 1971; Moore & Baron, 1973; Pritchard, 1969; Pritchard, Dunnette, & Jorgenson, 1972; Wiener, 1970). Other studies suggest that rewarding a recipient in advance increases the likelihood that he will perform a desired action (e.g., Doob, Freedman, & Carlsmith, 1973; Doob & Zabrack, 1971; Kephart & Bressler, 1958; Watson, 1965).

A strategy of giving recipients more than is merited by their past inputs may improve their subsequent performance for several reasons. For example, a norm or reciprocity may lead the overrewarded recipient to repay the allocator's generosity by working harder and more effectively (Berkowitz, 1972a; Blau, 1963, 1968). Alternatively, an unexpectedly high reward may stimulate the recipient's appetite for more reward by providing a sample of what he can obtain if he performs at a higher level. But whatever the reason for the facilitative effect of giving a recipient more reward than he has earned, past experience has probably taught most allocators that overreward can often induce recipients to increase their inputs. Results obtained by Greenberg and Leventhal (1974) confirm this suggestion. Subjects were asked to evaluate the effectiveness of raising rewards as opposed to reducing rewards as strategies for motivating failing performers. Subjects believed that giving high reward would be a more effective method for stimulating better work.

The fact that allocators recognize overreward is effective for stimulating better performance suggests they will sometimes use overreward to modify recipients' task behavior. Consequently, we may expect an allocator to deviate occasionally from a policy of giving equitable allocations, a policy which he regards as an effective long-term strategy for eliciting high productivity but one for which he may briefly substitute other strategies. For example, an allocator may adopt a strategy of using overreward when be believes it is urgent to elicit better work. To obtain rapid improvement, he may overreward poor performers, sometimes to such a degree that he completely violates the rule of equity.

A study by Rothbart (1968) provides indications of a tendency for allocators to use overreward as a technique for eliciting better performance. Subjects supervised the work of a performer to whom they delivered monetary reward over a number of trials. The subjects' motivation to elicit high performance was manipulated by promising some of them special payment if they could elicit a substantial improvement in his work. Those subjects who were most highly motivated to elicit better performance gave the worker higher reward than other subjects, and were more likely to reward him on trials on which he did poorly. Using a similar paradigm, Bankart and Lanzetta (1970) had subjects deliver reinforcements to a trainee who made correct responses on most trials, or incorrect responses on most trials. Subjects gave the poorer performer higher reward for correct answers and punished him less severely for errors.

Greenberg and Leventhal (1974) found further indications of the use of overreward to stimulate poor performers. Subjects took the role of management consultants and made recommendations about bonus pay for hypothetical groups of workers who had to meet a deadline that was approaching rapidly. The groups were described as performing badly and likely to fail to meet the deadline. Some subjects were instructed to distribute monetary reward so as to motivate the workers. Other subjects were told to reward them in accordance with performance. Subjects who were told to motivate the failing workers gave them much higher bonus pay. Results from another study (Greenberg & Leventhal, 1973) indicated that subjects' tendency to use overreward was directed primarily toward the worst performers in the failing group.

Other findings provide even more striking indication of deviations from equity among subjects who are told to motivate poor performers. In one case (Greenberg & Leventhal, 1973), subjects who sought to motivate recipients completely violated the equity norm by giving higher reward to members of a group that was likely to fail than to members of a group that was doing very well. In another study (Greenberg & Leventhal, 1974), male subjects who were trying to elicit better performance violated equity by giving higher reward to individuals who were lazy and unconcerned than to individuals who were very concerned about doing well.

One may wonder how these results can be reconciled with our claim that allocators believe allocating rewards equitably facilitates productivity. This question raises no problem if one recognizes that subjects in these studies were expected to induce substantial improvements in performance in a short period of time. Rothbart's subjects and Bankart & Lanzetta's subjects had little time to train the worker they supervised. Greenberg and Leventhal's subjects were in an "emergency" situation in which an important deadline was approaching. Under such conditions, allocators probably feel that extreme measures are necessary. Although they may believe that a policy of distributing rewards equitably is best in the long run, they adopt a different strategy when faced with the problem of producing immediate improvement. To accomplish this end, they may abandon the policy of following the equity norm in favor of a short-term strategy of overrewarding recipients whose work is inadequate.

We have seen that allocators sometimes overreward poor performers to elicit better performance. However, there are compelling reasons why an allocator will deviate from equity and adopt a strategy of overreward only briefly. First, prolonged use of a strategy of overrewarding poor performers might produce dissatisfaction among better performers and disrupt their task behavior. Second, continued overrewarding of poor performers might eventually retard their improvement by removing the incentive for doing better work. If their rewards remained high in spite of continuing poor work, they would have little reason to expend additional effort. Their tendency to perform at a modest level might only be strengthened. Furthermore, their reward expectancies would tend to rise and they might begin to feel it was unfair for the allocator to demand better performance (Blau, 1964, pp. 143–147; Marwell & Schmitt, 1967b). Thus, marked deviations from the equity norm for an extended period would probably encourage poor performance. So long as an allocator is very concerned about maximizing performance, he is likely to deviate only briefly from an equitable distribution of rewards and resources.

III. Equality and the Prevention of Conflict

A. CAUSES AND CONSEQUENCES OF DISSATISFACTION

In any allocation situation there is considerable potential for conflict between the allocator and recipients, or between the recipients themselves. The recipient's desire to maximize his own reward often generates dissatisfaction because it makes him feel his rewards are insufficient. His satisfaction is also greatly influenced by social comparison processes (Adams, 1965; Berkowitz, 1972b; Homans, 1961; Patchen, 1961; Walster, Berscheid, & Walster, 1973; Weick, 1966). If his rewards are lower than those of others, he is likely to respond negatively. For example, he may behave antagonistically toward the allocator and demand more reward than the allocator is willing or able to give. In addition, he may view other recipients as rivals who are vying with him for access to limited resources.

Dissatisfaction among recipients may have serious negative consequences for the allocator. He may be subjected to criticism and pressure from dissatisfied individuals who want him to modify his allocation decisions. Such criticism is inherently unpleasant and may also pose a threat to the allocator's authority and status. For example, results obtained by Michener and Lyons (1972) and Michener and Tausig (1971) suggest that if an allocator loses support and is criticized by some recipients, other recipients may also withdraw their support. Dissatisfied recipients may also jeopardize the allocator's position by complaining to his superiors, or to other parties whose support and approval he desires (Caplow, 1968; Miller, 1965; Smith, 1967). His position may be further weakened if recipients' dissatisfaction disrupts productivity. The allocator's status often depends on his success in maintaining recipients' performance at a high level. If task activities are seriously disrupted, he may be forced to vacate his position (Hamblin, 1958; Michener & Lawler, 1971). For these reasons, an allocator is likely to take steps to minimize recipients' dissatisfaction with his allocation decisions.

B. METHODS OF PREVENTING CONFLICT

1. Changing the Distribution of Reward

Allocators may prevent dissatisfaction and conflict by changing their distribution of reward. For example, Donnerstein and Donnerstein (1972) have shown that allocators give especially high reward to a recipient who is likely to retaliate if he is not treated properly. Subjects in their study administered rewards and punishments to a learner. Those subjects who expected to reverse roles with the learner gave him relatively high reward when they believed he belonged to an ethnic group that was inclined to use violence to achieve its rights. Presumably, subjects assumed the recipient would be less inclined to attack an allocator who treated him generously.

An allocator who is distributing rewards among members of a group may use similar tactics to appease potentially antagonistic individuals. However, he faces two problems not confronted by an allocator who deals with only one recipient at a time. First, he must discover which group members are dissatisfied before he can placate them by inflating their rewards. Second, his supply of reward is usually limited. Consequently, if he increases one recipient's share, he must do so at the expense of other recipients. The allocator must therefore weigh the beneficial effect of raising a dissatisfied recipient's share of reward against the potentially negative effect of reducing other recipients' shares.

Results from an unpublished study by the author provide evidence concerning an allocator's perception of which group members are most dissatisfied. Subjects estimated the satisfaction of each member of a hypothetical four-man work group as a function of the distribution of pay within the group. The group members differed in their performance and pay, with better performers receiving higher pay. The difference between the pay of the best and worst performer ranged in several steps from very small to very large. For each increase in the worst performer's pay there was a corresponding decrease in the best performer's pay. Subjects believed that poor performers who received low reward would be more dissatisfied. Furthermore, the less reward poor performers received the greater was the subjects' estimate of their dissatisfaction. The subjects also estimated the likelihood of conflict among group members. The more the pay of the best performer exceded that of the worst the more subjects believed there was likely to be conflict. Thus, as the difference in pay *decreased*, there was a steady reduction in the perceived likelihood of conflict.

These findings suggest that an allocator who hopes to minimize disruptive conflict will reduce the difference between recipients' rewards. By inflating the rewards of inferior performers who are poorly paid, the allocator placates those group members who are most dissatisfied and most likely to behave antagonistically. This suggestion is confirmed by the results of Leventhal, Michaels, and

Sanford (1972). Their subjects recommended a distribution of earnings in work groups that would meet for a number of sessions. The subjects were told each group would be rewarded in accordance with its performance but that the experimenters were uncertain as to how group earnings should be divided among the members. To show their recommendation, subjects divided a monetary reward among the members of a hypothetical group two times. The first time, they divided the reward as they thought best and gave much higher reward to better performers. Subjects received different instructions concerning their second allocation decision. In two conditions, they were told to divide the reward so as to prevent conflict and hostility, either among the group members, or between the group members and the experimenters. In comparison to a control group, subjects in these conditions showed a marked tendency to inflate the rewards of poorer performers at better performers' expense. Thus, subjects whose goal was to minimize interpersonal conflict gave less weight to differences in recipients' work contributions and reduced the difference between the rewards of good and poor performers. However, it should be noted that subjects stopped short of giving equal reward to all recipients. They still gave substantially higher reward to better performers.

2. Secrecy

Another strategy allocators may use to minimize antagonism is to impose secrecy about their distribution of reward. Evidence from the unpublished study cited above suggests that an allocator believes the likelihood of conflict among recipients depends on whether they are able to compare themselves to one another. Subjects were asked whether maintaining secrecy about the distribution of pay would help prevent conflict in the group. The greater the difference between the pay of the best and worst performers the more subjects believed that secrecy would prevent conflict. Thus, preventing recipients from comparing their rewards was seen as an effective means for minimizing dissatisfaction and conflict, especially when the disparity in rewards was great.

The strength of an allocator's desire to withhold information about his distribution of pay is likely to differ for different recipients. The more a group member is expected to feel dissatisfied, i.e., the lower his pay is in relation to other members' pay, the more the allocator should tend to withhold information from that recipient. This hypothesis has been confirmed by Leventhal, Michaels, and Sanford (1972). Subjects were asked to rate how much they desired to withhold information about the distribution of reward from each of several group members. It was found that the less the subject had given a recipient the more he desired to keep that recipient ignorant of the distribution of reward. Thus, subjects' desire to withhold information was strongest in the case of recipients who were most likely to feel dissatisfied.

We have seen that subjects believe the imposition of secrecy will help prevent conflict. This finding suggests that an allocator's decisions may be strongly affected by whether the distribution of reward is secret. If recipients have full knowledge of pay differences, those given lower pay are likely to experience heightened dissatisfaction and the danger of disruptive interpersonal conflict will increase. Accordingly, if an allocator believes recipients have complete information about his distribution of reward, he is likely to inflate the rewards of poorer performers in order to appease them. This hypothesis has also been confirmed by Leventhal, Michaels, and Sanford (1972). Subjects recommended a division of pay among four group members on two occasions, once under the assumption that all recipients would know what others were receiving and once under the assumption that the distribution of reward would remain completely secret. In both cases, subjects gave more to better performers. However, when there was full disclosure, subjects reduced the difference in pay by inflating the worst performer's share at the best performer's expense. When there was secrecy, subjects discriminated more sharply between the best and worst performers and reduced the inferior performer's share. Apparently, when social comparison among recipients is prevented, the perceived threat of conflict is reduced and allocators feel freer to give low reward to poor performers.

The evidence suggests that secrecy about the distribution of reward may strengthen an allocator's tendency to follow the equity norm in order to maximize productivity. In this regard, comments by Porter and Lawler (1968, p. 67) indicate there may be a tendency among organizational allocators who adopt merit (equity) pay plans to simultaneously impose secrecy about the distribution of pay. Our findings suggest that managerial allocators who attempt to maximize productivity by rewarding recipients in accordance with work contributions are likely to believe that disclosure of pay differences will create dissatisfaction among a significant number of worker recipients. Consequently, they may impose secrecy to prevent poorly paid workers from comparing themselves to others. Such secrecy might help minimize disruptive conflict. However, as Lawler (1965a, b, 1967, 1971, 1972) and Porter and Lawler (1968) have suggested, secrecy makes it difficult for recipients to perceive the link between pay and performance. Consequently, it may reduce the effectiveness of merit pay plans as a device for maximizing worker productivity. Thus, we have the curious phenomenon of a managerial allocator who distributes rewards equitably in order to maximize productivity but simultaneously undermines the impact of his allocation policy by imposing secrecy because he fears equitable allocations will cause dissatisfaction.

a. Secrecy by Recipients and Observers. Secrecy about the distribution of reward may be due to recipients as well as allocators. Results obtained by Johnson, Conlee, & Tesser (1974), and Tesser & Rosen (1972) indicate that a recipient whose outcomes are higher than those of others is reluctant to inform his co-recipients about the disparity between their rewards. It may be that the recipient who receives higher outcomes fears his less fortunate co-recipients will be envious and reject him because he seems to be profiting at their expense (Johnson, Conlee & Tesser, 1974). The highly rewarded recipient may also fear that full disclosure will cause poorly rewarded recipients to demand modifications in the distribution of rewards and resources, modifications that could seriously threaten his favorable position. Thus, recipients who believe they are highly paid may protect themselves by maintaining silence about the distribution of reward.

It has been suggested that both allocators and highly rewarded recipients have an interest in concealing information about the distribution of reward from recipients who receive low reward. There is also reason to believe that other observers may withhold information from poorly rewarded recipients. A number of studies indicate that a communicator avoids transmitting information about negative events to a victim even when the communicator is not responsible for the events and does not profit from them (e.g., Rosen & Conlee, 1972; Rosen, Johnson, Johnson, & Tesser, 1973; Rosen & Tesser, 1970). Thus, even disinterested observers who do not directly benefit from secrecy may help maintain it.

Given the variety of constraints on communication about rewards by observers, co-recipients, and allocators, it is not surprising that secrecy about pay is prevalent in many organizations (Caplow & McGee, 1958; Lawler, 1965a,b, 1967, 1971, 1972; Milkovich & Anderson, 1972). However, there are probably major exceptions to others' tendency to withhold information from poorly rewarded recipients. For example, individuals with positive feeling for a recipient may warn him if they believe he is seriously underrewarded. Or, a recipient who discovers he and his co-recipients are underrewarded may inform them of their common fate in order to initiate collective action to modify the distribution of reward (Caplow, 1968; Michener & Lawler, 1971).

b. Secrecy in Relation to Superiors. Just as secrecy can protect an allocator from the wrath of recipients, so may it protect him from his superiors. He is less likely to conform to his superiors' expectations if they do not scrutinize his decisions closely. However, if he expects his superiors to evaluate him carefully, he will modify his allocation decisions in directions which meet their approval. This suggestion is supported by the work of Donnerstein and Donnerstein (1973), Isen, Horn, and Rosenhan (1973), and Leventhal, Popp, and Sawyer (1973). It is also likely that an allocator will withhold or distort information about his decisions if he believes his superiors are likely to disapprove of them. This suggestion is consistent with the view that subordinates tend to avoid transmitting information which may tarnish their image (Collins & Guetzkow, 1964; Read, 1962).

C. THE EQUALITY NORM

The Instrumental Value of Equal Allocations

Many authors have suggested that an allocator's decisions are influenced by an equality norm (e.g., Garrett, 1973; Kahn, 1972; Lane & Coon, 1972; Lerner, 1974a; Leventhal, Popp, & Sawyer, 1973; Lichtman, 1972; Pruitt, 1972; Sampson, 1969). Thus, an allocator sometimes ignores differences in recipients' inputs and distributes rewards equally. He is especially likely to follow the equality norm in settings in which it is widely regarded as the most appropriate rule of allocation and others expect him to follow it. However, his decision to follow the equality norm is also influenced by a desire to obtain certain benefits associated with equal distributions. For example, equality of reward may foster harmony and solidarity (Bales, 1950). Studies of the effect of different distributions of reward on interpersonal relationships indicate that equal distributions tend to produce a high level of satisfaction and harmony among group members (e.g., Deutsch, 1953; Julian & Perry, 1967; Smith & Cook, 1973; Steiner, 1972). Consequently, the allocator who follows the equality norm as a criterion of fair distribution is also likely to elicit a high level of solidarity. Thus, we hypothesize that an allocator often follows the equality norm because he believes it helps resolve problems arising from the group's interpersonal environment (Collins & Guetzkow, 1964; Homans, 1950). More specifically, he believes equal allocations reduce negative socio-emotional behaviors such as dissatisfaction and antagonism. This speculation is supported by the author's unpublished study which found that subjects believe conflict among group members becomes less likely as the distribution of reward approaches equality.

Equality and Group Allocation Decisions. Studies of group allocation decisions are often cited as evidence of the influence of the equality norm (e.g., Gamson, 1964; Komorita & Chertkoff, 1973; Morgan & Sawyer, 1967; Wiggins, 1966). However, as Burnstein and Katz's (1972) work suggests, studies of group allocation decisions may yield a different picture of the influence of allocation norms than studies of individual allocation decisions. For example, the two types of studies yield different conclusions concerning the role of the equality norm as a source of sex differences in allocation behavior (Leventhal, 1973). Vinacke and his associates have studied the influence of subjects' sex on group allocation decisions (Bond & Vinacke, 1961; Uesugi & Vinacke, 1963; Vinacke, 1962). They found that female partners divided rewards equally regardless of initial differences in contributions. In contrast, male partners divided rewards unequally, with the individual whose inputs were greatest receiving the larger share. Vinacke and his associates accounted for these results by suggesting that female groups prefer equality because they are more concerned than males about preserving harmony and solidarity. This conclusion is consistent with the view that a desire for group harmony is associated with a preference for equalizing rewards. However, other results indicate that individual female allocators often do not follow the equality norm. In a study of individual allocation decisions, Leventhal and Lane (1970) found that a female allocator with low inputs did not divide rewards equally. Instead, she took less for herself than she gave to her partner. The reasons for the apparent discrepancy between this finding and findings from Vinacke's studies of group allocation decisions have been discussed elsewhere (Leventhal, 1973).

D. DEVIATIONS FROM EQUALITY

1. Equity and Equality as Opposing Norms

Research indicates that the equity and equality norms often operate as opposing forces in determining an allocator's decisions. The two norms may arouse incompatible response tendencies that must be reconciled by a compromise response which partially satisfies each norm. For example, subjects in a study by Leventhal, Michaels, and Sanford (1972) probably compromised between the opposing demands of the equity and equality norms. As reported earlier, subjects who were instructed to prevent conflict moved toward equality by reducing the difference between the rewards of the best and worst performers in a group. However, they stopped short of complete equality and gave substantially higher reward to the better performer. This response can best be understood as a compromise between the opposing demands of the equity and equality norms. The instructions to minimize hostility aroused a strong tendency to follow the equality norm. However, in all conditions, it was clearly implied that monetary reward was being given to stimulate productivity. Thus, subjects probably believed they were expected to follow a policy of distributing rewards in accordance with performance, i.e., to follow the equity norm. As a consequence, the subjects were influenced by both norms. They moved toward equalizing rewards to satisfy the requirements of the rule of equality, but stopped short of complete equality to satisfy the requirements of the rule of equity. This interpretation is supported by results from another experimental condition in the same study. In this condition, subjects were told to disregard the possibility of conflict among recipients. As a result, the effect of the equality norm was weakened and subjects showed a significant increase in the tendency to distribute rewards equitably, i.e., they increased the best performer's share and gave less to the worst. Thus, if an allocator's primary goal is to maximize productivity, he favors the equity norm because equitable allocations help maximize group productivity over the long run. If his primary goal is to minimize antagonism and maintain solidarity, he favors the equality norm because equal allocations foster interpersonal harmony.

Paradoxically, opposition between the norms of equity and equality may sometimes arise because the allocator believes a high level of harmony is necessary for effective group functioning. Dissatisfaction and antagonism may disrupt task activities. Consequently, if dissatisfaction is high, the allocator who desires to maximize productivity may move toward equalizing rewards in order to restore the solidarity that he considers necessary for effective performance. However, once dissatisfaction and conflict have been reduced to tolerable levels, he may revert to a policy of distributing rewards equitably in order to elicit high performance.

Confluence of the Equity and Equality Norms. Although the equity and equality norms often have opposing effects on allocation decisions, there are many situations in which the two norms are not in opposition. All too often, researchers have overlooked the fact that the two norms frequently dictate the same allocation response and have mutually supportive effects. For example, when recipients have similar task inputs, both the equality and equity norms will lead an allocator to distribute rewards evenly. Confluence of the two norms may also occur when available information about inputs is vague and contradictory. In such instances an unbiased allocator might choose to operate on the assumption that the recipients had similar inputs. Accordingly, both the equity and equality norms would dictate an equal distribution.

Leventhal, Popp, and Sawyer (1973, p. 758) have identified another factor that researchers sometimes overlook in studies concerned with the relative influence of the equality and equity norms. The allocator who is evaluating recipients' inputs often gives different weight to different aspects of their task behavior (Adams, 1965). Consequently, even when he desires to maintain equity, he may disregard certain differences in their performance and divide rewards evenly. For example, if an allocator believes total output is very important, and two recipients have similar output, he may focus on that aspect of their behavior and ignore differences in their effort. In such cases, the allocator will distribute rewards equally because he is following the equity norm, but giving little weight to differences in effort. However, outside observers might erroneously conclude he was following the equality norm.

2. The Allocator as a Co-Recipient

Bales (1950) and Lerner (1974b) have suggested that increased solidarity among group members fosters a more equal distribution of status and rewards. Accordingly, situational variables which increase solidarity should cause an allocator to equalize his distribution of reward. However, this suggestion may not always hold true when the allocator is a co-recipient, i.e., when he performs many of the same tasks as the recipients and shares in the rewards he gives them. An example of the allocator as co-recipient is the chairman of a subspecialty area *within* an academic department. Although the Area Chairman has extra responsibilities, his basic duties and status often remain similar to those of his colleagues. Because he is similar and shares rewards with them, his co-recipients are likely to compare their rewards to his. Furthermore, they are sensitive to the possibility that he can inflate his own rewards at their expense. If the allocator appears to take unfair advantage of his position, his co-recipients may behave very negatively toward him. To minimize antagonism, an allocator who is a co-recipient must reassure other recipients that his allocation decisions are not self-serving. He must allocate rewards in ways that demonstrate he is not abusing his authority. Consequently, he will tend to avoid (or conceal) allocation decisions which give the appearance of impropriety.

The preceding considerations suggest that an allocator whose performance is superior to that of his co-recipients is more likely to equalize the distribution of reward than an allocator whose performance is inferior. An allocator with poor performance will probably not divide rewards evenly because such a division might cause his fellow recipients to accuse him of profiting at their expense. The allocator could best demonstrate his fairness, not by following the equality norm, but by taking no more for himself than the small share merited by his modest performance. However, if his performance was superior, he could best maintain harmony by following the equality norm. By reducing his own share and taking no more than he gave to others, he could demonstrate his generosity and allay his fellow recipients' suspicions. Accordingly, when allocators desire to maintain solidarity, those with superior performance are likely to equalize rewards while those with inferior performance are not.

Results from several studies confirm these speculations. In each case, subjects worked on a task with a fictitious partner. The subject then received feedback about performance which indicated his performance was either better or worse than that of his co-worker. In addition, the subject was given the task of dividing group earnings. Feelings of solidarity and mutual dependence were also manipulated. Among allocators with superior performance, manipulations which heightened solidarity consistently increased the subjects' tendency to divide rewards equally. However, among allocators with inferior performance, the manipulations often had little effect. For example, Valentine (1971) found that instructions which emphasized group members' interdependence caused a subject with superior performance to reduce his own share and divide rewards equally. However, a subject with inferior performance did not equalize the distribution of reward, i.e., he did not increase his own share. Shapiro (1972, 1975) found that a subject with superior performance moved toward equalization by reducing his own share in response to an increase in anticipated interaction with his co-worker. However, subjects with inferior performance did not move toward equality. Mikula's (1974) results indicated that when subjects residing in a foreign country felt drawn together by virtue of their same nationality, those with superior performance reduced their own share and distributed rewards evenly. Subjects with inferior performance, on the other hand, took less than half the reward for themselves. Unlike other investigators, Lerner (1974a) did *not* find a stronger preference for equal distributions among subjects with superior performance. However, Lerner used children as subjects and it is questionable to compare their responses to those of older subjects studied by Valentine (1971), Shapiro (1972, 1975), and Mikula (1974).

Results indicate that when group solidarity is high, an allocator who is a co-recipient tends to avoid allocation responses that may raise doubts about his fairness and disrupt harmony. The allocator with superior performance is likely to take no more for himself than he gives to others because he believes an equal distribution will minimize suspicion and maintain solidarity. This interpretation receives support from the questionnaire responses of Shapiro's (1975) subjects. Superior performers who divided rewards equally expected to be evaluated more favorably than superior performers who took more for themselves. On the other hand, the allocator with inferior performance is likely to take less for himself than he gives to others because he fears they will react negatively to him if he equalizes the distribution of reward at their expense. This interpretation receives support from a study by Brickman and Bryan (1975). Observers reacted unfavorably to an allocator who equalized rewards at his co-recipient's expense.

IV.   Other Means of Influencing Recipients' Behavior

A.   CHOOSING AMONG ALTERNATIVE METHODS OF INFLUENCE

An allocator often employs other means of influencing recipients' behavior besides giving or withholding rewards (Cartwright, 1965; Marwell & Schmitt, 1967a, b; French & Raven, 1959; Raven & Kruglanski, 1970). His allocation response is only one member of a large family of responses he may direct toward recipients in order to influence their productivity and satisfaction. For example, an allocator who desires to elicit high performance may supervise recipients more closely, or teach them new skills. The allocator tends to use those methods of influencing recipients which he considers most effective for eliciting desirable behavior (Goodstadt & Hjelle, 1973; Goodstadt & Kipnis, 1970; Kipnis & Cosentino, 1969; Raven & Kruglanski, 1970). In addition, his choice of influence techniques is affected by factors such as the adequacy and costliness of available modes of response, his fear of retaliation, and anxiety about violating ethical standards (cf. Berscheid & Walster, 1967; Berscheid, Walster, & Barclay,

1969; Macaulay & Walster, 1971; Raven & Kruglanski, 1970; Walster, Berscheid, & Walster, 1973). Most importantly, the allocator's decision to use a given technique for influencing recipients' behavior affects the likelihood of his using other techniques. For example, Kipnis (1972) found that subjects made less use of one method for raising subordinates' productivity when alternative methods were available. Other studies indicate that the perceived range of available response options changes the frequency with which an allocator makes a specific response (e.g., Harrison & Pepitone, 1972; Leventhal & Bergman, 1969; Vidmar, 1972). Consequently, there may be marked changes in an allocator's distribution of reward as a function of the range and nature of other methods he can use to influence recipients. He may use these alternatives in place of or in addition to his allocation response. To the extent these alternative techniques prove effective, the allocator may find it less necessary to use his distribution of reward as a device for influencing recipients' productivity and satisfaction.

At this time, we shall not attempt to consider the full range of techniques an allocator can use to control recipients' behavior. Instead, we shall only consider techniques he uses to minimize dissatisfaction and the relation of these techniques to his allocation decisions.

B. MANIPULATING OTHERS' PERCEPTION

An allocator may use a variety of techniques to influence recipients' satisfaction with his allocation decisions. Some of his techniques affect the recipients' perception of the nature and causes of his decisions. Other techniques affect their perception of the value of the reward.

1. Secrecy

An allocator's use of secrecy to minimize dissatisfaction and conflict has already been discussed in detail. The evidence suggests that an allocator who is able to impose secrecy about his distribution of reward is less likely to appease inferior performers by inflating their rewards.

2. Altering the Perceived Locus of Decision

An allocator can reduce dissatisfaction and antagonism by manipulating others' perception of the causes of his decisions (Blau, 1963, p. 222; Cartwright, 1965; Collins & Guetzkow, 1964). If his decision is unpopular, he may encourage receivers to believe that factors beyond his control have forced him to make it. Like a harm-doer, he can escape retaliation by denying personal responsibility for his actions (Kelman & Lawrence, 1972; Macaulay & Walster, 1971; Walster, Berscheid, & Walster, 1970, 1973; Walster & Piliavin, 1972). The allocator's success in influencing others' perception of the causal locus of his decision is likely to affect his allocation response. If he can persuade recipients that circumstances beyond his control are dictating his decision, he may feel freer to give them low reward.

3. Justifying the Decision

An allocator may reduce dissatisfaction by providing poorly rewarded recipients with information which justifies his allocation decisions. For instance, he may give them incontrovertible evidence that other recipients have performed at a higher level. The allocator who is able to defend his decisions in this manner may be less reluctant to give low reward to poor performers.

4. Enhancing the Value of the Reward

An allocator may reduce antagonism by increasing recipients' estimate of the value of their rewards. To the extent he can inflate the perceived sufficiency of their share, he is less likely to modify his allocation response in order to placate them. The three techniques listed below enhance the perceived value of reward by modifying the frame of reference recipients use to evaluate their outcomes.

1. The allocator may encourage upward revaluation by providing information which indicates that the total amount of reward available for distribution was small. This would permit him to claim that the recipient's share of reward was quite large in relation to the limited resources that were available.

2. A recipient's choice of a comparison other is a critical determinant of his satisfaction with his outcomes. Accordingly, an allocator may reduce dissatisfaction by encouraging a recipient to shift his object of comparison in directions that enhance the apparent magnitude of the recipient's rewards. For example, the allocator may provide information about comparable recipients whose rewards are lower, or information which makes others with higher reward seem less comparable.

3. An allocator may induce upward revaluation by altering the time frame the recipient uses to evaluate his current rewards. By increasing the salience of the recipient's past rewards, or forthcoming rewards, the allocator can lead the recipient to believe that (a) in the long run his rewards are no lower than those of others, or (b) that his present rewards are much higher than they once were. The use of such techniques is consistent with comments by Weick (1966) and Schwab (1973, p. 311) concerning the importance of temporal perspective as a factor which affects recipients' evaluation of their rewards.

Preliminary findings from a study by Carl Greenberg and the author illustrate an allocator's use of the technique of reducing dissatisfaction by expanding recipients' temporal frame. The study examines mothers' methods of minimizing feelings of sibling resentment and jealousy on birthdays. Typically, when a child has a birthday, there is a special celebration in his honor and he receives many presents. Because he is the center of attention, his sibling(s) may feel neglected and resentful. Many mothers try to deal with these negative feelings by expanding the sibling's temporal frame of reference. They remind him that he, too, will receive presents when his birthday comes, or that he received gifts on his last birthday. By focusing on past or forthcoming rewards, the mothers try to show that all children in the family are being treated fairly. The mothers' behavior is reminiscent of that of some employers who attempt to assuage employees' dissatisfaction with small pay raises by pointing out that last year's raises were quite large, or that next year's raises will be bigger.

V. Regularization and Timing

A. REGULARIZING THE ALLOCATION RESPONSE

An allocator often makes repeated deliveries of reward to the same recipients. In such situations, he is likely to regularize his delivery of reward. He will establish a schedule which dictates the precise amount of reward he gives and the precise times at which he gives it. For example, a majority of parents allocate spending money to their children by giving an allowance, i.e., by delivering a specific amount to the child at regular intervals (Weinstein, 1972). Similarly, an employer usually pays his employees specified amounts on specified days of the month.

Allocators probably regularize their delivery of reward with respect to amount and timing because regularization has important benefits, both for the allocator and for the recipients. Regularization makes the environment more stable and predictable (Bales, 1950), and allows the allocator and recipient to synchronize their behavior more effectively (Thibaut & Kelley, 1959). In addition, regularization reduces dissatisfaction and antagonism because it increases recipients' certainty about future rewards and makes their reward expectancies more realistic. By delivering regular amounts at regular times, the allocator brings recipients' reward expectancies into closer alignment with their actual rewards. Recipients with more realistic expectancies are likely to be more satisfied (Porter & Steers, 1973). Thus, an allocator is likely to minimize dissatisfaction by following an agreed upon schedule of regular payments.

Regularization of the allocation response probably provides another important benefit for the allocator and recipients. For both parties, cognitive and emotional strain will be reduced. A firm commitment by the allocator to deliver rewards and resources in accordance with an accepted schedule will eliminate the necessity for spending inordinate time in making decisions, or in negotiations. Thus, the regularization of allocation responses provides an allocator with the benefit of reduced cognitive and emotional strain, as well as the benefit of reduced interpersonal conflict.

The Norm of Adhering to Commitments

The preceding analysis suggests that an allocator has much to gain by adhering to a schedule for delivering rewards. Furthermore, there is considerable evidence which indicates an allocator's decisions are influenced by a norm of adhering to commitments, i.e., an allocation norm which dictates that he reward recipients in accordance with commitments he has made to them (Leventhal & Whiteside, 1973; Pruitt, 1971, 1972; Thibaut, 1968; Thibaut & Gruder, 1969). Our analysis suggests that an allocator gains several benefits by following this norm. First, he reduces cognitive and emotional strain by eliminating the need for additional decision-making and negotiation. Second, he reduces the likelihood of conflict because recipients' expectancies are more realistic. Third, by following the norm, the allocator establishes a reputation for fairness and integrity. He gains others' respect by honoring his commitments.

B. TIMING THE DELIVERY OF REWARD

Our analysis of the regularization phenomenon suggests that decisions about when to deliver reward may be as critical a feature of the allocator's behavior as decisions about how much to deliver. In fact, there are probably many instances in which an allocator is more concerned about when to give than how much to give. For example, an experimenter who is using reward to shape a pigeon's behavior may be most concerned about giving a fixed reward at precisely the right moment—and so may a mother who is using candy as a reinforcer to toilet train her child. Unfortunately, there has been little theorizing or research which deals with factors that determine the timing of an allocator's response. Instead, most work has dealt with factors which determine how much he gives and to whom he gives it.

The present analysis of the timing of allocation responses assumes that an allocator's decision creates a plan for allocation, a plan which is the mediating link between his decision and his subsequent delivery of reward. An allocator may reach a decision about how and when to distribute rewards but not act on his plan until circumstances are deemed appropriate. The period of delay between the decision and the actual execution of the plan for delivering reward may be extremely brief or quite long.

To illustrate the utility of this simple conception, let us consider how the timing of allocation responses is influenced by an allocator's desire to preserve harmony. To prevent conflict, the allocator may delay his response, or terminate it prematurely. For example, an allocator who has formulated a plan for distributing rewards may sometimes delay his delivery of reward until recipients are likely to react favorably. In other instances, he may postpone his response if he discovers that his plan of allocation is likely to arouse more antagonism than he initially anticipated. The allocator may make this discovery in several ways. For example, if he informs some of the recipients about his plan and finds they disapprove, he may delay action and reconsider his options. Alternatively, he might discover his allocation plan was unacceptable to recipients if the first few individuals to whom he delivered reward responded very negatively. In such cases, the allocator might terminate his allocation response prematurely. Instead of carrying through his plan, he would take no further action until there was an opportunity to reformulate it. A decision made by George Washington in 1775 provides a good illustration of the premature termination of an allocation response to prevent disruptive conflict. Shortly after being appointed Commander-in-Chief of the Continental Army, Washington arrived in Cambridge to take command of the siege of Boston. He brought with him a set of appointments which assigned ranks in the new Continental Army to officers who already held rank in various state militia. In Wheeler's (1972, p. 59) words, he "arrived at Cambridge with continental commissions that established their relative seniority; but he had no sooner issued the first one—to Israel Putnam—than another general left camp in a huff because he was Putnam's senior in the Connecticut service and had no wish to be his junior in the Continental. Washington wisely decided to withold the rest of the commissions and refer the matter back to Congress for further consideration." Washington's good political skill led him to set aside an allocation plan that could have created serious antagonism and disunity. However, it is important to recognize that his decision to abort the plan for allocating ranks was possible only because his power in the social system was great enough to allow him to override the decisions of others and because the situation did not require immediate action. In many cases, an allocator may be unable to postpone action when he discovers his plan of allocation is creating serious problems. Pressures from his superiors or other situational demands may force him to execute the plan without delay in spite of the newly discovered problems.

C. DECISION-MAKERS AND DELIVERERS

The preceding analysis distinguished between the formulation of an allocation plan and the actual delivery of reward to recipients. In practice, these two aspects of the allocator's role may devolve on different individuals. It is therefore necessary to distinguish between decision-makers and "deliverers." Often, a decision-maker who formulates an allocation plan delegates the task of actually delivering the reward to other individuals who act as his agents. The behavior of these deliverers is frequently governed by comprehensive rules which are so specific that the deliverers have minimal freedom of decision. Instead of making allocation decisions, they merely follow instructions and use procedures established by others in the social system. Some examples of individuals who make delivery responses rather than allocation decisions are: a bank teller who cashes a check for a regular customer; a librarian who checks out books for a reader; and a food server in a cafeteria who fills a customer's plate. The allocation responses of the teller, librarian, and food server involve little choice. Their role requires only the routine execution of an allocation policy that has been established at an earlier time by persons of higher rank in the social system. The behavior of deliverers changes only if a decision-maker at higher levels changes the procedures they are required to follow.

It is clear that allocation roles vary greatly in the amount of discretion granted to the role occupant. Our analysis has dealt primarily with cases in which the allocator has considerable freedom of action. We have not been greatly concerned with whether the allocator's role requires him to actually deliver the reward into the recipients' hands, or whether the actual delivery of reward is delegated to another person. Our primary concern has been the behavior of decision-makers who formulate the allocation decision. However, it must be recognized that even when an individual's duties consist primarily of delivering reward in a prescribed manner and in prescribed amounts, he may have some slight freedom to vary his response. For example, a food server may give slightly larger portions to a customer he likes.

VI. Other Allocation Norms

It has been suggested that an allocator's tendency to follow a specific allocation norm is strongly influenced by his desire to obtain the pattern of benefits associated with that norm. Thus, an allocator may follow the equity norm to maximize productivity; follow the equality norm to reduce dissatisfaction and conflict; and follow the norm of adherence to commitments to foster harmony and reduce cognitive strain. Other allocation norms which provide other patterns of benefits are considered below.

A. THE RECIPROCITY NORM

A great deal of work suggests that a norm of reciprocity is an important determinant of social behavior (e.g., Berkowitz & Friedman, 1967; Blau, 1963, 1968; Goranson & Berkowitz, 1966; Gouldner, 1960; Schopler, 1970; Schopler & Thompson, 1968; Staub, 1972). For an allocator, following a rule of reciprocity has obvious advantages. The allocator who reciprocates recipients' past favors and services guarantees their continued willingness to interact with him and exchange their services for his rewards (Blau, 1963, 1968; Schopler, 1970). The effect of the reciprocity norm on an allocator's decisions has been demonstrated in many investigations (e.g., Garrett & Libby, 1973; Greenberg & Frisch, 1972; Kahn & Tice, 1973; Leventhal, Weiss, & Long, 1969; Pruitt, 1968; Stapleton, Nacci, & Tedeschi, 1973; Staub & Sherk, 1970; Wilke & Lanzetta, 1970).

B. NORMS AFFECTING RESPONSIVENESS TO RECIPIENTS' NEEDS

The views of several authors suggest that an allocator will give higher reward to recipients with greater need for the reward (e.g., Berkowitz, 1972a; Lerner, 1974a, b; Leventhal, Weiss, & Buttrick, 1973; Pruitt, 1972). For example, Lerner has postulated a norm of Marxian justice, i.e., a social rule which dictates that allocators reward recipients in accordance with their needs. However, Pruitt's (1972, p. 147) analysis indicates it may be necessary to adopt a more differentiated conception of the norms which govern an allocator's response to recipients' needs. Several different norms may influence his response.

Work by Berkowitz and others suggests that a norm of social responsibility will cause an allocator to reward recipients in accordance with their need for assistance. The operation of the norm is revealed in studies which demonstrate that an individual works harder to help others as their involuntary dependence upon him increases (e.g., Berkowitz, 1969; Berkowitz & Connor, 1966; Berkowitz & Daniels, 1963, 1964; Horowitz, 1968; Schopler & Matthews, 1965). Leventhal and Weiss (in press) obtained direct evidence of the influence of the social responsibility norm on allocation decisions. The subjects divided a monetary reward between themselves and a co-worker whose monetary resources were either greater or less than their own. Subjects attributed greater need for money to co-workers with lower resources and gave them higher reward. Furthermore, the subjects stated that their allocation decision was strongly influenced by a desire to help someone whose need was greater than their own.

Despite the substantial body of evidence consistent with the hypothesized influence of the social responsibility norm, several authors have questioned the potency of the norm (Berkowitz, 1972a; Schwartz, 1970; Schopler, 1970). Even though an allocator may believe recipients in need should get what they require, his allocation decision will not be strongly affected unless other factors activate the social responsibility norm. One such factor is the allocator's feeling of personal responsibility for the recipients' welfare. The importance of this factor is shown by Schwartz's (1970) work and also by studies which indicate that an allocator's willingness to reward needy recipients is a direct function of his emotional involvement and liking for them (Golightly, Huffman, & Byrne, 1972; Piliavin & Piliavin, 1969; Walster & Piliavin, 1972).

Pruitt (1972) has proposed the existence of another norm that may influence an allocator's responsiveness to recipients' needs. He suggests that in highly solidary dyadic relationships, a norm of mutual responsiveness exists. This norm imposes on each partner an obligation to satisfy the other's needs. Pruitt suggests that, in comparison to the social responsibility norm, the norm of mutual responsiveness operates in a much narrower range of interpersonal relationships, and generates a much higher level of concern for the other's welfare. However, the extent to which the norm of social responsibility and norm of mutual responsiveness are conceptually and empirically independent remains to be demonstrated.

A factor which further complicates the analysis of an allocator's responsiveness to recipients' needs is the necessity of distinguishing between the recipient's needs as the allocator perceives them and the recipient's needs as the recipient, himself, perceives them. Often, an allocator may find that his assessment of the recipient's needs differs from the recipient's self-assessment of needs (cf. Schopler, 1970, p. 235). The recipient's expressed desire may differ greatly from what the allocator believes the recipient actually requires to protect the recipient's welfare. Parent-child relationships are replete with instances of contradictions between recipients' expressed needs and the allocator's assessment of the recipients' "true" needs. For example, a child may frequently ask for candy but his mother may withhold it because she believes the child needs more nourishing food that is less harmful to teeth. In such cases, the allocator must decide whether to base his allocation decision on his assessment of the recipient's needs, on the recipient's own expressions of need, or on a weighted combination of the two.

One factor likely to affect an allocator's decision when such disagreements occur is whether he believes the recipient's stated need is harmful or improper. If it is, the allocator is unlikely to allocate in accordance with the recipient's expressed desires. For example, a physician may refuse to prescribe drugs for an addicted patient in spite of intense expressions of need because the physician believes the need is both harmful and improper. In such cases, the allocator may withhold the resource and encourage the recipient to suppress the undesirable need. Thus, one cannot predict an allocator's response to recipients' needs unless one knows whether the allocator approves or disapproves of the needs in question.

The study of an allocator's response to recipients' needs is further complicated by the influence of pragmatic considerations such as the desire to preserve harmony and maximize productivity. A recipient whose needs are unsatisfied is likely to behave antagonistically. Consequently, the allocator who seeks to maintain harmony will tailor his response to fit the recipient's desires. Similarly, the allocator who seeks to maximize productivity will try to give recipients the kinds and amounts of resources they need to perform task activities.

Work by Leventhal, Weiss, and Buttrick (1973) demonstrates the impact of another pragmatic factor on an allocator's response to information about recipients' needs, namely, his desire to conserve resources. Allocators are often concerned about minimizing waste and utilizing available resources as efficiently

as possible. Consequently, an allocator may be reluctant to give valuable resources to recipients who will not use them, to the exclusion of other recipients
who will. Leventhal, Weiss, and Buttrick confirmed this suggestion by manipulating subjects' concern about preventing waste. Some subjects believed the
resources they were distributing would deteriorate if not used promptly, i.e.,
there was high potential for waste. These subjects displayed a significantly
stronger tendency than others to give more resources to recipients who needed
them and were likely to use them. Thus, the more an allocator seeks to minimize
waste, the more he is likely to distribute resources in accordance with recipients'
needs.

A complex array of factors influences an allocator's response to recipients'
needs. These factors include a family of partially overlapping allocation norms,
namely, a norm of Marxian Justice, a social responsibility norm, and a mutual
responsiveness norm. Another important factor is the consistency between the
recipient's expressed desires and the allocator's beliefs about what is best for the
recipient's long-term welfare. In addition to such altruistic concerns, an allocator's responsiveness to recipients' needs is influenced by his desire to maximize
productivity, preserve harmony, and conserve valuable resources. These considerations suggest that the determinants of an allocator's response to recipients'
needs are more complex than has generally been recognized.

VII. Neglected Aspects of the Allocator's Role

We have examined the determinants of an allocator's decisions. However,
allocators perform many additional activities related to the problem of resource
allocation. For example, an allocator may: (1) promulgate rules which regulate
the manner in which recipients use resources; (2) preserve resources from deterioration, and defend them against unauthorized seizure; (3) increase the supply
of resources to replace current disbursements and meet future demands; and
(4) delegate allocation authority to others. Unfortunately, little theory or research has dealt with these four aspects of an allocator's behavior. Yet, they are
closely related to his allocation decisions. We shall present preliminary analyses
of these features of the allocator's role with the aim of initiating further studies
of these neglected aspects of his behavior.[3]

A. PROMULGATING RULES OF PROPER USE

An allocator may often promulgate and enforce rules concerning the manner
in which recipients may use the resources he gives them. For example, when

---

[3] I am indebted to Phyllis Hopkins, Richaurd Camp, and Jerald Greenberg for their
valuable contributions to the following formulation.

children receive regular allowances, parents may prohibit certain types of expenditures (Weinstein, 1972). Allocators in organizations also promulgate many rules concerning the proper use of resources. For example, a subject-pool coordinator in a psychology department may establish and enforce regulations concerning the proper treatment of subjects (human resources) by experimenters (recipients) who obtain subjects from the pool.

An allocator's decisions may be closely tied to his promulgation of rules of proper use. He may withhold reward until recipients are ready to comply with the rules and make his allocation responses contingent upon continued compliance. Thus, if a child makes improper expenditures, his parents may threaten to withhold his allowance. If a subject-pool coordinator learns that an experimenter is treating subjects badly, he may prohibit that experimenter from obtaining additional subjects.

B. PRESERVATION AND DEFENSE OF RESOURCES

An allocator must often take steps to preserve and defend the resources he controls. Efforts to preserve resources are necessary because many resources can deteriorate and lose their capacity to satisfy needs. For example, a housewife must store food under conditions that prevent deterioration. Similarly, she launders and mends clothes to keep them in usable condition.

An allocator may also have to defend resources against unauthorized seizure. Recipients who want more than the allocator is willing or able to give may sometimes try to circumvent him and obtain resources by improper means. For example, a young child may steal cookies when his mother is occupied elsewhere. Unauthorized seizure of resources is also common in organizations, ranging from padding of expense accounts, to theft of supplies. To defend resources, an allocator may punish acts of illicit seizure. He may also defend resources by the use of ecological control (Cartwright, 1965), i.e., by interposing environmental barriers between the recipients and the resources. For example, a mother might prevent cookie stealing by putting the cookie jar on a high shelf, or hiding it.

The occurrence or threat of unauthorized seizure may substantially alter an allocator's decisions. For example, he may reduce a recipient's rewards to punish acts of unauthorized seizure. Alternatively, if the allocator is powerless to prevent further seizures, he may increase a recipient's share of resources in order to appease him.

C. SUPPLYING ADDITIONAL RESOURCES

An allocator must often obtain additional resources in order to meet current and future demands. He must replace resources promptly to prevent depletion of the supply. He may also have to augment the supply because the number of recipients has increased. For example, when new faculty positions are created, a department chairman must obtain additional space and equipment.

Whatever the cause of increased demand for resources, an allocator will intensify his efforts to augment the available supply whenever the rate of resource distribution threatens to outstrip the rate at which resources are replenished. His attempts to augment the supply of resources may take a variety of forms. For example, he may appeal to his superiors for an increase in the total resources allotted to his group, or, if he anticipates a shortage of resources, he may institute a program of accelerated acquisition. Such a policy of hoarding would increase the supply of resources beyond current requirements and make it possible to survive a prolonged period of scarcity.

If an allocator cannot add or replace resources rapidly enough, he is likely to resort to other strategies to prevent depletion. First, he may reduce the rate at which he is dispensing resources. For example, he may withhold resources that are used for nonessential purposes. Second, he may conserve resources by reducing the number of recipients. Thus, when business is slow and financial resources are shrinking, an employer is likely to lay off personnel. Third, he may reduce the demand for resources by persuading recipients to lower their rates of consumption. By frightening them with the spectre of future shortages and appealing to their group allegiance, he can motivate them to use resources more frugally.

D. DELEGATION OF AUTHORITY

Allocators often control many resources, deal with a number of recipients simultaneously, and have many other responsibilities. Consequently, an allocator may find it necessary to delegate to others authority to make decisions about some of the resources he controls. In some cases, he may transfer the power of decision to the recipients themselves. Thus, an allocator may permit recipients who depend on him for their resources to allocate the resources themselves. An example would be a mother who allows her young child to help himself to food snacks, or spend his allowance as he pleases. Previously, she may have kept control of food and money and allowed the child to have them only at her discretion. The transition from allocator-control to self-allocation by the recipient is probably closely related to whether the allocator believes the recipient is able and willing to self-allocate at proper times, and in proper amounts. Thus, a mother may allow her child to take his own snacks only if she believes he will not abuse the privilege.

In other cases, an allocator may delegate allocation authority to aides and give them the task of distributing rewards and resources to recipients. Often, the aides remain accountable to him. In addition, he may use his power to reverse their decisions, or take away the authority he has given them. Of course, individuals to whom allocation authority is delegated may often have considerable discretion and operate with a high degree of autonomy. Future studies must examine the conditions which cause an allocator to grant greater or lesser degrees of autonomy to his aides, and support or overturn their allocation decisions.

VIII. Summary and Conclusions

Allocation norms are important determinants of an allocator's decisions. Each norm specifies criteria for identifying a fair distribution. However, several norms are often salient at one time and each may favor a different distribution of reward. Thus, an allocator must decide which allocation norm or combination of norms to follow. Often, he follows those norms which are approved and accepted by others. His choice among allocation norms is also influenced by the specific pattern of benefits associated with following each norm. Thus, an allocator may follow the equity norm because he believes that distributing rewards and resources in accordance with recipients' contributions will maximize performance and productivity over the long term. The benefits of equitable allocations stem from the fact that giving more to better performers reinforces and strengthens their task behavior, strengthens their loyalty to the group, and provides them with resources they need to carry out their work. Equitable allocations may also stimulate poor performers to quit the group and thereby upgrade the overall quality of group performance.

It must be emphasized that an allocator who desires to maximize productivity does not always closely follow a policy of distributing rewards equitably. For example, if he desires to elicit rapid improvement, he may employ a strategy of overreward. To motivate poor performers, he may sometimes give them higher reward than their performance merits.

Equitable distributions of rewards and resources may have negative side effects. For example, poor performers who receive low reward may be dissatisfied and behave antagonistically. Such negative reactions may interfere with task activity and threaten the allocator's position. Accordingly, an allocator usually desires to preserve harmony and may deviate from equity to do so. Instead of rewarding recipients in accordance with their contributions, he may follow the equality norm and distribute records evenly. Equal distributions appease poor performers by inflating their rewards. Consequently, the threat of disruptive interpersonal conflict is reduced. However, an allocator who desires to preserve harmony often stops short of complete equalization of rewards. His desire to minimize antagonism and simultaneously maximize productivity may lead him to reduce the difference between the rewards of good and poor performers but still give more to better performers.

An allocator may use other methods for influencing recipients' behavior besides his delivery of reward. For example, to reduce dissatisfaction and antagonism, he may maintain secrecy about his distribution of reward, or mislead recipients about the causes of his allocation decisions. In addition, he may enhance their estimate of the value of the rewards they have received. To the extent such strategies reduce dissatisfaction, they will affect the allocator's distribution of rewards and resources. He is less likely to inflate the rewards of poor performers.

Other rules of allocation besides the equity and equality norms benefit the allocator. For example, he can reduce cognitive and emotional strain by following a norm of adhering to commitments. Recipients will also be more satisfied in such cases because their expectations are met. By following the norm of reciprocity, the allocator can strengthen the bonds between himself and the recipients. A family of partially overlapping allocation norms affects the allocator's responsiveness to recipients' needs. These norms satisfy his altruistic desire to protect recipients' welfare. However, his response to recipients' needs also depends on pragmatic considerations such as his desire to conserve valuable resources, maximize productivity, and preserve harmony.

Many aspects of an allocator's behavior require further study and conceptualization. For example, processes involved in the regularization of allocation responses are not well understood. When allocators make repeated deliveries of reward to the same recipients, they are likely to establish a schedule for delivering specified amounts of reward at specified times. Little is known about the factors which determine the allocator's timing of his delivery of reward. An allocator often formulates plans in advance for distributing rewards and resources. However, he may not execute his plan until circumstances are appropriate. It is therefore necessary to distinguish between decision responses which formulate allocation plans and delivery responses which actually transfer rewards and resources to the recipients. In many social systems, the task of making allocation decisions is separated from the task of delivering rewards. Some individuals serve only as deliverers who carry out the actual transfer of resources but take no part in deciding how much various recipients are to receive.

Several other important aspects of the allocator's role require further study. For example, in conjunction with his allocation decisions, an allocator often promulgates and enforces rules concerning the manner in which recipients may use rewards and resources. In addition, he must often preserve resources from deterioration, or defend them from unauthorized seizure. Allocators are also called upon to augment the supply of reward and resources in order to meet increasing demands and prevent depletion of essential resources. Finally, an allocator may often delegate power and give others authority to distribute some of the resources and rewards he controls.

The analysis of allocation behavior has important theoretical and applied implications. For example, it is closely related to the study of leadership. A leader's control of rewards and resources is a major source of his authority over subordinates. Furthermore, the manner in which he handles problems of allocation is very likely to determine his success in facilitating group goals, and his ability to retain his position.

The study of allocators' behavior complements the study of recipients' behavior. Many studies have examined the effects of varying the amount and timing of rewards on recipients' behavior. Much less attention has been given to analyzing the behavior of the allocators who dispense rewards. Yet, to understand the influence of rewards on social behavior, it is necessary to understand the allocator as well as the recipient. It is the allocator who establishes many of the reward contingencies which control recipients' behavior. To a considerable extent, he determines the structure of the reinforcing environment.

The analysis of allocation behavior has important implications for planning programs to modify the behavior of individuals, groups, or organizations. In most settings, existing allocation practices tend to support existing patterns of recipient behavior. To change recipients' behavior, the distribution of rewards and resources must be changed, i.e., the behavior of the allocators who distribute them must be changed. Once allocators alter their practices, attendant changes in reinforcement contingencies will modify recipients' behavior. However, allocators may be reluctant to adopt new allocation policies. Furthermore, even if they are forced to adopt a new allocation plan, they may undermine its effectiveness by executing it improperly (Reppucci & Saunders, 1974; Rivlin, 1974). Thus, the problem of effecting change in individual or group behavior is, in part, a problem of modifying the behavior of allocators. More generally, the importance of studying allocation behavior derives from the fact that allocation decisions have profound effects on individual and group welfare. Allocation decisions determine the fate of groups and organizations.

DESERVING AND THE EMERGENCE
OF FORMS OF JUSTICE[1]

Melvin J. Lerner,[2] Dale T. Miller,[3]

and

John G. Holmes

UNIVERSITY OF WATERLOO
WATERLOO, ONTARIO, CANADA

[1] The research reported in this article was done at the University of Waterloo and supported by grants from the Canada Council S-70-1251 and S-73-0194.

[2] On Sabbatical leave: East-West Culture Learning Institute, East-West Center, Honolulu, Hawaii.

[3] Present address: Department of Psychology, University of Western Ontario, London, Ontario, Canada.

I. The Personal and Social Contract

A. DIVERGING PERSPECTIVES OF SOCIAL REALITY

The related themes of justice and deserving pervade the entire fabric of our society. Our mythology and religious systems abound with illustrations of industry and "goodness" triumphing over laziness and evil. On the basis of his experience with peers and adults, the child learns that deserving is the appropriate path to one's fate. Those who violate this relation by cheating or opportunistic acts will be punished sooner or later; those who are unjustly deprived will be compensated in the long run.

The evidence for the importance of the theme of justice in our society can be strikingly juxtaposed against the equally vivid signs of institutionalized injustice and widespread indifference to the fate of innocent victims. The most familiar way of integrating this apparently contradictory evidence is to portray the concern for justice and fairness as nothing more than a veneer, which masks the more basic attributes of self-interest, greed, and apathy. It is possible to make a case for the image of the typical citizen as someone whose concern for his fellow man goes only as far as his perceived self-interest will allow. The common expression, "What's in it for me?" provides an apt embodiment of the sentiment implied by this description.

On the other hand, there is an emerging body of evidence derived from systematic observation which indicates that this is a limited, and probably mistaken, image of the way people actually judge and react to events. The "social paradox" of layers of motivation that appear to be inconsistent and in virtual conflict—"egoism versus altruism"—may in fact be moved toward resolution by hypothesizing that most people not only care deeply about justice for themselves and others but also that justice and deserving are central organizing themes in their lives.

B. PRELIMINARY CONCEPTS OF JUSTICE AND DESERVING

Before looking at the evidence relevant to this hypothesis it is necessary to be somewhat more explicit about how the concepts of "justice" and "deserving" are used here. Although various theorists have treated the definition in a conceptually more systematic way, "deserving" refers essentially to the relation between a person and his outcomes. A person deserves an outcome if he has met the appropriate "preconditions" for obtaining it. If a person does not get the outcome or gets something judged to be of less value, then he has not received all he deserved. Of course, the outcomes in question can be negative rather than positive in nature.

Within any society there are rules which dictate what people should do to obtain rewards and avoid suffering, as well as a set of preconditions that should eventuate in gain or loss. Theoretical positions such as "distributive justice" (Homans, 1961) and "equity theory" (cf., Adams, 1965; Walster, Berscheid, & Walster, 1973; Leventhal and Anderson, 1970) have tried to describe more or less precisely the conditions that will lead a person to see his outcomes as fair and just and to predict his reactions to states of felt injustice. In a complex and changing society, however, the rules for determining the appropriate preconditions for specific desired outcomes are very often vague or in flux. The common ground of these various theories, including our own, is that in social situations where ambiguity exists, people turn to others for a stable referent: "I deserve what others who are like me have" (Festinger, 1954; Pettigrew, 1967).

The concept of justice introduces another person or humanlike figure into the scene. When another person is seen to be the cause of someone's outcome being less desirable than he deserves, then an injustice has occurred. Although the inflicter of injustice is usually identified as another person, the inflicter can also be an agency of society, or an abstract process such as "progress" or "social change." In any case, the inflicter of an injustice is assumed, at the time of the judgment, to have "caused" the person's outcomes to be less than deserved.

C. THE PSYCHOLOGY OF DESERVING: A DEVELOPMENTAL PERSPECTIVE

With these notions of deserving and justice in mind we can now approach the more substantive issue of the extent to which people care about justice and the way these concerns affect their lives. First, let us examine more carefully the question of why people care at all about justice and deserving. One possibility is suggested by a consideration of a developmental sequence, particularly the transition from living by the "pleasure" principle to living by the "reality" principle (Hall, 1954). Through a blending of structure and experience, a child eventually recognizes that it is to his long-term benefit to give up using the power he has at hand to gratify his impulses immediately. He adopts the alternative of incurring the costs of frustrated impulses and investing efforts on the *assumption* that an appropriately more desirable outcome will accrue to him in the future. In effect, the child makes a *"personal contract"* with himself to orient himself to the world on the basis of what he earns or deserves via his prior investments rather than on the basis of what he can get at any given moment. He learns and trusts that his world is a place where additional investments often entitle him to better outcomes, and that "earning" or "deserving" is an effective way of obtaining what he desires. As the child matures he places greater portions of his goal-seeking activities under the rules of deserving, so that in the normal course of events, he eventually finds that his life is committed and organized on the basis of "deserving" his outcomes.

D. PERSONAL CONTRACT AND JUSTICE

The link between the person's private endeavors to deserve his desired outcomes and his concern with the fate of others in his environment is based, at least in part, on potential threats to his "personal contract." One of these recurring threats is the person's desire for the immediate gratification of his urges and wants. The person often simply wants to let go, to do what feels good rather than what is sensible or right in terms of what he "deserves." The second type of threat derives from the "contract's" dependence on an "orderly" physical and social environment. In order to live by his "contract," the person must assume that if he does make the appropriate investments, his world is constructed so that the anticipated outcomes will follow. This is not always the case, of course. Seemingly fortuitous events or the planned acts of other people can intervene so that one's investments are wasted.

If for important functional and adaptive reasons the person wants to maintain his "contract," then any evidence that deserving efforts are not appropriately compensated presents a threat, especially in the face of pressing internal impulses for immediate gratification. Thus, if the person becomes aware that someone else who lives in and is vulnerable to the same environment has received undeserved suffering or failed to get what he deserved, the issue must arise as to whether the person himself can trust his environment. The viability of his "personal contract" becomes questionable. Obviously, then, to the extent that it is to the person's advantage to maintain his contract, he will be motivated to maintain and protect the belief that he lives in (or can create) an environment where each person's fate corresponds to what he deserves, in other words, a *"just world."* The adverse psychological consequences of a lack of trust in one's environment have been described in other sources (Erikson, 1950; Jessor *et al.,* 1968; Merton, 1957).

A second factor which links the person's private concern with deserving to the fates of those around him is the issue of *limited, desired* goals. Other than combat in which raw power generally prevails, there are roughly two ways in which contesting interests can be resolved. Often, some form of institutionalized competition is allowed to take place so that the person who invests the most in terms of effort and ability prevails. In other cases, the members agree to distribute the desired resource on the basis of a more direct assessment of each person's "investment" in it.

Both of these means of resolving contesting interests imply development of the kind of "social contract" described by Piaget (1932) and others (Blau, 1964; Gouldner, 1960). A crucial psychological link between the "personal contract" and these social norms is the person's recognition of an "equivalence" between himself and others. The child understands that, although he is separate and distinct from others, he can be in a similar "position" in relation to a desired outcome. The norms, then, protect the investments of the person, and by implication, everyone in his social world. In addition, they reduce the costs of destructive conflicts that would decrease the value of the limited goals, and preserve the increased benefits that accrue to living within an integrated social organization (Campbell, 1969). In one sense, the "two-way" social contract of norms provides the structured social reality that maintains the personal contract of each individual.

The major point to be made here is that the person, if he attempts to operate effectively in his environment, *will develop a sense of deserving and will become aware of the contingency of his own ability to deserve his outcomes upon the ability of other people to orient themselves similarly.* The personal contract can only be maintained in a "just world." In addition, most people who are successfully socialized in western society will have internalized the values of justice and deserving. Not only will the person judge himself on the basis of what he has earned and deserved, but he will base an important part of his *self-image* as a good person and a citizen on the perception of himself as someone who causes others no harm and who will act to correct injustices when they occur. Finally, the citizen of this society generally expects that other people will judge him by the extent to which he meets these norms of deserving and maintaining justice.

E. THE JUST WORLD HYPOTHESIS

If a person foresakes immediate gratification to orient himself toward future deserving, any evidence that social reality is not preserving *justice for others* is threatening, and should motivate the individual to restore his belief that he does live in a just world.

Although the "belief in a just world" is a tentatively held *hypothesis,* it is backed by strong, motivational forces. Any evidence that deserving for others is not maintained calls into question one's own prior commitments, efforts, unfulfilled investments, and present beliefs, and allows one's immediate impulses and desires to surface. To avoid these conflicts people should care strongly about seeing justice preserved for others.

There is a large body of evidence, both anecdotal and systematic, to indicate the extent to which people in this society want to believe that they live in a world where people ultimately get what they deserve. To witness one of the most compelling manifestations of this belief one has only to look at the way many people approach their religions. God, for instance, is perceived as one who ensures that the next life will "balance the scales" and that each person will get his just deserts. The "just world" belief also finds common expression in the "good guy/bad guy" or "ingroup/outgroup" theme which pervades both our present culture's media and most anthropological evidence (LeVine and Campbell, 1972). The "good guy" may experience temporary adversity and minor defeats at the hands of the "bad guy," but ultimately he triumphs. Whenever "goodness" does not triumph over "evil" people tend to experience stress and displeasure (Tannenbaum & Gaer, 1965).

The research designed to examine these hypotheses began with the assumption that people are motivated to believe they live in a "just world" where everyone gets what he deserves. Any evidence that this is not the case is "threatening" to this motive and therefore elicits efforts to eliminate the threat. These efforts may take the form of behavior designed to correct the unjust state of affairs—compensating the victim and/or punishing the inflicter of the injustice—if there is one. On the other hand, it was reasoned, if the person who witnesses the injustice, is unable, for various reasons, to reestablish justice he can persuade himself that no injustice has occurred, after all. The most functional change in his perceptions of the event would be to discover that the victim had done something for which he merited his fate. For example, Lerner (1965) found that observers persuaded themselves that whichever worker in a group task received an arbitrarily assigned large bonus was the one who had earned it by his comparatively outstanding performance.

We next turned our attention to the question of what happens if, for one reason or another, the observer cannot attribute the victim's fate to something he did or failed to do. This seemed to typify the most prevalent form of "victim situation" in our society and also afforded the best test of our theoretical ideas. What would happen if "innocent observers" were confronted with the suffering of an innocent victim? Certainly, the observers should be motivated to correct the injustice. What would happen then? According to our notions, the observers should initially be upset, disturbed, and then for the sake of their own comfort and security try to persuade themselves that the seemingly innocent victim was the kind of person for whom this suffering was not an inappropriate fate. All the observers had to do was decide that the victim was a less than desirable person, at least in some respects—selfish, unintelligent, crude, etc.—and then they could feel more comfortable. Unfortunately, it is relatively easy to see ourselves or anyone else, for that matter, in this negative light. All that is required is selective attention, recall, and emphasis concerning behaviors that we all exhibit from time to time.

Certainly, those who see what appears to be unjust suffering do not resort to this kind of derogation of a victim automatically and uniformly. They are probably in a state of conflict between maintaining a veridical but disturbing view of what is happening and indulging in the more comfortable solution of reducing the sense of injustice by derogating the victim. Other things being equal, most people if impotent to alter the state of affairs will sooner or later indulge in the latter more satisfying alternative. In a sense it is functional for the observer—at least on a short-term basis—since it enables him to maintain his belief that he lives in a world where he can deserve his fate.

To test these hypotheses we allowed students who believed they were involved in a study of cues of emotional arousal to watch an experiment on human learning over closed-circuit T.V. What they saw ostensibly was another undergraduate who was trapped by the "system" and "Dr. Stewart" into receiving severe electric shocks while trying to learn pairs of nonsense syllables. The results of a number of experiments involving this or a very similar paradigm showed that (a) most observers, if given the opportunity, would vote to end the victim's suffering and see to it that she received compensation for her suffering; (b) if they believed they were successful in rescuing and compensating the victim or that the victim would be compensated by Dr. Stewart in the end, they viewed her in a rather "neutral," objective light; (c) also, if they believed they both (the observer and the victim) had been vulnerable and the victim drew a critical slip which decided their respective fates, she was not derogated, and in fact was often seen in a very positive light; (d) on the other hand, the observer's evaluation of the victim became increasingly negative, the greater her undeserved suffering, and (e) the most derogation occurred when the victim was portrayed as the "martyr"—someone whose altruistic motives made her vulnerable to being exploited by Dr. Stewart; (f) as one might have expected, observers who were either informed that the purpose of the research was to study the way people react to victims in society and/or made aware that the victim was merely acting and not actually being shocked did not portray the "victim" in any negative manner or were they able to predict the derogation of the "innocent victim" or the "martyr" (Lerner and Simmons, 1966; Lerner, 1970; Lerner, 1971; Simons and Piliavin, 1972).

So it appears that, at least in the experimental situation we created, observers would try to rescue and compensate an innocent "victim," but barring that possibility, altered their evaluations of the victim's personal attributes as a function of the extent to which her fate was unjust. Other investigators employing the same or a similar experimental situation found that the reactions to undeserved suffering were not unique to the various samples we employed: Undergraduate and graduate students from the health professions at the University of Kentucky, high school students from Berkeley, California (Piliavin, Hardyck, and Vadim, 1967), housewives from a lower socio-economic area in one of the Canadian Maritime Provinces (Johnson and Dickinson, 1971), students from the University of Pennsylvania (Simons and Piliavin, 1972), and the University of Western Ontario (Sorrentino and Hardy, in press) altered their evaluations of the victim to fit her fate: the more undeserved suffering the lower the evaluation.

Experiments employing other situations have also demonstrated the observer's desire to find or create a correspondence between what happens to someone and what he deserves by virtue or his personal attributes. MacDonald (1971) confronted his subjects with the report of a stabbing in which the innocence of the victim was varied. The results revealed that the less responsible for his fate the victim was portrayed as being, the lower was his rated attractiveness. A somewhat similar study was reported by Jones and Aronson (1973). In a simulated jury context, a defendant was depicted as having raped (or attempted to rape) a married woman, a virgin, or a divorcee. Pretesting had established that subjects differentiated between these three categories in terms of respectability, with the virgin being most respectable, and the divorcee least respectable. Not surprisingly, subjects sentenced the same defendant to a longer term if they believed he raped a virgin than a divorcee. More interestingly, the victim of the rape was seen as personally more responsible for the event when she was either a virgin or a married woman than when she was a divorcee. The knowledge that innocent, highly respectable females can be raped is most threatening to one's belief that the world is just. To avoid the threat posed by this type of admission, it was necessary to find fault with the actions of the victim. The victim must not really be totally innocent; she must have contributed, at least in some small but significant way, to her fate (cf. Lerner and Simmons, 1966). In the case of the less respectable divorcee, there was less need to find a behavioral explanation. The rape of a divorcee does not pose as much threat to a belief in a just world as the rape of the much more "respectable" married woman or virgin.

A study reported by Lincoln and Levinger (1972) also demonstrated that innocent and uncompensated suffering often produces lowered evaluation of a victim. In their study, subjects were confronted with a black man who was the innocent victim of a policeman's attack. Subjects who were unable to rectify the injustice of the situation tended to lower their evaluation of the victim. Those observers who were able to lodge a public complaint against the assaulting policemen, however, showed no such victim condemnation.

F. INDIVIDUAL JUSTICE

Although the need or desire to believe one lives in a just world may be an important motive for most people, certainly the extent to which any of us are able to construe our experiences to fit this need will vary. Recognizing this, Rubin and Peplau (1973) devised a relatively direct and simple paper-and-pencil measure to assess the degree to which people would express the belief that they lived in a just world ("Just World Scale"). They assumed that the belief in a just world was a relatively stable and measurable dimension along which people would vary and the degree of acceptance of this belief should be predictive of people's reactions in a variety of situations. For example, in one study they found that people who scored highly on the JWS were relatively unsympathetic to peers who were less fortunate than they were in a draft lottery.

The construct validity of the JWS has been strengthened by a recent, factor analytic study (Lerner, 1973). Using a Canadian subject population, Lerner found that belief in a just world was associated with liking for winners (e.g.,

Americans) and dislike for losers (e.g., Indians and Metis). Consistent with this relationship, it was also found that responses of people who were high on the "Just World Scale" correlated with the belief that people can exercise control over their lives through effort and self-sacrifice.

Employing a different strategy, Sorrentino and Hardy (in press) examined the relationship between religiosity and perceptions of victims. In a situation similar to that used by Lerner and Simmons, subjects high or low in professed religiosity observed a person (learner) receiving either painful shocks (experimental condition) or no shock (control condition) for making errors in a serial learning task. The perceptions of the low-religious group revealed the just world effect, with the learner in the experimental condition (victim) being evaluated more negatively than the learner in the control condition. The individuals in the high-religious group, however, showed no difference across conditions. Thus, it would seem that people who have strong religious convictions do not appear to be threatened by more temporary and immediate imbalances in justice. For these people, it is the life after death that will be just, not the present life.

Of course, as the findings of Sorrentino and Hardy (in press) illustrate, not everyone who witnesses an injustice will derogate the victim when they are unable to reestablish justice by other means. Many of us recognize injustices, are disturbed by them, recognize our impotence to alter the state of affairs, and yet we do not resort to blaming the victim. Even in the initial experiment (Lerner and Simmons, 1966), approximately a third of the subjects condemned the experiment and Dr. Stewart, rather than the girl who was suffering. More recent research has been able to verify what most of us might guess to be an important determinant of whether one rejects the victim or maintains the distressing alternative of condemning the inflicter.

G. "IDENTIFICATION" WITH THE VICTIM

To a certain extent it is simply a matter of with whom we "identify." Identification, however, has various meanings, and fortunately the research has helped to delineate some of these. At one extreme is the experiment by Aderman *et al.* (1974). They employed three sets of experimental instructions, one of which requested that the subject imagine that he was the victim, a second which instructed him to watch the victim, and a third derived from the instructions employed by Lerner and Simmons. They report rejection of the victim in the latter two conditions but no condemnation when the subjects were identified with the victim in terms of imagining that the suffering was happening to them. Somewhat less explicitly, Chaikin and Darley (1973) had their subjects watch an event in which a supervisor "accidentally" ruined the product of his worker's good efforts. Half of their subjects were led to believe they were to be supervisors in the next situation, the other half thought they would be workers.

This was done to vary the subject's set in terms of identifying with either the supervisor or the worker—"that could be me." The results showed that when the consequences to the worker were serious—he was a victim of undeserved deprivation—those who anticipated being a worker blamed the supervisor, while those who expected to be a supervisor found him blameless and quite competent while condemning the worker as an undesirable person.

Stokols and Schopler (1973) employed the least direct form of "identification." They merely varied whether the subject expected to engage in a discussion about sexual mores with the victim or someone else. Before entering into the discussion all the subjects read a case history of the victim which had to do with her becoming pregnant and then having an abortion. At present she was doing fine. By changing certain parts of the history, Stokols and Schopler created additional experimental conditions involving greater or less severe consequences associated with the victim's fate, and greater or less responsibility on the victim's part for what happened to her—in one case she was careless in the use of contraceptives (responsible) and in the other she was the innocent victim of rape. Their results showed that the detached observers—those who did not expect to interact with the victim—saw the victim as a less desirable person as a function of the severity of her fate. The relative condemnation of the victim occurred whether she was portrayed as "careless" or "innocent." However, those who were identified with the victim in the sense of anticipating meeting and talking with her did not show any signs of lowering their evaluation of her as a function of her suffering. Apparently, those who were "identified" with her did not indulge themselves in the comforting mechanism of condemning the "innocent" victim for her fate.

II. The Development of the "Personal Contract" and Altruism

Our discussion of the evidence of the belief in a just world suggests that people, when confronted with undeserved suffering and deprivation which they cannot eliminate, frequently derogate the victim as a means of restoring their sense of justice. But in many situations people *do* have the power to maintain or restore justice, and the question may arise: what form, if any, will their concern for justice take in these situations? The theoretical model proposed here can provide the framework for some hypotheses. A dynamic interdependence was proposed between the development of the "personal contract" and social justice. The child who fulfills the conditions of his personal contract by restraining his impulses, feels *entitled,* first and foremost, to "appropriate" levels of personal deserving. Justice for others is essentially a "derived" requirement, that in certain circumstances may be less central in the child's personal world. Personal deserving then, is both conceptually and motivationally "prior" to justice for others.

A. CHILDREN'S DESERVING AND HELPING BEHAVIOR

Two recent studies provide more direct tests of these notions in the context of the latter type of situations. Long and Lerner (1974) enlisted grade-four children to test a toy for a toy company at either a "proper-pay" rate or at an "overpaid" rate. These children were later allowed to donate money to a poor orphan. The donating behavior was done either under anonymous conditions, or when the child believed the experimenter, the teacher, or future younger subjects would know what he did. A measure of each child's tolerance for delayed gratification was also taken. The delay of gratification measure was obtained as a rough index of the extent to which the child was affected by considerations of "deserving." The willingness to delay gratification—give up immediate rewards in favor of greater rewards to be obtained at a later time—was a necessary precondition for giving up the "pleasure" principle orientation and developing the "personal contract."

While there is some evidence of an association between scores on this paper-and-pencil measure of delay of gratification and measures of "social responsibility" (Mischel, 1961), Long and Lerner did not predict a simple positive relation between a child's willingness to delay gratification and the extent of his altruism or helping behavior. Instead, they expected that Hi DG children (those above the median of their class on Mischel's scale because they are more committed to a personal contract) would be more likely to follow the demands of deserving and justice which would appear as more, or less "altruism" depending on the situation. The Lo DG subjects (below the median) were expected to be more affected by the anticipated direct rewards and punishments.

The results were nicely consistent with these hypotheses. Children who were "overpaid" donated more money to the orphan than did children who were "properly paid." The difference between the two payment conditions suggests that the children were responding in terms of whether or not they deserved the amount they were paid. Apparently, the children were willing to give up more of their money—reduce their outcomes—when they believed they did not deserve the total amount they were given. This is similar, in essence, to what Adams and Jacobsen (1964) found with adults hired to do marketing interviewing.

The results also provided support for the important theoretical link between the child's concern with deserving and the willingness to delay gratification. In the "proper-payment" condition, Hi DG children donated considerably less than the Lo DG subjects. In the overpayment condition, however, the Hi DG children gave significantly more than their Lo DG counterparts. An examination of the interaction indicated that the effect of overpayment was due entirely to the donations of the Hi DG children, while the behavior of Lo DG children did not differ across conditions.

The Lo DG children donated relatively little under both levels of payment when they were anonymous. They simply "wanted" the money so they kept it if they thought their "selfish" acts would go undetected. The Hi DG subjects, on the other hand, responded according to what they felt they deserved regardless of who would know of their donations. In the proper-payment condition the Hi DG children gave little because they felt they deserved and had earned all the money. When they felt overpaid, however, their commitment to deserving motivated them to donate relatively large amounts to the poor orphan.

Important evidence for these inferences comes from the findings that the presence or absence of an audience affected only the behavior of the Lo DG children. These children, presumably because of their greater sensitivity to external sanctions than to the internal standards of deserving, donated substantially more money under surveillance than under nonsurveillance conditions.

A second study by Braband and Lerner (1973) probed more extensively the relationship between one's personal commitment to deserving and helping behavior. As with the Long and Lerner study, children high and low on delay of gratification were made to feel that they were "properly paid" or "overly rewarded" for their investments, in this case, in an essay-writing assignment. Unlike the Long and Lerner study, however, the "deservingness" of the recipient was also varied. In one condition, the victim, a child like themselves, had to copy out arithmetic problems by hand because his "carelessness" had caused the copying machine to break, while in the other condition, he had to copy out the problems because the copying machine had "accidentally" broken. The measure of helping behavior employed was the number of arithmetic problems the subject copied for the victim.

The only main effect to emerge from the analysis was for delay of gratification, revealing that the children scoring high on this measure helped significantly more than those scoring low. The variables of "own deservingness" and "other's responsibility" only affected the helping behavior of the Hi DG children. When these children felt that they did not deserve their outcomes (free time), they appeared to be sensitive to the variations in the legitimacy of the other's dependency and helped the "nonresponsible" victim more than the "responsible" victim. In the condition in which the Hi DG children had deserved their outcome, however, they were not nearly as responsive to the plight of the "nonresponsible" victim. In fact, they actually helped the "responsible" victim somewhat more than the "nonresponsible" victim in this condition.

Taken together, the results of Long and Lerner and Braband and Lerner provided good evidence that what had been portrayed as man's conflict between "egoism and altruism" may be instead, the conflict between two related commitments—his personal deserving and justice for others. Moreover, these studies strengthen the developmental model proposed earlier which associates the commitment to deserving with the ability to restrain impulses and forego immediate rewards and pleasures. Those children who had progressed more at that age in their willingness to delay gratification, appeared to be the ones most sensitive to issues of personal deserving and justice for others. The theory also helps us to make sense of the apparent paradox of a group of children who are both more generous and more responsive to indications of deserving on the part of others in one situation, and more "self-concerned" and insensitive in another context. The "key" is their perceived relative deserving and commitment to one's "personal contract."

B. ADULT DESERVING AND HELPING BEHAVIOR

The findings from Long and Lerner (1974) and Braband and Lerner (1973) suggested that threats to one's personal deserving may overshadow a concern for the plight of others. Those children most committed to their personal contract appeared to be responsive to the deprivation of others only when they had resources over and above their own appropriate or deserved share. The fact that this did not change when an audience was present suggests that they believed their behavior was justified and reasonable.

A study by Miller (1974) contrasts a person's strong desire to achieve justice for others when personal deserving is maintained with the defensive behavior that is evident when it is threatened. Subjects in this experiment were recruited for a concept formation task, the payment for which was $3. At the end of the task, the subjects were informed that there was an opportunity for participation in future, similar studies and were then taken to a secretary who paid them. At that point their experimenter thanked them for their help and left the scene.

At the secretary's office, subjects received one of four treatments. In all conditions, subjects were handed a written form which thanked them for their participation and asked them to indicate the number of additional sessions they would be willing to work. The experimental manipulation involved the amount of money subjects would be paid for each additional session and whether or not participation in these sessions would help a needy person. In two conditions, subjects were informed that they would receive a certain amount for each session ($3 or $2), with no mention made of a victim. In the other two conditions, subjects read about the case of a woman whose husband had deserted her and her two children. The case was allegedly brought to the attention of the Psychology Department by a local community organization. In response to the organization's request for assistance, the Psychology Department had decided to ask subjects to give up a portion of their sessional pay to assist the woman and her family. In one of these "helping" conditions, subjects were told that they would be paid $2 for each future session with another $1 going to the victim (2/1). In the other helping condition, subjects were told that both they and the victim would receive $1 for each session they signed up for (1/1). The dependent measure in this experiment was the number of 1-hour sessions subjects agreed to work.

The results indicated, not surprisingly, that the subjects were inclined to sign up for more sessions *to help the victim* (2/1) for a $2 payment than for a $1 payment (1/1). In fact, the size of the difference between these two conditions (11.9 versus 3.7 hours) suggests that subjects' behavior was not at all motivated by a desire to help, but instead, was simply a function of self-interest. A quite different conclusion was suggested, however, by a comparison of the $2 helping conditions (2/1) with the $2 (2/0) and $3 (3/0) nonhelping conditions. When the subjects expected to receive $2 for each session with an additional dollar being earned for the victim, they elected to work more sessions than subjects who were offered simply $2 (7.2) or $3 (7.4) pay for themselves for each session. On the basis of this comparison, it would seem that the behavior of subjects was guided in large part by a strong desire to help.

Another perspective on these same findings is provided by comparing the evidence for the pairs of cases where subjects' *total* pay ($2 or $3) is either kept constant or reduced in order to help others. In the $2 case, the subjects were willing to work significantly *less* if they lost earnings to help the family (1/1; $\overline{X}$ = 3.7) than if they simply received the total amount (2/0; $\overline{X}$ = 7.2) of pay themselves. Apparently when their personal deserving was threatened, the subjects' behavior supports our more negative images of man, and they *appear* to be relatively unconcerned with the suffering of others. However, a reversal of the value of the "dollar" per session is evident when the subjects have the opportunity to help and preserve a fair exchange on their own part at the same time. When the arrangement resulted in subjects maintaining a just hourly wage ($2), even with the loss of a dollar to the victim, subjects volunteered to work about 5 hours more than did subjects who were offered a $3 hourly wage but no opportunity to help a victim (11.9 versus 7.4).

This pattern of results was not mirrored by similar subjects who were removed from the very real choice points and conflicting motivations. Four groups of subjects were given detailed descriptions of the experimental situations and asked to predict how the "real" subjects would respond. They expected that people would react directly to only the incentives offered, with subjects in the 3/0 condition predicted to work most hours (2/0 the next, etc). A simple, rule-following or normative explanation does not appear sufficient to generate the experimental findings.

It is interesting that the $2 and $3 helping conditions elicited similar results. This suggests either that the subjective utility of the $2 and $3 did not differ for the subjects, or that there was something both additionally desirable and "aversive" about the latter arrangement. An example of this, predictable from various theories, is that for some subjects the $3.00 is viewed as an inequitable overpayment. The "overpayment" interpretation seems unlikely, however, in these circumstances. The subjects were paid $3 for their first session, and should, if anything, have perceived this amount as an appropriate payment. Also, nothing was communicated either implicitly or explicitly to the effect that this was overpayment. Typically, experiments on overpayment have very explicitly contrasted the earnings to appropriate pay levels, and have not demonstrated that people will actually *avoid* a job with high levels of payment, but rather they will adjust their "inputs" or perceptions in order to restore a form of "justice." The most likely conclusion then, is that both a $2 and $3 pay level seemed within a normal range in the Psychology Department and both amounts represented fair, just pay for the subjects' time and effort.

The evidence from the experiments by Long and Lerner (1974), Braband and Lerner (1973), and Miller (1974) provides good support for our theoretical model as it has been outlined thus far. The findings fit well with our hunches about why people care about deserving and how important it is to them. Also, we were able to show that an individual's preeminent concern for personal deserving, however, often restrains or diverts him from responding to the needs of others, with the consequences that his behavior often takes on a selfish appearance in certain specifiable situations (i.e., when his concern for personal deserving is threatened).

III. The Personal Contract and the World of Victims

A. JUSTICE-BASED THREATS TO THE PERSONAL CONTRACT: THE DILEMMA

In the research presented thus far, it has been relatively clear to the person when his standards of personal deserving have been sustained or threatened. In many circumstances, however, the question of where the appropriate level of entitlement lies may exacerbate the threat and conflict experienced by a person. Under these conditions of normative ambiguity, a person's behavior may appear inconsistent and defensive. His response is, in many cases, an attempt to secure and insulate the border of the world of personal deserving from the inroads and threats represented by the "insatiable" demands from the world of potential or actual victims.

When confronted with evidence of the pathogenic conditions under which many millions of people are forced to survive, a person is likely to ask, "What *can* I do?" "Even if I responded to the needs of all the victimized and underprivileged, I would have to devote everything I have in terms of time and money. And then, how much would I have been able to do? The only thing I would definitely accomplish is to put me and my family in the same deprived conditions as 'they' are."

At this point the person can emphasize the fact that he has earned and deserved what he has. He can also recount how he, and most people he knows and respects, pay taxes, donate money and/or effort to charities, service groups, and political organizations in order to correct the injustices which he and his friends care about deeply. Everyone knows that he is a decent person, neighbor, and citizen who does more than his share to help others.

It is important to recognize that this person probably knows, and has for some time, that ours is not a "just world." He also realizes, however, that it is not entirely "unjust," and that there are really at least two worlds and that two kinds of people inhabit them. Most people with whom he has direct contact do live in a relatively just world where, by and large, they are able to get what they deserve—to live by the terms of a "personal contract" with themselves. Other people, the "different" ones, the victims of serious poverty, chronic illness, etc., do not and probably cannot get what they deserve.

This "aware" person is forced then to decide, in effect, which world he wishes to live in—the world where he can earn and get what he deserves or the world of victims where he is continually responding to the unrequitable needs of those who have less than they deserve, those who need and deserve help. Essentially, he faces the conflict between "deserving" and "justice"—between living by his *personal contract* (i.e., living in a world where he can deserve his own outcomes) and the *derived requirement*—of justice— (i.e., that he sees to it that all others get what they deserve) (Lerner, 1971).

B. DEFENDING THE PERSONAL CONTRACT: SOCIAL REFERENTS

Happily for most people, the means of resolving this conflict are immediately available. Typically, when we are forced to act in those situations where the requirements of physical or social reality are vague (either because they are complex and contradictory or because they are ill-defined), we turn to others, especially those who are similar to us, for a definition of what is "really" happening in the situation (cf., Festinger, 1954; Pettigrew, 1967). One is able then, to "insulate" his sense of personal deserving by comparing oneself to appropriate others who share a similar environment and who also have personal contracts to uphold. Any action taken on behalf of victims which may threaten a person's ability to "deserve" his outcomes must therefore be viewed within the context of the potential helper's referent group. People belonging to the same referent group have roughly similar resources at their disposal. If one person in that group decides to unilaterally reduce his resources by giving some to a victim, he will no longer be getting what he "deserves." That is, he will be receiving less than others with investments similar to his own. Moreover, by asking a person to respond to an injustice, which is not responded to by other members of his group, a person is being asked to legitimize his private responsibility to correct injustices *as they exist and as he sees and feels them,* rather than doing simply what other "good" people do.

Why then must this person resist acting on behalf of an innocent victim? The answer is that if he allows himself to respond on the basis of what he "feels" when he becomes aware of an injustice, this will threaten the legitimacy of his use of "what others do" as the guide for his actions toward victims in general. Given the vast number of people in the world who deserve help, and can elicit the compelling "internal" reaction, how will he be able (i.e., what *criterion* will he be able to employ) to establish his own right to deserve those things he desires, to keep and enjoy what he has earned, and to protect those he loves from becoming victims? The person's social referents and models enable him to maintain the boundary that protects his personal deserving, and ensures that his genuine commitment to justice does not lead him to fall prey to the "other world"—the world of victims. Without the buffers and defences that surround and help define deserving, the personal contract would be meaningless, and he would be unable to function among the majority who live in a "just world."

The person, however, also has to come to terms with that part of him which perceives the essential similarity between himself and others who are victims, and therefore "needs" to react to reestablish justice. To handle this, he may engage in *"justice gestures."* He does his part. He learns to reduce the resources he has earned by an amount through taxes, donations, etc. *In this manner he is able to maintain his self and public esteem, and most important of all he continues to have what he deserves. He continues to deserve what others who are "similar" to him have.*

Unhappily for him, however, this solution to the problem is not entirely effective. If our ideas are valid, *the person who does not engage in cognitive changes to justify his reaction will remain continually vulnerable to the immutable demands of justice and deserving for others.* Every time a victim's suffering becomes salient this person will be upset, threatened, and motivated to reestablish justice. He will also almost invariably resist these impulses and maintain his publicly sanctioned solution to the conflict, but not without some pain and cost (Lerner, 1971).

Let us recapitulate our ideas to this point, in order to make the directions and implications clear. When people are faced with cases of injustice where helping would clearly violate personal deserving, little if any action is likely to be taken to restore justice for others (Long and Lerner, 1974; Braband and Lerner, 1973; Miller, 1974).

The above studies also suggest that in cases where people can help others and clearly maintain their personal deserving, they will often exert considerable effort or incur high costs to restore justice for others. In such situations, people also appear to be responsive to the degree and type of injustice. For instance, Braband and Lerner (1973) report that high DG children helped a "nonresponsible" victim more than one responsible for his fate when they had resources over and above what they deserved. This finding helps elaborate those of earlier studies in quite different contexts. A number of studies (Schopler and Matthews, 1965; Berkowitz, 1969; Horowitz; 1968) have shown that people in need of help are much more likely to receive it if their need was brought about by factors beyond their control than if their deprivation was of their own making.

Berkowitz (1973) has evidence that more help will be given where the need is seen as "legitimate." We would also expect people to be sensitive to such normal variations as the degree of need, the "class size," the consequences of failing to help, and so on, when their personal deserving is clearly maintained.

C. OTHER DEFENSES: SYMBOLIC THREATS

We have emphasized the point, however, that one's judgments of personal deserving are often ambiguous and fraught with uncertainty. The importance of social referents and models as one way of deriving clarity and reducing threat was presented. However, many people remain vulnerable to pleas of injustice even when they have the inaction of similar others to "protect" them. In many cases people therefore will choose to help in situations which offer them the protection of firm guidelines as to what can be expected of them or which enable them to avoid clear attributions that would legitimize their private responsibility to correct injustices. Characteristics of the victims that set limits on potentially insatiable demands would also help to buffer the threat to personal deserving.

This set of defenses serves a function similar to that of social referents in helping to reduce the ambiguity associated with personal deserving and justice for others by making the person sensitive to variations in levels and types of injustice, but in a way that may appear inconsistent with the notion of a just world. Apparently we learn to view a request for help not only from the perspective of what the demand is on the surface, but what it *implies* for one's own deserving: a *symbolic threat,* if you will. As a result, people are more likely to be responsive to cases of injustice that require little more than gestures, and avoid situations where effective acts are called for.

An interesting hypothesis which follows from this analysis is that when their own deserving is threatened or ambiguous often people will choose to help victims who received a low priority in the situations discussed above where personal deserving was clearly maintained. In these "threatening" circumstances, it is relatively "safe" psychologically to come to the aid of those who are either responsible for or deserve their fate, whose need is not comparatively high or not "legitimate," or who represent only a small class of individuals. In these situations, boundaries and limits are set that reduce the symbolic threat.

D. A FIELD STUDY OF THE EXCHANGE FICTION

The behavior of some fund-raising organizations indicates that they are not entirely insensitive to the problems of symbolic threat. Many employ a strategy, perhaps unwittingly, which may substantially reduce the threat posed by helping a victim, even a large class of victims. We refer here to the *exchange* of a service or a product for a contribution to a victim group. By selling a product (light bulbs, address stickers, magazine subscriptions, etc.) it appears that charities are able to collect more money than by simply soliciting contributions. Why should this be so? It may be that people simply feel the product is worth the money they give and their behavior is not at all affected by the fact that there is a victim group associated with the product. The high profit made in these types of exchanges, however, suggests that this is not the entire answer. Another explanation is that by receiving something in exchange for the help, people are able to obviate their feelings of commitment and vulnerability. In this type of arrangement people are provided with the fiction or the illusion that, while they may be helping victims, it is not an unconditional act of help. They are not legitimizing the status of the victims, nor are they assuming personal responsibility for reducing the victim's suffering. They are simply entering into an *exchange relationship* with the victim. Such an action does not make them vulnerable to future demands by the victim group which do not involve an exchange, nor does it make them vulnerable to the demands of similar victims who do not have anything to exchange.

Some evidence from a field study done by the present authors offers some preliminary support for the notion of an "exchange fiction" (Holmes, Miller, & Lerner, 1974). The experimenters presented themselves to subjects on the university campus as representatives of charitable organizations. In one case, appeals were made for donations to buy new uniforms for a children's softball team. In the other, the group was presented as more deserving and in greater need of help: requests were made for perceptually handicapped children who had difficult problems in coping with normal activities. The representatives were distributing decorative candles for $3.00 apiece for these groups. The subjects were told that $1.00 out of this amount would go to the charity. The "fairness" of the exchange *as a transaction* was varied in the presentations. The candles were described as normally selling for $2, $3, or $4 in most stores. In the $2.00 condition, the person was therefore paying $1.00 "extra" for the candle "in order to help the charity." The $3.00 condition represented a fair, competitive price for the produce, whereas the $4.00 condition was a "bargain" that could not be obtained elsewhere. Control conditions were also run where the representatives simply asked for $1.00 donations (the amount that would go to charity if one bought a candle) or $3.00 donations.

The type of transaction (or donation) had no apparent effect on contributions in the "low-need" conditions—the amount of giving was uniformly low (about 30 cents on the average). The subjects did not appear to be at all interested in the candles for their own sake. However, when the candles were sold for "fair" prices in the "high-need" conditions, the average contribution was about $1.75; the $3 and $4 "normal cost" conditions did not differ. On the other hand, contributions dropped sharply ($1.20) when the price did not represent a fair exchange (the $2 normal price). The $1 (or $3) *donation* control groups produced roughly equivalent amounts for the handicapped children (55 cents on the average), while the low-need, children's softball teams received somewhat less (36 cents).

There may be various explanations for the findings of this preliminary study. It is important, however, to recognize that the victim's need alone had relatively little effect in obtaining donations from the people in this experiment. Also, the product employed in the exchange—the candles—had little market appeal itself. It was the combination of these two that created the expected and interesting effects. The amount of donations obtained by the two control conditions where people were simply asked to donate multiples of a dollar to the low-need softball team or the "high-need" handicapped children did not differ strongly from each other. Also, the addition of the candle sale to the low-need condition did not lead to any increase in the amount obtained for the group. The sale of the candle only made a difference when combined with the opportunity to help victims. As we expected, our subjects were much more willing to give money to help the handicapped children when they were allowed to act as though—pretend—they were engaged in a "fair" economic exchange. Even the presentation of the candles as costing more than "normal" in order to help charity seemed to erode the illusion, and led to a marked decrease in contributions. These findings fit our theoretical ideas quite well. It appears that the "exchange fiction" served a disinhibiting function. It enabled people to comply with their desire to help the victims while protecting their defenses against the implicit threat of recognizing the "legitimacy" of the demand these and other victims have for their resources.

IV. Forms of Justice

A. DESCRIPTION OF THE DIMENSIONS

At the beginning of this chapter we offered some very general preliminary definitions of the focal concepts of deserving and justice. Deserving was defined essentially as equivalent to "entitlement," the person having met the appropriate preconditions for obtaining a given outcome. Justice, and particularly the notion of injustice, was equivalent to deserving in an interpersonal context in the sense that it referred to what happened to and among other people. Although these concepts initially were most broadly defined and virtually empty of content, the description of the development of the personal contract and the procedures we employed to vary and measure the perception of deserving and justice implied fairly specific criteria for determining what someone deserves. For the most part these criteria of "entitlement" were the familiar "inputs" of effort, self-deprivation, relative performance or contribution that are valued in social exchanges. In addition, it was recognized fairly early in our work that personal qualities, more or less desirable or valued personal attributes rather than some kind of behavior or performance, could be viewed as an "input" entitling someone to a more or less desirable fate.

Our ideas about the developmental origins of the commitment to deserving fit well with the more systematic approaches to exchange and equity theory in emphasizing the criteria of performance or personal cost and "investment" in determining what someone deserves. To be sure, the personal attributes component, job "seniority," social status, etc. were also recognized in the more formal exchange models. If one takes the perspective, however, of looking at the way people decide what they and others deserve, a much more complex picture emerges. In many cases, people do consider the relative value of their own and others' "inputs" and costs in coming to a decision about relative deserving. This is most often seen and precisely measured in the contemporary marketplace where there is a relatively cooperative exchange of goods and services. The quality or market value of the product of one's efforts, and risking or investing one's efforts and resources, all imply a certain degree of entitlement to specific desired resources. But there are obviously many other situations where the "relative" degrees of performance, investment, and cost are irrelevant in determining the allocation of a desired resource among people.

For example, where there are scarce resources—either because of the degree of demand for them, or because they are seen as indivisible—people often compete with one another directly or indirectly. Under these circumstances, "winning" is all that matters in deciding who gets the desired resource . . . the promotion, the fair maiden, the prize. Although one's prior efforts, investment, and costs may elicit some form of condolence or compassion they are not allowed to alter the decision as to who deserves what.

At the other extreme of the social spectrum one can see, even within our society with its strong ideological roots in capitalism and the operation of the free market, the allocation of great parts of our resources without regard to "investments," costs or even performance as described above. Instead one finds a variation of the socialist ideology where each gives according to his ability and each takes according to his needs. The most obvious example of this is the way the adults in most families allocate the family's resources. Their earnings are distributed, to a great extent, in terms of the legitimate "needs" of the various members, no matter how much each contributed in obtaining resources.

Wives, husbands, and children are entitled to and deserve to have certain needs met if and when the resources are available. For the most part these "needs" take precedence over all other considerations in determining what each person deserves and receives.

If these observations are valid what we have is a view of social man which leaves our assumptions about his commitment to deserving and justice intact, but adds a complex and, at times, contradictory image of the manifestations this commitment may take in our society. Obviously we need a systematic framework to organize these various forms which deserving and justice may take. Probably the easiest way to approach this kind of organization is from one of the various sociological perspectives for analyzing the structural components of our social fabric. Actually, if one is willing to make the not entirely inappropriate translation of deserving and justice to "norms" (and possibly values), then the problem is solved in that there are many analyses of the normative structure of our society already available. The ones we know of, however, do not satisfy our need to achieve some understanding of the psychological bases of social behavior. And so we are left with the task of constructing one of our own.

At this point we will outline, as briefly as possible, the basic structure of this framework and some of the relevant data.

In our daily commerce with other people we create or find ourselves in a variety of different relations. We are going to assume at this point that all these relations among members of the same society can be ordered within two dimensions. On one of these, the relationship can emphasize the way people are tied, psychologically, to each other. They are in an *identity* relation if there is a minimal psychological separation or distinction between them. What happens to one "happens" empathically to the other (Kagan, 1958; Hall, 1954; Piaget, 1932). People involved in a *unit relationship* do not "see" themselves in each other, but there is a perception of "belonging to" similar to Heider's (1958) sense of the term. There is no empathic connection but an awareness of a bond which links the participants. Unit relations most often appear where there is a strong perception of similarity and/or promotive interdependence. *Nonunit* relations (in contrast to the other two types) imply antagonistic, competitive relations. The participants are bound together—the fate of one is tied to the fate of the other—but bound together as contestants.

The second dimension is based on the perception of the other as a *"person"* or as a *"position."* The meaning of the term position as we use it is similar to that of role behavior and status, in that the considerations "attached" to it are essentially independent of the individual occupant (Kahn *et al.,* 1964). It is a relational concept and is often derived from our functions and place in a social organization. Piaget (1932), however, has provided a nice elaboration of the psychology of "positions." He described the process whereby the child develops an understanding of "equivalence" rather than identity or "sameness," i.e., that there are separate and distinct people who can be in the same position or relationship. The concept of equivalence as compared to role differentiation enables one to view interpersonal events in a way that is independent of particular objects or persons (e.g., the awareness that positions of "brother" or "middle" are trans-personal).

In contrast, the recognition of a *person* in one's environment is infused with a constancy which transcends time and space. As Heider (1958) has pointed out, we actively try to locate trans-situational attributes in others, so that we can better adapt in a stable and predictable social milieu.

The two dimensions of relationships that we have presented create six broad categories of situations that a person may experience (see Table I). We suggest that the type of situation in which a person perceives he is "located" will elicit the *form of justice* that he applies. Also, we expect that an individual can cope with internal conflict related to justice by changing or distorting his perception of the type of situation in which he is involved. But a discussion of such dynamics must wait for a later occasion.

In order to clarify the model, we shall present a short discussion of some research that seems to pertain to the three types of perceived relationship, and then discuss, when appropriate, the person—position distinction within each of the three categories.

TABLE I[a]
FORMS OF JUSTICE

Object of perception	Perceived Relationship		
	Identity	Unit	Nonunit
Person	Perception of O as self NEEDS	Perception of similarity, belonging with O PARITY	Perceptions of contesting interests and personal differences related to the claims LAW, DARWINIAN JUSTICE
Position	Perception of self in O's circumstances of need ENTITLEMENT SOCIAL OBLIGATIONS	Perception of equivalence with O EQUITY	Scarce resources, with equally legitimate claims within the "rules" JUSTIFIED SELF-INTEREST

[a]Adapted from M.J. Lerner (in press).

B. IDENTITY RELATIONS

Individuals who perceive themselves in *an identity relation* with others will be willing to pool their resources and distribute them to any person according to his needs, without regard to who was responsible for "earning" or deserving the resources. Experimental findings relevant to the contention that people will often ignore a person's investments in favor of his needs in judging what he deserves have come from the work of Berkowitz and his students on the "norm of social responsibility." This line of research has demonstrated that people will expend energy and effort for others who are dependent upon them for the attainment of legitimate goals (e.g., Berkowitz & Daniels, 1963; Berkowitz & Friedman, 1967). The greater the dependent other's need, the greater will be the person's effort on his behalf. When people "identify" or sympathize with the suffering or deprivation of others and are in a position to do something about it, they feel compelled to intervene.

The work of Leventhal and his colleagues indicates that the behavior of people under such circumstances will be guided more by comparative need than by equity considerations. For example, in one study (Leventhal & Weiss, in press) it was found that subjects, when given the opportunity to divide joint earnings with a co-worker, were likely to give more money to their partner when his monthly income was relatively low than when it was high. Presumably, the allocation pattern was based on the perception of need. In another study (Leventhal and Whiteside, 1973), subjects were given the task of allocating grades as compensation for performance. Predictably, it was found that the better the performance the higher the grade allocated—the justice of "equity." However, when the subjects believed that the allocation of grades could serve an important function in helping a deficient student's development, equity considerations were set aside. The poorest performers were given the highest grades, apparently as a form of therapeutic incentive. The major point to make here is that in these studies, subjects' helping behavior was affected more by the need of the other person than by their inputs. Their behavior was still guided by considerations of justice and deserving, however.

C. UNIT RELATIONS

When individuals find themselves in *a unit relationship* with other participants the justice of parity may become salient under certain circumstances. Parity specifies that individuals receive equal outcomes regardless of inputs.

Lerner (1974), for instance, found that a subtle variation in instructional set greatly affected allocation behavior. When kindergarten-age children were defined as a "team," they distributed rewards to themselves and others on the basis of "parity"—equal reward regardless of inputs. The parity rule was followed whether the allocation was made by one of the "team workers" or an impartial supervisor. When defined as "co-workers" rather than "team members," however, subjects' allocation behavior more closely adhered to the principle of equity—reward dependent on input. In one condition, the application of the equity rule actually resulted in subjects allocating more reward to the others than themselves. In other words, subjects appeared motivated to maintain justice in the distribution of desired resources even at the cost of their own immediate gain.

The important point to be made here is that under both sets of instructions the children appeared to have taken what they felt they *deserved*. Under team instructions, they "deserved" parity with their partner, and so took about half. Under nonteam instructions they deserved outcomes matching their inputs, and so they took either more or less than half, depending on what was appropriate.

In both the "team" and "co-worker" conditions, the children were in one sense functionally interdependent. The co-worker situation involved an "equivalence" of roles. The children were in similar *positions* and were "related" by function and "common predicament." That is, they were susceptible to common rules, structure, and goals. However, their positions were also "separate," and would remain unchanged if another child were to "occupy" the role. Deserving in this case seems to have followed the rules of "equity," where a person is entitled to an amount correspondent with his inputs.

On the other hand, the children were related in a rather different way in the "team" situation. Their goals were "promotively interdependent," and a sense of "belonging" may have been evident. Tajfel (1970) has demonstrated the ease with which children develop a sense of "we-ness" in team situations. The perception of similarity as *persons* seems to develop in such relationships. In this case, the children followed the rules of "parity," and divided the resources equally.

Benton (1971) also provides evidence for the determinants of "equity" and "parity" forms of justice. He had one member of a pair of preadolescent children either lose or win the right for both of them to play with a pair of more or less preferred toys. An equity prediction would state that the subject who won the opportunity for the pair had invested the most and so the desirability of his outcome should be proportionally greater. Benton found that girls, whether they were "winners" or "losers," preferred equal outcomes for themselves and their partners, *if* the partner was a friend or at least moderately attractive. This alternative was also preferred by most of the boys when they were "losers." On the other hand, the "winning" girls who were paired with nonfriends, and most of the "winning" males followed an equity solution.

D. NONUNIT RELATIONS

There is at least one additional form of justice which has an extremely important effect on our behavior. The justice of rules and laws includes by far the most structured and pervasive aspect of justice in our lives. In effect, laws and rules provide the framework within which each person can pursue his own private interests. Once the rules are established, then each person need no longer be concerned with issues such as needs or investments outside of the framework in determining what another person deserves. Of course, if someone violates the rules, that will constitute an injustice. Any outcome acquired within the rules, however, is considered just and deserved.

Legalistic justice is often relatively inhuman and unsatisfying in comparison with those forms where the participants' needs and investments are taken into consideration. It is the last alternative before resorting to naked power as a way of deciding who gets what. Legalistic justice is most likely to be employed where individuals are in a *nonunit relationship* (i.e., where they share a bond but one which is antagonistic or has a clear conflict of interest).

A number of diverse studies offer support for this speculation. For example, Lerner and Becker (1965) found that when people anticipated entering into a cooperative situation in which they and the other person would compete for all the desired resources—only one of them would get everything—they elected to interact with someone who was "different" from them in personality and values rather than someone who was similar. When the interaction was to be cooperative and supportive, they chose the similar other. Krauss (1966) also found that high similarity and attraction between the participants led to avoidance of a competing strategy in favor of a cooperative one.

There are also studies which more directly examine behavior in situations where two or more people, with equally legitimate claims, desire the same outcomes. The natural law seems to be that of pursuing one's "justified self-interest" when it is a "him or me" situation. It is entirely legitimate to do what one can within the rules to get the desired outcome—the promotion, the beautiful woman, the best job, and only one left, etc. For example, in an experiment by Lerner and Lichtman (1968), two undergraduate women learned that one of them would have to receive severe electric shock while the other would not. One of them was then given the choice of the condition she preferred—via manipulations surrounding a table of random numbers. The vast majority of these women chose the desirable condition for themselves. Moreover, while they attributed responsibility to themselves for their own good fortune and the other person's suffering, they exhibited little evidence of guilt. Not only was there no devaluation of the other subject whom they had caused to suffer, but they expressed quite freely the notion that "anyone would have done" as they did. Their act seems best explained by suggesting that in certain "competitive" relations where a winner and a loser will basically emerge, one can pursue his "justified self-interest."

A study by Lerner (1971) did not find the Lerner and Lichtman results for male subjects. The choice of shock or nonshock for oneself was about evenly divided for males, and whichever condition they chose for themselves, they were inclined to condemn the other person (cf. Davis and Jones, 1960; Glass, 1964). Why should males feel guilty about choosing the nonshock condition for themselves while females do not? Lerner speculated that in this situation of parallel competition it was not appropriate for *men* to use the desire to avoid pain as a means of justifying causing another person to suffer. To test this hypothesis, Lerner altered the Lerner and Lichtman situation slightly by giving the "fortunate" male subject the choice between a shock condition and one where he could earn a considerable amount of money. With this manipulation, he was able to replicate the Lerner and Lichtman findings. The men overwhelmingly chose the positive incentive condition and there was no sign of condemnation or guilt. Apparently, men felt justified in allowing the other subject to suffer in this situation because they had won the right to choose their fate and, unlike the avoidance of shock, the reward of money was sufficiently attractive to justify seeking it.

More interesting than the perceptions of those subjects who chose the fate were the perceptions of those less fortunate subjects who believed they were about to suffer. The male subjects only condemned the person who caused them to suffer for illegitimate reasons—to avoid physical pain. The person who caused the subject to suffer in order to gain a large amount of money was not devalued by his "victim." In other words, subjects in all conditions tended to apply the same "objective" norms in determining the appropriate reaction in a situation where one of each pair was to suffer.

E. PERSON–POSITION: SOME IMPLICATIONS

The evidence, shown above, was not intended to be exhaustive or even complete in the sense of providing examples of all the various forms of justice and their determinants. Except for the Lerner and Benton experiments which identified some of the conditions for eliciting either the justice of "Equity" or "Parity," we did not attempt, at this time, to deal with the important distinction between the perception of *Person* or *Position* within the three kinds of relations. There are some important implications which should be mentioned, at the least, before we end this discussion of the forms of justice.

For example, in nonunit relations the distinction between the perception of *Person* with its trans-situational component and *Position* which is trans-personal can be very important. What is implied by this distinction can be found in the familiar distinction between a "game" and a "fight." The admonition to a contestant not to "take it so personally" is an attempt to keep the interaction at the level of "position" rather than "person." The psychology of the *Nonunit Person* situation derives from the awareness of conflicting interests and permanence of outcome. That is, there must be a winner and a loser and these fates are attached to people. In other words, there is invariably an invidious, enduring personal comparison at stake: the superior, better winner, and the inferior, worse loser. Thus the law and the courts are what keep the contesting parties from raw combat. On the other hand, *Nonunit Position* relations, since they are trans-personal, have a social history and a future independent of the particular participants. One may have lost a contest, a competition, but one is not an inferior person. Since the relationship is *Positional* it could have been anyone who won or lost and it might be someone else, next time, who wins or loses.

Similarly, the *Person-Position* distinction in *Identity* relations can be quite important. Again it is easiest to discuss at this time in terms of everyday examples rather than experimental evidence, primarily because there are virtually no experimental data available. In any case, the distinction here can be described simply as the perception that the event is actually "happening" to oneself—"I am feeling his suffering"—versus the understanding that one could be in his position—"That could be me." Also, the trans-personal aspect of position implies that there are later consequences associated with being in that position. The demand, therefore, associated with *Identity-Position* is in terms of what is valuable in the long run for the dependent person. What this boils down to, often, is the distinction between doing something to make the other person feel better (Identity-Person) versus being concerned with doing what is "good" for him (Identity-Position).

V. Some Concluding Thoughts

It is quite possible that the findings generated by the studies described in this chapter could be subsumed under a small number of relatively simply propositions. One could postulate certain norms and rules of social behavior, and after the fact "explain" the various reactions to violations of these norms in an apparently more parsimonious system. Even greater parisomony could be achieved by reducing these propositions to a derivation of the "law of effect." It is far less likely, however, that one could have made similar progress in the other direction. That is, by starting with the "law of effect" or propositions about norms and "distress," could one have generated the variety of experiments and studies reported here? What these studies represent is a sequential dialogue between the perspective of social psychology—the concepts, theories and analytic techniques, on the one hand—and the events and experiences which we see happening around us and within ourselves.

It must have been obvious to the reader that our dialogue did not always follow a "linear," deductive form, and our research efforts were often better at raising questions than providing the answers. In fact, some of the most intriguing findings come embarrassingly close to the cardinal sin of *seeming* to be "contradictory." Nevertheless there are the detectable and distinct outlines of a pattern and set of themes, and eventually it was hoped that a greater sense of order and understanding was achieved. The main questions guiding the dialogue were rather simple and familiar ones, having to do with such issues as "justice," "helping," and "victims." At times, however, the questions were difficult to phrase in language which was sufficiently explicit to enable us to apply the social psychologist's perspective, and yet also provide a minimal bias in terms of an implicit theoretical explanation.

This kind of problem—the conceptual language and theoretical propositions—is the most vulnerable aspect of our approach. We may appear at times to be conceptually sloppy and theoretically unsophisticated ... often on the fringes of a "bubba" psychology. This, however, was a calculated, and we think, desirable approach at this stage in our understanding of "justice"-related phenomena and the development of our science and craft. We did not hesitate to choose our concepts from sources as diverse as Freud, Piaget, Mead, Parsons, and Marx, and, at times, we retranslated some others into our own language such as the "Personal Contract" and finally, even invented our own—e.g., the "exchange fiction." Needless to say, at any given point the reader could have rescued himself from the sense of outrage, or confusion (only temporary, of course) generated by this approach by turning to one of the other chapters in this book more committed to a systematic scientific approach to "equity" and its "theories."

Although the subheadings provided a structure for integrating material in this chapter, there were a few questions and observations that were central in its organization. The earliest research we did was directed at trying to integrate and explain the apparent contradictions in the way people react to the deprivation or suffering of others. Their reactions can and do vary from extreme compassion and help, on the one hand to indifference or derogation on the other—even toward the same person at different times. How can this be? The integrating theme we arrived at was that of "justice." In effect, the answer was that there is "good" suffering and "bad" suffering, depending upon whether the victim deserves his fate or not.

This notion in its various forms may or may not be a complete (or evan valid) answer for the original question, but the data and thinking generated by the initial efforts raised in a most compelling way the issue of why people care about justice and how important a theme it is in people's lives. There were then, and still are, various answers available to those questions. The ones we were aware of, however, did not satisfy us for various reasons. Mainly, they were too "reductionistic" in the sense that they translated or "reduced" the concern with justice to the status of a relatively trivial manifestation of other more familiar psychological processes or motives. This approach was esthetically unappealing—"dull"—and also seemed to be a poor strategy. For example, everyone knows that people care about justice because they are taught to. They are "socialized" via reinforcement and modelling and the norms and rules are more or less "internalized."

All this probably does go on, but before we accept this as "a" or "the" explanation there are a few observations we should consider. First, the theme of justice has played a preeminent role in the norms and expressed values of western civilization, and, second, one can make a case, if you take the evidence at face value, that the themes of deserving and justice play a central role in most people's lives—or at least those we know about. So, it appears that there may be something special about the concern with justice, and rather than reduce this concern to norms and social learning, it might be worthwhile to look for a process or some processes that are "isomorphic" with this central organizing theme. And that is how we came to the hunch about the "personal contract."

That worked rather well and made good sense except that we then discovered that there were problems most people had to face, for example, conflicts created by various aspects of the person's commitment to deserving for himself and justice for others. Once we had made inroads into understanding something about these conflicts and how people attempt to deal with them, we then learned that the situation was even more complex than that. We came to the obvious conclusion that people used different criteria to decide what a given person deserved—was entitled to receive. At times it was the familiar notions of effort, ability, or a combination in terms of "performance." In other circumstances, however, these investments were totally ignored and the mere "outcomes" as defined within the system defined deserving. "The winner deserved to win." In yet other circumstances, these were ignored and the person's expressed or inferred state of "need" was the sole factor in determining the distribution of the desired resources. How could this be? How could we explain or at least provide some system for all of these "forms" which judgments of deserving and justice take in this and other societies?

Certainly we had to move beyond the "personal contract" to do this. Also we suspected that if we could provide some system for organizing the various criteria people employ in determining the form deserving and justice would take in a given situation, we also might come closer to answering our original questions as to when people care for and help others and when they ignore or harm them. These considerations and others led to the "Forms of Justice Model" and some promising data which partly came from and partly helped create the theory.

As it stands, the model is no more than a beginning. For example, it relies on "perceived relationships" with the other person and leaves us with the substantial, but not unfamiliar problem of what determines this perception. Fortunately, we do know something about this issue; certainly enough to make a start at research to examine critically the structure of the model. It is on that note of more questions raised and hints as to possible answers that we end this chapter.

EQUITY AND THE LAW: THE EFFECT OF A HARMDOER'S "SUFFERING IN THE ACT" ON LIKING AND ASSIGNED PUNISHMENT[1]

William Austin

UNIVERSITY OF VIRGINIA
CHARLOTTESVILLE, VIRGINIA

Elaine Walster

and

Mary Kristine Utne

UNIVERSITY OF WISCONSIN
MADISON, WISCONSIN

I. Introduction

Scholars have long been interested in questions of "justice," "fairness," and "equity." Aristotle was among the first to propose an "equity" theory of justice.

[1] This research was supported in part by National Science Foundation Grant GS 30822X.

163

He alluded to two forms of justice: (1) *Equal Justice* (rewards are distributed equally among men); (2) *Distributive Justice* (rewards are distributed in proportion to men's merit). The Aristotelian conception has been elaborated by such modern social psychologists as Homans (1961), Adams (1965), and Walster *et al.* (1973; in press).

In this paper we will briefly review equity theory,[2] speculate concerning its possible usefulness in illuminating the legal process, and present some preliminary research findings.

II. Theoretical Background: The Equity Formulation

Equity theory is a strikingly simple theory. Essentially it consists of four propositions:

Proposition I: Individuals will try to maximize their outcomes (where outcomes equals rewards minus costs).

Proposition II: Groups can maximize collective reward by evolving accepted systems for "equitably" apportioning rewards and costs among members. Thus, members will evolve such systems of equity and will attempt to induce members to accept and adhere to these systems.

The only way groups can induce members to equitably behave is by making it more profitable to behave equitably than inequitably. Thus, groups will generally reward members who treat others equitably and generally punish (increase the costs for) members who treat others inequitably.

Walster *et al.* define an "equitable relationship" to exist when the person scrutinizing the relationship (i.e., the scrutineer—who could be Participant A, Participant B, or an outside observer) perceives that all participants are receiving equal relative outcomes from the relationship, i.e.,

$$\frac{Outcomes_A - Inputs_A}{(|Inputs_A|)^{k_A}} = \frac{Outcomes_B - Inputs_B}{(|Inputs_B|)^{k_B}}$$

A. DEFINITION OF TERMS

Inputs (I) are defined as "the participant's contributions to the exchange, which are seen (by a scrutineer) as entitling him to rewards or costs." The inputs that a participant contributes to a relationship can be either assets (entitling him to rewards) or liabilities (entitling him to costs).[3]

---

[2] Readers who are familiar with the equity theory of Walster *et al.* (1973) should skip to Section III.

[3] The restriction of this formula is that Inputs cannot equal zero.

In different settings, different inputs are seen as entitling one to rewards or costs. In industrial settings, assets such as "capital" or "manual labor" are seen as relevant inputs—inputs that legitimately entitle the contributor to reward. In social settings, assets such as physical beauty or kindness are generally seen as assets entitling the possessor to social reward. Social liabilities such as boorishness or cruelty are seen as liabilities entitling one to costs. In accident cases, such inputs as "intent," "fault," and "negligence" may be of primary importance.

Outcomes (O) are defined as the positive and negative consequences that a scrutineer perceives a participant has incurred as a consequence of his relationship with another. Following Homans (1961), we shall refer to positive outcomes as "rewards" and negative outcomes as "costs." The participant's total outcomes in a relationship are equal to the rewards he obtains from the relationship minus the costs he incurs.

$$k_A = \text{sign}(I_A) \times \text{sign}(O_A - I_A)$$

$$k_B = \text{sign}(I_B) \times \text{sign}(O_B - I_B)$$

[The exponents k_A and k_B simply take on the value +1 or −1, depending on the sign of A and B's inputs and the sign of their gains (outcomes − inputs).] [4]

B. WHO DECIDES WHETHER A RELATIONSHIP IS EQUITABLE?

In Proposition II, we argued that societies develop norms of equity and teach these systems to their members. Thus, within any society there will be a general consensus as to what constitutes an equitable relationship. However, the equity formulation makes it clear that ultimately, equity is in the eye of the beholder. An individual's perception of how equitable a relationship is will depend on *his* assessment of the value and relevance of the various participants' inputs and outcomes. Participants themselves, even after prolonged negotiation with one another, often do not agree completely as to the *value* and *relevance* of various inputs and outcomes. One person may feel that a distinguished family name is a relevant input, entitling him to positive outcomes. His partner might disagree.

If participants do calculate inputs and outcomes differently—and it is likely that they will—it is inevitable that they will differ in their perceptions of whether or not a given relationship is equitable. Moreover, "objective" outside observers are likely to evaluate the equity of a relationship quite differently than do participants.

---

[4] The exponent's effect is simply to change the way relative outcomes are computed. If $k = +1$, then we have $(O - I)/|I|$, but if $k = -1$, then we have $|I| \times (O - I)$. Without the exponent k, the formula would yield meaningless results when $I < O$ and $O - I > 0$, or $I > O$ and $O - I < 0$.

A simple example illustrates the application of the equity formula. Assume that an employer (Person A) and his accountant (Person B) have an equitable relationship. Assume, for example, that both their relative outcomes = +10:

$$\frac{\$100,000}{|\$10,000|} = \frac{\$10,000}{|\$1,000|}$$

If the accountant embezzles $10,000 from his employer, he creates a marked inequity:

$$\frac{\$100,000 - \$10,000}{|\$10,000|} \neq \frac{\$10,000 + \$10,000}{|\$1,000|}$$

By convention, equity theorists term an individual who intentionally takes larger relative outcomes than he deserves an *"exploiter"* or a "harmdoer." The member of the relationship whose outcomes are reduced is the *"victim."*

C. THE PSYCHOLOGICAL CONSEQUENCES OF INEQUITY

Proposition III: When individuals find themselves participating in inequitable relationships, they become distressed. The more inequitable the relationship, the more distress individuals feel.

According to equity theory, both the harmdoer and the victim experience distress after an exploitative encounter. (Evidence in support of this contention is reviewed in Austin and Walster, 1974). Theorists have labeled their distress reactions in various ways. The exploiter's distress may be labeled "guilt," "shame," "dissonance," "empathy," "conditioned anxiety," or "fear of retaliation." The victim's distress may be labeled "anger," "shame," "humiliation," "dissonance," or "conditioned anxiety." Most agree, however, that the distress felt by harmdoers and victims arises from two sources.

First, when children engage in inequitable relations, they are sometimes punished. Soon the performance of (or acquiescence in) unjust acts arouses conditioned anxiety. Such distress may have a cognitive component: The harmdoer may attribute his distress to a fear that the victim, the victim's sympathizers, legal agencies, or even God will retaliate against him. The victim may fear that his fellows will ridicule him or consider him a "pushover" and "fair game" for subsequent exploitation.[5] Discomfort emanating from these sources has been labeled *retaliation distress.*

Harmdoing may produce discomfort for a second reason. In our society there is an almost universally accepted (if not followed) moral code that one

---

[5] Data from Brown (1968) indicate that victims do indeed experience "retaliation distress." Brown found that when subjects were informed that others thought they had been "suckered," they were more likely to show face-saving behaviors. Brown interpreted his data as evidence of subjects' desire to bolster their self-esteem *and* to avoid future exploitation.

should be fair and equitable in his dealings with others. [See Fromm (1956) for an interesting discussion of the pervasiveness of the "fairness" principle.] In stating that "individuals accept a code of fairness" we do not mean that everyone internalizes exactly the same code, internalizes it to the same extent, or follows that code without deviation. Juvenile delinquents and confidence men, for example, often seem to behave as if the exploitation of others is completely consistent with their self-concept. However, evidence suggests that even deviants do internalize norms of fairness. It is true that they may repeatedly violate such norms for financial or social gain, but such violations do seem to cause some distress. Deviants evidently experience sufficient discomfort that they are motivated to try to convince others that their actions were equitable. For example, some deviants argue that the inputs of those they victimize are so negative that to exploit them is in fact to give them "what they deserve." Anecdotal evidence on these points comes from interviews with confidence men (Goffman, 1952; Roebuck, 1964) and delinquents (Sykes and Matza, 1957).

Participating in a profoundly inequitable relationship—"taking" others or being "taken"—threatens the self-concept of almost any individual. The tension that accompanies such inconsistent acts has been discussed in great detail by cognitive dissonance theorists (Bramel, Taub, & Blum, 1968). In addition, guilt theorists have extensively analyzed the reactions of harmdoers (Arnold, 1960; Maher, 1966). Researchers have only begun to study victims' cognitive and affective reactions (Austin and Walster, 1974). Discomfort emanating from these sources has been termed *self-concept distress*.

There is compelling evidence that individuals become distressed when they get too much as well as when they get too little. No one would argue that a given inequity is as distressing for the harmdoer as for the victim. Aesop acidly observed that, "The injuries we do and those we suffer are seldom weighted on the same scales." It is clear why a harmdoer would be less disturbed by an inequity than his victim. Although both participants must endure the discomfort of knowing they are in an inequitable relationship, the harmdoer can at least console himself that he is benefitting materially from his discomfort. His victim has no such consolation—he is losing in every way from the inequity. Abundant data support the assumption that an injustice is less disturbing to the beneficiaries of the injustice than their victims (see, e.g., Blumstein & Weinstein, 1969; Pritchard *et al.*, 1972; Austin & Walster, 1974).

Presumably, individuals are motivated by retaliation distress and self-concept distress to restore equity to their inequitable relationships.

Proposition IV: Individuals who discover they are in an inequitable relationship attempt to eliminate their distress by restoring equity. The greater the inequity that exists, the more distress they feel, and the harder they try to restore equity.

D. TECHNIQUES BY WHICH INDIVIDUALS REDUCE THEIR DISTRESS

1. Restoration of Actual Equity

One way participants can restore equity to their unjust relationship is by allowing the exploiter to compensate his victim. Many studies indicate that a harmdoer will often exert considerable effort to make restitution (see, e.g., Walster & Prestholdt, 1966; Berscheid & Walster, 1967; Schmitt & Marwell, 1972). Parallel evidence indicates that a victim's first response to exploitation is to seek restitution [Leventhal & Bergman, 1969; Marwell, Schmitt, & Shotola, 1971]. If the exploiter refuses to make restitution, the victim may settle for "getting even" by retaliating against the exploiter (Thibaut, 1950; Ross *et al.*, 1971).

2. Restoration of Psychological Equity

Participants can reduce their distress in a second way. They can distort reality and convince themselves (and perhaps others) that their ostensibly inequitable relationship is, in fact, perfectly fair. Individuals use several techniques to rationalize exploitation. A number of studies demonstrate that harmdoers may rationalize their harmdoing by derogating their victim, by denying responsibility for the act, or by minimizing the victim's suffering (Brock & Buss, 1962; Glass, 1964; Sykes & Matza, 1964). Cressey (1955) reports that embezzlers commonly insist that they merely "borrowed" the money (denial of responsibility) and that, in any case, the company "did not really miss it" (minimization of harmdoing). There is even some sparse experimental evidence (Austin & Walster, 1974; Leventhal & Bergman, 1969) that under the right circumstances, victims will even justify their own exploitation. Legal theorists have observed, with some puzzlement, that victims do tend to accept (if not justify) their own exploitation. [For example, Maurer (1940) notes that confidence men and perpetrators of assault can rarely be prosecuted; their victims simply refuse to sign complaints.]

3. Actual versus Psychological Equity Restoration

Obviously, now we must confront a crucial question. Can we specify when a person will try to restore actual equity to his relationship? When he will settle for restoring psychological equity instead? Equity theory states that a person follows a Cost-Benefit strategy when deciding how he should respond. Theoretically, two situational variables are crucial determinants of a person's response: (1) the adequacy of the possible techniques for restoring equity, and (2) the cost of the possible techniques for restoring equity. There is evidence that harmdoers and their victims prefer techniques that completely restore equity to ones that only partially restore equity (see, e.g., Berscheid & Walster, 1967; Berscheid, Walster, & Barclay, 1969). There is complementary evidence that they prefer techniques with little material or psychological cost to techniques with greater cost (see, e.g., Weick & Nesset, 1968). Whether an individual responds to injustice by attempting to restore actual equity, by distorting reality, or by doing a little of both, will thus depend on the costs and benefits he thinks are associated with each strategy.

The preceding discussion has focused upon *participants'* equity behavior. Participants are not the only possible agents of equity restoration, however. The participants' friends, social workers, the courts, etc., may all observe inequity, become distressed by it, and intervene to right existing wrongs. Are there any data on how such impartial observers respond to inequity?

E. THE IMPARTIAL OBSERVER

According to equity theorists, impartial observers tend to react to injustice in much the same way that participants do—with one qualification: Observers react less passionately than do participants. The discovery that observers' reactions faintly echo participants' fiery ones should come as little surprise. Human beings are able to empathize with others. An observer who empathizes with a harmdoer may well share his embarrassment and rationalizations; the observer who empathizes with his victim may well share the victim's anger and indignation. If, as seems likely, the feelings we empathize with are less intense than the ones we experience, it is understandable that observers react less intensely to inequity than do actual participants.

Evidence that impartial observers react to injustice in much the same way as do participants comes from a wide variety of sources:

Restoration of actual equity. When participants are unable—or refuse—to restore equity, impartial observers often intervene and attempt to set things right (Lerner & Simmons, 1966; Lerner & Matthews, 1967; Baker, 1974). Indeed, social welfare and legal structures are designed, in part, to prod harmdoers into "paying their debt" to their victims and to society (Schafer, 1960).

Restoration of psychological equity. Complementary research documents that when "impartial" observers of injustice are powerless to reestablish actual equity, they too tend to settle for restoring psychological equity. For example, Lerner (1971) argues that even the most impartial of observers possesses an intense desire to continue to believe that people get what they deserve. In an impressive body of research, he documents observers' eagerness to convince themselves that people get what they deserve and deserve what they get (Lerner, 1965, 1970; Lerner & Simmons, 1966; Lerner & Matthews, 1967).

Chaiken and Darley (1973) provide impressive evidence that an observer's reaction to an event will depend on whether he identifies with the perpetrator or the victim of an inequity. The authors asked college students to watch a video-taped accident. These judges carefully observed a supervisor showing a worker how to perform his job. When the worker finally finished his task, the supervisor stood up, remarking, "I guess that's it." As he pushed away from the workbench, it began to wobble; the worker's carefully completed project toppled over and was destroyed. As a consequence of this accident, the worker lost the bonus he expected. The authors predicted that if the observers expected to become supervisors themselves, their sympathies would be with the supervisor, and they would be motivated to perceive the event as an accident. Conversely, when they expected to be workers themselves, their sympathies would be with the worker, and they should severely condemn the supervisor for his carelessness. These predictions were confirmed.

On the basis of the existing evidence, we must conclude that although "impartial" observers can certainly evaluate the fairness of an interaction more objectively than can participants, even the most aloof of judges is personally motivated to right existing wrongs, and—failing that—at least to convince himself that this is a just world—a place where exploiters are somehow entitled to their excessive benefits and the deprived somehow deserve to suffer.

III. Equity Theory and the Law

There is no social psychological theory in existence that will give us a complete understanding of the American legal system . . . or even a complete understanding of even a tiny part of the legal system. Yet, even a superficial glance at equity theory makes it evident that the theory must have *some* relevance to the legal process. Equity theory deals with men's perceptions of fairness and justice. It seems reasonable to suppose that men's perceptions should have some impact on their judicial decisions.

Aristotle (1912 translation) was keenly aware of the key role equity principles played in judicial decision making. According to Aristotle, equity served as a corrective device for the "blind" and universal application of laws:

> Equity, though just, is not legal justice, but a rectification of legal justice. The reason for this is that law is always a general statement, yet there are cases which it is not possible to cover in a general statement. In matters, therefore, where, while it is necessary to speak in general terms, it is not possible to do so correctly, the law takes into consideration the majority of cases, although it is not unaware of the error this involves. And this does not make it a wrong law; for the error is not in the law or the lawgiver, but in the nature of the case: the material of conduct is essentially irregular. When therefore the law lays down a general rule, and thereafter an exception arises which is an exception to the rule, it is then right, where the lawgiver's pronouncement, because of its absoluteness, is defective and erroneous, to rectify the defect by deciding as the lawgiver would himself decide if he were present on the occasion, and would have enacted, if he had been cognizant of the case in question. (*Nicomachean Ethics*, 1137b)

The application of equity principles enables judges to consider mitigating circumstances (i.e., inputs) in handing down sentences (i.e., outcomes).

Modern-day equity theorists have considered the legal system from the perspective of the harmdoer, the victim, or an impartial observer.

A. THE HARMDOER'S PERSPECTIVE

Macaulay and Walster (1971) used an equity theory framework to examine the impact of the legal system on the harmdoer. They confronted two questions: To what extent do existing laws and informal legal procedures encourage restitution and reconciliation? To what extent do existing legal procedures foster self-justification, i.e., derogation, denial, and minimization? They concluded that:

> On its face, American law is consistent with the goal of supporting compensation. . . . For example, the common-law of torts consists of rules which say a wrong-doer must compensate his victim. In addition, the legal system in operation provides more avenues to restitution than are available in its formal rules. A wide variety of informal procedures encourage compensation. For example, criminal sanctions are sometimes used as leverage to induce restitution. A police officer may decide not to arrest a shoplifter if the wrong-doer is not a professional thief and if the stolen items are returned; a district attorney may decide not to prosecute if the amount embezzled is returned. (p. 179)

They also acknowledged, however, that other legal rules and procedures exist which dilute a harmdoer's incentive to restore equity. The legal necessity of determining who is at fault, the inevitable delays in securing judgments, the costs of litigation, and the existence of impersonal insurance systems, all tend to emphasize bargaining and to deemphasize exact equity restoration. They conclude:

> The tendency in the law, then, is not to support the ideal of having the wrong-doer make good the harm he has done, but to support the best balance of self-interest possible between harmdoer and victim, in light of bargaining skill and position. Rather than develop the harmdoer's best motives, the system tends to guard against his worst since the potential of litigation forces him to strike some bargain rather than to ignore totally the victim's claim. (p. 182)

The American legal system, then, exerts some pressure on wrongdoers to restore equitable relations with others, but this pressure must vie with competing pressures toward other competing goals.

B. THE VICTIM'S PERSPECTIVE

As yet, equity theorists have not scrutinized the legal system from the victim's perspective.

According to equity theory, the victim's assignment of the probable Costs and Benefits of possible courses of action should determine whether he demands restitution or justifies his own exploitation. For example, theorists argue that the oppressed will demand justice only if they are confident that legal or revolutionary action can be successful. Otherwise they will apathetically accept the status quo (Davies, 1969; Gurr, 1970; Ross *et al.*, 1971). Unfortunately, equity principles have not been applied in examining legal settings from the victim's viewpoint.

C. THE IMPARTIAL OBSERVER'S PERSPECTIVE

This paper will take the perspective of impartial observers—such as judges, jurors, and courtroom spectators.

Specifically, we will attempt to determine the extent to which a judge's or juror's discovery that a harmdoer has suffered will alter their liking for him and dampen their desire to punish him further.

Legal philosophers have never been able to agree on *why* we punish wrongdoers. Should we punish men to: Restore equity? Rehabilitate them? Protect society by isolating them? Set a harsh example for other potential harmdoers? They cannot agree. In spite of philosophers' disagreements, most observers seem to feel that to *some* extent, wrongdoers should expiate their crimes by suffering (Sharp & Otto, 1910; Rose & Prell, 1955; Fry, 1956). For example, Durkheim (1933) insists:

> And in truth, punishment has remained, at least in part, a work of vengeance. It is said that we do not make the culpable suffer in order to make him suffer; it is nonetheless true that we find it just that he suffer.
> . . .In supposing that punishment can really serve to protect us in the future, we think that it ought to be above all an *expiation* of the past. The proof of this lies in the minute precautions we take to proportion punishment as exactly as possible to the severity of the crime; they would be inexplicable if we did not believe that the culpable ought to suffer because he has done evil and in the same degree. (p. 88)

If we do punish wrongdoers, *at least in part,* to "set things right," a second question immediately arises. Is it possible for a defendant to "pay for" his crime—or convince the jury he has—before he ever comes to trial? Will judges and jurors perceive that the defendant has partially "paid for" his crime . . . if he reveals he suffered from intense remorse . . . if he was accidentally injured while committing the crime . . . if he volunteers financial restitution . . . if he was held in lengthy pretrial detention . . . if he suffered in ways in no way connected with his crime? We will explore these questions throughout the balance of the paper.

Many legal scholars have remarked that a criminal's suffering "weighs heavily" on the minds of judges and juries. The bank robber who is crippled when making a getaway may get an unusually light sentence. The mother whose child is killed when she runs a stop sign might be treated with similar leniency. Equity theory makes some intriguing predictions as to the effect that a defendant's suffering might have on a judge's and juror's liking for him and their eagerness to punish him.

1. The Harmdoer's Suffering: Its Impact on Liking and Sentencing

Let us consider a typical case: A trusted accountant embezzles $10,000 from his employer. The employer catches him. He is enraged at his accountant's exploitative behavior and complains to their mutual friends, clients, and, finally, to the police. Then the embezzler's troubles begin. His outside clients abandon him in droves, he suffers business losses, his wife divorces him, and he faces the threat of imprisonment.

How will such information affect jurors? How will they react if the embezzler's losses are described as negligible compared to his crime (i.e., say $10)? If they "balance out" his crime (say $10,000)? If they far exceed his crime (say $100,000)?

Equity theorists would predict that jurors will take information concerning the embezzler's suffering into account when deciding how much restitution he owes the victim and/or society. When the embezzler has lost only $10 as a consequence of his crime, he has made only the most token of atonements. When he has lost $10,000 or $100,000 as a result of his $10,000 embezzlement, however, he has, in a sense, completely "paid" for his theft. Thus, we would expect jurors to feel he had a more severe punishment "coming to him" when he has lost only $10 than when he's lost $10,000 or $100,000.

2. Contingency of Suffering

According to equity theory, "an equitable relationship exists when all participants are receiving equal relative outcomes *from the relationship.*" This statement suggests that the *context* in which a harmdoer suffers should be an important determinant of whether his suffering "counts" as atonement or whether it is judged to be irrelevant to his relationship with the victim. For example, if the jurors know that the irate employer ruined the embezzler's outside business in order to punish him for his theft, the embezzler's suffering is clearly a "consequence of his relationship with the victim." Under these conditions, the embezzler's suffering may well be considered partial atonement for his theft. If, on the other hand, the jurors learn that a playmate accidentally shot the embezzler when he was a child, his early suffering will probably not be seen as an outcome of his relationship with the employer, and it will probably not be considered to be partial atonement for his theft. It should not "count."

On the basis of this reasoning, we would predict that how relevant to the harmdoer/victim relationship the harmdoer's suffering is, will determine whether or not the exploiter's suffering counts against the debt he owes the victim and/or society.

3. Harmdoer's Suffering and Liking

Clarence Darrow declared in 1933 that:

> Jurymen seldom convict a person they like, or acquit one they dislike. The main work of a trial lawyer is to make a jury like his client, or at least to feel sympathy for him; facts regarding the crime are relatively unimportant. (Sutherland, 1966, p. 442)

Kalven and Zeisel (1966) point out that jurors' liking and sympathy for the defendant and plaintiff have a dramatic impact on the way they evaluate evidence.

Thus the first thing equity theorists might ask is: Does a harmdoer's suffering affect the jurors' liking and sympathy for the defendant?

According to equity theorists, a person will evaluate another person differently depending on the *function* that he thinks his expressions of liking will have. They note that "expressions of liking" can serve to (1) compensate or punish another, (2) mirror one's justifications, or (3) simply to reflect one's mood.

1. *Expression of Liking as Compensation:* Sometimes, people are keenly aware that their expressions of regard for someone will have actual consequences for that person's life. We know that if we report that an acquaintance is a "dislikable, repulsive, filthy crook," our listeners will probably not be eager to invite him to dinner . . . or to offer him a job. If we say he is "likable, charming, and conscientious," he may well reap those social benefits.

In any case, if, when courtroom spectators, character witnesses, or jurors discuss the defendant's personality or character, they know that their answer may have practical consequences for the defendant; they cannot help but equate "expressions of liking" with "conferring reward or punishment."

Under conditions which make connections between "expressed liking" and "reward versus punishment" salient, equity theorists would expect a linear relationship between the harmdoer's suffering and the witnesses' expressed liking for him. When an embezzler has not paid sufficiently for his crime, spectators, witnesses, and jurors should be motivated to express disapproval and disliking, in the hope that he will be punished. When he has already suffered overmuch, they should express approval and liking, in an effort to compensate him for his suffering.

Previous research has documented the eagerness of impartial observers to reward the deprived with public praise and to punish the overbenefited with public condemnation (Walster *et al.,* 1966; Lincoln & Levinger, 1972).

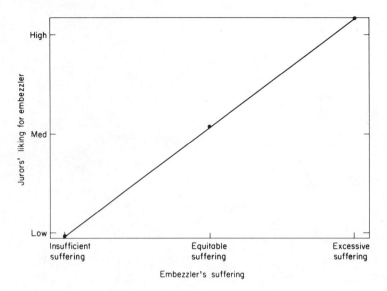

Fig. 1. The relationship predicted between the embezzler's suffering and jurors' liking for him: Expressions of liking as compensation.

2. *Expressions of Liking as Justification:* Sometimes, individuals know that they are powerless to right social wrongs. Nothing they can do—including praising another, gossiping about him, etc.—will have any conceivable effect on his fate. The lawbreaker may be so poor he can never make restitution to his victim; he may be so old he could never serve out an appropriate sentence. It also may be clear to the juror that the "guilty" defendant will be released on a technicality. In such cases, observers are left with only two options: they can acknowledge the irremediable inequity *or* they can justify its existence. They can convince themselves that the participant deserved his excessively lenient or excessively harsh treatment. In such cases, observers' "expressions of liking" may simply reflect their consoling justification of the status quo. For example, if the courtroom spectator or juror learns that the ubiquitous embezzler has gotten away with an excessively lenient punishment ($10), and he can do nothing to right this injustice, he might be motivated to convince himself that extenuating circumstances were such that the defendant only deserved that little punishment; that the defendant is a likable fellow who really did not deserve to suffer. On the other hand, when he learns that the embezzler has received an excessively harsh penalty ($100,000 worth), the observer might be motivated to convince himself that in fact the embezzler is a despicable fellow who deserved what he got. ("Probably this was not the first time he embezzled from his firm; only the first time he had been *caught*.")

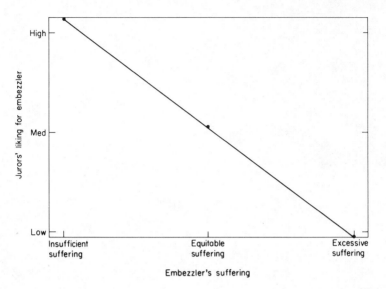

Fig. 2. The relationship predicted between the embezzler's suffering and jurors' liking for him: Expressions of liking as justification.

Previous theorists have documented that impartial observers' "expressions of liking" often reflect their intense desire to "derogate" or "aggrandize" another (Sykes & Matza, 1957; Davis & Jones, 1960; Berkowitz, 1962; Davidson, 1964; Glass, 1964; Walster & Prestholdt, 1966; Lincoln & Levinger, 1972; Katz *et al.*, 1973).

3. *Expressions of Liking as Emotion:* Sometimes individuals have reactions to others which have nothing to do with equity restoration—they simply feel what they feel even though it does not do them or anyone else a bit of good. As Homans (1961) points out, one tends to feel contented when he and his acquaintances are being treated equitably and to feel distressed when they are treated inequitably. Since people have a strong tendency to dislike those who are associated with unpleasantness and injustice (Berscheid & Walster, 1967), we might expect people to have a positive reaction to the defendant who has paid in full for his crime and a negative one to the defendant who has either escaped punishment or been overly punished. It is easy to acknowledge that we tend to dislike wrongdoers, in part because they confront us with the unsettling realization that injustice exists. It is harder to admit that one might feel some anger at the excessively tormented person because he reminds us of the same thing. Yet, psychologists have observed that we do feel some resentment toward anyone—harmdoer or victim alike—who threatens our comfortable world. To the extent that spectators' and jurors' expressions of "liking" simply reflect their "mood," we would expect the defendant's suffering and liking to be related as shown in Fig. 3.

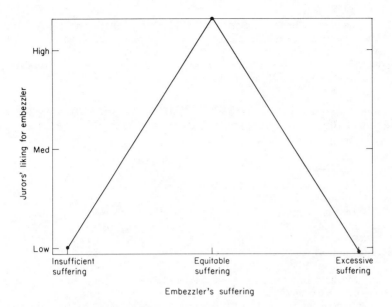

Fig. 3. The relationship predicted between the embezzler's suffering and jurors' liking for him: Expressions of liking as emotion.

It is apparent, then, that the expected relationship between a harmdoer's suffering and observer's liking for him is a complicated one. It should depend on the immediate situation. An inquirer may get quite different replies if the observer believes his expressions of liking can facilitate restitution or retaliation, only support his justifications, or strictly reflect his mood.

Suffering and liking: the evidence. Some theorists have long been aware that liking might serve as a compensation; others were aware that liking might serve as a justification; still others were aware that liking could reflect emotionality. Unfortunately, heretofore, no one ever put these observations together. No one realized "liking" might serve three distinct functions.

Thus, there is little information as to the conditions which motivate individuals to use expressions of liking in one or another way. For this reason, Utne (1974) attempted to determine whether or not, under appropriate circumstances, courtroom spectators may respond to the simple question: "How much do you like Defendant X?" in the three ways we have proposed.

Utne (1974) asked college students to act in the role of courtroom spectators. The criminal case she gave them was a completely fictional account of the circumstances surrounding an embezzlement. She explained:

There is currently a great deal of interest in the contributions psychology can make to our understanding of the legal process. Unfortunately, most of the psychological principles used to answer questions about courtroom processes have not developed from the study of courtroom situations. Rather, theories have been "borrowed" from other research areas and 'stretched to fit' the legal applications. The study you are participating in today is an attempt to fill in some of the gaps in our understanding of the courtroom decision-making process. You will be asked to play the role of a courtroom spectator, and will answer questions about an actual court case as if you had just observed the case. (p. 12)

Then she asked them to read an "actual court case." Actually she gave them a fictionalized account of the circumstances surrounding an embezzlement. The summary brief was as follows:

FACTS OF THE CASE
(Names, places and dates have been changed to insure the anonymity of the people involved.)
The defendant, Robert Brown, is a 32-year-old white male. He is a practicing accountant in Oakdale, a midwest city of approximately 250,000.
Plaintiffs are Smith, owner of a drycleaning store, and Jones, owner of a carry-out food outlet. Plaintiffs also work and reside in Oakdale.
In June of 1962, Smith and Jones opened their businesses. Defendant Brown, a certified public accountant, was retained at this time to manage their books and in general act as financial overseer for the businesses.
Although initially in debt, by January 1, 1964, the businesses were prospering. The successful working association of Brown, Smith, and Jones continued.
Two years later, winter of 1966, plaintiffs realized that although daily cash receipts had increased tremendously, their total profits had not increased accordingly. Both Smith and Jones were earning a modest, comfortable yearly income, but relative to the great expansion of their businesses, net income was too low.
Aware that something was amiss, Smith and Jones hired another accountant to privately review their books and find the source of the discrepancies. After a careful and extensive investigation, this accountant reported gross irregularities in the books.
Smith and Jones went immediately to their attorney for counsel, and on February 5, 1966, brought suit against Robert Brown for embezzlement under grounds as set forth in Ill. Stat. 277.04.
During the trail Brown admitted embezzling almost $100,000 of Smith's and Jones' money over a two-year period. (pp. 13–14)

Immediately following this case description, mock spectators were told of the sentence given the defendant. All were told of the *possible* range of punishment:

THE SENTENCE. The possible range of punishments Brown could have received according to the law varied from a minimum of $10,000 fine (no repayment of embezzled money) with a suspended sentence, to a maximum of $200,000 repayment–plus–fine, and 40 years in prison. (p. 14)

Manipulation of independent variables. The actual sentence given the defendant varied across experimental conditions:

Excessive punishment condition. Robert Brown was given the especially severe punishment of $100,000 repayment to Smith and Jones, plus $100,000 fine, and 40 years in prison without consideration for parole until 20 years had been served.

Equitable punishment condition. Robert Brown was given the moderate punishment of paying back all the money he had taken from Smith and Jones ($100,000), plus paying their expenses for trying to get their money back (legal, court costs). In addition, a deterrent punishment was given—2 years in prison with a chance for parole after 6 months.

Insufficient punishment condition. Robert Brown was given the especially light punishment of paying a $10,000 fine. He was not required to repay Smith and Jones. Brown was given no deterrent punishment such as a prison term, but rather received a suspended sentence. (p. 15)

After reading these facts of the case, students were told:

You have just read the details of Robert Brown's embezzlement, trial and sentencing. Now we are going to present a hypothetical situation, and ask you to role-play, to "put yourself in someone else's shoes" and respond as you think that person would respond, given the particular circumstances. Here's the situation.

The perceived effect of expressions of liking was manipulated by varying the role description:

1. Jurors in the *Compensation Condition* were led to believe their responses would have actual consequences for the defendant:

A current legal trend is to consider community standards in the assignment of criminal penalties. The recent Supreme Court pornography ruling, which declared that definitions of obscenity rest with local-level authorities, is an example of this principle. Your town is partaking in this trend by conducting an experimental court procedure. After a case has been tried and sentence determined, courtroom spectators from the community are asked to anonymously complete questionnaires asking about their feelings regarding the trail, the people involved, the verdict and the sentence. *The responses are read by the presiding judge, and he uses them as the primary factor in determining a new sentence when the defendant appeals his sentence.* This procedure worked extremely well in two recent appeals, where one sentence was made lighter, another heavier, on the basis of community responses to the original case.

You have just observed the trail of *Smith and Jones vs. Brown,* and are answering the 'community opinion' questionnaire. Thoughtfully and carefully consider the details of the case and the decision of the court when you answer the questions. Remember, your feelings about Robert Brown will be crucial in determining what his appealed and reconsidered punishment will be. (p. 16)

2. Subjects in the *Justification Condition* were told their responses would have no effect on the defendant's legal situation. Utne tried to stimulate justification by presenting a possible rationale for the defendant's sentence.

Subjects were expected to "pick up" on the one more appropriate to their particular punishment level.

> [*Discussion of trend of interest in community standards.*] Your town is partaking in this trend by conducting a survey of people's responses to local court decisions. After trial and sentencing of a case, courtroom spectators from the community are asked to anonymously complete questionnaires asking about their feelings regarding the trial, the people involved, the verdict and the sentence. *The responses will in no way affect the case or any other. In fact, the presiding judge has decided that he will not even read the responses.* He argues that as judge it is his duty to guide the public on the basis of his expert legal knowledge, and not to be influenced by the latest whimsy of public opinion. There are too many emotional factors operating in the atmosphere of a courtroom already, he feels. The questionnaires will be reviewed by a panel set up to assess public attitudes in general.
>
> You have just observed the trial of *Smith and Jones vs. Brown,* and are answering the "community opinion" questionnaire. Carefully and thoughtfully consider the details of the case and the decision of the court when you answer the questions. For example, you may feel like the jurors who commented that Robert Brown was a contemptible criminal, willing to take advantage of the trust placed in him by his friends. He was a man with no regard for morals or principles, these jurors said, and they felt he showed no remorse in his actions.
>
> Or you might feel as some of the jurors did that Robert Brown was a good, hardworking man who'd helped his friends and community for years, and unfortunately gave in to a very human temptation. In their view, the carelessness of his partners in ignoring their own financial matters made it especially easy for this basically good man to make a mistake.
>
> Whatever your feelings are about the case, please consider the facts carefully when answering the questions. Remember, Robert Brown has already been tried by a jury and his sentence determined by an experienced judge. Your responses will in no way affect the trial verdict or Brown's sentence. (pp. 17–18)

3. Finally, subjects in the *Emotion Condition* were encouraged to give a purely emotional expression of liking for the defendant.

> [*Discussion of trend of interest in community standards.*] Your town is partaking in this trend by conducting a survey of people's responses to local court cases and decisions. After trial and sentencing of a case, courtroom spectators from the community are asked to anonymously complete questionnaires asking about their feelings regarding the trial, the people involved, the verdict, and the sentence. The responses are not meant to affect the court or its decisions in any way. They are to be merely a gauge of the people's direct, emotional reactions to lawbreakers and lawbreaking.
>
> You have just observed the trial of *Smith and Jones vs. Brown* and are answering the "community opinion" questionnaire. A rational, analytical response is *not* what is wanted here. *Of primary importance in answering these questions is that you be in touch with your feelings, unafraid to say whatever comes into your mind.* There may be features of the case that just "ticked off" a response in you. For example, one of the jurors commented that any person in

Robert Brown's position, a defendant in a criminal proceeding, just naturally aroused feelings of warmth and sympathy which couldn't help but influence his decision. Another juror noted the opposite response in himself, that anyone on trial for lawbreaking like Robert Brown was made him experience feelings of disgust and contempt, feelings which also influenced his decision.

No matter what your feelings about Robert Brown and his case are, don't be afraid to express them. Give your first, immediate 'gut response' to the embezzler Robert Brown, and his trial.

Finally, the subjects were asked about their reactions to the case. Included in the questions was the critical question:

"How much do you like the defendant?"
1. Very greatly like
2. Moderately like
3. Slightly like
4. Slightly dislike
5. Moderately dislike
6. Very greatly dislike

Utne's data provide compelling support for equity theorists' contention that: (1) Expressions of liking *can* serve three different functions, and (2) the amount of punishment given a defendant ("too much," "just right," "not enough") does interact with the subject's motivation ("Compensation," "Justificaton," "Emotional expression") in determining his expressed liking for the defendant.

In the *Compensation Condition,* spectators knew that any expressions of liking/disliking could have practical consequences for the defendant. As pre-

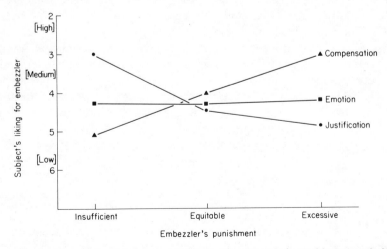

Fig. 4. The relationship secured between the embezzler's punishment and the Ss liking for him as a person.

dicted, under these conditions, observers expressed moderate dislike for the Insufficiently punished defendant ($\overline{M}$ = 5.10), slight dislike for the Equitably treated defendant ($\overline{M}$ = 4.05), and moderate liking for the Excessively punished one ($\overline{M}$ = 3.05). (These mean differences are significant, F = 33.67, 8/171 d.f., p < .01.)

In the *Justification Condition,* spectators knew that they were powerless to alter the defendant's prison sentence. Their expressions of liking were expected to reflect their acceptance of the status quo. As predicted, under these conditions, observers slightly liked the Insufficiently punished defendant ($\overline{M}$ = 3.00), slightly disliked the Equitably punished defendant ($\overline{M}$ = 4.45), and moderately disliked the Excessively punished one ($\overline{M}$ = 4.90). (F = 109.26, 8/171, d.f., p < .01.)

In the *Emotion Condition,* spectators were encouraged to simply express their mood. They were expected to like the Equitably treated defendant most and the Inequitably treated defendants—i.e., the Insufficiently *and* Excessively punished defendants—least. This prediction was *not* confirmed. Regardless of whether the defendant had been Insufficiently punished, Equitably punished, or Excessively punished, *S*s slightly disliked him ($\overline{M}$ = 4.30, 4.25, and 4.20, respectively).[6] (F = .33, 8/171 d.f., n.s.).

We have, earlier in this section, noted Clarence Darrow's statement emphasizing the importance of liking for the legal process. Undoubtedly, Darrow's—and Kalvan and Zeisel's—observations are correct: Jurors' liking for the defendant and the plaintiff must have *some* impact on the way they process information and on their ultimate decisions. However, Utne's data suggest that the link between "liking" and the "processing of information" and "sentencing behavior" is not as simple as theorists have supposed. The legal process is just that—a process. Courtroom interactions are ongoing, dynamic processes. Jurors constantly receive new information about their own roles as jurors, about the defendant and the plaintiff, and about their ability to affect the situation, e.g., their freedom to set penalties, and so on. Nor is liking static. The opinions one forms of others are constantly being altered by the input of new information. One's affective orientations, in turn, filter incoming information, and shape one's critical decisions. For example, jurors might enter the courtroom, naively assuming that they will have the power to set things right. They will have the

---

[6] Utne reports that her *Emotional Liking* manipulation failed for many students. She cites the comments of a typical boy who complained that he was so "into" the study—so determined to be a good, rational, sensible respondent—that he was completely thrown when finally asked to spontaneously express liking for the defendant. "How can I be spontaneous," he wrote, "when I've got all these *facts* to think of?" Utne recommends that experimenters who wish to conceptually replicate her study should use another strategy to motivate *S*s to express "gut" reactions.

power to decide the defendant's guilt/innocence, and in a few instances, to give him an appropriate sentence.

During the course of the trial, the testimony might yield new information which arouses a *strong* emotional response in the jurors; their liking for the defendant might then be colored by those feelings.

When the judge issues his instructions, however, the jurors may discover that they have far less power than they had thought. The jury deliberation may further reinforce their feeling of powerlessness: They may discover that all the other jurors want to let the "guilty" defendant go . . . or they may discover that the defendant will be let off on a legal technicality in spite of the jury's unanimous decision that he is guilty. Under these conditions, the disenchanted jurors might resign themselves to the status quo.

Each of the preceding events should affect the juror's liking for the defendant and the victim—and their liking, in turn, should color their reaction to new information and affect their sentencing behavior. It is clear that the link between "liking" and sentencing behavior may be an indescribably complex one.

Initially, we proposed that there would be a link between the juror's perception of the defendant's suffering and his liking for him. Utne (1974) demonstrated that this suffering and liking *are* linked. Liking, in turn, presumably affects the juror's evaluation of evidence and his sentencing. This relationship has not been empirically tested, but has been noted by legal scholars.

Second, we proposed that there should be a link between the juror's perception of the defendant's suffering and his sentencing behavior. Since the liking/sentencing relationship may be so complex, and since we do not yet know how much of an impact liking has on sentencing, we might do well to turn directly to our second question. We might ask directly: What impact does a defendant's suffering have on the spectators' and jurors' desire to punish him further?

3. Harmdoer's Suffering and Sentencing

Many theorists and lawyers believe that jurors will be sympathetic toward defendants who claim they have endured great remorse or great personal and financial losses.

In two recent and highly publicized legal cases—the Watergate burglaries of the Democratic party headquarters and the resignation and conviction of ex-Vice President Spiro Agnew—the defendants used appeals to sympathy—with varying success.

(1) E. Howard Hunt was convicted of breaking into the Democratic party national headquarters during the 1972 Presidential election campaign. He was convicted of burglary and given a preliminary sentence of 6 to 20 years in prison. In his testimony during his trial, before a grand jury, and before a Senate

184 W. AUSTIN, E. WALSTER, AND M. K. UTNE

special investigation, Mr. Hunt pleaded for leniency on the basis of his suffering from the crimes he committed. During the Senate hearings he noted:

> Now I find myself confined under a sentence which may keep me in prison for the rest of my life. I have been incarcerated for six months. For a time I was in solitary confinement. I have been physically attacked and robbed in jail. I have suffered a stroke. I have been transferred from place to place, manacled and chained, hand and foot. I am isolated from my motherless children. The funds provided me and others who participated in the break-in have long since been exhausted. I am faced with an enormous financial burden in defending myself against criminal charges and numerous civil suits. (as reported by *UPI*, 1973)

Hunt's attempt to win sympathy and leniency has thus far failed to either reduce his prison sentence or to increase public support for his predicament.

(2) In ex-Vice President Agnew's case, Elliot Richardson, the United States Attorney General in the government investigation and prosecution of charges of bribery and tax fraud, called for leniency on the grounds that the Vice President had suffered substantially. Richardson stated:

> I am firmly convinced that in all the circumstances leniency is justified. I am keenly aware, first, of the historic magnitude of the penalties inherent in the vice president's resignation from his high office and his acceptance of a judgment of conviction for a felony.
>
> To propose that a man who has suffered these penalties should, in addition, be incarcerated in a penal institution, however briefly, is more than I as head of the government's prosecuting arm, can recommend or wish. (as reported by *AP*, 1973)

Agnew was fined only $10,000 and put on 3-year probation on only one charge of tax evasion. The prosecutors dropped all other charges.[7]

In their classic survey of jury trials, Kalven and Zeisel (1966) found evidence that jurors do take a harmdoer's suffering into account when deciding on a penalty. These authors found that when a defendant reports great remorse, suffers in the commission of the crime, endures lengthy pretrial detention, or even when he has suffered misfortunes unconnected to the crime, jurors tend to be lenient. Consider, for example, the presiding judges' descriptions of why jurors, in a potpourri of cases, were more lenient than they should have been:

Defendant suffers as a consequence of crime:

---

[7] At the time of this publication, it appears that the "ultimate" example of appeals to the redemptive value of a wrongdoer's suffering has occurred. President Ford justified his full and absolute pardon for former President Nixon by citing Nixon's, and the Nixon family's, profound suffering.

'YOUR HONOR, CAN WE JUST TAKE THE PARDON AND GO? . . . WE'VE SUFFERED
ENOUGH ALREADY!'

While the Court sitting without a jury would have found him guilty, there was
no difficulty for the Court to understand why a jury of laymen would find the
defendant not guilty. The police chief and his witnesses were six-foot, one-inch
men, weighing over 200 pounds, and the defendant was about five-foot seven,
weighing about 118 pounds. . . The police. . .beat the defendant up before they
got him into the car. (p. 237)

Defendant suffers remorse:

The authors report two cases in which the defendant's remorse is sufficiently
marked to come to the judge's attention. One report read:

A young Negro who apparently was sorry for his act. (p. 205)

Defendant suffers pretrial detention:

The jury felt sorry for the defendant because he had been in jail for over two
months and the lumber allegedly stolen was worth $2.50. I think the jury had a
Jean Valjean complex. (p. 264)
. . . It is customary for the judge in sentencing to give the defendant credit for the
time he has already spent in jail; the jury, however, would at times not only give
him credit, but would set him free. (p. 303)
. . . The defendant is charged with the rape of his ten-year-old daughter and at the
first trial of his case is found guilty and sentenced to life imprisonment. On
appeal, a new trial is granted with a change of venue. At the second trial the jury
hangs. The case is tried a third time, and it is for this third trial that we have the

judge-jury report. At this trial it is disclosed that the defendant has at that point been in jail for thirteen months. The extraordinary reaction of this third and last jury, which acquits, is set forth by the judge as follows: They were out just 30 minutes. The jury took up a collection of $68 and gave it to the defendant after the case was over. (p. 304)

Defendant suffers—suffering unrelated to crime:

Defendant did not testify but the evidence shows that, during the years in question, his home burned, he was seriously injured, and his son was killed. Later he lost his leg, his wife gave birth to a premature child which was both blind and spastic. These, however, are only a portion of the calamities the defendant suffered during the years he failed to file his income tax return. The jury cannot bring itself to add to the misfortune of the defendant. The judge gives full recognition to the point, adding: "This is a typical case of the jury exercising the power of pardon." (p. 305)

Kalven and Zeisel conclude, on the basis of these reports, that jurors' decisions are markedly influenced by whether or not the defendant has suffered—even if his suffering is unrelated to his crime.

In a study with grade school children, Austin *et al.* (1973) tested the notion that children would assign harmdoers who suffer insufficiently in the course of their act more punishment than harmdoers who suffer appropriately or excessively. Austin *et al.* asked the children to read a story describing two boys—Steve and Bob. Steve was described as the harmdoer; Bob was the victim. During recess, while the two boys were playing baseball, Steve deliberately tripped Bob. Bob fell down and sprained his ankle and cut his lip. Steve lost his balance and fell down *in the act* of tripping Bob. Steve's suffering was then systematically varied: In the *Insufficient Suffering* condition, his suffering was *slight* (he received "a few scratches on his hands"). In the *Moderate* condition, he received "some painful cuts on his hands and knees." In the *Excessive* condition, he "broke his arm and leg."

The story then reported that the school principal had appointed a student panel to decide how much punishment Steve should receive. "The principal tells the panel to decide how many hours Steve should have to stay after school. You are on the panel. How many hours would you say Steve should have to stay after school?" Students were asked to indicate their opinion on a "Punishment scale," which ranged from 0 to 7 hours.

Austin *et al.* found that students did assign Steve a harsher penalty when he had suffered insufficiently than when he suffered moderately or excessively.

Finally, Austin (personal communication) recently conducted two studies in an attempt to demonstrate that jurors do take a criminal's "suffering in the act" into account when settling on an appropriate sentence.

In both studies, Austin asked college students to read a synopsis of the proceedings of an actual trial. First, they read an eye-witness account of the crime: [In Study 1, the defendant's crime was a relatively minor one (purse snatching). In Study 2, the defendant's crime was a far more serious one. (He had not only snatched a purse, but he had severely beaten his female victim, causing her to be hospitalized for 10 days.)]

After allegedly committing his crime, the defendant attempted to escape from the scene (and from the police). In the process, Austin claimed, the purse-snatcher had suffered not at all, moderately, or excessively. [In Study 1, the defendant was said to have suffered not at all, moderately (i.e., receiving cuts and bruises and a broken arm), or excessively (paralyzed from the neck down). In Study 2, the defendant was said to have suffered not at all, moderately (i.e., suffering cracked ribs and a broken leg), or excessively (paralyzed from the neck down).]

Finally, students were told that, after deliberating for only ten minutes, a jury had convicted the defendant.

Students were asked to play the role of presiding judge. They were asked to carefully study the synopsis and then to recommend an "appropriate" sentence (within the minimum-maximum set by law).

In both studies, Austin found strong support for the "Suffering in the Act Hypothesis." The more the defendant was said to have suffered in the "get away," the smaller the prison sentence mock judges gave him (see Tables I and II).

TABLE I
NUMBER OF MONTHS ASSIGNED TO PRISON AS A
FUNCTION OF A CRIMINAL'S SUFFERING AND SEX OF THE
OBSERVER (AUSTIN) FOR LOW CRIME SEVERITY
(PURSE SNATCHING)[a]

	Amount of criminal suffering			
	None	Moderate	Excessive	$\bar{M}$
Male observer	15.83	10.83	3.44	10.04
Female observer	22.72	14.39	7.89	15.00
$\bar{M}$	19.28	12.61	5.67	

[a]The range of the prison sentence set by the law was 0 (suspended sentence) to 60 months in prison.

TABLE II

NUMBER OF MONTHS ASSIGNED TO PRISON AS A
FUNCTION OF SEX AND CRIMINAL'S SUFFERING FOR HIGH
CRIME SEVERITY (AUSTIN: STUDY 2)[a]

	Amount of criminal's suffering			
	None	Moderate	Excessive	$\overline{M}$
Male observer	75.22	73.17	11.00	53.13
Female observer	78.33	73.33	21.00	57.56
$\overline{M}$	76.78	73.25	16.00	

[a]The range of the prison sentence set by the law was 0 (suspended sentence) to 180 months in prison.

In an ingenious set of laboratory experiments, Legant (1973a) tested the hypothesis that the length of time a defendant was detained between arrest and trial would effect the sentence jurors assigned him.

In one experiment, Legant asked student jurors to review a single case report. The report described the defendant and the circumstances surrounding his offense. For the sake of generality, several crimes of varying severity were presented. For example, in one set of case studies, the defendant stole items from a car. In one report, he removed the hubcaps alone from a car. In another case, he stole the hubcaps and tires. In a third report, the hubcaps, tires, and as many items as he could carry were stripped from the car. In a set of cases related to heroin offenses, the defendant merely possessed heroin, sold it to users on the street, or acted as a "wholesaler" for street pushers. In a set of cases involving purse-snatching incidents, the defendant grabbed the purse and fled, took it and pushed his victim down in the process, or took it and beat his victim up before retreating. Legant systematically varied how long the criminal had ostensibly been detained. Various reports stated that the criminal was held in pretrial detention a short time (2 days), a moderate amount of time (1 month), or a long period of time (1 year). In the second study, male registered voters watched a video tape of an "actual trial."

The scene of the tape was an actual courtroom of the New Haven Circuit Court. The *dramatis personae* included a court clerk, robed judge, and a stenographer, as well as a public defender, prosecutor, and the star of the show—the defendant. The clerk pounded his gavel to open court and the judge entered. The case was announced, the attorneys were introduced, and a brief blackout signalled the entrance of the jury. Then the public defender called his client to the stand. Information about the defendant and his crime emerged during the questioning. The defendant was a 25-year-old high school dropout. At the time of his arrest, he was a packer in a factory. The defendant admitted that he had removed either the radio (low severity condition) or the radio, tires, radiator, battery, and tape deck (high severity condition) from a car. He claimed, however, that he assumed that the car was abandoned. In the course of his testimony, the defendant also revealed that he had been held in pretrial detention.

Legant emphasized the period of pretrial detention to mock jurors in the following way: The public defender asked the defendant if he had lost his job upon arrest. This question enraged the defendant. He complained that he "couldn't pay no $500 bail to get out," that he *had* lost his job, and had had to spend a short time (a week), a longer time (a month), or a long time (a year) in jail "without a trial." He continued to mutter briefly, while the prosecutor shouted, "Objection" twice and urged the judge to instruct the witness to confine his remarks to answering the questions. The judge did so.

Legant's results were startlingly negative. In neither study did pretrial detention affect the length of sentence observers suggested for the defendant—or their liking for him.

In summary, then, observational data and survey data (Sharp & Otto (1910a,b), Kalven & Zeisel, 1966) provide consistent support for the contention that jurors will take the harmdoer's suffering into account when calculating how severely he should be punished. Laboratory experiments provide inconsistent evidence in support of this contention.

Unfortunately, no one has yet tested the intriguing hypotheses that a harmdoer's suffering in the act will "count" more than will suffering unrelated to his criminal activity.

IV. Discussion

Legal theorists have never been able to agree on the nature of justice (Brandt, 1962; Rawls, 1971). Thus, judges and jurors are often forced to decide on its nature themselves. Let us consider an example.

Why Should the Defendant Be Punished? As we noted earlier, penal theorists have never been able to agree on *why* we punish wrongdoers; nor do legislators tell judges the objectives of punishing or what the punishment should be (Frankel, 1973). Since theorists cannot agree on why or how much society should punish wrongdoers, the problem of deciding falls to the judge and jury. Of course, judges' and jurors' decisions are subject to some legal restraints. For example, often judges must impose a minimum sentence if they are to impose any sentence at all. Yet, judges and jurors—by default and choice—still exercise enormous discretion (Gaudet *et al.*, 1933). In fact, some scholars have argued that discretionary decision-making is the foremost aspect of the Western legal system (Davis, 1959). Discretion is deliberately written into the legal system. (The writing of minimum-maximum sentences by legislatures exemplifies this fact.) U.S. District Court Judge Marvin Frankel (1973) admitted that he was appalled by "the unbridled power of the sentencers [including himself] to be arbitrary and discriminatory." In addition, the dominant evolutionary trend in American judicial behavior seems to be toward a Realist decision-making style (Chambliss & Seidman, 1971)–a style which would increase judges' and jurors' discretion still further. Slogans such as, "Make the punishment fit the criminal, not the crime," press for even more discretion in sentencing behavior.

Since impartial observers possess so much discretion currently (and may possess even more in the future), jurors' informal perceptions as to the nature of justice and equity are likely to have an enormous impact on their judicial decisions.

This realization leads us to two conclusions:

What Is and What Should Be. Obviously, legal theorists must continue to try to hammer out an adequate theory of social justice. They should try to provide judges and jurors with some systematic guidelines as to how they *ought* to behave. Legislators should try to formulate precise across-the-board sentencing principles (Wasserstrom, 1961).

At the same time, social psychologists and lawyers should try to ascertain what *is*. They should try to ascertain what practices judges and jurors are following currently. For example, they should try to ascertain how important various potential extralegal factors are in determining conviction and sentencing. For example, do jurors presently follow equity dictates in making their decisions? Or, as is more likely, do they try to compromise between their desire for perfect equity and their conflicting desires to ignore laws they dislike, ignore "trivial" complaints, give young men a second chance, etc. Only research can tell us what informal "rules" judges and jurors are currently following.

Once we know how things ought to be, and how they are, we can begin to investigate the best way to induce jurors to behave as we think they should.

No existing social psychological theory (or collection of theories) can tell us very much about the legal system in action. Yet, in embarking on such an ambitious project as the one detailed above, the utilization of some social psychological theories such as equity theory has several potential advantages: (1) Such theories give us an orderly framework for analyzing the legal system in action; (2) they give us a framework for uncovering and categorizing factors which presently affect judicial decisions; (3) they remind us that unless decisions are *perceived* to be equitable, those who come into contact with the legal system will perceive the system to be unjust.

INCREMENTAL EXCHANGE THEORY: A FORMAL MODEL FOR PROGRESSION IN DYADIC SOCIAL INTERACTION[1]

L. Rowell Huesmann

UNIVERSITY OF ILLINOIS
CHICAGO CIRCLE, CHICAGO, ILLINOIS

George Levinger[2]

UNIVERSITY OF MASSACHUSETTS
AMHERST, MASSACHUSETTS

[1] The authors' names are listed alphabetically, the first having contributed especially to the formalization and the second to the model's theoretical motivation. We are indebted to our two excellent co-workers: Philip E. Long, who created the initial computer program for RELATE, and John Goldin, who worked intensively on several simulation experiments. Robert Abelson, Icek Ajzen, Henry Alker, and Robert Wyer have provided constructive suggestions that have improved this paper.

[2] This work was initiated at Yale University where LRH taught and GL was an NIMH Special Research Fellow in the Department of Psychology in 1970–1971. It was supported by Grants HD-04319 from the U. S. Public Health Service and GS-33641 from the National Science Foundation to George Levinger. The Yale Computer Science Department generously made available its PDP-10 computer facility.

I. Introduction

In attempting to understand interpersonal relationships, social psychologists have relied primarily on research on static structures and stable states. Yet an important characteristic of social relationships is their gradual development over time. Social psychological theory has not emphasized longitudinal changes in interpersonal behavior, but has focused on the ahistorical aspects of interpersonal relations. Laboratory studies have, of course, investigated changes in relationships that occur over a short time span. But such research is suited for understanding problems in the near term rather than for illuminating longer interaction sequences. Longitudinal research on the development of relationships has seldom been carried out; it is expensive, it yields correlational rather than experimental data, and it poses many practical problems.

Given the difficulties of studying longitudinal changes in dyadic relationships, it is important to build abstract models so that the effects of hypothetical determinants can be examined before beginning one's field research. Such models should possess reasonable generality and a priori plausibility. One medium for model building is computer simulation, which enables us to test the effects of varying combinations of factors on sequential changes in artificial relationships.

In this paper we present a general model of dyadic social interaction stated in the language of computation science. We call our computer program "RELATE" and the theory underlying it "incremental exchange theory." Actually, RELATE is a general framework within which many theories can be formulated about particular instances of pair involvement. The RELATE program brings two hypothetical actors together for an interaction. It simulates the development of the actors' relationship in accord with the basic tenets of our theory *and* the user's own subtheory. Since RELATE does not understand English, it can only accept specific theories stated in the language of computation science. Hence, RELATE discourages "hand waving" by its users or comments such as "you know," "sort of," and "generally." Indeed, RELATE's value to social psychology may stem as much from the theorizing behaviors it forces upon its users as from its own substantive theory.

Several frameworks have been used in the past for modeling pair behavior. We have drawn upon them in constructing the RELATE model. Let us briefly review the most relevant of these approaches before proceeding with a description of incremental exchange theory and RELATE.

II. Formal Approaches to Dyadic Interaction

A. TWO-ACTOR MATRIX MODELS

1. Thibaut and Kelley's Exchange Matrices

One paradigm that has drawn the attention of social psychologists during the last decade is the two-person outcome matrix, first generalized to diverse forms of social interaction by Thibaut and Kelley (1959). Using a schema derived from economic game theory, they put forth a conceptual framework that draws on the traditions of both reinforcement and cognitive theories, and utilizes familiar psychological concepts such as reward and cost in a payoff matrix. The interaction between two persons is considered by casting one person in the role of Row actor and the other as the Column actor. Each actor has available a repertoire of responses, varying in number and kind across situations. The intersection of the actors' responses yields an outcome to each, as specified by the payoffs in the cell at the intersection of the row and column selected. "Bimatrices" of this sort have been used for conceiving of interaction in laboratory games such as Prisoner's Dilemma, and also for conceiving of many other sorts of encounters (see Wolf & Zahn, 1972).

Despite its potential usefulness, Thibaut and Kelley's conception of the exchange matrix has so far been primarily illustrative; it has produced few unique insights or novel data. For one thing, the paradigm itself contains no rationale for coordinating actors' hypothetical payoffs with empirical data about outcome values. There exists no specified means for converting the raw payoffs used in existing experimental research on dyadic games into the theoretically defined subjective utilities upon which Thibaut and Kelley's hypothetical actors presumably base their behavior.

A second limitation derives from a predominantly static use of the game matrix. Characteristically, writings on exchange theory treat outcome matrices as though they remain stationary during interaction. Yet, in the living world, a pair's outcomes and response options usually change over time either gradually or dramatically, depending upon factors associated with the situation and the stage of a relationship.

A third limitation of the approach has been its individualistic orientation to problems that are often supra-individual in nature. To quote a recent critic of exchange theory:

> Thibaut and Kelley assume that each individual has at his disposal a sort of internal "clock" or scale which determines the comparison level (C.L.) and which indicates the profit that he might obtain if he engaged in a relationship alternative to the one in which he is engaged at present. If this profit is greater, he abandons the current relationship; if not, he stays with it. . . . What appears to me significant is the attempt to construct a theory of collective processes on the basis of an individualistic theory [Moscovici, 1972, p. 26].

Conceptions of social exchange based on Thibaut and Kelley's suggestions have neglected to account for the transformation of personal outcome preferences through social interaction or group membership. This same limitation attends other theories of social exchange, such as those of Homans (1961) or Blau (1964), which ignore one partner's gratification from the other partner's own good outcomes.

2. Mathematical Game Models

Another body of social psychological work has been tied to game-theoretic models of dyadic interaction. Beginning with the interest aroused by the Prisoner's Dilemma in the 1950's (Deutsch, 1958; Luce & Raiffa, 1957), social psychologists started to use game matrices for work on problems of conflict and cooperation. Such game situations seemed to present an avenue for attaining systematic knowledge about how partners might achieve accommodation in other mixed-motive situations.

Mathematical analyses of the Prisoner's Dilemma (Harris, 1969; Amnon Rapoport, 1967; Anatol Rapoport, 1966) and of other games (Wyer, 1969) led to some interesting insights into the psychology of cooperation *in games*. Rapoport (1967) introduced the ideas of interstate transitions and the discounting of future payoffs into models of game behavior, while Wyer (1969) proposed that actors weight their co-actor's payoffs differentially over the course of an interaction sequence. None of these game-theoretic models, however, linked incremental changes in payoffs with the depth of dyadic involvement. Moreover, it has been difficult to use the social psychology of laboratory games for informing the social psychology of everyday life. That realization has led to disenchantment with purely game-theoretic approaches toward social behavior (see Nemeth, 1972).

B. COMPUTER SIMULATION MODELS

Another avenue leading toward modeling of social interaction has been the use of computer simulation. Two simulation models were particularly influential for our own work: HOMUNCULUS (Gullahorn & Gullahorn, 1963) and ALDOUS (Loehlin, 1965).

1. HOMUNCULUS

One imaginative attempt to model dyadic interaction was stimulated by Homans' (1950, 1961) enumeration of axioms for social behavior. On the basis of some of Homans' propositions, Simon (1957) constructed mathematical models to provide predictions of social behavior. Simon's (Newell, Shaw, & Simon, 1958) introduction of computer simulation into psychology influenced Gullahorn and Gullahorn's (1963) use of Homans' principles in a computer program designed to model social behavior.

The Gullahorns' program, called HOMUNCULUS, simulated the interaction between an actor and his social environment. Most often that environment consisted of just one other actor. HOMUNCULUS was essentially a determinate model of behavior, which applied Homans' propositions in order to select an actor's behavior in the context of a well-defined social situation. Each action then became part of the actor's characteristics and could play a part in determining new actions. The actor was defined by a hierarchical structure of lists of personality characteristics and situation-action pairings of moderate complexity. To classify the actor's actions, the Gullahorns used Bales' (1950) twelve-category scheme for classifying interpersonal behavior. Despite its inventiveness, the HOMUNCULUS model has not yet contributed substantially to the social psychology of interpersonal behavior. Its complexity has made it hard to conceive of action or interaction in its terms.

2. ALDOUS

Another computer model of dyadic social interaction, which arises more directly out of reinforcement theory, was Loehlin's (1965) ALDOUS model. An ALDOUS actor could engage in three general types of interaction with his environment: approach, withdrawal, or attack. It appears that Loehlin was primarily interested in showing how actors can modify their behavior purely on the basis of positive and negative reinforcements. While his experiments show interesting sequences of individual and inter-individual accommodation as a result of such reinforcement, ALDOUS has produced little new knowledge concerning dyadic interaction in general.

Despite their limitations, each of these formal approaches to social interaction contributed to the development of our own model. We now turn to a discussion of the theory underlying the RELATE model: incremental exchange theory.

III. Central Features of Incremental Exchange Theory

Incremental exchange theory assumes that an essential characteristic of any social relationship is its change over time. To represent dyadic interaction, the theory employs dyadic exchange matrices like those of Thibaut and Kelley (1959). But while earlier theorists used a single static matrix to represent a relationship, we use a set of systematically linked payoff matrices to represent a relationship. The fundamental assumption of incremental exchange theory is that the expected value of a dyad's rewards increases as the depth of the relationship increases. By "depth" we mean the level of a pair's mutual involvement (Levinger & Snoek, 1972).

Consider the elementary situation that constitutes the absence of any relation between two isolated individuals—a point of "zero contact" (Levinger & Snoek, 1972). At that point, the outcome associated with a continued "stay apart" response is assumed to have a payoff of zero, while the expected payoff for mutual approach (i.e., a two-person encounter) may be greater or less than zero, depending on the anticipated pleasure of the meeting.

As a relationship proceeds, we propose that expected payoffs, in general, change from relatively small to quite large, and that the variability of payoffs increases in range. Interpersonal rewards characteristically increase if involvement deepens; conversely, if involvement recedes, they decline (Levinger & Snoek, 1972). Associated with the increase of rewards at deeper levels, however, is an increase in the potential losses entailed by noncoordination. Thus one loses little if stood up by a blind date, but it would be quite hurtful to be ignored by someone dear. Familiarity may breed reward, but it also breeds the capacity to hurt (Aronson, 1970).

In each "state" of a relationship, the actors' behaviors lead to an immediate outcome having a separate payoff value for each actor (Thibaut & Kelley, 1959). Furthermore, the outcome results in a *transition* to either the same or a different interpersonal "state"—where either the same set or a different set of behaviors and payoff values is applicable.

If both members' outcomes at the early stages of a relationship are satisfying compared to those outcomes they can obtain in alternative relationships, the pair moves into states of deeper involvement (Altman & Taylor, 1973; Levinger & Snoek, 1972; Thibaut & Kelley, 1959). If the actors experience reward from each other, they are likely to invest more in the relationship and to become more interdependent (Huston, 1973). Conversely, if interaction is unrewarding, investment in the relation diminishes; all else being equal, they will minimize contact (Thibaut & Kelley, 1959).

As people get to know one another—as they transit from superficial to deeper states of involvement—their options in interaction seem to widen. In initial contacts, behavior tends toward stereotype or etiquette. Later in a relationship, a larger number of behaviors become appropriate (Altman & Taylor, 1973).

People also consider the *costs* of interaction. Regardless of the expected rewards, particular behaviors in particular situations are costly to some people.

Thus a shy person finds it expensive to say "hello," particularly to a stranger, even if it is likely that the stranger will respond warmly to his greeting (Jung, 1923). A proud man finds it costly to offer an apology, even if he knows it is justified and it would relieve the tension. A submissive subject fears to seize control over a task, even if he is assigned the leader role (Ghiselli & Lodahl, 1958; Smelser, 1961). Regardless of the potential outcome, then, varying basic costs are associated with differences among actors, among actions, and among situations.

Irrespective of how deeply he is involved, an individual often anticipates rewards in a dyadic interaction long before they occur. Yet even when future rewards appear clearly higher than present rewards, a person may prefer present rewards because of a *discount* (Klineberg, 1968; Mischel, 1966). One values deferred rewards less than present rewards to the extent that one is unsure about the future: "A bird in the hand is worth two in the bush." In some situations, however, deferred outcomes may be valued more than present ones.

Given that human actors consider the future, how do they evaluate it? In social interaction, an actor is sensitive to the other's probable responses in choosing his own actions. Persons differ in how far into the future they look, but they do try to anticipate their partner's most likely actions and responses. Either implicitly or explicitly one estimates the probability of the occurrence of each of the co-actor's alternative actions (Ajzen & Fishbein, 1970; Rapoport & Chammah, 1965). Of course, one person's estimates of the other's probable behavior are likely to change over the course of interaction (Wyer, 1969). Each person *learns* about the other's probable future actions from the nature of his past actions (Lott & Lott, 1972). In real life, another's past behavior exercises an obvious effect on one's current estimates of what he is likely to do next.

IV. The Premises of Incremental Exchange Theory

Incremental exchange theory is an attempt to move beyond earlier theories of exchange by incorporating assumptions about sequential process. To state the above premises of incremental exchange theory more formally, one needs a framework within which to cast the theory. We have chosen the methodology of computer simulation and call our framework the RELATE model.

A. INTRODUCTION TO THE RELATE MODEL

RELATE is a program for simulating social interaction between two persons. It is a finite-state process model, based on the conception that the current interpersonal state is determined solely by the previous state and by the behaviors selected by the two actors while in that previous state. Aside from determining the next state of the relationship, these two behaviors result in an interactive outcome with separate payoffs for each actor.

An interpersonal state refers to a given level of interpersonal involvement in a relationship between two persons. The deeper a relationship, the greater is the partners' mutual investment and the greater are their expected outcomes (Levinger, Senn, & Jorgensen, 1970; Levinger & Snoek, 1972). A state is defined in terms of five major variables:

1. The *behaviors* available in the state. Each actor has a set of mutually exclusive behavior options. The actions available to one actor may be quite different from those available to his co-actor. During any time unit, both actors choose their behavior simultaneously.[3]

2. The *cost* of each behavior, independent of its payoff.

3. A separate *payoff matrix* for each actor. If Actor 1 selects behavior i and Actor 2 selects behavior j, the payoff for Actor 1 is in row i and column j of his payoff matrix. The payoff for Actor 2 is in row j and column i of his matrix.

4. Each actor's initial *estimate of the probability* that his co-actor will choose any given behavior. A probability estimate of zero, for any of the co-actor's behaviors, would indicate that the actor is unaware that his co-actor has that option or believes there is no chance that he will use it. Estimates in any state are permitted to change during the course of interaction.

5. A *state transition matrix* which specifies which state follows each possible behavior outcome. Transitions are not probabilistic; if Actor 1 selects behavior i and Actor 2 behavior j, the next state will definitely be the state specified in row i and column j of the matrix. This next state may be either the same state, a state of deeper social interaction, or a state of lesser social interaction.

B. FORMAL BASIS OF INCREMENTAL EXCHANGE THEORY

The premises of incremental exchange theory can be stated as rules within the RELATE framework. These rules specify some processes or structures precisely and constrain others. They pertain to (1) an actor's decision-making procedures, (2) the array of potential payoffs and costs associated with his behaviors, (3) transitions across states, (4) the actor's consideration of the future, (5) his learning from past outcomes, (6) his estimation of the other's probable behavior, and (7) the termination of a relationship. These rules are formalizations of principles of incremental exchange theory.

---

[3] One of the problems with exchange matrices is that the behaviors available to an actor cannot depend on the co-actor's behavior choice. Yet in life they often do. If one member of a pair decides to walk away, the other cannot very well continue to talk to him. RELATE resolves this difficulty by using sequential state transitions to represent such dependencies. An actor may decide to talk to his co-actor at the same time his co-actor decides to depart. This leads the pair to a new state where conversation is impossible.

1. Decisions

The decision-making model is described in detail later; however, it is based upon three premises.

1.1. An actor chooses that behavior (from any given set of options) which maximizes a weighted sum of his own and his co-actor's expected payoffs for a fixed period of time into the future (his depth of search).

1.2. The weight accorded to the co-actor's payoffs increases with the depth of the relationship. At early stages, the other's payoffs receive insignificant weight; at later stages, increasing weight is accorded to the payoffs received by the co-actor.[4]

1.3. In making any particular decision, an actor considers payoffs from both current and potential future states. The relative weighting of the present and the future is determined by the discount he employs in his search strategy.

2. Payoffs and Costs

It is assumed that, as interaction deepens, payoffs increase in value and also in variability. So-called deeper states represent greater investment by the actors and greater potential payoffs than do earlier states. Furthermore, it becomes more costly to terminate the relationship at a later state than at an earlier state.

2.1. In deeper states the average immediate potential payoff for an actor is greater (more positive) than in shallower states.

2.2. In deeper states, the entries in an actor's payoff matrices have higher variability.

2.3. A fixed cost for initiating a behavior is associated with each behavior and the state in which it is exercised.

2.4. The cost of terminating a relationship increases with the increasing depth of the relationship.

3. Transition Across States

Interaction is not confined merely to one static matrix of behavior options and outcomes. The typical interpersonal relationship offers opportunities not only to repeat interaction within the same payoff matrix, but also to move forward in the relationship, to move backward, or to terminate the relationship entirely. Transitions from any given behavioral state depend upon the outcomes experienced in that state.

3.1. A transition is determined solely by the previous interpersonal state and the outcome arrived at through the actors' behavior in that state.

---

[4] Concern for a co-actor's outcomes may indeed by *chronologically* curvilinear. In other words, later in a relationship, when the partner is taken more for granted, the actor may easily become less concerned with his or her outcomes. In the present version of the theory, though, we assume that concern for a co-actor increases directly with depth of involvement.

3.2. Consider any two outcome cells, X and Y in State$_t$, where both actors' payoffs are higher in Cell X than in Cell Y. Any transition to a new state from the more positive Cell X must then be to at least as deep a state as the transition from the less positive Cell Y.

4.   Consideration of the Future

At any given moment, an actor assesses the payoffs associated with the options then available to him. In this assessment, the other's probable behavior in the present and in future states is taken into account. Payoffs expected from future interaction with the other are weighted by a discount factor which is specified for the particular relationship.

4.1. An actor always searches out those outcomes to be expected within the present interaction state. In other words, he always examines all potential outcomes at the Depth of 1. Actors also may look into the future beyond the present state, searching to a Depth of 2, 3, 4, etc., according to their predisposition to seek out the future.

4.2. Present payoffs are worth 100% of their par value. Future payoffs are discounted to be worth from 0 up to 100% of par value.

If future states are discounted to 0%, the actor's depth of search is effectively equal to 1.

5.   Estimating the Other's Probable Behavior

In any given state, the actor will possess expectations about his co-actor's likely behaviors.

5.1. An actor's subjective probabilities for his co-actor's behaviors depend initially on the actor's experience with comparable co-actors, and subsequently also on his learning from his experience with this particular co-actor.

6.   Learning from Past Outcomes

In interpersonal relationships, actors frequently encounter each other in states that have been previously experienced.

6.1. If an actor selects behavior X in some state, then—if that state should recur—his co-actor will have increased his estimate of the relative probability of the actor's behavior X. The amount by which one actor increases his subjective probability of another's behavior after a single trial is his "speed of learning." Of course, in some relationships learning does not occur.

7.   Termination of the Relationship

Thibaut and Kelley's exchange theory assumes that if a person's outcomes in a dyadic relationship fall below some critical point of comparison, he will leave the relationship (1959, p. 81). The following premise is consonant with that assumption.

7.1. An actor terminates a relationship if the expected payoff from a competing relationship minus the cost of terminating the current one exceeds the *expected payoff from the current relationship* by an amount sufficient to overcome the effect of past credits and debits.

In any situation being modeled, the RELATE program allows the theoretician freedom to specify exactly how past credits and debits shall affect termination. He can specify whatever function of credits and debits he wishes.

V. The RELATE Model

Having specified the premises of incremental exchange theory within the framework of the RELATE model, we can now elaborate the details of this model.

A. DECIDING ON A BEHAVIOR

The actors' decision processes are modeled with a tree searching optimization procedure developed by artificial intelligence researchers for intelligent game playing (Slagle & Lee, 1971). In any state an actor may consider (i.e., "look ahead") a specifiable number of decisions into the future. For each possible decision he might make, he must also consider all decisions his co-actor might make. These potential decision sequences can be represented as a tree that contains an enormous number of nodes if the actor looks ahead more than a few decision steps. For example, if four behaviors are available in every state, a look-ahead of five decision steps results in a tree with 4^{10} (over 1,000,000) sequences that would be considered.[5]

Our model assumes that, prior to selecting a behavior, each actor engages in a decision process that is *equivalent* to generating the tree of potential sequences representing a look-ahead of n decision steps. He then "backs up" the payoffs attainable to the top of the tree.

This backing up of payoffs is best viewed as assigning an outcome value to each node in the tree. An actor selects the behavior leading to the immediate node with the highest backed-up value.

The backing up of values from a set of nodes to their parent node is accomplished with recursive equations. Suppose Actor 1 is at a decision level in

---

[5] While the current RELATE model operates as though all people are maximizers, the RELATE framework is general enough that "satisficing" actors can be simulated too. Essentially, a RELATE actor wants a payoff at least as large as a parameter SAT. If he cannot find a payoff as large as SAT, he will settle for the best available. In the current version of RELATE the value of SAT is infinity; therefore, people behave as maximizers.

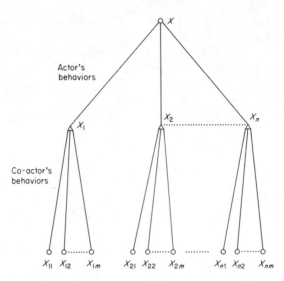

Fig. 1. Two levels of an actor's decision tree as modeled by RELATE. Node X represents one actor's decision point; nodes $X_1 \ldots X_n$ represent his co-actor's decision points for the same time; and nodes $X_{11} \ldots X_{nm}$ represent the actor's perceived decision points one step further ahead in time.

the tree attempting to determine the value of a particular node X. This situation is diagrammed in Fig. 1.

Let X be a node where Actor 1 makes a decision.

Let $X_1 \ldots X_n$ be X's daughter nodes (Actor 2 makes a decision at these nodes).

Let $X_{i1} \ldots X_{im}$ be X_i's daughter nodes (Actor 1 makes a decision at these nodes).

Let $V1\ (X)$ be the backed-up value of node X to Actor 1.

Let PAY 1 (X_{ij}) be the immediate payoff to Actor 1 associated with node X_{ij}.

Let d be the discount parameter for Actor 1.

Let L be the decision level in the tree. Accordingly, the values are backed up by equations:

$$V1\ (X) = \max V1\ (X_i) \quad \text{for } i = 1 \text{ to } n \qquad (1)$$

$$V1\ (X_i) = \sum_{j=1}^{m} \left\{ [\text{PAY } 1\ (X_{ij}) + V1\ (X_{ij})] \cdot \text{Prob (Actor 2 choosing behavior leading from } X_i \text{ to } X_{ij}) \right\} \cdot d^{\,L} \qquad (2)$$

The node X_{ij} is the same type of node as node X (i.e., Actor 1 to move) and its value would have been previously derived with the same recursive equations. It can be seen in Eq. (2) that an actor's payoff at node X_{ij} is the sum of his immediate payoff at that node plus the backed-up value of future payoffs attainable from that node. At the deepest decision level, $L = N$,

$$V1\ (X_i) = \sum_{j=1}^{m} \left\{ \text{PAY } 1\ (X_{ij}) \cdot \text{Prob (Actor 2 choosing behavior leading from } X_i \text{ to } X_{ij}) \right\} \cdot d^N \tag{3}$$

This decision procedure is deterministic, not probabilistic. Probability plays a role in the model only insofar as each actor estimates the "probability" of his co-actor's actions at each time point (or node in the tree); transitions from state to state are fully determined by the outcomes. Thus, repeated executions of the program with any given set of data lead to precisely the same repeated result. This does not mean that one can easily predict how the model will behave. The simplest way to know the outcome of any given relationship is to execute the decision algorithm.

B. DISCOUNT

Future payoffs are discounted in this model by being multiplied by d^L, where d is a discount parameter and L is the number of decision steps forward from the current state. For the current state, $L = 0$; thus payoffs in the current state are always worth 100% of their point value. The discount parameter d indicates the degree to which future payoffs are considered to be either less or more attractive than their par value. If $d = 0$, then future payoffs are entirely ignored; if $0 < d < 1$, then future payoffs are worth less than current payoffs; if $d = 1$, future and current payoffs are weighted equally; if $d > 1$, then future payoffs are considered more valuable than current payoffs. For example, if the discount were .50, a payoff of "4" would be worth $.5^1 (4) = 2$ at one step ahead, and $.5^2 (4) = 1$ at two steps ahead, and so on.

C. DEPTH OF SEARCH

The depth of an actor's look-ahead is absolutely limited by a specific parameter provided to the decision algorithm; however, when the discount parameter is below 1, the practical limit on the depth of search will frequently be determined by the discount. For example, if d were equal to .20, very little would be anticipated from potential payoffs more than 2 steps in the future— i.e., $d^3 = .2^3$ is only .008—and possible payoffs any farther forward would be weighted even less.

D. LEARNING ABOUT THE CO-ACTOR

Our model is designed to allow each actor to alter his conception of his co-actor over the course of the interactions in two ways. First, every transition to a new joint state modifies the conceptions the actors have of each other. Moving to a new state not only may locate the actors' immediate behavior options in a new matrix with new payoffs, etc., but it permits them to look ahead to another set of nodes one step farther down the tree.

The second learning mechanism is more subtle. In selecting a behavior, each actor uses probability estimates for his co-actor's behaviors. The *initial* estimates for each state are put in as parameters of the model. However, on the basis of his actual experience in any state, the simulated actor will change his subsequent probability estimates of the other's behavior if he ever returns to that state. In other words, the behavior previously selected by the co-actor is considered more likely to be *repeated if the same state recurs in the future;* accordingly, the estimated probability for that behavior is increased and the estimates for the remaining behaviors are decreased proportionately. Hence, if $\text{Prob}_t\,(b_i, S)$ is the probability estimate of behavior b_i in State S at time t, and if b_i is selected then

$$\text{Prob}_{t+1}\,(b_i, S) = (1 - \theta)\,\text{Prob}_t\,(b_i, S) + \theta \tag{4}$$

$$\text{Prob}_{t+1}\,(b_j, S) = (1 - \theta)\,\text{Prob}_t\,(b_j, S) \qquad [\text{for } j \neq i] \tag{5}$$

where θ is the learning parameter, and where $0 \leqslant \theta \leqslant 1$.

E. WHAT THE MODEL DOES NOT SAY

Having specified the **RELATE** model in detail, it seems appropriate to make some disclaimers. First, the **RELATE** model is intended to be a general framework within which a variety of specific theories of dyadic interaction can be stated. Many aspects of the model remain to be elaborated and must be specified before any particular dyadic relationship can be simulated. However, these aspects are clearly revealed as a finite set of parameters, e.g., payoff matrices, transition matrices, learning rates. Furthermore, any subtheory stated within the **RELATE** framework must be consonant with the basic premises underlying **RELATE**.

Second, the **RELATE** model specifies some processes at a more detailed level than others. Eventually, one might describe each process in terms of simple information processing operations. At present that goal is beyond the realm of possibility. Thus, **RELATE**'s description of social learning with a linear-incremental learning equation is a macroscopic approximation of more microscopic phenomena. One useful property of the **RELATE** model is that specific micro-structures can be substituted at any time without necessitating other changes in the model.

Third, while some of the rules of incremental exchange theory are certainly testable, others are neither verifiable nor falsifiable. For example, Rule 2.3, that fixed costs are associated with behaviors, is not testable because fixed costs cannot be empirically distinguished from payoffs. Similarly, Rule 3.1, that a transition is determined solely by the previous state and the behaviors chosen, and Rule 4.1, that an actor always searches out all those outcomes to be expected in the present state, are hardly falsifiable. Such rules receive support on the basis of RELATE's overall predictive power. In contrast, rules such as 1.2, that the weight accorded to the co-actor's payoffs increases with the depth of the relationship, and 2.1, that in deeper states the average immediate expected payoff for an actor is greater than in shallower states, should be testable if depth can be operationally defined.

Finally, the RELATE model uses processes which are intended to be analogous but not necessarily identical to human decision-making processes. We do not assert that people have payoff matrices stored in memory for every state of a relationship or that they search through the tree of possible decisions as in chess; rather, we suggest that one can predict how people behave by modeling their decisions in this way.

People's memory structures and cognitive operations need not be identical to the model's, but they should be computationally analogous. Newell and Simon (1972), for example, have illustrated how people can quickly solve massive tree searching problems with heuristic techniques.

VI. Applications of the RELATE Model

In the remainder of the paper we will show how the RELATE model yields insights into four specific topics of dyadic interaction: altruism, interpersonal similarity, self-disclosure, and romantic involvement. In each of these areas, the model can make some testable predictions and serve as a heuristic for productive research. A heuristic is a "rule of thumb" that helps to guide one toward a solution to a problem or toward the truth about a phenomenon.

RELATE is a heuristic framework in that it enables us to generate hypotheses that might otherwise not be identified. It helps us locate the conditions under which a given phenomenon will occur, and to pinpoint the assumptions and parameter values required for its occurrence. For applications to sequential interaction, where empirical research is costly and difficult, a heuristic model is especially valuable for moving research into a productive direction.

VII. Altruistic Behavior

"Altruism" generally refers to one person's concern with an other (alter), as indicated by one's active assistance to the other at significant cost to the self. In this paper, altruistic behavior will refer to any action that has both of the following characteristics: (a) it yields the actor himself an immediate payoff lower than the maximum available to him, and (b) it gives his co-actor a payoff greater than the co-actor would receive if the actor selected his own maximal payoff. As Krebs (1970, p. 298) has pointed out, "the fact that man acts altruistically does not mean that he is altruistic"; altruistic actions do not necessarily confirm one's altruistic intent. Yet the occurrence of an altruistic act is of interest regardless of why it happens. For this reason we define an altruistic act solely in terms of assessed rewards and costs, even though others (e.g., Berkowitz, 1972a) have suggested that definitions of altruism should not ignore the subject's inner motivation.

The explanation of altruistic actions in two-person interactions presents a problem for any theory of social behavior that assumes humans try to maximize their personal gain. Concern for a co-actor's outcomes certainly does occur in deep interpersonal relationships (a man races into a burning house to rescue a member of his family, when he would not try to rescue someone he knows only superficially). Even in surface contacts, an actor is frequently guided by moral principles or social pressures to sacrifice personal gain (a driver will run off the road to avoid a strange child). However, in the absence of either a deep relationship or moral principle, it seems difficult to explain the occurrence of altruistic actions.

This difficulty may be seen another way. In early interaction states, two actors often have low payoff correspondence. Few of their behaviors yield equally satisfactory outcomes for both; there is a low correlation between their respective payoffs. Yet, for a relationship to deepen beyond surface contact, the actors must choose actions giving both of them desirable payoffs. If each individual tries to maximize solely his *own* current gain, outcomes with desirable payoffs for both actors seem unlikely. Yet actors do select altruistic acts, and outcomes do occur that have desirable payoffs for both actors.

A. EMPIRICAL RESEARCH ON ALTRUISM

Most research on altruism has unfortunately dealt with altruistic acts by strangers (Krebs, 1970). From these studies, it is difficult to draw conclusions about altruism in longitudinal interpersonal relations. Nevertheless, several findings are of interest. Daniels and Berkowitz (1963) found that subjects performed more altruistic acts for "supervisors" whom they were told they would like than for those they were told they would dislike. Apparently, the anticipation of liking someone increases one's altruism toward that person. Also, a co-actor who is perceived to be attractive is also perceived to be altruistic (Friedrichs, 1960). With a strange co-actor, though, two crucial variables in determining the occurrence of altruism have been the actor's belief that the co-actor will reciprocate and the actor's perception of the social norm (Goranson & Berkowitz, 1966; Frisch & Greenberg, 1968; Pruitt, 1968; Berkowitz & Friedman, 1967). Finally, a theme running throughout the research is that the anticipation of future interaction with the co-actor enhances the likelihood of altruistic behavior. All these findings are consonant with RELATE's predictions.

B. MODELING ALTRUISM VIA RELATE

The RELATE model can treat altruism in either of two ways. First, in accord with Rule 1.2, the RELATE actor weights the alter's payoffs to an increasing degree as the relationship between them deepens. Correspondingly, the actor's payoffs transcend his initial individualistic interests; they are affected by developments in the relationship and his behavior is thereby also affected. Thus the man who risks his life for a family member does so because he is deeply affected by the other's own payoffs. We refer to such actions as "true altruism."

Second, RELATE can account for altruistic behavior in shallow relations, where one's concern for alter's own payoffs is nil. Even when actors maximize purely their own gains, altruistic actions will occur if interaction is viewed in the longitudinal context of a continuing relationship rather than a static event. This second form of altruism may be labeled "self-seeking altruism."

a. Simulating self-seeking altruism. To demonstrate the occurrence of self-seeking altruism, we designed a two-actor relationship with five potential interaction states and two behaviors per state: an altruistic behavior and a nonaltruistic behavior. If both actors selected the altruistic behavior in any of these states, they would progress to the next deeper state of involvement. If either or both chose the nonaltruistic behavior, however, their relation would transit back to a lower state of involvement. In accord with a basic premise of incremental exchange theory (Rule 2.1), the deeper the mutual involvement represented by a state, the greater was its mean payoff. In every state, though, the nonaltruistic behavior had the greater immediate expected payoff. In game theory terms, we were considering a relationship consisting of an interconnected sequence of five Prisoner Dilemma states. Since our goal was to demonstrate that "altruistic" behavior could occur even when the actor does not consider his co-actor's payoffs, the actor's parameters were set so that he completely ignored his partner's payoffs in all five stages of involvement.

Following these principles, we constructed and simulated the relationship called Relationship I in Table I. The simulation began with the two actors in the second lowest state of involvement, State 2. Table I shows that if either actor selects the nonaltruistic behavior (NA) in State 2, the interaction moves into State 1, which contains less desirable payoffs for both actors. In contrast, repeated joint selections of behavior A, the altruistic choice, will successively

TABLE I

TRANSITION AND PAYOFF MATRICES FOR TWO RELATIONSHIPS
USED TO SIMULATE THE OCCURRENCE OF ALTRUISM

		State 1[a]		State 2		State 3		State 4		State 5	
Prescribed transition from present state into next state											
					Co-actor's behavior						
		A	NA	A	NA	A	NA	A	NA	A	NA
Actor's behavior	A	2	1	3	1	4	2	5	3	5	4
	NA	1	1	1	1	2	2	3	3	4	4

Payoffs received by actor[b]

Relationship I
Δ States[c] = 6.0
Δ Rows[d] = 10.0

						Co-actor's behavior									
		A	NA		A	NA		A	NA		A	NA		A	NA	
Actor's behavior	A	4	-26	-11[e]	10	-20	-5	16	-14	1	22	-8	7	28	-2	13
	NA	14	-16	-1	20	-10	5	26	-4	11	32	2	17	38	8	23

Relationship II
Δ States[c] = 5.0
Δ Rows[d] = 10.0

						Co-actor's behavior									
		A	NA		A	NA		A	NA		A	NA		A	NA	
Actor's behavior	A	5	-25	-10	10	-20	-5	15	-15	0	20	-10	5	25	-5	10
	NA	15	-15	0	20	-10	5	25	-5	10	30	0	15	35	5	20

[a]In State 1, an *A–A* outcome leads forward to the matrix of State 2, while any other outcome leads to State 1 (see Fig. 2). This set of transition matrices applies to both Relationships I and II.

[b]The co-actor's payoffs are given by the symmetric matrix.

[c]"Δ States" is the difference in expected payoffs between each row of each state and the same row in the next deeper state of mutual involvement.

[d]"Δ Rows" is the difference in expected payoffs between the two rows of each payoff matrix.

[e]The marginal numbers refer to the actor's expected values from Responses A and NA, respectively, when he has no information about the co-actor's probable response.

lead to states of deeper interaction: to States 3, 4, and 5. In this series, State 5 is conceived to be the deepest state of pair involvement. Figure 2 shows the state transitions possible in this relationship.

   b. Results. The output from the simulation of Relationship I is shown in Table II and diagrammed in Fig. 3. The parameter settings for this simulation are shown in Table II. The actors began interacting in State 2 and both chose the "altruistic" behavior. Hence, they moved into the next deeper state of involvement, State 3. Here they also selected altruistic behaviors. They progressed to State 4, selected the altruistic behaviors again, and progressed to the fifth and deepest state. Here, though, both chose the nonaltruistic alternative and re-

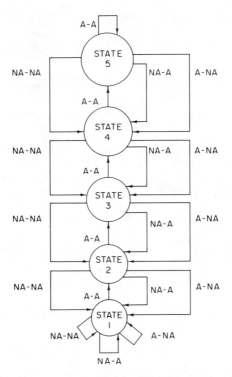

Fig. 2. State transition diagram for all relationships used to simulate self-seeking altruism. (See Table I.)

turned to State 4. From then on, the interaction alternated between States 4 and 5, altruistic behavior always being selected in the fourth state and nonaltruistic in the fifth state.

Why did this happen? In States 2, 3, and 4, the greater potential payoffs in the deeper states were sufficient to induce a self-seeking actor to behave altruistically so that he could reach deeper involvement and the possibility of higher payoffs. But in State 5 no further progress to a deeper state was possible; the actors found it more profitable therefore to select the immediately gratifying nonaltruistic alternative.

Does this simulation imply that two people in a dyadic interaction will behave altruistically until they reach a point where deeper involvement cannot be achieved? Perhaps this will happen in some situations. But it is more likely that by the time no deeper involvement can be achieved, each actor will have begun to weight his co-actor's payoffs and true altruism will occur. (In this simulation, no such weightings have been employed.) The RELATE model does

TABLE II

SUMMARY OF THE SIMULATIONS OF RELATIONSHIPS DIAGRAMMED
IN FIGURE 2 SHOWING WHEN THE ACTORS ARE ALTRUISTIC

State	EV(A)[a]	EV(NA)[a]	ΔEV[a]	Actor's[b] behavior	Actor's immediate payoff	Actor's cumulative payoff
Relationship I (Δ States = 6.0, Δ Rows = 10.0)						
2	3.00	1.00	2.00	A	10	10
3	22.50	13.00	9.50	A	16	26
4	46.00	37.00	9.00	A	22	48
5	62.50	64.00	−1.50	NA	8	56
4	46.00	37.00	9.00	A	22	78
5	62.50	64.00	−1.50	NA	8	86
4[c]	46.00	37.00	9.00	A	22	108
Relationship II (ΔStates = 5.0, Δ Rows = 10.0)						
2	3.75	5.00	−1.25	NA	−10	−10
1	−7.50	0.00	−7.50	NA	−15	−25
1	−7.50	0.00	−7.50	NA	−15	−40
1[c]	−7.50	0.00	−7.50	NA	−15	−55

[a]The second and third columns show the backed-up expected values (EV) for altruistic and nonaltruistic behavior, respectively. The fourth column contains the difference between columns 1 and 2 which governs the choice of behavior in that state; positive differences lead to A choices, and negative differences lead to NA choices.

[b]Since all parameters were set at identical values for both actors in these simulations (Discount = 1.0, Depth of Search = 5, Initial Probability Estimates = 50/50, and Learning Rate = 0.0), the co-actor always chose the same behavior as the actor.

[c]In both of these simulations RELATE's termination routine was inhibited, and the simulations were stopped by the experimenter.

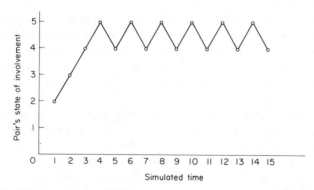

Fig. 3. The pattern of state transitions observed in simulating Relationship I of Table I. (See Table II.)

assert that altruistic acts can occur in shallow interactions without either actor caring about the other's rewards, simply because such acts further the self-seeker's efforts to reap the benefits of deeper involvement.[6]

As one would expect from a heuristic theory, these results suggest more questions than they answer. What types of actors would be most likely to display self-seeking altruism? In what situations would self-seeking altruism be most likely to occur? Rewards in future states must obviously be higher, but how much higher? What influence does the actor's estimate of his co-actor's probable behavior have upon his own decision? How will the actor's propensity to be altruistic change as he gains experience with his co-actor? While empirical data are lacking, the RELATE program can be used to derive some predictions.

   c. *Payoff matrices.* In order for an actor to choose an altruistic behavior, the increments in his payoffs between the current state and the next state reached as a result of the act must be large enough to overcome the advantage in immediate payoffs for the nonaltruistic act. But how great must the increment be? In Relationship I this increment, called Δ States, was 6.0; self-seeking altruism occurred when Relationship I was simulated. In contrast, Relationship II in Table I had a Δ States of only 5.0; here self-seeking altruism did not occur. In Relationship II, the increment between states was not sufficient to overcome the immediate advantage of one's nonaltruistic action, but on all other parameters Relationship II was identical to Relationship I.

   Mathematical analysis of RELATE's decision algorithm suggests that the occurrence of self-seeking altruism does not depend on any other characteristics of the payoff matrices than the increment in mean payoffs across states (Δ States) and the difference in mean payoffs between the altruistic and nonaltruistic rows of the matrices (Δ Rows). Additional simulations have verified that the relative values of Δ States and Δ Rows completely determine whether or not self-seeking altruism occurs, as long as the actors are not "learning" about each other (θ = 0). If Δ Rows and Δ States remain constant, the entries in the matrices can be altered in any manner without affecting the outcome of the simulation. Figure 4 shows which values of Δ States and Δ Rows will produce self-seeking altruism under the parameter settings used in Table I—that is, when the actors (a) are not learning anything from the other's behavior (θ = 0); (b) are searching five steps into the future; and (c) are not discounting the future (d =

---

[6] Analogies to the international arena are readily imaginable. It is not uncommon for self-seeking international actors to engage in overtly altruistic actions in order to build deeper nation-to-nation involvements (e.g., trade relationships) that return ample benefits.
   Even Berkowitz's (1972a, p. 65) notion of an individual's "selfless action on behalf of others" based on "internalized standards of conduct" reverts *ultimately* to the actor's own benefit. For one learns early in life that one's generous actions create a healthy interpersonal climate, contributing to a wholesome society which in turn rebounds to the benefit of the actor himself.

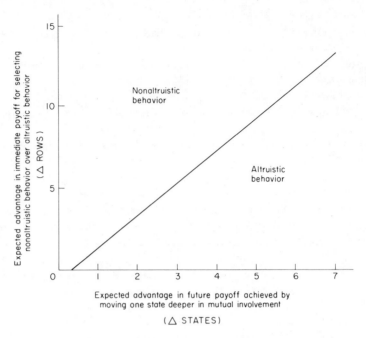

Fig. 4. The occurrence of self-seeking altruism as a function of differences between current and future payoff matrices.

1). The slope of the indifference line separating the altruistic from the non-altruistic region was ascertained through computer simulation.

From the RELATE model one can conclude that, no matter how much the immediate cost of being altruistic is increased, a person will behave altruistically if his payoffs in deeper states of involvement are incremented in proportion to the slope of the indifference line. Furthermore, the actor should not care about the exact distribution of his payoffs as long as his expected payoffs in deeper states are incremented sufficiently. Finally, neither the distribution nor the expected values of his co-actor's payoffs should affect his choice of behavior.

d. Depth of search and discounting. Mathematical analysis of RELATE's decision algorithm also revealed that either decreasing an actor's depth of search into the future or increasing his discount for future payoffs will decrease the slope of his indifference line. For example, if the depth of search were reduced from 5 to 2, the slope of the indifference line in Fig. 4 would be reduced from 2 to .5. In other words, the less the actor looks ahead, and the more he discounts the future of the relationship, the less altruistic will be his present behavior. However, no matter how little he discounts the future or how deeply he examines it, he will not behave altruistically if outcomes of future states are less rewarding than those found in current states.

    e. Estimates of the co-actor's probable behavior. Figure 5 shows the results of another set of simulations. They indicate that the more likely an actor thinks it is that his co-actor will behave altruistically, the more likely he is to behave similarly. Such a finding is the opposite of what a self-maximization model predicts for a *static* mixed-motive payoff matrix of this type (a Prisoner's Dilemma matrix; see Gallo and McClintock, 1965). RELATE predicts that, in a series of situations of this sort, a person will tend to be altruistic.

    f. Effects of learning about the co-actor. So far, our discussion of altruism has been limited to situations in which actors learn nothing about each other ($\theta = 0$). What happens in the more realistic situation where each actor learns to change his view of the co-actor's probable behavior?

    To answer this question, some of the previous relationships were simulated at two different rates of learning ($\theta = .20$, and $\theta = .50$). The actors' *initial*

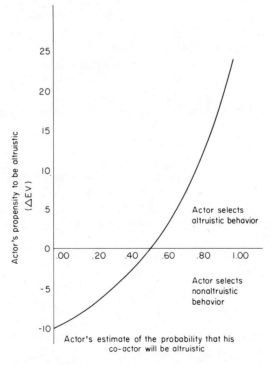

Fig. 5.   An actor's propensity to behave altruistically as a function of his estimate that his co-actor will behave altruistically.

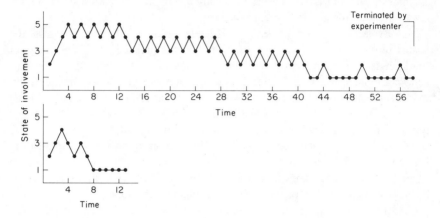

Fig. 6. The pattern of state transitions observed in simulating two variations of Relationship I. The upper graph is the output from simulating a pair of slow learners (θ=.20); the lower graph is the result from a simulation of fast learners (θ=.50).

behaviors remained exactly the same as when no learning (θ = 0) had been permitted. Their initial actions were still determined completely by the association between current and future payoffs shown in Fig. 4. However, the learning rate greatly affected what eventually happened in these relationships. Results of nine simulations at different rates of learning are summarized in Table III, and two of the runs are shown in detail in Fig. 6. Each simulation was terminated when it reached a "steady state," that is, when the relationship cycled in one or two states and the probability estimates had converged to 1.0 or 0.0.

As Table III indicates, a pair whose members rapidly (θ = .50) change their estimates of each other's probable behaviors is less likely to reach a steady state of mutual involvement than a pair that learns more slowly. Apparently, learning quickly that one's co-actor will be altruistic at a shallow level of involvement removes some of an actor's incentive to be altruistic in order to advance to a deeper level. This result can explain the empirical finding that altruistic acts considered inappropriate to a pair's level of involvement are less likely to be reciprocated than ones that are (Kiesler, 1966; Schopler & Thompson, 1968).

C. THE UTILITY OF ALTRUISM

In a world where self-seeking is advocated by many "successful" persons in public life, there is an inclination to deride various forms of helpfulness. Practical men view altruism as soft-headed. "Irrational" is a label applied to Biblical injunctions such as "Love thy neighbor as thyself." As our practical

TABLE III

LEVELS OF INVOLVEMENT WHEN RELATIONSHIPS REACH
"STEADY-STATE"[a] AS A FUNCTION OF THE ACTORS' LEARNING RATE
AND PAYOFF MATRICES

Payoff matrices[b]		Learning rate			
		$\theta = .20$		$\theta = .50$	
Difference in column sums	Difference in diagonal sums	Final steady-state[a]	Time to steady-state	Final steady-state	Time to steady-state
−8	12	State 4–State 5	21	State 4–State 5	14
0	12	State 4–State 5	21	State 4–State 5	14
+8	12	State 4–State 5	21	State 4–State 5	14
−8	30	State 4–State 5	21	State 1	19
0	30[c]	State 4–State 5	26	State 3–State 4	19
+8	30	State 4–State 5	25	State 3–State 4	13
−8	48	State 1	57	State 1	13
0	48	State 4–State 5	28	State 2–State 3	12
+8	48	State 4–State 5	21	State 2–State 3	12

[a]Steady-state was reached when the relationship settled in a single state or a cyclical pattern of transitions was established and the actor's probability estimates approached unity so no further learning was possible.

[b]In all these relationships the difference in expected values between rows (Δ Rows) was 10 and the difference between states (Δ States) was 6, the same as Relationship I of Table I.

[c]This is Relationship I.

world careens from one crisis to another, however, the limits of self-seeking interpersonal relations become increasingly visible.

The RELATE model is one attempt to provide a rational solution to this issue. Its focus is purely on dyads, but the pair may serve as the prototype for analyzing more complex relationships. By showing how others' payoffs can be weighted into own payoffs, and by demonstrating a technique for assessing the consequences of own behavior, RELATE suggests ways in which humans can optimize interpersonal functioning. The demonstration is, of course, entirely artificial, but the model suggests how social theory may help bridge the gap between "practical self-interest" and "true altruism."

Consider, for instance, the simulation shown in Fig. 3. Under the payoff conditions of Relationship I (see Table I), altruistic behavior was the actor's rational choice whenever the pair was located in States 1 through 4, but not in

State 5 (the highest possible state in this simulation). Pure self-interest dictated that an actor choose cooperation, an immediate self-sacrifice, in order to reach the potential higher payoffs in future states. Having reached the maximum, though, self-interest required a noncooperative choice; Fig. 3 therefore shows that later interaction between these two self-seekers cycles indefinitely between States 4 and 5. In living relationships, though, partners do continue to act altruistically in later states, for they increase the weight of the other's payoffs in considering their own payoffs. Thus RELATE demonstrates the insufficiency of mere self-seeking and the importance of concern for one's co-actor for maintaining a deeper relationship.

VIII. Similarity and Attraction

It is beyond the scope of this paper to review research on similarity and dyadic interaction. The weight of evidence indicates that there is a positive association between attraction to a stranger and his perceived similarity in attitudes, values, or other characteristics (Byrne, 1971). For long-term interpersonal relationships, there is also evidence of a positive association between attraction and *perceived* similarity (Curry and Emerson, 1970; Levinger and Breedlove, 1966; Newcomb, 1961). The evidence is weaker concerning the association between attraction and *actual* pre-acquaintance similarity (Curry & Kenny, 1974; Levinger, 1972).

Levinger and Breedlove (1966) suggested that actual similarity (or agreement) would correlate with attraction only to the extent that such similarity promotes the achievement of a pair's interpersonal goals: "The more that agreement is *instrumental* for furthering the goals of the . . . relationship, the higher should be the correlation with . . . satisfaction" (p. 368). Neither their study nor subsequent research has yet succeeded in explaining what sorts of actual similarity are generally instrumental. The RELATE model, however, can help delimit our search for the sort of actual similarity most likely to further the development of dyadic relations.

To model the effect of similarity, we will first define "similarity" unambiguously in the language of RELATE. In what different ways can RELATE actors be similar? Two actors can display varying degrees of similarity on any of the variables defining them: on behavior options, behavior costs, estimates of the co-actor's probable behavior, discounting of the future, learning rates, or payoff matrices. The difficulty is to decide what similarity shall mean in terms of these parameters.

Similarity has generally been measured by agreement on a set of attitude questions and/or sameness on socio-cultural, physical, or intellectual traits.

Within the RELATE model, it is necessary to distinguish between similarity on *permanent traits* not under behavioral control and similarity manifested in *behavior preferences,* e.g., political attitudes, moral principles, or recreational preferences. While a co-actor's permanent traits may be important for affecting an actor's payoffs, those characteristics are not under the co-actor's control. The subtheory used to construct the initial payoff matrices would take account of each actor's traits in determining payoffs. For some people and for some traits, the more desirable characteristic in a co-actor will be identical to the actor's own characteristic. For other people and other traits this will not be true. In either case, trait similarity only determines the initial values placed in the payoff matrices representing a relationship.

Similarity of *behavior preferences,* on the other hand, directly affects the outcome of a RELATE interaction. Here, the RELATE framework forces us to recognize two different types of similarity in behavior preferences: *symmetry* and *payoff correspondence.* These two types of similarity can be illustrated with an example. (a) Suppose the payoff John receives from giving a present to Susan is the same as the payoff Susan receives from giving a present to John. Obviously, John and Susan are similar in their feelings about giving presents to each other. This type of similarity represents *symmetry* between John's and Susan's payoff matrices. (b) In contrast, suppose that John gains the same payoff from *receiving* Susan's present as Susan gets from *giving* the present. Here the two actors are similar in their feelings about Susan giving John a present. This type of similarity is represented by similar payoffs for the two actors within one cell of the payoff matrix. In other words, the payoffs in the cell for Susan giving and John receiving are the same for both actors. This type of similarity will be called *payoff correspondence.*

What does the RELATE model predict about these two types of similarity? The model predicts that payoff correspondence is directly relevant to whether or not a relationship deepens, but that symmetry is not. In particular, the greater the payoff correspondence among cells in a state, the greater are the chances that the pair will progress to the next deeper state of involvement.

To see why payoff correspondence affects the development of a relationship and symmetry does not, let us look at the example in Table IV. Three 3 × 3 payoff matrices are shown. For both actors, and in all three cases, the average immediate payoff for each behavior is 5.0. However, Matrix A has perfect payoff correspondence; Matrix B has perfect symmetry; Matrix C has neither, although some degree of symmetry and payoff correspondence occurs in any matrix. As a function of the actors' behaviors, let us allow transitions from the present state of the relationship to states up to two levels of involvement deeper and one level shallower. The transition matrices must be constructed to obey Rule 3.2. The following directions will accomplish this:

TABLE IV: MATRICES FOR SIMULATING THE EFFECTS OF SIMILARITY ON DYADIC INVOLVEMENT

Inputs

Payoff matrices [a]

(In each cell: co-actor's immediate payoff above diagonal / actor's immediate payoff below diagonal; marginals are actor's expected immediate payoff.)

Co-actor's behaviors →, Actor's behavior ↓

A — Perfect corresp.

			marg.
4 / 4	3 / 3	8 / 8	5.0
9 / 9	5 / 5	1 / 1	5.0
2 / 2	7 / 7	6 / 6	5.0
5.0	5.0	5.0	

B — Perfect symm.

			marg.
4 / 4	9 / 3	2 / 8	5.0
3 / 9	5 / 5	7 / 1	5.0
8 / 2	1 / 7	6 / 6	5.0
5.0	5.0	5.0	

C — Neither

			marg.
4 / 2	3 / 9	8 / 4	5.0
9 / 7	5 / 5	1 / 3	5.0
2 / 6	7 / 1	6 / 8	5.0
5.0	5.0	5.0	

State transition matrices [b]

Co-actor's behaviors →, Actor's behavior ↓

A — Perfect corresp.

+1	+1	+2
+2	+1	−1
0	+2	+2

B — Perfect symm.

+1	+1	0
+1	+1	−1
0	−1	+2

C — Neither

0	+1	+1
+2	+1	−1
0	−1	+2

Outputs

Backed-up expected payoffs (immediate + future) [c]

Co-actor's behaviors →, Actor's behavior ↓

A — Perfect corresp.

			marg.
5 / 5	4 / 4	10 /10	6.3
11 /11	6 / 6	0 / 0	5.7
2 / 2	9 / 9	8 / 8	6.3
6.0	6.3	6.0	

B — Perfect symm.

			marg.
5 / 5	4 /10	8 / 2	5.7
10 / 4	6 / 6	0 / 8	5.3
2 / 8	6 / 0	8 / 8	5.3
5.7	5.3	5.3	

C — Neither

			marg.
4 / 2	4 /10	9 / 5	5.7
11 / 9	6 / 6	0 / 2	5.7
2 / 6	6 / 0	8 /10	5.3
5.7	5.3	5.7	

Frequency of occurrence of outcomes

Co-actor's behaviors →, Actor's behavior ↓

A — Perfect corresp.

+1	+1	+2 50%
+2	+1	−1
0	+2	+2 50%

B — Perfect symm.

+1	+1	+1 100%
+1	+1	−1
0	−1	+2

C — Neither

0	+1 25%	+1 25%
+2 25%	+1	−1 25%
0	−1	+2

---

[a] The number above the diagonal in each square is the co-actor's immediate payoff and the number below the diagonal is actor's immediate payoff. The marginals are an actor's expected immediate payoff for each behavior under the assumption that each of the co-actor's behaviors are equally probable.

[b] The numbers in the transition matrices represent transitions to states of deeper mutual involvement (+1 and +2), to states of less involvement (−1), and to the same state (0). The text describes how these transitions were selected in accordance with the rules of incremental exchange theory (e.g., Rule 3.2).

[c] The discounted, expected future payoffs in the states to which the pair could transit were given by the numbers on the transition matrices (this satisfied Rule 2.1 of incremental exchange theory). Therefore, the backed-up expected payoffs are the sum of the immediate payoffs and

If both actors' payoffs > 5, then move to State$_{t+2}$:
if both actors' payoffs > 2, then move to State$_{t+1}$:
if both actors' payoffs > 1, then stay in State$_t$:
otherwise, move to State$_{t-1}$:

Transition matrices constructed according to those directions are shown below the payoff matrices in Table IV. Note that there are many more opportunities to advance deeper from the state of perfect payoff correspondence (Matrix A). Furthermore, in all three matrices, the cells which lead to deeper states are cells with high payoff correspondence.

What are the chances that the actors will select behaviors which lead to a +2 transition? Since both actors look ahead, and higher payoffs occur in those future states reached by +2 transitions, the expected gain associated with a cell is increased when it has a +2 transition. In the illustrative matrices of Table IV, we have used the transition numbers −1, 0, +1, and +2 as the discounted expected future payoffs associated with transitions. Adding these expected future payoffs to the expected immediate payoffs gives the values in the third set of matrices in Table IV for the backed-up expected payoffs.

If we examine these total expected payoffs, we can see which behaviors the actors would choose. The percentages in the cells of the final set of matrices in Table IV indicate the expected frequency of each dyadic choice. Thus the perfectly correspondent state has a 50% chance of being followed by the +1 state and a 50% chance of being followed by the +2 state. The perfectly symmetric state offers no chance of any +2 transition, but certainty of +1 transition. Matrix C offers an equal 25% chance of being followed by either the same state or states −1, +1, or +2 levels different from the current one.

This example has shown analytically why high payoff correspondence is the type of similarity that is most likely to advance an interpersonal relationship. Comparable analyses will assist future empirical studies on the effects of similarity on attraction. A practical problem will be to specify real world payoff correspondence on the basis of predictive rather than post hoc criteria.

IX. Self-Disclosure

A common characteristic of social relationships is reciprocal disclosure of feelings and personal information. Jourard (1971) has outlined many of the factors affecting disclosure and proposed that *reciprocity* is central to disclosure in dyads. Altman (1973) has reviewed the variations on this theme, and concludes that

> For the most part, conceptualizations have been vague, point to the phenomenon as fairly universal, say little about factors which may accelerate or slow down its occurrence, and only grossly identify potential underlying mechanisms. (p. 251)

TABLE V

A SIMULATION OF SELF-DISCLOSURE IN FOUR HYPOTHETICAL RELATIONSHIPS

	Inputs				Outputs				
	Actor's immediate payoff matrix	Immediate transition matrix	Actor's expected future payoffs		Actor's total expected payoffs (immediate + future)				
			New state	Payoff	Derived payoff matrix		Expected payoffs		

1. Strangers

Co-actor's behavior[b]

Actor's behavior[b]:

	ND	D
ND	0	2
D	1	3

	ND	D
	1.0	1.0
	1.0	1.0

1.0 No further contact: 0

Co-actor's behavior — Actor's behavior

	ND	D
ND	0	2
D	1	3

Actor's estimate of probability of co-actor disclosing

	0%	50%	100%
	0	1	2
	1	2	3
D-ND 1 1	+1	+1	+1

2. Acquaintances

Co-actor's behavior

Actor's behavior:

	ND	D
ND	0	2
D	1	3

	ND	D
	2.0	2.1
	2.2	2.3

2.0 Continuing friendship: 4
2.1 Actor gets added power: 6
2.2 Co-actor gets added power: -6
2.3 Greater friendship: 10

Co-actor's behavior — Actor's behavior

	ND	D
ND	4	8
D	-5	13

Actor's estimate of probability of co-actor disclosing

	0%	50%	100%
	4	6	8
	-5	4	13
D-ND -9 5	-9	-2	+5

3. Friends

Co-actor's behavior[b]

Actor's behavior:

	ND	D
ND	0	2
D	1	3

	ND	D
	3.0	3.1
	3.2	3.3

3.0 Continuing friendship: 10
3.1 Actor gets added power: 12
3.2 Co-actor gets added power: 4
3.3 Greater intimacy: 20

Co-actor's behavior — Actor's behavior

	ND	D
ND	10	14
D	5	23

Actor's estimate of probability of co-actor disclosing

	0%	50%	100%
	10	12	14
	5	14	23
D-ND -5 9	-5	+2	+9

4. Intimates

Co-actor's behavior

Actor's behavior:

	ND	D
ND	0	2
D	1	3

	ND	D
	4.0	4.0
	4.0	4.0

4.0 Continuing intimacy: 20

Co-actor's behavior — Actor's behavior

	ND	D
ND	20	22
D	21	23

Actor's estimate of probability of co-actor disclosing

	0%	50%	100%
	20	21	22
	21	22	23
D-ND 1 1	+1	+1	+1

[a]The derived payoff matrix is computed by adding the immediate payoff to the expected payoff in the resulting future state. The total expected payoff is then calculated from this matrix for each of three probability estimates by the actor.

[b]ND, no self-disclosure; D, self-disclosure.

Altman (1973) goes on to propose a theory integrating two ideas: (1) that reciprocity is a social norm, and (2) that disclosure is rewarding to both discloser and recipient. At shallow stages of involvement, social norms play a primary role in disclosure while at deeper stages the positive outcomes associated with disclosure play the more important part. As Rubin (1974) has pointed out, one interesting characteristic of disclosure concerns the surprising degree of intimacy that people often display in disclosures to strangers. Altman's theory predicts that *reciprocity* of disclosure will be high among strangers, but only for non-intimate topics. Reciprocity of intimate disclosure of topics will peak at moderately deep levels of involvement and be least at both the shallowest and deepest ends according to his theory.

What assumptions must be made within the incremental exchange framework to yield parallel predictions about dyadic disclosure? The central assumption is that the act of self-disclosure in the short run is rewarding to the discloser, even if it is not reciprocated by the recipient. Given this premise, reasonable assumptions about actors' payoffs can produce a RELATE simulation that accords well with observed data.

In considering predictions about self-disclosure, one must remember that predictions pertain only to average behavior; innumerable situational and interpersonal variables will affect the actual occurrence of disclosure. Further, among the several different aspects of disclosure one must be careful to specify the dependent variable. Shall one try to predict, for example, the frequency of an actor's disclosure, the intimacy of disclosures that do occur, or the likelihood that a particularly intimate item will be disclosed? Or is one making predictions about a dyad's tendency toward reciprocation?

Using the RELATE framework, we will model predictions about one actor's preference for self-disclosure over nondisclosure, and about the payoffs he receives from disclosure. Table V presents the matrices we constructed for several hypothetical cases. Four levels of mutual involvement are represented: (1) strangers, (2) acquaintances, (3) friends, and (4) intimate companions. The *immediate* payoffs for disclosure are the same at each level of involvement; disclosure is assumed to have a slightly positive payoff, higher than for nondisclosure whether or not the co-actor reciprocates. The transition matrices and expected payoffs for future states are constructed in accordance with the rules of incremental exchange theory, and are also based on assumptions about the potential structure of payoffs and costs that would follow from either disclosure or nondisclosure. The transitions prescribed in Table V reflect our assumption that neither stranger nor intimate relationships are much changed by particular instances of disclosure, while acquaintanceships and friendships may be affected substantially.

Strangers. At this minimal level of involvement, there is no significant prospect for future interaction. Hence the immediate payoff constitutes the only payoff that an actor considers. Table V suggests that disclosure is slightly preferred over nondisclosure, although expected payoffs are low no matter what the actor believes will be done by his co-actor.

Acquaintances. If two people see each other repeatedly, the situation is different; they seriously consider payoffs in future states. A RELATE actor evaluates the state that would result if he discloses intimate information and his co-actor does not. If that happens, the co-actor obtains power, which he may use to the actor's potential harm. Such an eventuality would contain potentially high negative payoffs. Unless the probability of reaching that state is perceived to be low, its negative payoffs overcome the slightly positive immediate payoffs for disclosure; thus nondisclosure seems preferable.

Table V suggests that acquaintances prefer nondisclosure unless they believe that their disclosure will be reciprocated. On the average, there is a preference for nondisclosure. If reciprocal disclosure is believed rather likely, however, the actor will make disclosures. Reciprocation does yield much higher payoffs than it does for strangers, since it tends to move acquaintances toward friendship.

Friends. What happens when acquaintances have moved deeper toward friendship? At this point, the other's nonreciprocation is less threatening, since an actor does not fear that a friend will hurt him. Furthermore, potential future payoffs from reciprocal disclosure are now larger, since reciprocation strengthens friendship ties. Consequently, unless one believes that the friend is almost certain *not* to reciprocate, one is prone to disclose intimacies to a friend. Table V suggests that preferences for self-disclosure will be quite strong if reciprocation from a friend is believed likely, much stronger than for strangers or acquaintances; payoffs will also be much greater. Such outcomes depend, of course, on both actors' beliefs that the other is likely to reciprocate and that deeper involvement with their friend will be highly rewarding. If either actor does not wish deeper involvement, or if either believes that the other is unlikely to disclose intimacies, the pair will not progress beyond this point in their relationship.

Intimates. Finally, let us consider a deeply involved pair. In reaching their current interpersonal state, the partners have previously engaged in many intimate disclosures; each member has learned much about the other. Each member possesses much power over the other. It appears, then, that single acts of nonreciprocation now possess little significance, for both members already know very much about each other. Accordingly, current outcomes are dictated primarily by immediate payoffs for disclosure. Table V therefore suggests that intimate companions will slightly prefer disclosure over nondisclosure, but the difference is no greater than that held by strangers. However, the absolute value of either act is far greater than in less intimate relationships.

The above predictions are summarized in Fig. 7. One curve shows an actor's gains from choosing disclosure over nondisclosure; the other curve plots the

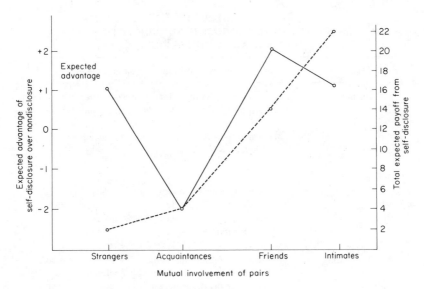

Fig. 7. The model's predictions about an actor's gain from self-disclosure to his co-actor as a function of their level of involvement.

expected value of disclosure. These predictions are derived from the rules of incremental exchange theory, from the premise that on the average self-disclosure itself has an immediate positive payoff for both discloser and recipient, and from other assumptions about payoff levels and transitions that follow from varying outcomes. Other assumptions could, of course, lead to quite different predictions. While there are insufficient longitudinal data to test these RELATE predictions empirically, it appears that they describe existing findings as well as any other theory.

X. Romantic Involvement

One fascinating longitudinal relationship is a romantic involvement. We have discussed some processes relevant to such an involvement, but many other processes also affect its course. It is not possible to compare a simulation of romantic involvement with parallel empirical data, because adequate longitudinal data do not exist. Data that do exist pertain mainly to initial interactions between potential romantic partners (see Berscheid & Walster, 1974), or to data from longer relationships collected at time points that are months apart (see Levinger, Senn, & Jorgensen, 1970).

To simulate the development of a romantic involvement via the RELATE

TABLE VI
STATES AND BEHAVIORS IN THE SIMULATION
OF ROMANTIC INVOLVEMENT

State	Behavior options (for either person)
1. Meeting	1. Initiates a friendly interaction with other. 2. Responds warmly. (Adopts a warm stance toward other person.) 3. Responds coolly. (Adopts a cool stance toward other.)
2. Request	1. Asks for a date. 2. Takes a warm stance toward other. Says "yes" if other asks for a date. 3. Seems cool toward other. Says "no" if other asks for a date.
3. Begin dating	1. Actively communicates liking for the other person. 2. Nonverbally (i.e., nonexplicitly) communicates liking for the other person. 3. Nonverbally communicates *dis*liking for the other person.
4. Disclosure	1. Makes very intimate disclosures. Shows great interest in hearing other's disclosures. 2. Makes only moderately intimate disclosures. 3. Does not volunteer personal self-disclosure and expresses only polite interest in other's disclosures. 4. Expresses clear disinterest in either making or hearing disclosures.
5. Romance	1. Actively tries for deepening romantic involvement. Wants to see the other more often. 2. Takes a positive stance toward other. Responds warmly. 3. Accepts present involvement but does not want any deepening of romantic involvement. 4. Dislikes present involvement. Expresses rejection of the other person.
6. Sex	1. Initiates sexual behavior more intimate than one's own usual standard. 2. Accepts sexual behavior more intimate than usual standard, if it is proposed. 3. Restricts sexual behavior to usual standard for the situation. 4. Restricts sexual behavior to *less* than usual standard.

TABLE VI (*continued*)

State	Behavior options (for either person)
7. Harmony	1. Yields completely to the other's wishes. 2. Emphasizes compromise rather than conflict. 3. Negotiates and bargains. Emphasizes formal agreement.
8. Future	1. Proposes plans that involve the other person in the future (e.g., 6 months from present). 2. Adopts an accepting stance toward future plans (though status of future is not made explicit). 3. Rejects future planning.
9. Commitment	1. Openly declares against romantic involvement with others by either partner. 2. Expresses *dis*interest in other romantic prospects. 3. Expresses interest in other romantic prospects. 4. Declares that self and other should maintain interest in other romantic contacts.
10. Permanence	1. Initiates "semi-public" action that implies permanency. 2. Adopts a positive stance toward actions implying permanency. 3. Rejects only actions that imply permanency without rejecting the current relationship with the other person.
11. Proposal	1. Suggests marriage. 2. Accepts suggestion of marriage, if it is made. 3. Rejects marriage at this time, without implying rejection of the other person. 4. Rejects other person and, therefore, marriage to that person.

model, one must first state a subtheory within our framework. Our subtheory specified 11 potential states of a pair's involvement. These states and the behaviors available in the states are shown in Table VI. To arrive at reasonable values for the payoff matrices, transition matrices, and other parameters, a scaling study was conducted.[7] Each subject in the study received a brief per-

---

[7] John Goldin carried out this study.

sonality sketch of two hypothetical actors: John and Susan. John was described as attractive, but shy and introverted; Susan was described as attractive and extroverted. Initially, each subject ranked the 11 states in order of their relative depth of involvement. After completing this ranking, subjects filled in each of the 11 payoff matrices for the actor of their own sex, and then compared the payoffs across states. Finally, the subjects constructed transition diagrams for the relationship and suggested appropriate values for the other parameters. The payoffs that subjects had supplied were then normalized so that both actors' payoffs were on the same scale in each state. The scaled values obtained for a male and a female subject (graduate students in social psychology) provided the input for the simulation of romantic involvement described below.

The simulation began with the hypothetical actors meeting as strangers. The course of the romance is summarized in Fig. 8. It can be described as follows:

John and Susan first meet in a class. Susan initiates a friendly interaction, and asks John for a date at the same time as John is asking her. On their initial dates, they both actively (though nonverbally) communicate liking for each other. However, neither is willing to be very intimate in their disclosure to the other.

After a period of time in this situation, John learns that Susan is willing to disclose intimacies in response to his disclosures, and he confides in her completely. This leads the pair into active striving for a deep romantic involvement. They both initiate sexual behaviors more intimate than their standard. They establish a pattern of interaction where Susan is willing to yield completely to John's wishes, though John is not ready to reciprocate. When John proposes

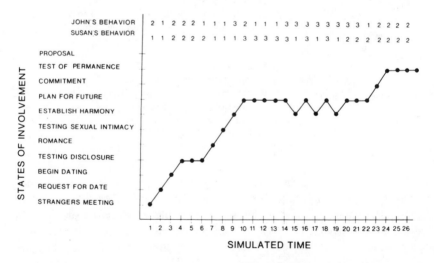

Fig. 8. The pattern of state transitions observed in a simulation of romantic involvement. The behaviors the hypothetical male (John) and the hypothetical female (Susan) selected at each point in time are noted at the top and described in Table VI.

future plans for the pair, however, Susan is evasive and noncommittal. As a result, John stops proposing such plans and the pair remains in this situation for some time (i.e., alternating between the state called "Establish harmony" and the state "Plan for future"). Finally, Susan adopts a more positive stance toward the future; John, detecting this, proposes future plans again. This time Susan accepts the plans, and they both express disinterest in alternative romantic prospects. They move into a state of semi-permanency, where each partner adopts a positive stance toward actions implying real permanency, though neither proposes marriage.

While we know of no hard data with which to compare the course of this relationship, the behaviors within sections of this simulation agree with anecdotal evidence and intuitive knowledge. Susan, the extrovert, initiated interaction at a shallow level, but was reluctant to get deeply involved. John, the introvert, was passive at first, but later initiated movement into a deep relationship. The pair had to establish a pattern of reciprocal disclosure early in the relationship in order to advance deeper. Perhaps, however, the most interesting aspect of the simulation was the way in which the pair reached commitment. John learned that his proposal to consider future plans was not welcomed and he stopped proposing. After a time, though, Susan detected that their relationship would begin to regress if she failed to become more positive toward future plans. She became so. John then proposed future plans again, and the hurdle was overcome.

RELATE's simulation of the development of a romantic involvement is interesting, but this example depends completely on views of a hypothetical pair by a few participating subjects. More representative simulations await further research. Readers should note that different views about what states are preferred or probable will lead to results entirely different from those depicted here.

The present simulation, then, is illustrative rather than definitive. While it is unlikely that we will soon attain novel insights about real life pairs from such simulations, a reward-cost model of deeper relationships does have applicability. Current findings by the second author and his co-workers are that people can meaningfully report on their rewards and costs in current and past relationships, and that they can compare such rewards and costs. Preliminary findings indicate that as relations deepen there is a general increase in the structure of expected payoffs; it appears that while actual payoffs do not necessarily increase greatly, the probability of positive payoffs becomes considerably higher. As relationships deepen, costs deriving from increased commitments and obligations also increase. This scheme also enables us to analyze sex-role stereotypes about a deeply involved partnership: The female partner is judged to invest more highly in the relationship at a higher cost than the male partner, but is also believed to derive significantly higher rewards. Such work illustrates how the simulation model can serve as a heuristic for research entirely unconnected with computer formalization or mathematical abstraction.

XI. Conclusions

This paper has described a general theoretical framework for modeling dyadic interaction. The framework, which we call "incremental exchange theory," was built in order to move beyond current theories of social exchange. It incorporates two major assumptions: (1) that the potential goodness of interaction outcomes varies directly with depth of pair involvement, and (2) that pair development implies a sequential movement from one outcome matrix to another, the direction and amount of movement being contingent on current outcomes. The ensuing RELATE computer model incorporates two operations that advance it beyond current exchange conceptions. One feature is the differential weighting of the co-actor's payoffs in the actor's assessment of own rewards; this moves the model beyond heretofore "individualistic" conceptions, and allows us to account for the influence of alter's feelings on the actor's own choices. A second feature is the body of state-to-state transition rules, which allow us to proceed beyond the limitations of static matrix conceptions. The formal basis of the RELATE model is intended to be so general as to adapt it for application to a wide variety of dyadic problems.

In brief, the RELATE model treats any pair relationship as a finite set of interpersonal outcome matrices or states. Any actor's perspective upon those states hinges on his view of the transitions from state to state, which in turn depend on the outcomes that either do or can occur at any given point in the anticipated sequence. In choosing his behavior from his available options at any given moment, the actor bases his choice on some combination of present and future considerations—as affected by the behavior options and payoffs in each possible state, perceived transitions between states, his depth of search into the future, his discounting or accentuation of future payoffs and costs, and by his initial estimates of his partner's own actions as modifiable through learning about the partner's actual behavior during interaction.

In assessing the merits and limitations of the present model, it is important to note its flexibility and its tentativeness. One purpose of the model is to permit us to test the implications of simplifying assumptions for specifying longitudinal sequences, in order to guide the design of actual empirical research. For that purpose, the RELATE model has several limitations. The major ones are the following: (1) Incremental exchange theory, on which the model rests, is not a complete theory; it cannot completely specify the rules of social behavior, because those rules are largely unknown. (2) The model itself contains a large number of parameters, which render it complex and also make its predictions difficult to disconfirm. (3) Most of the concepts within the model, such as payoffs, costs, or discounts, are extremely difficult to define operationally. Its impact, therefore, is mainly that of a meta-theory that *points* to avenues of theoretical development.

In viewing these limitations, readers may note that they are similar to those of earlier exchange theories. As Simpson (1972, pp. 14–18) has suggested, theories of social exchange have excluded from their domain various problems that must be dealt with before they can fruitfully be applied. Like other reinforcement approaches, social exchange theories offer no substantive theory of what constitutes rewards or costs (see Levinger, 1974). Our present effort does not escape this criticism.

The RELATE model contains many parameters. For any given application, it is left to the user to specify states, behaviors, payoffs, costs, probability estimates, discounts, depth of search. In practice, then, the model is hard to use. One reason for introducing these parameters is to call attention to the complexity rather than to evade it. For instance, it would be possible to lump a behavior's costs into the same term as its payoffs; but it seems more accurate to assume that costs can occur prior to and independent of outcomes. RELATE's user must decide how to employ the various parameters. If the user wishes, he can greatly simplify the model by appropriate choices of parameters.

The RELATE model has been applied to a variety of central issues in the social psychology of dyadic relations which have been extremely resistive to theoretical advance. Our applications have illustrated RELATE's solution to the following knotty problems: (1) how altruism can occur in shallow interactions; (2) what sorts of "similarity" are most clearly linked to interpersonal attraction; (3) how degree of self-disclosure is likely to vary across different levels of intimacy; and (4) how romantic involvements develop within a longitudinal perspective of incrementing payoffs. It would be tempting to consider other dyadic phenomena, such as aggression, divorce, persuasion, or attitudinal convergence. However, "subtheories" compatible with RELATE remain to be developed.

The model, then, is a heuristic framework for integrating current ad hoc theories of a variety of dyadic phenomena which are usually treated as distinct topics, and are poorly tied to one another. This is the major rationale for this model. To put it in the word's of Abelson's (1968, p. 326) assessment of several other computer simulation models of social behavior: RELATE can serve as "a spur to the better articulation of theories."

COMMENTARY

George C. Homans

HARVARD UNIVERSITY
CAMBRIDGE, MASSACHUSETTS

I have been much interested in studying the papers included in this volume. Each of them has added to my own understanding of what has come to be called equity theory, though they have not increased my fondness for that phrase itself. What follows is a series of reflections on the papers, reflections not wholly exhaustive and systematic but not wholly random either. If the space devoted to criticism in comparison with the space devoted to praise seems itself inequitable, remember that praise, though much more rewarding than criticism, usually requires much less argument.

After restating briefly my own general view of the problem of distributive justice as an aspect of equity theory, I shall turn in succession to the following subjects: the probable limitations of some of the propositions stated in the papers; the limitations of equity theory itself; the possible extensions of the theory, and finally the problem of the integration of the theory with a more general theory of social behavior, particularly in the relations between equity, status, and power.

My own interest in equity began with an interest in distributive justice, which I believe to be only one aspect of equity. Ever since Aristotle's discussion of the subject in his *Nichomachean Ethics,* the study of distributive justice has been concerned with the relationship between two further relationships: first, the relationship between at least two persons or groups in the amounts of reward they receive, when the distribution of reward results from direct exchange between the parties or when it is made by some third party, such as a boss, an organization, or even a market; and second, the relationships between the same persons or groups in the amounts of contribution, however that be defined, which they make to the direct or indirect exchange. When the ratio of their rewards is equal, as perceived by *all* the parties, to the ratio of their contributions, then the distribution of rewards is said to be fair, just, or equitable. Thus distributive justice always entails a comparison by the parties of the contributions each makes and the reward each receives, but what they compare is not the subjective value and cost of the rewards and contributions—for there can be no comparison of subjective values—but rather the outward and visible amounts of the rewards and contributions. Thus workers in a factory compare their earnings but not how much these earnings "mean" to each of them.

Note that if all parties are to accept a distribution as just, they must agree on three different points. First, they must agree on the rule of distributive justice itself: that rewards ought to be proportional to contributions. Second, they must agree on what kinds of rewards and contributions are to be legitimately taken into account in applying the rule. Third, they must agree in their assessment of the amounts of these contributions each makes and the amounts of these rewards each receives. Experience seems to indicate that people are much more likely to reach agreement on the rule itself than on the other two issues. They agree on the rule but not on its concrete applications.

Two of the papers (Austin, Walster & Utne; Leventhal) seem at times to imply that a rule of equality of reward between persons is a different rule from one of distributive justice. It need not be so. If the persons are equal in contributions, then their equality in reward meets the conditions of distributive justice; the ratio of contributions is still equal to the ratio of rewards.

The student of distributive justice is concerned next with the reaction of persons or groups to distributions of reward that they consider, under the rule, too low, too high, or about right, that is, fair. The rule of distributive justice represents in a very general way what people expect in the way of reward. Why it does so I shall suggest later. When people do not get as much reward as they expect, they are, by the frustration-aggression proposition, apt to feel some degree of anger and to take aggressive action against the source or beneficiary of their frustration, in this case, the source or beneficiary of the injustice, provided that such action does not cost them too much in other ways. Accordingly social scientists are not interested in injustice merely for its own sake. The anger and possible aggression it provokes alter the hitherto existing balance of power among the persons concerned, for the readiness to take aggressive action is always a factor in power.

If people get more than they expect, they are apt to feel some degree of guilt and even to do something to compensate their victims for the injustice of which they are the sources or beneficiaries, again provided that it does not cost them too much. The question of the origin of their guilt is an interesting one, discussed in the Austin-Walster-Utne paper. Perhaps it represents the anxiety precipitated in the beneficiaries by their knowledge that the victims may be expected to take aggressive action against them. But it has long been recognized that the beneficiaries of injustice are much less likely than the victims to be disturbed by it, and are often and easily able to persuade themselves that their contributions are really superior to those of the victims, so that they deserve their superior rewards after all.

Finally, there are the people who, even if they need more of a certain kind of reward, feel nevertheless that they are getting as much of it as they deserve under the rule of distributive justice. Such people are, by the obverse of the frustration-aggression proposition, apt to be approving of, and nonaggressive toward, the source of the reward, that is, the source of justice. To this extent, justice makes for social harmony.

After this general statement I begin the main body of my paper with some critical remarks. Some of the papers in this volume state certain propositions as if they were generally true when I believe that they hold good only within special circumstances. Consider the Huesmann-Levinger paper on "Incremental Exchange Theory." This is the only paper that is not specifically concerned with equity but rather with social exchange in general, and it is the only one that presents a formal model suitable for use in computer simulation. The model incorporates the notion that interaction between persons in a dyad must be treated sequentially, that it develops by steps, and that reward or punishment at any particular step, that is, after any one of the persons has acted, affects the probability that he or she will take the action again. Any model that pretends to be realistic must incorporate this notion, which lies at the heart of every behavioral psychology. The model also embodies the notion that persons will forgo immediate in favor of future rewards to the extent that they perceive the latter to be of higher value than the former and that they will be successful in gaining them. This also is realistic, though the paper does not specify the kind of past experience a person must have had in order to discount the present in this way.

So far so good. But then the authors say: "The expected value of a dyad's rewards increases as the depth of their relationship increases. By 'depth' we mean the level of a pair's mutual involvement." In all fairness, investigators must be allowed to build any assumptions they like into their computer models. They are entitled to ask what the social world would be like if the assumptions were true. It is well to examine possible worlds, and the computer may help us do so. Sooner or later, however, we compare them with real ones. In the present case I do not think that the assumption, if I understand it aright, holds good generally. If it did, I believe, for instance, that there would be fewer divorces than in fact there are. The proposition may well hold good in particular circumstances, but the authors do not suggest what they may be. In general I suspect that it runs up against some kind of law of diminishing returns, notably the effect of satiation.

The authors clearly label the proposition in question as being only an assumption, though it plays an important part in their model. A little later they present, without any qualification, a set of results of computer simulations as indicating that "the more likely an actor thinks it is that his co-actor will behave altruistically, the more likely he is to behave similarly." This conclusion may follow from computer simulation under the given assumptions; the behavior may also occur in real life when the circumstances fit the assumptions, but I cannot believe the conclusion to be generally true. An actor may well behave so as to reward his co-actor if he knows that the latter will be in contact with him later and able to punish him if he does not do so. But is this altruism? Since I am sure that one of the assumptions of the model is inadequate, I suspect that conclusions drawn from this and other assumptions are apt to be even more inadequate.

This same paper illustrates the recurring difficulties psychologists encounter in trying to deal with the notion of altruism. Citing one kind of example of altruism Huesmann and Levinger write: "Even in surface contacts, an actor is frequently guided by moral principles or social pressures to sacrifice personal gain (a driver will run off the road to avoid a strange child)." But does he really sacrifice personal gain? If he would have come under heavy criticism for not trying to miss the child, his action avoids this punishment and so is a personal gain. Amazing as it may seem, even living up to a moral code some persons may experience as a personal gain. I think it quite unscientific to discuss altruism as if it were a problem of balancing personal gain against something else. It is rather a problem of balancing different personal gains against one another. Indeed all the gains and losses that affect the behavior of persons are personal. What else could they be?

The same tendency to make statements that sound as if they were generally true but probably are not appears in Leventhal's paper. I do not argue that all of his propositions are of this sort, yet he does write this: "Numerous studies conducted in laboratory and field settings indicate that reward systems which closely tie a recipient's rewards to his performance often do elicit better performance." "Sometimes" would be a better word than "often" here. If the proposition were often true, we should expect systems of wage payment by piecework to be more effective in eliciting really high production than in fact they are. What usually happens is that employees at piecework wages do not increase their production beyond a certain point, embodied in a group norm. This does not mean that the finding is not true but only that it does not hold good for the full range of values of the variables. We must look for the conditions that limit its generality, especially the influence of alternative social rewards to be obtained by actions other than increased production. Leventhal certainly recognizes later in his paper that rewarding the members of a group according to a principle of distributive justice need not always be associated with high productivity by the group.

Austin, Walster, and Utne hold that equity theory is "a strikingly simple theory" consisting essentially of four propositions. Perhaps I should like to make it even simpler, for I am not sure that their Proposition II is either true or necessary. Let us give it a close look: "Groups can maximize collective reward by evolving accepted systems for 'equitably' apportioning rewards and costs among members. Thus members evolve such systems of equity and will attempt to induce members to accept and adhere to these systems."

Remember how much the acceptance of a system of distributive justice requires of members of a group. Agreement on the general principle that the ratio of contributions equal the ratio of rewards is the least of their problems. They must also agree on what dimensions are to be held relevant to the assessment of contributions and rewards, and finally how members are to be ranked along these dimensions.

The members of a group do not find it easy to reach agreement on these issues and thus establish distributive justice as a reality and not an ideal. But I concede that they sometimes do, though probably only for a short time and only if the members are few in number. Why do they do so at all? The proposition says that by so acting they can "maximize collective reward" and therefore they will so act. Let us not look too closely at the assumption that what members of a group "can" do, they "will" necessarily do, but turn rather to the other part of the proposition: that the establishment of a system of distributive justice will indeed maximize collective reward.

I believe it is demonstrable that distributive justice maximizes collective reward only if one specifies very carefully what kind of collective reward one has in mind. Since injustice creates resentment, the establishment of just conditions obviously ought to increase the rewards of the former victims of injustice and even to increase the rewards of the former beneficiaries by obviating the threat which the resentment on the part of the victims presents to them.

But does the establishment of distributive justice increase the overall rewards of the members of a group? Remember always that there are rewards and rewards and that they are usually in competition with one another. Although the establishment of distributive justice tends to increase social harmony, which may indeed be to every member's benefit, it is far from clear that in general it also increases the physical productivity of the group, which may also bring reward, though of a different kind. Increased productivity may, for instance, depend on innovations in methods, and yet innovation is the great enemy of justice, because it usually goes along with a change in the contributions made by individual members and subgroups and hence with a change in their claims for reward—claims that the others may not immediately be ready to concede. A just society is apt to be a static society.

I do not believe that "equity theory" needs Proposition II in the Austin-Walster-Utne paper, although I am prepared to accept their other three propositions.

Austin *et al.* also say: "By convention, equity theorists term an individual who intentionally takes larger relative outcomes than he deserves an 'exploiter' or a 'harmdoer'." Let me say at once that, if I am an equity theorist, I do not use these terms by convention or in any other way. I am prepared to speak of "victims" but not of "exploiters" or "harmdoers." Let us be careful how we use these "moral" words! Who determines what "he" deserves? He may judge that he does deserve larger relative outcomes. It takes at least two to establish justice or injustice. And suppose he does not deserve it, but still takes the larger outcome; he is not necessarily a "harmdoer." The increased resources he thereby commands may, wisely invested, enable him to increase the future rewards of the whole group he belongs to. Yet no doubt there will be plenty of persons to curse him in the short run.

This last statement by Austin *et al.* leads me to offer a wholly unscientific aside. Look at the kind of propositions I have recently been commenting on: One person's altruistic behavior increases the likelihood of another's. The rewards from an interpersonal association increase the deeper it becomes. Equitable reward improves a person's performance. An equitable system of reward in a group increases collective rewards. And so on. The characteristics common to these propositions are that they state a direct, not an inverse, relationship between two variables and that an increase in both variables is morally "good." Or a decrease in both variables is morally "bad": thus an unjust person is necessarily a "harmdoer." Seldom is it suggested that an increase in one good may produce a decrease in another, or that good may come out of evil.

This amuses me. How liberal and how American these assumptions are! Their authors would say that "All things work together for good to them that love God"—if they read the Bible or believed in God. (And all things work together for evil to them that don't.) What nice people they all are! I do not say that they are biased, but only more sensitized to certain kinds of relationships than to others. Certainly the relations they are concerned with often hold good—evil may indeed come out of evil—but, alas!, they do not hold good across the board. These social psychologists sometimes remind me of the innocent American heroines of a Henry James novel before they have been had by the subtle and wicked Europeans. Perhaps to be subtle is indeed to be wicked, but I sometimes wish they would take the advice that one of the characters in *The Portrait of a Lady* (Chapter LI) offered Isabel, the heroine: "Don't try to be too good. Be a little easy and natural and nasty; feel a little wicked, for the comfort of it, once in your life!" That is, consider a wider range and complexity of propositions about human behavior.

I think it would be better to rely on experience—experience, for instance, as it appears in the record of history—than on *some* of the research social psychologists apparently do rely on. I distrust, particularly, research in which the investigator asks subjects to report what they would do in situations they do not in fact face, like the study reported in the Leventhal paper in which "subjects took the role of management consultants and made recommendations about bonus pay for hypothetical groups of workers," or in the research of Edward

Thorndike, who asked subjects to assess how much money paid in cash they would take in return for having, for instance, their left arms cut off at the elbow. This exercise, it seems to me, was utterly meaningless. Not only were the actual subjects unlikely ever to have to answer such a question in real life, but any persons whatever are unlikely to do so. It is a shame that the man who formulated the Law of Effect should ever have lent himself to such a waste of time. We must always be concerned with what people actually do. What they say about their actions may bear some relation to the actions themselves—or it may not. What they say they would do in a situation in which they do not have to bear the costs or gain the rewards is bound to be still further removed from reality. A good experiment in social psychology is one in which the subjects at least believe that their actions make some serious difference, some serious gain or loss, to themselves.

A point of the greatest importance made in some of these papers is the one Karl Weick has expressed as: "Man does not live by equity alone." Thus the beneficiary of inequity may do nothing to compensate the victim, and the victim nothing to force the compensation. For the former, his gain from injustice may be too great, and his fear of reprisal from the victim too low. For the latter, his loss by inequity may be too little in view of the danger to himself of trying to take reprisals. More generally, equity may cede to power—but I shall have more to say on the subject of power later in this paper.

As I have pointed out (Homans, 1974; p. 250), most of the action in justice occurs not over the generalized rule of distributive justice (equity) but over what dimensions for comparing the contributions and rewards of different individuals and groups shall be used in applying the formula. The existence of dimensions on which different persons and groups can be compared seems to depend on some degree of similarity between them. Thus persons who hold different jobs may make it an issue of justice that they receive the same pay. If no such dimensions can be found, the question of inequity does not arise. The same holds for secrecy about the contributions and rewards of individuals. Secrecy sometimes has its advantages. I believe it is just as well for the morale of professors in my university that in theory and often in fact no one but the Dean of the Faculty knows the amount of individual salaries. The same perhaps holds for the case in which it is difficult to determine what the contributions of individuals to a joint task may be—but I am not sure. This situation may really call in justice for an equal distribution of the collective reward, if it can be divided.

The Lerner-Miller-Holmes paper introduces some other important cases in which the rule of distributive justice is either modified or treated as wholly irrelevant. One of these is the case of need. But need seems not to work alone. It is especially likely to make justice irrelevant to the distribution of reward when the needy person is especially intimately related to those who have the rewards to distribute. As the authors say: "The most obvious example of this is the way the adults in most families allocate the family's resources. Their earnings are distributed, to a great extent, in terms of the legitimate 'needs' of the various members, no matter how much each contributed in obtaining resources." That is, if one of the children needs eyeglasses and the others do not, the parents will not begrudge that one the eyeglasses, even though he or she has contributed no more than the others to the well-being of the family. But the parents might well begrudge paying for the glasses of a child they were not responsible for. "Responsible for" in this case means, I suspect, "someone whom others would blame them for not taking care of." "Am I my brother's keeper?"—"Yes, if he is really your brother." That is, need and responsibility combine to make justice irrelevant. On the other hand, let us not assume too quickly that distributive justice is irrelevant within the family. If it were, children would never accuse their parents of playing favorites. In the absence of differences between children in their needs for money, most American parents would not be apt to distribute allowances unequally, or if they did, they would be apt to do so on some equitable principle, such as increasing the allowance with age.

Children are not the only persons to whom we distribute goods on the grounds of need and not of distributive justice, or at least not of justice alone. We distribute them individually or collectively out of charity rather than justice to the "unfortunate," that is, especially to the needy whose neediness is not their own fault. Even here I suspect justice comes in. An example is the unemployed. Certainly many of them are not unemployed through any fault of their own. Yet we usually do not intend to provide an unemployed person with more money by relief than the least well-paid employed person can earn by working. That is, we still preserve some relationship between relative contribution to the economy and relative reward—though of course other considerations beside justice, such as the problem of motivation, come in here. The very least the papers show—and they show in fact much more—is the necessity for further examination of the relationships between need, "responsibility," and distributive justice.

Lerner, Miller, and Holmes also argue that, when people compete for scarce resources, the question of distributive justice does not arise between them. "Under these circumstances, 'winning' is all that matters in deciding who gets the desired resource ... the promotion, the fair maiden, the prize. Although one's prior efforts, investment, and costs may elicit some form of condolence or compassion, they are not allowed to alter the decision as to who deserves what." This may well be true of competition for the fair maiden—though even here we used to say, "None but the brave deserve the fair"—but it is not often true of promotions. Here not only the person who awards the promotion but also the persons who are competing for promotion and the organizations to which they belong, such as a labor union, bring all sorts of notions of distributive justice into their actions and reactions. As usual, the different parties may not consider the same dimensions to be relevant to the just distribution of promotions. One may cite the relative skill of the competitors, another their seniority as relevant to the decision, but all imply that they accept the general rule of proportionality between contributions and rewards. Yet even though their argument does not apply fully to promotions, Lerner, Miller, and Holmes certainly point to an important limitation on the applicability of distributive justice. It is worth asking, though I shall not try to answer it here, what makes the difference between the promotion and the fair maiden.

It is obvious that in many cases of competition, especially games, people raise the question of equity, of fairness, not over the results of the competition but over the procedures by which the result is reached: the competition must have been fair, the competitors must have obeyed the rules, due process must have been followed. Note that distributive justice as Aristotle used the phrase is concerned with results not with the process of reaching them, not with procedural justice. Perhaps we should not lump everything remotively concerned with fairness together under the single rubric of equity theory, but use different names to indicate what sorts of equity we are talking about. We might then be better able to recognize how the different kinds are related to one another. Thus procedural justice in games is meant to ensure distributive justice, to ensure that the best man will win. But there are obviously conditions in which at least some people consider procedural justice irrelevant. Accordingly "all's fair in love and war." Note that the fair maiden comes in again. What's different about her? Perhaps the more valuable the gain and correspondingly the more painful the loss in zero-sum games, the more likely is equity to be disregarded. Finally, procedural justice may bring about what some people would consider injustice of a different kind. Thus procedural justice in the form of equal educational opportunity may lead to what some Americans believe to be gross injustices of result, such as large differences in income between persons. In any event, the papers in this volume should lead us to consider more carefully the relationships, under varied circumstances, between different forms of equity.

Some of the papers are concerned, very properly, with pointing out some of the limits of equitable behavior: man does not live by equity alone. Others are more concerned with extensions of equity theory. The notion of distributive justice as developed by Aristotle and, much more recently, by social psychologists and sociologists has been concerned with the behavior of persons who are themselves the direct beneficiaries or victims of justice or injustice. Equity theory is now being extended to consider the behavior of persons who are observers, judges, of the justice of the exchanges between others. Such extension is particularly characteristic of the Austin-Walster-Utne and the Lerner-Miller-Holmes papers in this volume. The latter asks the crucial questions how and why a person convinces himself, or fails to convince himself, that he lives in an essentially just world. Of course, "essentially" is vague, but I do believe that some such conviction is a necessary condition for the integrity of many persons' behavior. The authors put forward the interesting idea that, in order to live by his "personal contract"—in effect, to establish what we used to call his ultimate "deserts" by taking actions that postpone immediate gratifications—a person must assume that, "if he does make the appropriate investments, his world is constructed so that the anticipated outcomes will follow." That is, he must believe the world to be a just one. Many people never acquire this conviction.

Of those who look forward to extensions of equity theory, Adams and Freedman, in a thoughtful survey of the present state of the field, express the largest hopes for its future. They write, for instance: "equity theory may, indeed, eventually result in a comprehensive theory of social relationships." Or again: "It is logical that equity theory has the capacity to be generalized to social influence and social learning." The picture they seem to present is one of a theory gradually spreading out to encompass not only new fields but even the whole of social behavior. Here I am in disagreement. I doubt that equity theory will provide the general propositions that will eventually be used to explain all the principal features of social behavior. My belief is that in what is usually called behavioral psychology we already possess for this purpose a set of propositions obviously far more general than those of equity theory. They are, in fact, more general than those of any social psychology, for they can be used to explain both the social and the nonsocial behavior of individuals, both when individuals are interacting with other individuals and when they are interacting with the nonhuman environment. In my view one of our jobs as social psychologists is to show how the propositions of equity theory themselves follow from these more general propositions. My own program strikes me as almost the reverse of the Adams-Freedman one. In practice the two might come out at much the same place. If I am right, Adams and Freedman, in an effort to extend equity theory, could not help discovering that they had to use propositions different from and more general than those of equity theory itself.

I confess that I do not much like these phrases with the word "theory" in them. We have had so many of them in psychology: balance theory, dissonance theory, exchange theory, and now equity theory. I can appreciate their *ad hoc* or, to use a fancier word, heuristic value as labels for the study of certain classes of phenomena. But they too often give the impression that they come and go like fads, which is unfortunate, because the phenomena themselves are of permanent importance. If the effort to formulate theory means the statement of the findings within these fields in as general a form as possible, I am wholly in favor of the effort. Were I not, I should not be writing this commentary. Yet the findings of these particular "theories" always turn out to be partial. We must remember that in the long run there is only one theory we want to develop—a theory of human behavior—indeed, a theory of the behavior of organisms (see Skinner, 1938) in general.

Though the papers in this volume extend equity theory in a number of ways, what they do not much try to do is relate equity to other kindred social phenomena about which a good deal is already known. Thus I do not hear much in these papers about either status or power, though they have close if somewhat ambiguous relations with equity.

When the ledger clerks in an accounting department I once studied (Homans, 1974, pp. 242–45) complained that they ought to get paid just a couple of dollars a week more than the cash posters because their job was more responsible, they were not simply addressing themselves to a problem of distributive justice, to the fact that they felt their compensation was unfairly low. They were also addressing themsleves to a problem of status. Everyone knew about the relative pay rates of groups in the department: pay was an outward and visible sign of status, and the fact that the ledger clerks were receiving the same pay as the cash posters was a sign, a stimulus to observers, that threw into doubt the overall superiority of the clerks to the posters in status. It was not just money they were losing but social consideration. Sometimes it is difficult to separate the reaction to injustice from the reaction to a threat to a person's or a group's status.

Again, when a full-time worker in a supermarket says that when he works in company with a part-time worker, he has got to work faster than the other (see Homans, 1974, p. 215), he is not addressing himself to any marked degree to a problem in the relative distribution of rewards between the two of them. The speed at which the full-timer works may increase the rewards of the company, but even that is not really what is at stake. What is at stake is the security of a person's status. If one person is superior to another in one respect, such as being a full-timer rather than a part-timer, he must, if he is to maintain his overall superiority in status, be superior to another in another respect, too, that of speed. Status I believe to be rewarding not only, as we say, "in itself" but also because it is a stimulus affecting the future behavior of others toward the person whose status is in question.

These issues are at one and the same time issues of distributive justice and what is called *status congruence* or *status equilibration*. (See Homans 1974; pp. 200–202.) How similar the two are to one another! The problem that faces a ledger clerk is getting the company to increase the rewards the company gives her; the problem that faces a full-timer is increasing the contributions he gives the company. (In social exchange, one person's reward is another person's contribution.) However, in the cases of both equity and status, the condition that people say is proper or appropriate, and treat behaviorally as such, is the one in which a person's rank on at least one dimension—and several may be relevant—is in line with his rank on another, in comparison with the ranks of other persons on the respective dimensions. What are the relations between equity and status? Under what conditions is inequity more powerful in its effect on a person's behavior than a threat to his or her status? And why are equity and status-congruence similar? It takes a theory more general than either "equity theory" or "congruence theory" to explain why.

Finally, the authors of these papers have little to say about the relationships between equity and power, though if we are not just concerned with equity theory but with a general theory of social behavior, these relationships are of the first importance. By *power* I mean a situation in which the powerful person is himself able to affect the outcomes of the less powerful one and not a situation, which I call *authority,* in which one person can get some control over the behavior of another, not because he can himself affect the other's outcomes but because obedience to his orders has resulted in the other's obtaining favorable outcomes from the external physical or social environment. (See Homans, 1974, pp. 70–93.)

The question of power arises particularly in connection with Leventhal's paper. He does not refer to power explicitly, but his allocator—someone responsible for the allocation of rewards to others—obviously has it very much in mind, as allocators in real life always must. An allocator can seldom afford to consider only how he *ought* to redistribute the rewards at his disposal, so as, for instance, to increase the productivity of the members of his group. He must also consider whether he *can* redistribute them, especially when the rewards at his disposal are in short supply—as they always are—and he has to face competing demands for them. Leventhal writes: "Several factors probably limit an allocator's tendency to use a strategy of giving low reward to force nonproductive recipients from the group. First, it may be very difficult or costly to obtain or train competent replacements." Note, however, that by this standard the recipients are *not* unproductive. They are not unproductive if the cost of obtaining their services is less than the cost of obtaining those of others. In terms of the relation between cost and benefit they are *more* productive than the others. Indeed these recipients are in a strong power-position over against the allocator: it appears that his trying to get rid of them would hurt him more than it would hurt them, and it is this condition, sometimes called "the principle of least interest," that is the essence of power. Note that if the allocator were in the stronger power position he would probably not lower the rewards of nonproductive recipients in order to force them out of the group; he would give them no rewards at all. That is, he would fire them.

Leventhal writes: "Equitable allocations ensure that recipients whose behavior is most useful have greatest access to essential resources." Let us be very careful in our use of language here. "Essential resources" is ambiguous. One may, for instance, hire a number of laborers and provide them with "essential resources" in the form of excellent shovels, but still not pay them much. Let us talk of rewards rather than resources, for rewards are what equitable allocations have to do with. Rewards may indeed be resources to the recipients, but resources, as in the case of the shovels, are not always rewards. Or rather, the shovels are rewards for the contractor not the laborers.

The variable "degree of usefulness" is also ambiguous. Consider the peasants in the economy of medieval societies. In one sense, what activity could possibly be more useful than theirs? They produced the food on which the lives of all the members of society depended. Yet in general they received low rewards, often no more than a bare subsistence. Why? Because though their behavior was highly useful, there were a great many of them and they replaced themselves readily. It is not usefulness in some absolute sense but the ability to provide services the supply of which is low relative to demand that determines the degree of "access to essential resources" in Leventhal's proposition. Only when peasants became, through war, pestilence, and famine, relatively more scarce did their rewards in medieval society tend to rise, in the form of lower rents and higher wages.

But usefulness in this new relative sense is the same thing as power. Remember that, if a person is to gain power through his ability to provide services the supply of which is low relative to demand, the demand in question need not come, so to speak, from the population at large. It need only come from persons who are themselves powerful. Thus guards often get power not because people at large demand their services but because the tyrant does. Remember also that the ability to punish is a scarce service as well as the ability to reward, for the ability to punish usually entails the ability to withdraw the punishment, and that is a reward. The power to kill is also the power to spare.

If one person or group has greater power in either the good or the bad (coercive) sense than another person or group, it is usually able to command greater rewards than the other. This is what we mean when we say that the person or group in question has greater bargaining power. Thus is produced a kind of proportionality between contributions and rewards that looks very much like distributive justice. But if power and equity are similar, why do we need both concepts?

I believe power to be the more primitive phenomenon that lies behind distributive justice (and for that matter behind status congruence). But this does not mean that power is identical with justice. Might may make right but that does not mean it *is* right. How do we get from one to another? As one of the noble Romans in Plutarch's *Lives* (I cannot retrieve the reference now) once asked the inhabitants of a conquered city: "Why do you prate of justice to us who have swords by our sides?" The reaction of people to injustice follows as a special case from the frustration-aggression proposition: they react with anger because they have not gotten what they expected in the way of reward. What they expected is what has usually occurred in the past. And what very generally has occurred in the past is that power differences have produced a direct relationship between a person's ability to provide goods scarce in relation to demand and the value of the rewards he receives (see Homans, 1974, p. 250.)

Unfortunately the goods that some people offer in social exchange are not as rare in fact as they think they are. Accordingly they do not get what they expect in the way of reward; they say that they are being treated unfairly, and are angry. The tendency for expectations to get out of line with realities is encouraged by changes in the relation between a group and its external environment, by the entrance of new kinds of goods into social exchange, and by fluctuations of old goods in value. All of these things produce changes in power relationships.

As the Austin-Walster-Utne paper reminds us, injustice is a curse of the weak not the strong; for the strong, the more powerful, just because they are that, can successfully insist on getting what they think they deserve. This does not mean that the weak complain more about injustice than do the strong. A group that is increasing in power may complain with particular vehemence that it has been unjustly treated hitherto, precisely because it is now able to make its demands effective. (See the Adams-Freedman paper on the instrumental uses of inequity.) We are now more concerned, however, with the weak than with the strong.

The great point to remember is that their very anger at the injustice done them tends to make up for their weakness in other respects. Anger allows the victims of injustice to accept greater costs in attacking its beneficiaries than they would otherwise have accepted. So far as the beneficiaries wish to avoid the attack, their power has decreased, and they may go some distance toward disgorging their gains. If the threats or actual attacks fail, the evidence is that all parties come in time to acquiesce, if somewhat ruefully, in the new dimensions along which contributions and rewards are to be ranked and to acquiesce in the new positions they occupy on the rankings. Justice depends on expectations, and expectations in the long run on actualities. What is, is always becoming what ought to be. Several of the papers in this volume, especially those of Lerner-Miller-Holmes and Austin-Walster-Utne, suggest processes by which inequitable conditions are rationalized as equitable after all. Except perhaps for some philosophers, an equitable distribution of rewards may simply be a distribution by relative power—provided only that the relative powers of the parties, power and countervailing power, have managed to remain equal and constant for some considerable period of time. An inequitable distribution may be no more than one that no longer reflects the actual distribution of power.

REFERENCES

Abelson, R.P. Simulation of social behavior. In G. Lindzey and E. Aronson (Eds.), *Handbook of social psychology*, Vol. 2. Cambridge, Mass.: Addison-Wesley, 1968.

Adams, J.S. Toward an understanding of inequity. *Journal of Abnormal and Social Psychology*, 1963, 67, 422–436.

Adams, J.S. Inequity in social exchange. In L. Berkowitz (Ed.), *Advances in experimental social psychology*, Vol. 2. New York: Academic Press, 1965. Pp. 267–299.

Adams, J.S. A framework for the study of modes of resolving inconsistency. In R.P. Abelson, E. Aronson, W.J. McGuire, T.M. Newcomb, M.J. Rosenberg, & P.H. Tannenbaum (Eds.), *Theories of cognitive consistency: A sourcebook*. Chicago: Rand McNally, 1968. Pp. 655–660.

Adams, J.S., & Jacobsen, P.R. Effects of wage inequities on work quality. *Journal of Abnormal and Social Psychology*, 1964, 69, 19–25.

Adams, J.S., & Rosenbaum, W.E. The relationship of worker productivity to cognitive dissonance about wage inequity. *Journal of Applied Psychology*, 1962, 46, 161–164.

Aderman, D., Brehm, D., & Katz, L. B. Empathetic observation of an innocent victim: The just world revisited. *Journal of Personality and Social Psychology*, 1974, 29, 342–347.

Ajzen, I., & Fishbein, M. The prediction of behavior from attitudinal and normative variables. *Journal of Experimental Social Psychology*, 1970, 6, 466–487.

Altman, I. Reciprocity of interpersonal exchange. *Journal for the Theory of Social Behaviour*, 1973, 3, 249–261.

Altman, I., & Taylor, D.A. *Social penetration: The development of interpersonal relationships*. New York: Holt, Rinehart, Winston, 1973.

Arnold, M.B. *Emotion and personality, Vol. 2. Psychological aspects*. New York: Columbia University Press, 1960.

Aronson, E. Some antecedents of interpersonal attraction. In W.J. Arnold and D. Levine (Eds.), *Nebraska symposium on motivation*, 1969. Lincoln: University of Nebraska Press, 1970.

Atkinson, J.W. Motivational determinants of risk-taking behavior. *Psychological Review*, 1957, 64, 359–372.

Atkinson, J.W. Towards experimental analysis of human motivation in terms of motives, expectancies, and incentives. In J.W. Atkinson (Ed.), *Motives in fantasy, action, and society*. Princeton, N.J.: D. Van Nostrand, 1958. Pp. 288–305.

Atkinson, J.W. *An introduction to motivation*. Princeton, N.J.: D. Van Nostrand, 1964.

Austin, W. Studies on "Equity with the world": A new application of Equity theory. Unpublished Ph.D. dissertation, University of Wisconsin, 1974.

245

246   REFERENCES

Austin, W., & Walster, E. Reactions to confirmations and disconfirmations of expectancies of equity and inequity. *Journal of Personality and Social Psychology,* 1974, **30,** 208–216.

Austin, W., & Walster, E. Participants' reactions to "Equity with the world." *Journal of Experimental Social Psychology,* 1974, **10,** 528–548.

Austin, W., Walster, E., & Pate, M.A. The effect of "Suffering in the act" on liking and assigned punishment. Unpublished research report, University of Wisconsin, 1973.

Baker, K. Experimental analysis of third-party justice behavior. *Journal of Personality and Social Psychology,* 1974, **30,** 307–316.

Bales, R. F. *Interaction process analysis.* Cambridge, Mass.: Addison-Wesley, 1950.

Bales, R.F. Task roles and social roles in problem-solving groups. In I.D. Steiner, & M. Fishbein (Eds.), *Current studies in social psychology.* New York: Holt, Rinehart, & Winston, 1965. Pp. 321–333.

Bankart, C.P., & Lanzetta, J.T. Performance and motivation as variables affecting the administration of rewards and punishments. *Representative Research in Social Psychology,* 1970, **1,** 1–10.

Bandura, A. Social-learning theory of identificatory processes. In D.A. Goslin (Ed.), *Handbook of socialization theory and research.* Chicago: Rand McNally, 1969. Pp. 213–262.

Baskett, G.D. Interview decisions as determined by competency and attitude similarity. *Journal of Applied Psychology,* 1973, **57,** 343–345.

Bauer, R.A. (Ed.) *Social indicators.* Cambridge, Mass.: MIT Press, 1966.

Benton, A.A. Productivity, distributive justice, and bargaining among children. *Journal of Personality and Social Psychology,* 1971, **18,** 68–78.

Berkowitz, L. Resistance to improper dependency relationships. *Journal of Experimental Social Psychology,* 1969, **5,** 283–294.

Berkowitz, L. The self, selfishness and altruism. In J. Macauley & L. Berkowitz (Eds.), *Altruism and helping behavior.* New York: Academic Press, 1970. Pp. 143–151.

Berkowitz, L. Social norms, feelings, and other factors affecting helping behavior and altruism. In L. Berkowitz (Ed.), *Advances in experimental social psychology,* Vol. 6. New York: Academic Press, 1972. Pp. 63–108. (a)

Berkowitz, L. Frustrations, comparisons, and other sources of emotion arousal as contributors to social unrest. *Journal of Social Issues,* 1972, **28,** 77–91. (b)

Berkowitz, L. Reactance and the unwillingness to help others. *Psychological Bulletin,* 1973, **79,** 310–317.

Berkowitz, L., & Connor, W. H. Success, failure, and social responsibility. *Journal of Personality and Social Psychology,* 1966, **4,** 664–669.

Berkowitz, L., & Daniels, L.R. Responsibility and dependency. *Journal of Abnormal and Social Psychology,* 1963, **66,** 429–436.

Berkowitz, L., & Daniels, L. R. Affecting the salience of the social responsibility norm: Effects of past help on the response to dependency relationships. *Journal of Abnormal and Social Psychology,* 1964, **68,** 275–281.

Berkowitz, L., & Friedman, P. Some social class differences in helping behavior. *Journal of Personality and Social Psychology,* 1967, **5,** 217–225.

Berscheid, E., Boye, D., & Walster, E. Retaliation as a means of restoring equity. *Journal of Personality and Social Psychology,* 1968, **10,** 370–376.

Berscheid, E., & Walster, E. When does a harm-doer compensate a victim? *Journal of Personality and Social Psychology,* 1967, **6,** 435–441.

Berscheid, E., & Walster, E. A little bit about love. In T.L. Huston (Ed.), *Foundations of interpersonal attraction.* New York: Academic Press, 1974. Pp. 335–381.

Berscheid, E., Walster, E., & Barclay, A. Effect of time on tendency to compensate a victim. *Psychological Reports,* 1969, **25,** 431–436.

Blake, R.R., Rosenbaum, M., & Duryea, R.A. Gift-giving as a function of group standards. *Human Relations,* 1955, 8, 61–73.

Blau, P.M. *The dynamics of bureaucracy: A study of interpersonal relations in two government agencies.* (Rev. ed.). Chicago: University of Chicago Press, 1963.

Blau, P.M. *Exchange and power in social life.* New York: Wiley & Sons, 1964.

Blau, P.M. Social exchange. In D.L. Sills (Ed.), *International encyclopedia of the social sciences.,* Vol. 7. New York: Macmillan Co., 1968. Pp. 452–458.

Blood, R.O., Jr., & Wolfe, D.M. *Husbands and wives.* New York: The Free Press, 1960.

Blumstein, P.W., & Weinstein, E.A. The redress of distributive injustice. *American Journal of Sociology,* 1969, 74, 408–418.

Bock, R.D., & Jones, L.V. *The measurement and prediction of judgment and choice.* San Francisco: Holden-Day, 1968.

Bond, J.R., & Vinacke, W.E. Coalitions in mixed-sex triads. *Sociometry,* 1961, 24, 61–75.

Braband, J., & Lerner, M.J. "A little time and effort" . . . Who deserves what from whom? Unpublished manuscript, University of Waterloo, 1973.

Bramel, D., Taub, B., & Blum, B. An observer's reaction to the suffering of his enemy. *Journal of Personality and Social Psychology,* 1968, 8, 384–392.

Brandt, R.B. (Ed.) *Social justice.* Engelwood Cliffs, N.J.: Prentice Hall, 1962.

Brickman, P., & Bryan, J.H. Moral judgment of theft, charity, and third-party transfers that increase or decrease equality. *Journal of Personality and Social Psychology,* 1975, 31, 156–161.

Brock, T.C., & Buss, A.H. Dissonance, aggression, and evaluation of pain. *Journal of Abnormal and Social Psychology,* 1962, 65, 197–202.

Brock, T.C., & Buss, A.H. Effects of justification for aggression in communication with the victim on post-aggression dissonance. *Journal of Abnormal and Social Psychology,* 1964, 68, 403–412.

Brown, B.R. The effects of need to maintain face on interpersonal bargaining. *Journal of Experimental Social Psychology,* 1968, 4, 107–122.

Brown, B.R. Face-saving following experimentally induced embarrassment. *Journal of Experimental Social Psychology,* 1970, 6, 255–271.

Brown, B.R., & Garland, H. The effects of incompetency, audience acquaintanceship, and anticipated evaluative feedback on face-saving behavior. *Journal of Experimental Social Psychology,* 1971, 7, 490–502.

Burnstein, E. Interdependence in groups. In J. Mills (Ed.), *Experimental social psychology.* New York: Macmillan Co., 1969. Pp. 307–405.

Burnstein, E., & Katz, S. Group decisions involving equitable and optimal distribution of status. In C.G. McClintock (Ed.), *Experimental social psychology.* New York: Holt, Rinehart, & Winston, 1972. Pp. 412–448.

Burnstein, E., & Wolosin, R.J. The development of status distinctions under conditions of inequity. *Journal of Experimental Social Psychology,* 1968, 4, 415–430.

Byrne, D. *The attraction paradigm.* New York: Academic Press, 1971.

Campbell, D.T. Ethnocentric and other altruistic motives. In D. Levin (Ed.), *Nebraska symposium on motivation.* Lincoln, Neb.: University of Nebraska Press, 1969. Pp. 283–312.

Caplow, T. *Two against one: Coalitions in triads.* Englewood Cliffs, N.J.: Prentice-Hall, 1968.

Caplow, T., & McGee, R.J. *The academic marketplace.* New York: Basic Books, 1958.

Cartwright, D. Influence, leadership, control. In J.G. March (Ed.), *Handbook of organizations.* Chicago: Rand McNally, 1965. Pp. 1–47.

Chaikin, A.L., & Darley, J.M. Victim or perpetrator: Defensive attribution and the need for order and justice. *Journal of Personality and Social Psychology,* 1973, 25, 268–276.

Chambliss, W.J., & Seidman, R.B. *Law, order and power.* Reading, Mass.: Addison-Wesley, 1971.

Collins, B.E., & Guetzkow, H. *A social psychology of group processes for decision making.* New York: John Wiley & Sons, 1964.

Cressey, D. *Other people's money.* Glencoe, Ill.: Free Press, 1955.

Curry, T.J., & Emerson, R.M. Balance theory: A theory of interpersonal attraction? *Sociometry,* 1970, **33,** 216–238.

Curry, T.J., & Kenny, D.A. The effects of perceived and actual similarity in values and personality in the process of interpersonal attraction. *Quality and Quantity,* 1974, **8,** 27–44.

Daniels, L., & Berkowitz, L. Liking and response to dependency relationships. *Human Relations,* 1963, **16,** 141–148.

Davidson, J. Cognitive familiarity and dissonance reduction. In Leon Festinger (Ed.), *Conflict, decision, and dissonance.* Stanford, California: Stanford University Press, 1964. Pp. 45–60.

Davies, J.C. The J-curve of rising and declining satisfactions as a cause of some great revolutions and a contained rebellion. In H.D. Graham & T.R. Gurr (Eds.), *Violence in America: historical and comparative perspectives.* New York: Signet, 1969. Pp. 671–709.

Davis, K.C. *Discretionary justice: A preliminary inquiry.* Baton Rouge: Louisiana State University Press, 1959.

Davis, K.E., & Jones, E.E. Changes in interpersonal perception as a means of reducing cognitive dissonance. *Journal of Abnormal and Social Psychology,* 1960, **61,** 402–410.

Day, R.C., & Hamblin, R.L. Some effects of close and punitive styles of supervision. *American Journal of Sociology,* 1964, **16,** 499–510.

De Greene, K.B. *Sociotechnical systems.* Englewood Cliffs, N.J.: Prentice-Hall, 1973.

Deutsch, M. The effects of cooperation and competition upon group process. In D. Cartwright & A. Zander (Eds.), *Group dynamics.* Evanston, Ill.: Row, Peterson, 1953. Pp. 319–353.

Deutsch, M. Trust and suspicion. *Journal of Conflict Resolution,* 1958, **2,** 265–279.

Deutsch, M., & Krauss, R.M. Studies of interpersonal bargaining. *Journal of Conflict Resolution,* 1962, **6,** 52–76.

Donnerstein, E., & Donnerstein, M. Variables in interracial aggression: Potential ingroup censure. *Journal of Personality and Social Psychology,* 1973, **27,** 143–150.

Donnerstein, E., & Donnerstein, M. White rewarding behavior as a function of the potential for black retaliation. *Journal of Personality and Social Psychology,* 1972, **24,** 327–333.

Doob, A.N., Freedman, J.L., & Carlsmith, J.M. Effects of sponsor and prepayment on compliance with a mailed request. *Journal of Applied Psychology,* 1973, **57,** 346–347.

Doob, A.N., & Zabrack, M. The effect of freedom-threatening instructions and monetary inducement on compliance. *Canadian Journal of Behavioural Science,* 1971, **3,** 408–412.

Durkheim, E. *The division of labor in society* (George Simpson, Transl.). New York: The Free Press, 1933.

Einhorn, H.J. Use of non-linear, non-compensatory models as a function of task and amount of information. *Organizational Behavior and Human Performance,* 1971, **6,** 1–27.

Emery, F.E., & Trist, E.L. The causal texture of organizational environments. *Human Relations,* 1965, **18,** 21–32.

Erikson, E.H. *Childhood and society.* New York: W.W. Norton & Co., 1950.

Festinger, L. A theory of social comparison processes. *Human Relations,* 1954, **7,** 117–140.

Frankel, M. *Criminal sentences: Law without order.* New York: Hill & Wang, 1973.

Freedman, J.L., & Fraser, S.C. Compliance without pressure: The foot-in-the-door technique. *Journal of Personality and Social Psychology,* 1966, **4,** 195–202.

French, J.R.P., & Raven, B.H. The bases of social power. In D. Cartwright (Ed.), *Studies in social power.* Ann Arbor, Mich.: Institute for Social Research, 1959. Pp. 150–167.

Friedrichs, R.W. Alter versus ego: An exploratory assessment of altruism. *American Sociological Review,* 1960, **25**, 496–508.

Frisch, D.M., & Greenberg, M.S. Reciprocity and intentionality in the giving of help. *Proceedings of the 76th Annual Convention of the American Psychological Association,* 1968, **3**, 383–384.

Fromm, E. *The art of loving.* New York: Harper & Row, 1956.

Fry, M. Justice for victims. In M.H. Rubin (Ed.), *Compensation for victims of criminal violence: A round table.* Atlanta: Emory University Law School. (*Journal of Public Law,* 1956, **8**, 115–253.)

Galanter, E. The direct measurement of utility and subjective probability. *American Journal of Psychology,* 1962, **75**, 208–220.

Gallo, P.S., & McClintock, C.G. Cooperative and competitive behavior in mixed-motive games. *Journal of Conflict Resolution,* 1965, **9**, 68–78.

Gamson, W.A. Experimental studies of coalition formation. In L. Berkowitz (Ed.), *Advances in experimental social psychology,* Vol. 1. New York: Academic Press, 1964. Pp. 81–110.

Garrett, J.B. Effects of Protestant ethic endorsement upon equity behavior. Paper presented at the meeting of the American Psychological Association, Montreal, August, 1973.

Garrett, J.B., & Libby, W.L., Jr. Role of intentionality in mediating responses to inequity in the dyad. *Journal of Personality and Social Psychology,* 1973, **28**, 21–27.

Gaudet, F.J., Harris, G.F., & St. John, C.W. Individual differences in the sentencing tendencies of judges. *Journal of Criminal Law and Criminology, XXIII* (Jan.–Feb., 1933), 811–813.

Ghiselli, E.E., & Lodahl, T.M. Patterns of managerial traits and group effectiveness. *Journal of Abnormal and Social Psychology,* 1958, **57**, 61–66.

Glass, D.C. Changes in liking as a means of reducing cognitive discrepancies between self-esteem and aggression. *Journal of Personality,* 1964, **32**, 520–549.

Goffman, E. On cooling the mark out: Some aspects of adaptation to failure. *Psychiatry,* 1952, **15**, 451–463.

Goldner, F.H. Demotion in industrial management. *American Sociological Review,* 1965, **30**, 714–724.

Golightly, C., Huffman, D.M., & Byrne, D. Liking and loaning. *Journal of Applied Psychology,* 1972, **56**, 521–523.

Goode, W.J. The protection of the inept. *American Sociological Review,* 1967, **32**, 5–19.

Goodman, P., & Friedman, A. An examination of the effect of wage inequity in the hourly condition. *Organizational Behavior and Human Performance,* 1968, **3**, 340–352.

Goodman, P.S., & Friedman, A. An examination of Adams' theory of inequity. *Administrative Science Quarterly,* 1971, **16**, 271–288.

Goodstadt, B.E., & Hjelle, L.A. Power to the powerless: Locus of control and the use of power. *Journal of Personality and Social Psychology,* 1973, **27**, 190–196.

Goodstadt, B., & Kipnis, D. Situational influences on the use of power. *Journal of Applied Psychology,* 1970, **54**, 201–207.

Goranson, R.E., & Berkowitz, L. Reciprocity and responsibility reactions to prior help. *Journal of Personality and Social Psychology,* 1966, **3**, 227–232.

Gouldner, A.W. The norm of reciprocity: A preliminary statement. *American Sociological Review,* 1960, **25**, 161–178.

Graf, R.G., & Green, D. The equity restoring components of retaliation. *Journal of Personality,* 1971, **39**, 581–590.

Greenberg, J., & Leventhal, G.S. Violating equity to prevent group failure. *Proceedings of the 81st annual convention of the American Psychological Association,* 1973, 215–216.

Greenberg, J., & Leventhal, G.S. Sex differences in the use of reward to elicit high performance. Paper presented at the meeting of the Midwestern Psychological Association, Chicago, May, 1974.

Greenberg, M.S. A preliminary statement on a theory of indebtedness. In M.S. Greenberg (Chm.), Justice in Social Exchange. Symposium presented at the Western Psychological Association, San Diego, September, 1968.

Greenberg, M.S., & Frisch, D.M. Effect of intentionality on willingness to reciprocate a favor. *Journal of Experimental Social Psychology,* 1972, 8, 99–111.

Gullahorn, J.T., & Gullahorn, J.E. A computer model of elementary social behavior. *Behavioral Science,* 1963, 8, 354–362.

Gurr, T.R. *Why men rebel.* Princeton, N.J.: Princeton University Press, 1970.

Hall, C.S. *A primer of Freudian psychology.* Toronto: New American Library of Canada, 1954.

Hamblin, R.L. Leadership and crises. *Sociometry,* 1958, 21, 322–335.

Harris, R.J. Note on "Optimal policies for the Prisoner's Dilemma." *Psychological Review,* 1969, 76, 363–375.

Harrison, M., & Pepitone, A. Contrast effect in the use of punishment. *Journal of Personality and Social Psychology,* 1972, 23, 398–404.

Heider, F. *The psychology of interpersonal relations.* New York: John Wiley & Sons, 1958.

Holmes, J.G., Miller, D.T., & Lerner, M.J. Symbolic threat in helping situations: The "exchange fiction." Unpublished manuscript, University of Waterloo, 1974.

Homans, G.C. *The human group.* New York: Harcourt, Brace, & World, 1950.

Homans, G.C. Status among clerical workers. *Human Organization,* 1953, 12, 5–10.

Homans, G.C. *Social behavior: Its elementary forms.* New York: Harcourt, Brace, & World, 1961.

Homans, G.C. *Social behavior: Its elementary forms* (Rev.). New York: Harcourt, Brace, Jovanovich, 1974.

Horowitz, I.A. Effect of choice and locus of dependence on helping behavior. *Journal of Personality and Social Psychology,* 1968, 8, 373–376.

Huesmann, R.L., Long, P.E., & Levinger, G. RELATE: A computer program for simulating dyadic interaction. Technical report, Department of Psychology, University of Illinois at Chicago Circle, 1974.

Huston, T.L. Ambiguity of acceptance, social desirability, and dating choice. *Journal of Experimental Social Psychology,* 1973, 9, 32–42.

Isen, A.M., Horn, N., & Rosenhan, D.L. Effects of success and failure on children's generosity. *Journal of Personality and Social Psychology,* 1973, 27, 239–247.

Jaques, E. *Equitable payment.* New York: John Wiley & Sons, 1961.

Jessor, R., Graves, T.D., Hanson, R.C., & Jessor, S.L. *Society, personality and deviant behavior: A study of a tri-ethnic community.* New York: Holt, Rinehart & Winston, 1968.

Johnson, R.E., Conlee, M.C., & Tesser, A. Effects of similarity of fate on bad news transmission: A reexamination. *Journal of Personality and Social Psychology,* 1974, 29, 644–648.

Johnson, R.W., & Dickinson, J. Class differences in derogation of an innocent victim. Unpublished manuscript, University of St. Xavier, 1971.

Jones, C., & Aronson, E. Attribution of fault to a rape victim as a function of respectability of the victim. *Journal of Personality and Social Psychology,* 1973, 26, 415–419.

Jones, E.E. *Ingratiation.* New York: Appleton-Century-Crofts, 1964.

Jourard, S.M. *Self-disclosure.* New York: Wiley & Sons, 1971.

Julian, J.W., & Perry, F.A. Cooperation contrasted with intra-group and inter-group competition. *Sociometry,* 1967, **30,** 79–90.

Jung, C.G. *Psychological types.* London: Routledge, 1923.

Kagan, J. The concept of identification. *Psychological Review,* 1958, **65,** 296–305.

Kahn, A. Reactions to generosity or stinginess from an intelligent or stupid work partner: A test of equity theory in a direct exchange relationship. *Journal of Personality and Social Psychology,* 1972, **21,** 116–123.

Kahn, A., & Tice, T.E. Returning a favor and retaliating harm: The effects of stated intentions and actual behavior. *Journal of Experimental Social Psychology,* 1973, **9,** 43–56.

Kahn, R.L., Wolfe, D.M., Quinn, R.P., & Snoeck, J.D. *Organizational stress: Studies in role conflict and ambiguity.* New York: John Wiley & Sons, 1964.

Kalven, J., Jr., & Zeisel, H. *The American jury.* Boston: Little, Brown, 1966.

Kaplan, R.M., & Swant, S.G. Reward characteristics in appraisal of achievement behavior. *Representative Research in Social Psychology,* 1973, **4,** 11–17.

Katz, I., Glass, D.D., & Cohen, S. Ambivalence, guilt, and the scapegoating of minority group victims. *Journal of Experimental Social Psychology,* 1973, **9,** 423–436.

Kelley, H.H., Thibaut, J.W., Radloff, R., & Mundy, D. The development of cooperation in the "minimal social situation." *Psychological Monographs,* 1962, **76,** No. 19.

Kelman, H.C., & Lawrence, L.H. Assignment of responsibility in the case of Lt. Calley: Preliminary report on a national survey. *Journal of Social Issues,* 1972, **28,** 177–212.

Kephart, W.M., & Bressler, M. Increasing the responses to mail questionnaires: A research study. *Public Opinion Quarterly,* 1958, **22,** 123–131.

Kiesler, S.B. The effect of perceived role requirements on reactions to favor-doing. *Journal of Experimental Social Psychology,* 1966, **2,** 198–210.

Kipnis, D. Does power corrupt? *Journal of Personality and Social Psychology,* 1972, **24,** 33–41.

Kipnis, D., & Cosentino, J. Use of leadership powers in industry. *Journal of Applied Psychology,* 1969, **53,** 460–466.

Klineberg, S.L. Future time perspective and the preference for delayed reward. *Journal of Personality and Social Psychology,* 1968, **8,** 253–257.

Komorita, S.S., & Chertkoff, J.M. A bargaining theory of coalition formation. *Psychological Review,* 1973, **80,** 149–162.

Krauss, R.M. Structural and attitudinal factors in interpersonal bargaining. *Journal of Experimental Social Psychology,* 1966, **2,** 42–55.

Krebs, D. Altruism—an examination of the concept and a review of the literature. *Psychological Bulletin,* 1970, **73,** 258–302.

Kuhn, T.S. *The structure of scientific revolutions.* Chicago: University of Chicago Press, 1962.

Landau, S., & Leventhal, G.S. A simulation study of administrators' behavior toward employees who receive job offers. In press.

Lane, I.M., & Coon, R.C. Reward allocation in preschool children. *Child Development,* 1972, **43,** 1382–1389.

Lane, I.M., & Messé, L.A. Equity and the distribution of rewards. *Journal of Personality and Social Psychology,* 1971, **21,** 1–17.

Lane, I.M., Messé, L.A., & Phillips, J.L. Differential inputs as a determinant in the selection of a distributor of rewards. *Psychonomic Science,* 1971, **22,** 228–229.

Lanzetta, J.T., & Hannah, T.E. Reinforcing behavior of "naive" trainers. *Journal of Personality and Social Psychology,* 1969, **11,** 245–252.

Lawler, E.E. Managers' perceptions of their subordinates' pay and of their superiors' pay. *Personnel Psychology*, 1965, **18**, 413–422. (a)

Lawler, E.E. Should managers' compensation be kept under wraps? *Personnel*, 1965, **42**, 17–20. (b)

Lawler, E.E. Secrecy about management compensation: Are these hidden costs? *Organizational Behavior and Human Performance*, 1967, **2**, 182–189.

Lawler, E.E. *Pay and organizational effectiveness: A psychological view*. New York: McGraw-Hill, 1971.

Lawler, E.E. Secrecy and the need to know. In H.L. Tosi, R.J. House, & M.D. Dunnette (Eds.), *Managerial motivation and compensation*. East Lansing, Mich.: MSU Business Studies, 1972.

Lawler, E.E. III. Equity theory as a predictor of productivity and work quality. *Psychological Bulletin*, 1968, **6**, 596–610.

Lawler, E.E. III, Kopkin, C.A., Young, T.F., & Fadem, J.A. Inequity reduction over time in an induced overpayment situation. *Organizational Behavior and Human Performance*, 1968, **3**, 253–268.

Legant, P. The deserving victim: Effects of length of pre-trial detention, crime severity, and juror attitudes on simulated jury decisions. Dissertation, Yale University, 1973. (a)

Legant, P. Equity theory and the law: Suggestions for future research, Presented in a symposium at the meeting of the American Psychological Association, Montreal. August, 1973. (b)

Lerner, M.J. Evaluation of performance as a function of performer's reward and attractiveness. *Journal of Personality and Social Psychology*, 1965, **1**, 355–360.

Lerner, M.J. The desire for justice and reactions to victims. In J. Macaulay & L. Berkowitz (Eds.), *Altruism and helping behavior*. New York: Academic Press, 1970. Pp. 205–229.

Lerner, M.J. Deserving vs. justice: A contemporary dilemma. Department of Psychology, University of Waterloo. Waterloo, Ontario, Canada. Research Report #24. May 15, 1971.

Lerner, M.J. "Belief in a just world" versus the "Authoritarian" syndrome . . . but nobody liked the Indians. Unpublished manuscript, University of Waterloo, 1973.

Lerner, M.J. The justice motive: 'Equity' and 'parity' among children. *Journal of Personality and Social Psychology*, 1974, **29**, 539–550. (a)

Lerner, M.J. Social psychology of justice and interpersonal attraction. In T. Huston (Ed.), *Foundations of interpersonal attraction*. New York: Academic Press, 1974. Pp. 331–351. (b)

Lerner, M.J. The Justice motive in social behavior. *Journal of Social Issues*. In press.

Lerner, M.J. Justified self interest and the responsibility for suffering: A replication and extension. *Journal of Human Relations*, 1971, **19**, 550–559.

Lerner, M.J., & Becker, S. Interpersonal choice as a function of ascribed similarity and definition of the situation. *Human Relations*, 1962, **15**, 27–34.

Lerner, M.J. & Lichtman, R.R. Effects of perceived norms on attitudes and altruistic behavior toward a dependent other. *Journal of Personality and Social Psychology*, 1968, **9**, 226–232.

Lerner, M.J., & Matthews, G. Reactions to the suffering of others under conditions of indirect responsibility. *Journal of Personality and Social Psychology*, 1967, **5**, 319–325.

Lerner, M.J., & Simmons, C.H. Observers' reaction to the "innocent victim": Compassion or rejection? *Journal of Personality and Social Psychology*, 1966, **4**, 203–210.

Leventhal, G.S. Equity and the economics of reward distribution. Paper presented at the meeting of the American Psychological Association, Honolulu, September, 1972.

Leventhal, G.S. Reward allocation by males and females. Paper presented at the meeting of the American Psychological Association, Montreal. August, 1973.

Leventhal, G.S., Allen, J., & Kemelgor, B. Reducing inequity by reallocating rewards. *Psychonomic Science,* 1969, **14,** 295–296.

Leventhal, G.S., & Anderson, D. Self-interest and the maintenance of equity. *Journal of Personality and Social Psychology,* 1970, **15,** 57–62.

Leventhal, G.S., & Bergman, J.T. Self-depriving behavior as a response to unprofitable inequity. *Journal of Experimental Social Psychology,* 1969, **5,** 153–171.

Leventhal, G.S., & Lane, D.W. Sex, age, and equity behavior. *Journal of Personality and Social Psychology,* 1970, **15,** 312–316.

Leventhal, G.S., & Michaels, J.W. Extending the equity model: Perception of inputs and allocation of reward as a function of duration and quantity of performance. *Journal of Personality and Social Psychology,* 1969, **12,** 303–309.

Leventhal, G.S., & Michaels, J.W. Locus of cause and equity motivation as determinants of reward allocation. *Journal of Personality and Social Psychology,* 1971, **17,** 229–235.

Leventhal, G.S., Michaels, J.W., & Sanford, C. Inequity and interpersonal conflict: Reward allocation and secrecy about reward as methods of preventing conflict. *Journal of Personality and Social Psychology,* 1972, **23,** 88–102.

Leventhal, G.S., Popp, A.L., & Sawyer, L. Equity or equality in children's allocation of reward to other persons? *Child Development,* 1973, **44,** 753–763.

Leventhal, G.S., & Weiss, T. Status congruence, perceived need and the response to inequitable distributions of reward. In press.

Leventhal, G.S., Weiss, T., & Buttrick, R. Attribution of value, equity, and the prevention of waste in reward allocation. *Journal of Personality and Social Psychology,* 1973, **27,** 276–286.

Leventhal, G.S., Weiss, T., & Long, G. Equity, reciprocity, and reallocating rewards in the dyad. *Journal of Personality and Social Psychology,* 1969, **13,** 300–305.

Leventhal, G.S., & Whiteside, H.D. Equity and the use of reward to elicit high performance. *Journal of Personality and Social Psychology,* 1973, **25,** 75–83.

LeVine, R.A., & Campbell, D.T. *Ethnocentrism: Theories of conflict, ethnic attitudes, and group behavior.* New York: Wiley, 1972.

Levinger, G. Little sandbox and big quarry: Comment on Byrne's paradigmatic spade for research on interpersonal attraction. *Representative Research in Social Psychology,* 1972, **3,** 3–19.

Levinger, G. A three-level approach to attraction: Toward an understanding of pair related-ness. In T.L. Huston (Ed.), *Foundations of interpersonal attraction.* New York: Academic Press, 1974.

Levinger, G., & Breedlove, J. Interpersonal attraction and agreement: A study of marriage partners. *Journal of Personality and Social Psychology,* 1966, **3,** 367–372.

Levinger, G., Senn, D.J., & Jorgensen, B.W. Progress toward permanence in courtship: A test of the Kerckhoff-Davis hypotheses. *Sociometry,* 1970, **33,** 427–443.

Levinger, G., & Snoek, J.D. *Attraction in relationship: A new look at interpersonal attraction.* Morristown, N.J.: General Learning Press, 1972.

Lichtman, R.J. Values and the distribution of rewards. Paper presented at the meeting of the Southeastern Psychological Association, Atlanta. April, 1972.

Lincoln, H., & Levinger, G. Observers' evaluations of the victim and the attacker in an aggressive incident. *Journal of Personality and Social Psychology,* 1972, **22,** 202–210.

Loehlin, J.C. "Interpersonal" experiments with a computer model of personality. *Journal of Personality and Social Psychology,* 1965, **2,** 580–584.

Long, G.T., & Lerner, M.J. Deserving, the 'personal contract' and altruistic behavior by children. *Journal of Personality and Social Psychology,* 1974, **29,** 551–556.

Lott, A.J., & Lott, B.E. The power of liking. In L. Berkowitz (Ed.), *Advances in Experimental Social Psychology,* Vol. 6. New York: Academic Press, 1972. Pp. 109–148.

Luce, R.D., & Raiffa, H. *Games and decisions.* New York: Wiley, 1957.

Macaulay, S., & Walster, E. Legal structures and restoring equity. *Journal of Social Issues,* 1971, **27**, 173–188.

MacCorquodale, K., & Meehl, P.E. On a distinction between hypothetical construct and intervening variables. *Psychological Review,* 1948, **55**, 95–107.

MacDonald, A.P., Jr. More on the Protestant Ethic. *Journal of Consulting and Clinical Psychology,* 1971.

McGuire, W.J. The yin and yang of progress in social psychology: Seven koan. *Journal of Personality and Social Psychology,* 1973, **26**, 446–456.

Maher, B.A. *Principles of psychopathology: An experimental approach.* New York: McGraw-Hill, 1966.

Marwell, G., & Schmitt, D.R. Dimensions of compliance-gaining behavior: An empirical analysis. *Sociometry,* 1967, **30**, 350–364. (a)

Marwell, G., & Schmitt, D.R. Attitudes toward parental use of promised rewards to control adolescent behavior. *Journal of Marriage and the Family,* 1967, **29**, 500–504. (b)

Marwell, G., Schmitt, D.R., & Shotola, R. Cooperation and interpersonal risk. *Journal of Personality and Social Psychology,* 1971, **18**, 9–32.

Maurer, D.W. *The big con.* Indianapolis: Bobbs Merrill, 1940.

Mead, M. *Growing up in New Guinea.* New York: Morrow, 1951.

Merton, R.K. *Social theory and social structure.* Glencoe: The Free Press, 1957.

Messé, L.A. Equity in bilateral bargaining. *Journal of Personality and Social Psychology,* 1971, **17**, 287–291.

Messé, L.A., & Lichtman, R.J. Motivation for money as a mediator of the extent to which quality and duration of work are inputs relevant to the distribution of rewards. Paper presented at the meeting of the Southeastern Psychological Association, Atlanta, 1972.

Michener, H.A., & Lawler, E.J. Revolutionary coalition strength and collective failure as determinants of status reallocation. *Journal of Experimental Social Psychology,* 1971, **7**, 448–460.

Michener, H.A., & Lyons, M. Perceived support and upward mobility as determinants of revolutionary coalitional behavior. *Journal of Experimental Social Psychology,* 1972, **8**, 180–195.

Michener, H.A., & Tausig, M. Usurpation and perceived support as determinants of the endorsement accorded formal leaders. *Journal of Personality and Social Psychology,* 1971, **18**, 364–372.

Midlarsky, E., & Bryan, J.H. Affect expressions and children's imitative altruism. *Journal of Experimental Research in Personality,* 1972, **6**, 195–203.

Midlarsky, E., Bryan, J.H., & Brickman, P. Aversive approval: Interactive effects of modeling and reinforcement on altruistic behavior. *Child Development,* 1973, **44**, 321–328.

Mikula, G. Nationality, performance, and sex as determinants of reward allocation. *Journal of Personality and Social Psychology,* 1974, **29**, 435–440.

Milkovich, G.T., & Anderson, P.H. Management compensation and secrecy policies. *Personnel Psychology,* 1972, **25**, 293–302.

Miller, D.C. Supervisors: Evolution of an organizational role. In R. Dubin, G.C. Homans, F.C. Mann, & D.C. Miller (Eds.), *Leadership and productivity.* San Francisco: Chandler, 1965.

Miller, D.T. Altruism and hedonism: Two forms of justice? Unpublished doctoral dissertation, University of Waterloo, 1974.

Miller, L.K., & Hamblin, R.L. Interdependence, differential rewarding, and productivity. *American Sociological Review,* 1963, **28**, 768–778.

Mischel, W. Preference for delayed reinforcement and social responsibility. *Journal of Abnormal and Social Psychology,* 1961, **62**, 1–7.

Mischel, W. Theory and research on the antecedents of self-imposed delay of reward. In B.A. Maher (Ed.), *Progress in experimental personality research.* Vol. 3. New York: Academic Press, 1966. Pp. 85–132.

Moore, L.M., & Baron, R.M. Effects of wage inequities on work attitudes and performance. *Journal of Experimental Social Psychology,* 1973, 9, 1–16.

Morgan, W.R., & Sawyer, J. Bargaining, expectations, and the preference for equality over equity. *Journal of Personality and Social Psychology,* 1967, 6, 139–149.

Moscovici, S. Society and theory in social psychology. In J. Israel & H. Tajfel (Eds.), *The context of social psychology: A critical assessment.* New York: Academic Press, 1972.

Nardi, A.H. Person-perception research and the perception of life-span development. In P.B. Baltes & K.M. Schaie (Eds.), *Life-span developmental psychology.* New York: Academic Press, 1973. Pp. 285–301.

Nemeth, C. A critical analysis of research utilizing the Prisoner's Dilemma paradigm for the study of bargaining. In L. Berkowitz (Ed.), *Advances in experimental social psychology,* Vol. 6. New York: Academic Press, 1972.

Newcomb, T.M. *The acquaintance process.* New York: Holt, Rinehart, & Winston, 1961.

Newell, A., Shaw, J.C., & Simon, H.A. Elements of a theory of human problem-solving. *Psychological Review,* 1958, 65, 151–166.

Newell, A., & Simon, H.A. *Human problem solving.* Englewood Cliffs, N.J.: Prentice-Hall, 1972.

Patchen, M. A conceptual framework and some empirical data regarding comparisons of social rewards. *Sociometry,* 1961, 24, 136–156.

Pepitone, A. The role of justice in interdependent decision making. *Journal of Experimental Social Psychology,* 1971, 7, 144–156.

Pettigrew, T. Social evaluation theory: Convergences and applications. In D. Levine (Ed.), *Nebraska symposium on motivation.* Lincoln: University of Nebraska Press, 1967. Pp. 241–311.

Piaget, J. *The moral judgment of the child.* London: Rutledge & Keegan Paul, 1932.

Piliavin, I., Hardyck, J., & Vadim, T. Reactions to a victim in a just or non-just world. Paper read at Society of Experimental Social Psychology meeting, Bethesda, Md. August, 1967.

Piliavin, J.A., & Piliavin, I.M. Distance and donations. Unpublished paper, 1969.

Pondy, L.R., & Birnberg, J.G. An experimental study of the allocation of financial resources within small hierarchical task groups. *Administrative Science Quarterly,* 1969, 14, 192–201.

Porter, L.W., & Lawler, E.E. *Managerial attitudes and performance.* Homewood, Ill.: Richard D. Irwin, 1968.

Porter, L.W., & Steers, R.M. Organizational, work, and personal factors in employee turnover and absenteeism. *Psychological Bulletin,* 1973, 80, 151–176.

Pritchard, R.D. Equity theory: A review and critique. *Organizational Behavior and Human Performance,* 1969, 4, 176–211.

Pritchard, R.D., Dunnette, M.D., & Jorgenson, D.O. Effects of perceptions of equity and inequity on worker performance and satisfaction. *Journal of Applied Psychology Monograph,* 1972, 56, 75–94.

Pruitt, D.G. Reciprocity and credit building in a laboratory dyad. *Journal of Personality and Social Psychology,* 1968, 8, 143–147.

Pruitt, D.G. Indirect communication and the search for agreement in negotiation. *Journal of Applied Social Psychology,* 1971, 1, 205–239.

Pruitt, D.G. Methods for resolving differences of interest: A theoretical analysis. *Journal of Social Issues,* 1972, 28, 133–154.

Puzo, M. *The godfather.* New York: Putnam, 1969.

Rapoport, Amnon. Optimal policies for the Prisoner's Dilemma. *Psychological Review,* 1967, **74,** 136–148.

Rapoport, Anatol. *Two-person game theory.* Ann Arbor: University of Michigan Press, 1966.

Rapoport, A., & Chammah, A. *Prisoner's dilemma.* Ann Arbor: University of Michigan Press, 1965.

Raven, B.H., & Kruglanski, A.W. Conflict and power. In P. Swingle (Ed.), *The structure of conflict.* New York: Academic Press, 1970. Pp. 69–109.

Rawls, L. *A theory of justice.* Cambridge, Mass.: The Belknap Press, 1971.

Read, W.H. Upward communication in industrial hierarchies. *Human Relations,* 1962, **15,** 3–15.

Reppucci, N.D., & Saunders, J.T. Social psychology of behavior modification: Problems of implementation in natural settings. *American Psychologist,* 1974, **29,** 649–660.

Rest, S., Nierenberg, R., Weiner, B., & Heckhausen, H. Further evidence concerning the effects of perceptions of effort and ability on achievement evaluation. *Journal of Personality and Social Psychology,* 1973, **28,** 187–191.

Rhode, J.G., & Lawler, E.E. Auditing change: Human resource accounting. In M.D. Dunnette (Ed.), *Work and nonwork in the year 2001.* Monterey, Calif.: Brooks/Cole, 1973. Pp. 153–177.

Rivlin, A.M. Social experiments: Promise and problems. *Science,* 1974, **35,** 183.

Roebuck, J. The "short con man." *Crime and Delinquency,* 1964, July, 240–246.

Rose, A.M., & Prell, A.F. Does the punishment fit the crime? *The American Journal of Sociology,* 1955, **61,** 247–259.

Rosen, S., & Conlee, M.C. News valence and available recipient as determinants of news transmission. *Sociometry,* 1972, **35,** 619–628.

Rosen, S., Johnson, R.D., Johnson, M.J., & Tesser, A. Interactive effects of news valence and attraction on communicator behavior. *Journal of Personality and Social Psychology,* 1973, **28,** 298–300.

Rosen, S., & Tesser, A. On reluctance to communicate undesirable information: The MUM effect. *Sociometry,* 1970, **33,** 253–263.

Rosenberg, N. *Technology and American economic growth.* New York: Harper & Row, 1972.

Rosenhan, D., & White, G.M. Observation and rehearsal as determinants of prosocial behavior. *Journal of Personality and Social Psychology,* 1967, **5,** 424–431.

Ross, A.S. Modes of guilt reduction. Paper read at Eastern Psychological Association, New York, April, 1966. Unpublished Doctoral Dissertation, University of Minnesota, 1965.

Ross, M., Thibaut, J., & Evenbeck, S. Some determinants of the intensity of social protest. *Journal of Experimental Social Psychology,* 1971, **7,** 401–418.

Roth, P. *Portnoy's complaint.* New York: Random House, 1969.

Rothbart, M. Effects of motivation, equity, and compliance on the use of reward and punishment. *Journal of Personality and Social Psychology,* 1968, **9,** 353–362.

Rubin, Z. Lovers and other strangers: The development of intimacy in encounters and relationships. *American Scientist,* 1974, **62,** 182–190.

Rubin, Z., & Peplau, A. Belief in a just world and reaction to another's lot: A study of the national draft lottery. *Journal of Social Issues,* 1973.

Ruch, L.O., & Holmes, T.H. Scaling of life change: Comparison of direct and indirect methods. *Journal of Psychosomatic Research,* 1971, **15,** 221–227.

Sampson, E.E. Studies of status congruence. In L. Berkowitz (Ed.), *Advances in experimental social psychology,* Vol. 4. New York: Academic Press, 1969. Pp. 225–270.

Schafer, S. *Restitution to victims of crime.* London: Stevens & Son, Ltd., 1960.

Schmitt, D.R., & Marwell, G. Withdrawal and reward allocation as responses to inequity. *Journal of Experimental Social Psychology,* 1972, 8, 207–221.

Schopler, J. An attribution analysis of some determinants of reciprocating a benefit. In J. Macaulay and L. Berkowitz (Eds.), *Altruism and helping behavior.* New York: Academic Press, 1970. Pp. 231–238.

Schopler, J., & Matthews, M.W. The influence of the perceived causal locus of partner's dependence on the use of interpersonal power. *Journal of Personality and Social Psychology,* 1965, 2, 609–612.

Schopler, J., & Thompson, V.D. Role of attribution processes in mediating amount of reciprocity for a favor. *Journal of Personality and Social Psychology,* 1968, 10, 243–250.

Schwab, D.P. Impact of alternative compensation systems on pay valence and instrumentality perceptions. *Journal of Applied Psychology,* 1973, 58, 308–312.

Schwartz, S.H. Moral decision making and behavior. In J. Macaulay and L. Berkowitz (Eds.), *Altruism and helping behavior.* New York: Academic Press, 1970. Pp. 127–141.

Shapiro, E.G. Equity and equality in the allocation of rewards in a dyad. Paper presented at the meeting of the American Sociological Association. New Orleans. August, 1972.

Shapiro, E.G. Effect of expectations of future interaction on reward allocations in dyads: Equity or equality. *Journal of Personality and Social Psychology,* 1975, 31, 873–880.

Sharp, F.C., & Otto, M.C. A study of the popular attitude toward retributive punishment. *International Journal of Ethics,* 1910, 20, 341–357. (a)

Sharp, F.C., & Otto, M. Retribution and deterrence in the moral judgments of common sense. *International Journal of Ethics,* 1910, 20, 428–458. (b)

Simon, H.A. A formal theory for interaction in social groups. In H.A. Simon (Ed.), *Models of man.* New York: Wiley, 1957.

Simons, C.W., & Piliavin, J.A. The effect of deception on reactions to a victim. *Journal of Personality and Social Psychology,* 1957, 21, 56–60.

Simpson, R.L. *Theories of social exchange.* Morristown, N.J.: General Learning Press, 1972.

Skinner, B.F. *The behavior of organisms.* New York: Appleton Century Crofts, 1938.

Slagle, J.R., & Lee, R.G.T. Application of game tree searching techniques to sequential pattern recognition. *Communications of the A.C.M.,* 1971, 14, 103–110.

Smelser, W.T. Personality influences in social situations. *Journal of Abnormal and Social Psychology,* 1961, 62, 535–542.

Smith, R.J., & Cook, P.E. Leadership in dyadic groups as a function of dominance and incentives. *Sociometry,* 1973, 36, 561–568.

Smith, W.P. Power structure and authoritarianism in the use of power in the triad. *Journal of Personality,* 1967, 35, 64–90.

Sorrentino, R.M., & Hardy, J.E. Religiousness and derogation of an innocent victim. *Journal of Personality,* in press.

Stapleton, R.E., Nacci, P., & Tedeschi, J.T. Interpersonal attraction and the reciprocation of benefits. *Journal of Personality and Social Psychology,* 1973, 28, 199–205.

Staub, E. Instigation to goodness: The role of social norms and interpersonal influence. *Journal of Social Issues,* 1972, 28, 131–150.

Staub, E., & Sherk, L. Need for approval, children's sharing behavior and reciprocity in sharing. *Child Development,* 1970, 41, 243–252.

Steiner, I.D. *Group process and productivity.* New York: Academic Press, 1972.

Stephenson, G.M., & White, J.H. An experimental study of some effects of injustice on children's moral behavior. *Journal of Experimental and Social Psychology,* 1968, 4, 460–469.

Stevens, S.S. The measurement of loudness. *Journal of the Acoustical Society of America*, 1955, 27, 815–829.

Stokols, D., & Schopler, J. Reactions to victims under conditions of situational detachment: The effects of responsibility, severity, and expected future interaction. *Journal of Personality and Social Psychology*, 1973, 25, 199–209.

Sutherland, E. *Principles of criminology*. Philadelphia: J.B. Lippincott, 1966.

Sykes, G.M., & Matza, D. Techniques of neutralization: A theory of delinquency. *American Sociological Review*, 1957, 22, 664–670.

Tajfel, H. Experiments in intergroup discrimination. *Scientific American*, 1970, 223, 96–102.

Tannebaum, P.H., & Gaer, E.P. Mood changes as a function of stress of protagonist and degree of identification in a film-viewing situation. *Journal of Personality and Social Psychology*, 1965, 2, 612–616.

Taynor, J., & Deaux, K. When women are more deserving than men: Equity, attribution, and perceived sex differences. *Journal of Personality and Social Psychology*, 1973, 28, 360–367.

Tesser, A., & Rosen, S. Similarity of objective fate as a determinant of the reluctance to transmit unpleasant information: The MUM effect. *Journal of Personality and Social Psychology*, 1972, 23, 46–53.

Thibaut, J.W. An experimental study of the cohesiveness of underprivileged groups. *Human Relations*, 1950, 3, 251–278.

Thibaut, J. The development of contractual norms in bargaining: Replication and variation. *Journal of Conflict Resolution*, 1968, 12, 102–112.

Thibaut, J., & Faucheux, C. The development of contractual norms in a bargaining situation under two types of stress. *Journal of Experimental Social Psychology*, 1965, 1, 89–102.

Thibaut, J., & Gruder, C.L. Formation of contractual agreements between parties of unequal power. *Journal of Personality and Social Psychology*, 1969, 11, 59–65.

Thibaut, J.W., & Kelley, H.H. *The social psychology of groups*. New York: Wiley and Sons, 1959.

Tornow, W.W. The development and application of an input-outcome moderator test on the perception and reduction of inequity. *Organizational Behavior and Human Performance*, 1971, 6, 614–638.

Uesugi, T.K., & Vinacke, W.E. Strategy in a feminine game. *Sociometry*, 1963, 26, 75–88.

Utne, M.K. Functions of expressions of liking in response to inequity. Thesis submitted in partial fulfillment of the requirements of Master of Arts at the University of Wisconsin-Madison, August 2, 1974.

Valentine, R.J. The effect of group unity on reward allocation behavior. Unpublished Master's thesis, North Carolina State University, 1971.

Vershure, B. Employees' length of service, productivity level, age, subjects' sex, and the equitable distribution of rewards. Unpublished Master's thesis, Wayne State University, 1974.

Vidmar, N. Effects of decision alternatives on the verdicts and social perceptions of simulated jurors. *Journal of Personality and Social Psychology*, 1972, 22, 211–218.

Vinacke, W.E. Power, strategy, and the formation of coalitions in triads under four incentive conditions. Technical Report No. 1. October, 1962.

Vroom, V.H. *Work and motivation*. New York: Wiley, 1964.

Walster, E., Berscheid, E., & Walster, G.W. The exploited: Justice or justification? In J. Macaulay & L. Berkowitz (Eds.), *Altruism and helping behavior*. New York: Academic Press, 1970. Pp. 179–204.

Walster, E., Berscheid, E., & Walster, G.W. New directions in equity research. *Journal of Personality and Social Psychology,* 1973, **25**, 151–176.

Walster, E., & Piliavin, J.A. Equity and the innocent bystander. *Journal of Social Issues,* 1972, **28**, 165–189.

Walster, E., & Prestholdt, P. The effect of misjudging another: Over-compensation or dissonance reduction? *Journal of Experimental Social Psychology,* 1966, **2**, 85–97.

Walster, E., Walster, G.W., Abrahams, D., & Brown, Z. The effect on liking of underrating or overrating another. *Journal of Experimental Social Psychology,* 1966, **2**, 70–84.

Walster, E., Walster, G.W., & Berscheid, E. *Equity theory and research.* Boston: Allyn & Bacon. In press.

Wasserstrom, R.A. *The judicial decision.* Stanford: Stanford University Press, 1961.

Watson, J.J. Improving the response rate in mail research. *Journal of Advertising Research,* 1965, **5**, 48–50.

Weick, K.E. The concept of equity in the perception of pay. *Administrative Science Quarterly,* 1966, **11**, 414–439.

Weick, K.W., & Nesset, B. Preferences among forms of equity. *Organizational Behavior in Human Performance,* 1968, **3**, 400–416.

Weiner, B., & Kukla, A. An attributional analysis of achievement motivation. *Journal of Personality and Social Psychology,* 1970, **15**, 1–20.

Weinstein, A.G., & Holzbach, R.L. Impact of individual differences, reward distribution, and task structure on productivity in a simulated work environment. *Journal of Applied Psychology,* 1973, **58**, 296–301.

Weinstein, G.W. Making allowances: A parents' guide. *Money,* November, 1972, 52–62.

Wheeler, R. *Voices of 1776.* New York: Thomas Y. Crowell, 1972.

Wicker, A.W., & Bushweiler, G. Perceived fairness and pleasantness of social exchange situations. *Journal of Personality and Social Psychology,* 1970, **15**, 63–75.

Wiener, Y. The effects of "task- and ego-oriented" performance on two kinds of overcompensation inequity. *Organizational Behavior and Human Performance,* 1970, **5**, 191–208.

Wiggins, J.A. Status differentiation, external consequences, and alternative reward distributions. *Sociometry,* 1966, **29**, 89–103.

Wiggins, J.A., Dill, F., & Schwartz, R.D. On "status liability." *Sociometry,* 1965, **28**, 197–209.

Wilke, H., & Lanzetta, J.T. The obligation to help: The effects of amount of prior help on subsequent helping behavior. *Journal of Experimental Social Psychology,* 1970, **6**, 488–493.

Wolf, G., & Zahn, L. Exchange in games and communication. *Organizational Behavior and Human Performance,* 1972, **7**, 142–187.

Wright, P.H., & Crawford, A.C. Agreement and friendship: A close look and some second thoughts. *Representative Research in Social Psychology,* 1971, **2**(2), 52–69.

Wyer, R.S. Prediction of behavior in two-person games. *Journal of Personality and Social Psychology,* 1969, **13**, 222–238.

Yukl, G. Toward a behavioral theory of leadership. *Organizational Behavior and Human Performance,* 1971, **6**, 414–440.

SUBJECT INDEX

6
7
8
9
0
1
2
3
4